THE CAMBRIDGE COMPANION TO THEATRE HISTORY

Scholars, amateur historians and actors have shaped theatre history in different ways at different times and in different places. This *Companion* offers students and general readers a series of accessible and engaging essays on the key aspects of studying and writing theatre history. The diverse international team of contributors investigates how theatre history has been constructed, showing how historical facts are tied to political and artistic agendas and explaining why history matters to us. Beginning with an introduction to the central narrative that traditionally informs our understanding of what theatre is, the book then turns to alternative points of view – from other parts of the world and from the perspective of performers in fields such as music theatre and circus. It concludes by looking at how history is written in the 'democratic' age of the internet and offers a new perspective on theatre history in our globalised world.

David Wiles is Professor of Theatre at Royal Holloway, University of London.

Christine Dymkowski is Professor of Drama and Theatre History at Royal Holloway, University of London.

A complete list of books in the series is at the back of this book

THE CAMBRIDGE
COMPANION TO
THEATRE HISTORY

EDITED BY
DAVID WILES
Royal Holloway, University of London

and

CHRISTINE DYMKOWSKI
Royal Holloway, University of London

CAMBRIDGE
UNIVERSITY PRESS

CAMBRIDGE UNIVERSITY PRESS
Cambridge, New York, Melbourne, Madrid, Cape Town,
Singapore, São Paulo, Delhi, Mexico City

Cambridge University Press
The Edinburgh Building, Cambridge CB2 8RU, UK

Published in the United States of America by Cambridge University Press, New York

www.cambridge.org
Information on this title: www.cambridge.org/9780521766364

First published 2013

Printed and bound in the United Kingdom by the MPG Books Group

A catalogue record for this publication is available from the British Library

Library of Congress Cataloguing in Publication data
The Cambridge companion to theatre history / [edited by] David Wiles,
Christine Dymkowski.
p. cm. – (Cambridge companions to literature)
ISBN 978-0-521-76636-4 (hardback)
1. Theater – History. I. Wiles, David. II. Dymkowski, Christine, 1950–
PN2101.C36 2012
792.09–dc23
2012020522

ISBN 978-0-521-76636-4 Hardback
ISBN 978-0-521-14983-9 Paperback

CONTENTS

v

NOTES ON CONTRIBUTORS

HAZEM AZMY is co-convener (with Marvin Carlson) of the Arabic Theatre Working Group of The International Federation for Theatre Research (IFTR/FIRT). Before gaining his Ph.D. at the University of Warwick with a thesis on post-9/11 performance realities, he was based in his home country, Egypt, where he continues to maintain an internationally oriented career as theatre and interdisciplinary humanities researcher, university teacher, theatre and literary critic, translator, and cross-cultural *animateur*.

CHRISTOPHER BAUGH is Professor at the University of Hull and Emeritus Professor of Performance and Technology at the University of Leeds. His writing on baroque and romantic theatre includes *Garrick and Loutherbourg* (1990); 'Stage Design from Loutherbourg to Poel', in J. Donohue (ed.), *The Cambridge History of British Theatre* (2004); 'Philippe de Loutherbourg: Technology-driven Entertainment and Spectacle in the Late Eighteenth Century', in the *Huntington Library Quarterly* (2007); 'Scenography and Technology 1737–1843', in J. Moody and D. O'Quinn (eds.), *The Cambridge Companion to British Theatre, 1737–1843* (2007); and 'Shakespeare and the Rhetoric of Scenography 1770–1825', in C. Dymkowski and C. Carson, *Shakespeare in Stages* (2010).

JACKY BRATTON is Research Professor of Theatre and Cultural History at Royal Holloway, University of London. She works on the culture of the long nineteenth century; her most recent book is *The Making of the West End Stage: Marriage, Management and the Mapping of Gender in London, 1830–1870*. She is working on an edition of plays from the works of Dickens, intended to demonstrate that the classic novelist was also a classic dramatic artist by stealth, probably the greatest creator of plays the nineteenth century produced.

GILLI BUSH-BAILEY, Reader in Women's Theatre History at Royal Holloway, University of London, has contributed chapters to *The Performing Century: Theatre in Nineteenth-Century Britain* (ed. T. C. Davis and P. Holland, 2007) and to *The Cambridge Companion to the Actress* (ed. M. B. Gale and J. Stokes, 2007), where she writes on seventeenth-century actresses and female playwrights, a work begun in her first monograph, *Treading the Bawds* (2006). She has extended her published work on actresses and managers in nineteenth-century theatre with *Performing Herself: AutoBiography and Fanny Kelly's Dramatic Recollections* (2011). Her interest in practice-based research in theatre history informed her collaborative work with Jacky Bratton, which includes the co-authored special edition of *Nineteenth-Century Theatre and Film* (2002). Her research and publication work follows on from her first career as a professional actress.

MARVIN CARLSON is the Sidney E. Cohn Distinguished Professor of Theatre, Comparative Literature and Middle Eastern Studies at the Graduate Center of the City University of New York. He is the author of over 300 articles and many books on the history and theory of the theatre, most recently *The Theatres of Morocco, Tunisia, and Algeria* (2011) with Khalid Amine. He is the founding editor of the journal *Western European Stages*. He is the recipient of many major theatre awards and has been awarded an honorary doctorate from the University of Athens.

ZACHARY DUNBAR is Senior Lecturer in Music Theatre and Classical Acting at Central School of Speech and Drama, University of London. He has published essays in *Theorising Performance: Greek Drama, Cultural History and Critical Practice* (2010), *Theatre Noise: The Sound of Performance* (2011), *Studies in Musical Theatre* (2011), and *Choruses: Ancient and Modern* (forthcoming 2013). A concert pianist and freelance theatre director/writer, his original works have been staged in the UK and in Europe.

CHRISTINE DYMKOWSKI was until October 2012 Professor of Drama and Theatre History at Royal Holloway, University of London. Co-founder of the IFTR/FIRT working group on Feminist Theatre/Women in Theatre, she has written extensively on Edwardian and contemporary women playwrights and directors, including a case study of Cicely Hamilton's *Diana of Dobson's* for *The Cambridge History of British Theatre* (2004). Her work on Shakespeare includes *Harley Granville Barker: A Preface to Modern Shakespeare* (1986); *The Tempest* in Cambridge University Press's Shakespeare in Production series (2000); '"Ancient [and Modern] Gower": Presenting Shakespeare's *Pericles*', in P. Butterworth (ed.), *The Narrator, the Expositor and the Prompter in European Medieval Theatre* (2007); and '*Measure for Measure*: Shakespeare's Twentieth-century Play', in *Shakespeare in Stages*, which she co-edited with Christie Carson (2010). She is also Theatre History editor of the forthcoming New Variorum *Tempest*.

JOSETTE FÉRAL, presently professor at La Sorbonne Nouvelle (Paris 3), previously taught at the Université du Québec à Montréal. She has published several books, including *Théorie et pratique du théâtre, au-delà des limites* (2011), *Mise en scène et jeu de l'acteur*, Vol. I, II and III (1997, 1999, 2007), *Trajectoires du Soleil* (1999), *Rencontres avec Ariane Mnouchkine* (1995), and *La culture contre l'art: essai d'économie politique du théâtre* (1990). She has also edited several works on the theory of the theatre, the most recent ones being *Pratiques performatives: Body Remix* (2012) and special issues of *Theatre Research International* on 'Genetics of Performance' (2008), of *Yale French Studies* (with Donia Mounsef) on 'The Transparency of the Text: Contemporary Writing for the Stage' (2007), and of *SubStance* on 'Theatricality' (2002).

ERIKA FISCHER-LICHTE is Director of the Institute for Advanced Studies on 'Interweaving Cultures in Performance' (since 2008) and spokesperson of the International Doctoral School 'InterArt' (since 2006) at Freie Universität Berlin. She has had guest professorships in the USA, Russia, India, Japan, China and Norway. President of the International Federation for Theatre Research from 1995 to 1999, she is a member of the Academia Europaea, the Academy of Sciences at Goettingen, the National Academy of Sciences *Leopoldina*, and the Berlin-Brandenburg Academy of Sciences. Among her many publications are *Theatre, Sacrifice, Ritual: Exploring Forms of Political Theatre* (2005) and *The Transformative Power of Performance: A New Aesthetics* (2008).

BARBARA HODGDON is Professor of English (retired) at the University of Michigan. She is the author of *The Shakespeare Trade: Performances and Appropriations*, *The End Crowns All: Closure and Contradiction in Shakespeare's History*, two books exploring Shakespeare's *Henry IV, Parts One and Two* as texts and performances, and many essays, primarily on performed Shakespeare, stage and film. She is the editor of the Arden 3 edition of *The Taming of the Shrew* and the co-editor of *A Blackwell Companion to Shakespeare and Performance*.

STEFAN HULFELD is Professor of Theatre and Cultural Studies at the University of Vienna, Austria. Born and educated in Switzerland, he graduated in theatre studies and German literature from the University of Berne. With grants from the Swiss National Science Foundation, he was guest researcher at the Free University of Berlin, at the Biblioteca e Raccolta Teatrale del Burcardo in Rome and at the British Library in London. His second book *Theatergeschichtsschreibung als kulturelle Praxis* (2007) is a study in theatre historiography from the sixteenth to the twentieth centuries.

MARIUS KWINT studied cultural history at Aberdeen University and wrote his doctoral thesis at Oxford University on the history of the circus in England. He has worked as a research fellow in history of design at the Victoria and Albert Museum and Royal College of Art, London, and as lecturer in history of art at Oxford. He currently teaches visual culture at the University of Portsmouth and is guest curator for the 2012 exhibition *Brains: The Mind as Matter* at the Wellcome Collection, London.

FIONA MACINTOSH is Director of the Archive of Performances of Greek and Roman Drama (APGRD) and Fellow of St Hilda's College, University of Oxford.

She is the author of *Dying Acts* (1994), *Greek Tragedy and the British Theatre 1660–1914* (2005, with Edith Hall), and Sophocles' *Oedipus Tyrannus* (Plays in Production series, Cambridge University Press 2009). She has edited a number of APGRD volumes, most recently *The Ancient Dancer in the Modern World: Responses to Greek and Roman Dance* (2010).

ROS MERKIN is a Reader in Drama at Liverpool John Moores University. Her research mainly focuses on local and regional theatre and includes *The Glory of the Garden: English Regional Theatre and the Arts Council 1984–2009*, which she edited with Kate Dorney, and *Liverpool Playhouse: A Theatre and its City* for the theatre's 100th anniversary.

DIEGO PELLECCHIA received his Ph.D. from Royal Holloway, University of London, with a thesis on the history of the reception of Noh theatre in the West. He practises Noh chant and dance with Master-Actor Udaka Michishige (Kongō School) and has performed both in Japan and abroad as a member of the International Noh Institute. His research looks at the interactions of aesthetics and ethics of Noh in the international context.

GRANT TYLER PETERSON has published work on British alternative theatre history, gender and sexuality. He holds an MA from UCLA and a Ph.D. from Royal Holloway, University of London. His recent research, funded by HEFCE, presents a historiographical study of street theatre practices, focused on one of Britain's longest operating street theatre troupes, the Natural Theatre Company. He has been a Visiting Lecturer at University of Winchester, Bath Spa University, and Royal Holloway.

THOMAS POSTLEWAIT teaches in the doctoral programme of the School of Drama, University of Washington. His early publications include *William Archer on Ibsen: The Major Essays* (1984), *Prophet of the New Drama: William Archer and the Ibsen Campaign* (1986), and the co-edited *Interpreting the Theatrical Past* (1989). Between 1991 and 2011 he served as editor of the award-winning series, Studies in Theatre History and Culture, at the University of Iowa Press, which published over forty books. In recent years he has co-edited *Theatricality* (2003) and *Representing the Past: Essays in Performance Historiography* (2010) and published *The Cambridge Introduction to Theatre Historiography* (2009).

WILLMAR SAUTER, Professor of Theatre Studies at Stockholm University, Sweden, has long studied audiences and reception processes. He has also written on Swedish theatre history, from Bronze Age rock carvings to the free group movement in the 1960s. His interest in the theories of the theatrical event is documented in his book *The Theatrical Event* (2000) and summarised in *Eventness* (2006). A founding member and first chairman of the association of Nordic Theatre Scholars, he has also been President of the International Federation for Theatre Research (IFTR/

FIRT) and Dean of the Faculty of the Humanities at Stockholm University; he is presently the chair of the Research School of Aesthetics.

DAVID WILES is Professor of Theatre at Royal Holloway, University of London. He has published nine books, seven of them with Cambridge. These include *Theatre and Citizenship: The History of a Practice* (2011) and *A Short History of Western Performance Space* (2003). He has published extensively on Greek theatre, taking a special interest in the use of masks and performance space, and on Elizabethan theatre. His books have been shortlisted for the Runciman, Criticos and STR prizes.

S. E. WILMER is Professor of Drama and Head of the School of Drama, Film and Music at Trinity College Dublin. He is the author of *Theatre, Society and the Nation: Staging American Identities* (2002) and (with Pirkko Koski) *The Dynamic World of Finnish Theatre* (2006). Books that he has edited or co-edited include *National Theatres in a Changing Europe* (2008), *Native American Performance and Representation* (2009), and (with Audrone Zukauskaite) *Interrogating Antigone in Postmodern Philosophy and Criticism* (2010). He has also served as a visiting professor at Stanford University and the University of California at Berkeley.

ACKNOWLEDGEMENTS

After this project was commissioned, the editors and contributors met for a two-day symposium on 'Why Theatre History?', at the Department of Drama and Theatre, Royal Holloway, University of London, on 18–19 June 2010. We are grateful for the constructive comments from members of the audience, which helped to shape the volume. We are also grateful to the Society for Theatre Research and to the Department for financial support of the symposium. We thank Diego Pellecchia for assembling the index.

Every effort has been made to secure necessary permissions to reproduce copyright material in this work, though in some cases it has proved impossible to trace copyright holders. If any omissions are brought to our notice, we will be happy to include appropriate acknowledgements in any subsequent edition.

PART ONE

Why?

I

DAVID WILES

Why theatre history?

We, the editors and contributors to this volume, are united by a shared conviction that history matters. We all wish to resist 'presentism', which may be defined as a belief that the past is irrelevant because its inhabitants, people just like us, are now irretrievably gone. We sense that our students are disempowered by their lack of appropriate maps of the past, yet we find it difficult to endorse standard accounts of the theatrical past because we have a different set of priorities. We find it a challenge, using available textbooks, to engender passion about the past, because these books do not explain why the past should matter to us, in the here and now. This lack of intellectual engagement with the theatrical past is a rather surprising state of affairs given that, in the domain of mass culture, there is a vast public following for historical novels and films, for museums and for heritage sites.

In the political domain there is a clear perception that history matters. When the contributors to this volume gathered for a conference in London in the summer of 2010, the teaching of history was being debated in the wider world. Niall Ferguson, a controversial historian of empire, drew media attention at a literary festival because the incoming Conservative Minister of Education, Michael Gove, leapt up and invited him to help shape the new schools curriculum. In his speech Ferguson lamented that his children had left school having learned history only in fragments, their knowledge seemingly confined to Henry VIII, Adolf Hitler and Martin Luther King, isolated moral case studies that offered no sense of how historical events interconnect. The left-wing press was fierce in its condemnation. The *New Statesman*, for example, concluded its attack on Ferguson and the new government by declaring that

> Michael Gove's wish to re-engineer how history is taught to children is, quite simply, about social control. It is part of a broader political discourse that seeks, ultimately, to replace the messy, multivalent web of Britain's cultural inheritance with one 'big story' about dominance and hierarchy, of white over black, west over east, rich over poor. But history is not about the big story, the single

story, the story told by the overculture. History is not about 'celebrating' the past, nor about making white kids feel good about their cultural inheritance. History is a process of exploring the legacy of the past, and questioning it – including the ugly, uncomfortable parts. No wonder the Tories want to tear it up and start again.[1]

There is a fatal flaw in this argument, for how can you explore and question the 'legacy of the past' unless you are taught what that legacy is? There is an assumption here that big stories are necessarily right-wing stories, which is clearly fallacious if, for example, we think of how radicals in the French Revolution were fired by big stories from Republican Rome, or of the economic models of society developed by Karl Marx. The *New Statesman*'s moral agenda concerned diversity and multiculturalism, and the journal feared, no doubt with reason, that the new Minister was attached to a national story that would downplay diversity.

Like those educationalists whom Ferguson attacks and for similar ethical reasons, theatre historians have retreated from big stories, stories that catch the imagination and connect to the public domain, out of fear that they will prove inherently elitist or nationalist, racist or masculinist. It is much easier to take on board, without ethical qualms, the moral drive towards inclusiveness and plurality, the drive to embrace oppressed minority and marginalised groups in the present. But in abandoning the big, public stories, theatre historians have lost the ability to point up the interconnectedness of past events. If theatre history is to be harnessed to ends other than right-wing nationalism, there is a conundrum to be resolved, and we have sought to confront the problem directly in this volume. All of the contributors are intent that they should not be the voice of an 'overculture', and all of us honour the principle of diversity, yet we are concerned that attention to the rich diversity of the contemporary world may allow no intellectual space for looking backwards. Therefore, we shall set out what we see as legacies of the theatrical past in the first section of this book, before offering alternative pictures of how events are interconnected. The problem is one of balance: how to weigh a synchronic (or contemporary) awareness of global diversity and the equal rights of all human beings against a diachronic (or historical) awareness that sets out how our multifarious world came to be as it is and thus how we might change it. We shall keep reaching in this volume for points of intersection between a vertical line that cuts into the past and a horizontal line that reaches sideways to the diversity of the present.

Indeed, we cannot study the past without studying the present, for the present changes the past. As Hazem Azmy pointed out in our meeting, the attack upon New York on '9/11' changed Egyptian history retrospectively.

After 2001, the world seemed to be a different place, and accounts of the past had to be rethought and rewritten. Any historian needs to interrogate the present in order to ask important questions of the past. A historian of theatre must do this if she or he is to quarry documents and assemble data to some useful end. But in what way is our historical work going to be useful? We cannot escape the 'why?' behind our activity. Why does the past matter to *us*? When we confronted this question at our conference, three forms of answer emerged.

The first might be described as an aesthetic response: 'I love the theatre, and I love thinking about what I love.' One participant spoke of a love/hate relationship. Most theatre historians practise their profession because of an emotional attachment of this kind: they love going to the theatre, or some theatre, and as creative beings they imagine how they would love theatre better, or even better, if it were different, and at least in some respects more like the way it once was. Theatre audiences are more engaged when they have a sense of history, just as a sporting audience will be more excited when it knows the history of the game and of the team. Theatre practitioners have repeatedly looked to the past, to old stories, old spatial arrangements, and old techniques, in order to challenge and renew present practices. Historians thus have one role as servants to the art of contemporary theatre-making.

Then there was a more personal response, which relates to the fact that many who write about the theatre and its history are also practitioners of theatre. 'The stories told about me didn't fit.' No historian can work without empathy, without placing herself or himself in the world of the past, and we interrogate the past to find out who we are as individuals, and sometimes also who we are as artists.

Finally there was politics and the belief that 'I am making an intervention'. The title of Ngũgĩ wa Thiong'o's essay collection *Moving the Centre* provided a compelling image in our discussions, relating both directly to our project in Part III of this volume and metaphorically to the idea that we should present history from the perspective of those who feel marginalised by their class, their profession, their gender, their race and so forth. 'Moving the centre' has two aspects: first, a challenge to the established centre of power, an act of transfer, and second, consolidation around a new centre. While challenging authority has been the ideal of modernist art for well over a century, building community does not enjoy the same prestige in critical writing, and yet from the perspective of a new or multi-cultural nation this may be a more pressing and progressive project. Historians shape identities, and new identities seek out their historians. The *New Statesman* places its emphasis on overthrowing old stories, but the world also needs from its historians a repertory of new stories.

The idea of an 'intervention' presupposes that historians are not trapped in an ivory tower that encloses intellectual thought and prevents ideas from touching the 'real' world. In totalitarian regimes it is all too clear that ideas are dangerous, but in places like the UK and the USA it is less easy to see how historical analysis feeds into historical change: the processes are slow and indirect. In her book *New Readings in Theatre History*, Jacky Bratton demonstrates that theatre historians in the eighteenth and early nineteenth centuries were engaged in a battle for institutional power. Authority was wrested from the theatrical profession and passed over to a middle-class voice that spoke of literary merit and thereby lent legitimacy to political strategies designed to control the auditorium. It is much harder to see such processes at work in our own world, because it is so close to us, and we have to be all the more alert. Knowledge was power in the eighteenth century, and so it remains today.

NOTE

1 Article posted by Laurie Penny on 1 June 2010: www.newstatesman.com/blogs/the-staggers/2010/06/history-british-ferguson.

PART TWO

When?

Theatre historians always work with a map of the past in mind. To put it less metaphorically, they write with some sense of a temporal continuum, where one phase leads to the next, linked by complex relations of cause and effect. The historian's task is to impose order upon the chaos of events that were once lived and experienced by a multiplicity of confused human beings, and, though hindsight brings undoubted benefits, there is always something arbitrary about the retrospective imposition of order. Historians are interested in moments or processes of change, because only by identifying change can they map continuities, but they differ radically in the kinds of changes that they think significant. Their priorities stem from different aesthetic tastes and different ethical priorities regarding the world they themselves inhabit.

In this section we shall look at how theatre historians within the European or Western tradition have mapped the past. The story that we shall explore in the next four chapters belongs to an intellectually and politically dominant tradition. This narrative seeks to track the journey that brought us to where we are now, and, for all its many byways and detours, it comprises a single story that countless historians of theatre have each tried to retell in their own way. It is a story that always needs to be challenged, and creative historiography necessarily involves questioning received versions in the light of new understandings or intuitions about the present. Historians never work on a blank slate. It is impossible to look at the past objectively as a set of unmediated events because past events always come to us packaged up as stories, and sources are always shaped and ordered by someone. Just as the Greek tragedians kept telling the same old stories of Oedipus or Orestes in new ways for new purposes, so historians keep reshaping old stories in order to accomplish their own intellectually creative work. It is necessary to see how historians have previously configured the past in order to configure it afresh.

This volume is not a theatre history but a 'companion' to theatre history, and we do not want to offer the reader a potted or predigested history of our own. Our aim in the following four chapters will be to provide the reader with certain core reference points and to explore how different historians have articulated them. In these chapters we have to 'do' some history in order to clarify the historiographic principles at stake. If we do not give you, the reader, some sense of the maps that historians have drawn in the past, we risk leaving you disempowered, as though 'theatre history' were a mystery accessible only to an educated few, unknowable and therefore easy to dismiss as unimportant.

There are two ways of organising history: genealogically and sequentially. The genealogist traces a family line from the present back as far as he or she can go, sifting through the records. There is much to be said for this approach, which asks directly and bluntly, how did we get to be where we are now? How do we uncover our roots? While amateur family historians get much pleasure from genealogies, members of other families find less to rivet them. Sequential stories are much more exciting because they begin at the beginning, and the reader is forever in suspense to know what happens next. Successful historians are good storytellers who demonstrate how, by unexpected routes, one thing leads to another. This is the conventional way of doing history, but it risks being more duplicitous than genealogy, for it may all too easily imply that the progress of the narrative equates with the progress of humankind, and that there is an inevitability in the outcome such that no alternative present becomes conceivable. Though each of the four chapters in Part II has its own chronological order, we have reversed chronology by taking modernism first and classical antiquity last. We have done this in order to point up the genealogical logic that lies buried beneath our crafted stories. To assist the reader, we have followed this introduction with a brief timeline that sets out in standard chronological order some of the major events to which the contributors allude.

In the four chapters of Part II we shall carve theatre history into four pieces, unashamedly reflecting tradition. The first is organised around the idea of modernism, an important concept in all branches of the arts. It could be said that modernism helped the arts know that they were 'arts' and not mere crafts, since the movement is associated with the autonomy of the artist, whose selfhood is invested in his or her art, and who is characteristically a critic of 'society', which is conceived in turn as something separate from the solitary artist. 'Modernism' stands in a problematic relationship to the notion of 'modernity', invoked by economic historians, political historians and historians of ideas to describe the impact of world-changing phenomena like industrialisation and empire. Whatever the relationship of modernism to modernity, we are hard put to escape the idea of the 'modern' as a device for conceiving how an alien world transformed itself into *our* world.

The concern of the second chapter, spanning roughly the seventeenth to the nineteenth centuries, is a period that, from the perspective of today's English and American theatre repertoire, appears to be a kind of Dark Ages, for it has bequeathed to us few plays (as distinct from operas) that overtly contribute to contemporary culture. From the perspective of France, Germany or Italy, the picture looks rather different. An old-fashioned phrase, 'the Age of Reason', captures one major feature that distinguishes this period from the age of modernism, for there was little interest in the unique subjectivity of the artist, and theatre was pre-eminently seen as a craft. The focus of this chapter will be upon the evolution of the theatre as the space of a distinctive encounter between actor and audience, its lineaments still recognisable today. An aesthetic vocabulary drawn from the visual arts will be deployed as a more helpful tool than a literary vocabulary for describing processes of theatrical change.

The starting point for Chapter 4 is defined by the appearance at around the first millennium of scripts that dramatise parts of the biblical story. Much harder to define is the point when this period ends. For English theatre historians, Shakespeare acts as a centre of gravity, since the volume of scholarship accumulated around him and the importance of his plays in the modern global repertoire make him an inescapable presence; moreover, English historians have the added convenience that the monarch was executed in 1649, and public theatres were suppressed, returning in a more regulated and curtailed form when monarchy was eventually restored. In England but not on the continent a decisive break point seems to be available in the middle of the 1600s. This chapter will explore some of the strategies that historians of England and of Europe have adopted in order to devise meaningful labels that order theatrical activity within the period that the chapter has demarcated.

Chapter 5 is devoted to classical antiquity when theatre is said to have been invented. Rather than speak of invention, we are on safer ground if we say that dramatic texts, buildings and sculptural images from Greece and Rome have until recently provided a model for theatre practitioners, a recurrent model constantly adapted to serve ever-changing needs. This chapter will examine how practitioners and historians alike have devoted themselves to reconstituting the seminal theatre of antiquity. The chapter sits last in Part II in order to emphasise that antiquity can only be seen and portrayed through the lens of multiple past reinterpretations. Over the centuries the same set of data has been repeatedly reorganised to create radically different pictures of the classical world, so it is a rash historian today who will claim to be telling the reader that this is how ancient theatre *really* was. More vividly than any other field, the study of ancient theatre lays bare the dialectic of past and present involved in all historical study. We need to use our experience of the present in order to imagine the past, while at the same time the otherness of the past makes us see ourselves more clearly. There is no escaping from that entanglement, for any serious historian.

Indicative timeline

c. 430 BCE	Sophocles' *Oedipus the King* (often considered the masterpiece amongst the Greek tragedies that survive from 472–405 BCE)
55 BCE	The Theatre of Pompey (first permanent stone-built theatre in Rome)
c. 960	Hrosvitha writing plays in Saxony – in Latin
c. 1150	Montecassino Passion Play performed in Italy – in Latin
1376	First reference to the Passion Play in York – performed in English
1487	A Roman comedy performed in Latin in Ferrara in Italy (seen as a key moment for the 'renaissance' of drama)
1518	Machiavelli's *The Mandrake* (classical-style comedy written in colloquial Italian)
1548	Religious plays prohibited in Paris (and in England there are local prohibitions over the next thirty years)
1585	Staging of *Oedipus the King* in Italian translation at the Teatro Olimpico in Vicenza (a unique experiment launching a classical-style theatre building)
1589	Medici wedding in Florence (considered to introduce a 'baroque' style)
c. 1601	Shakespeare's *Hamlet* at the Globe Theatre
1605	Inigo Jones and Ben Jonson's *Masque of Blackness* at the court of James I (early use of Italian stage techniques)
1611	Flaminio Scala prints his collection of *commedia dell'arte* scenarios in Venice
1660	Two playhouses licensed in London by the restored monarchy (sets a pattern for the next two centuries)
1677	Racine's *Phèdre* (adaptation of Greek/Roman tragedy, performed in Paris)

1737	Licensing Act reinforces the monopoly of two playhouses in London (Harlequinades and similar unscripted pieces might still be performed elsewhere).
1758	Diderot publishes his *Discourse on Dramatic Poetry* (an important French 'enlightenment' text idealising private emotion and domestic naturalism)
1771/2	De Loutherbourg works with the English actor–manager David Garrick at Drury Lane (introducing a more romantic and pictorial style of theatre)
1841	Staging of Sophocles' *Antigone* at the Prussian court theatre, with music by Mendelssohn (first serious attempt at reconstructing the ancient style, and using a translation not an adaptation)
1872	Publication of Nietzsche's *Birth of Tragedy out of the Spirit of Music* (associated with the music theatre experiments of Wagner, and later seen as a modernist manifesto)
1881	Emile Zola's essay on naturalism in the theatre; Ibsen writes *Ghosts*
1895	William Poel founds the Elizabethan Stage Society (seen as a foundational moment in the attempt to create an authentic Elizabethan staging)
1896	Staging of *Ubu Roi* causes a riot in Paris (and came to be seen as an early landmark in the era of high modernism)
1920	Max Reinhardt stages *Everyman* at the first Salzburg Festival (part of a post-war quest for collective theatrical activity; an early engagement with medieval theatre)
1922	Meyerhold lectures on biomechanics in Moscow (associated with the aesthetic movement known as Constructivism)
1953	Première of Beckett's *Waiting for Godot* in Paris (apparently insignificant at the time, but construed as a landmark in retrospect; according to the director, the play jettisoned three-quarters of the theatre of the past)

2

STEFAN HULFELD[*]

Modernist theatre

From the perspective of Western culture, 'modernity' can be summed up as an era that began in around 1500, shaped by the emergence of capitalism, industrialisation, secularisation and rationalism. By contrast, 'modernism' is characterised by developments during the transition from the nineteenth to the twentieth century in the sphere of culture, which correlate with political and social upheavals, technological innovation and aesthetic experimentation. The terms 'modernity' and 'modernism' are the subject of controversies striking at the very self-image of Western culture. This debate is made ever more complex when seen through the lens of the twenty-first century within a globalised world: the modern age? post-modern? Were we ever 'modern'?

In academic discussions, the terms 'modern theatre' and 'modernist theatre' entail a difference of focus in respect of timescale and subject matter. However, the language of theatre history is often inconsistent. For instance, in *The Oxford Illustrated History of Theatre*, John Russell Brown divides the period since 1500 into two sections: 'From the Renaissance to 1700' and 'European and Western Theatres from 1700'. The notion of modernity does not come into play, though it could have served as a pointer to the influence of capitalism, industrialisation, secularisation and rationalism upon theatre since 1500. The time-span between 1500 and 1700 is split into four chapters based on national criteria (Italy, Spain, England, France), whereas the span between 1700 and 1970 fills four chronologically organised chapters that include 'Eighteenth-Century Theatre' and 'Nineteenth-Century Theatre' before 'Modern Theatre: 1890–1920' comes to be investigated. The mismatch here between a strictly limited time-frame and the expansive adjective 'modern' is striking. This chapter by Martin Esslin covers what is normally regarded as 'modernist' theatre, namely Naturalism and the movements that distinguished themselves from it: Symbolism, Futurism, Expressionism, etc. We see that theatre historiography

---

[*] This chapter was translated from the German by Linda Bartholomai (New York) with David Wiles.

tends not to discuss under the sign of 'modern' the *longue durée*, which is to say the long time-span of theatre's evolution since 1500, but tends rather to trace developments in smaller segments. If it does not differentiate between 'modern theatre' and 'modernist theatre', this is perhaps because our everyday language fails to do so, using 'modern' essentially as a relational concept setting a boundary to what constitutes the present. Or perhaps theatre historiography fails to address modernity because it has decided to take as its subject matter the opposition between Naturalism and Anti-Naturalism that theatre practitioners like to describe as 'modern'.

Divisions into periods are arbitrary. This insight will shift our focus to the process of writing or producing history – that is, to the historiographic assumptions and patterns of interpretation adopted by those who write theatre history. Alfred Jarry's *Ubu Roi* is a case in point, exemplifying the creation of the 'modernist' narrative. The story recounted is about the shock effect of a staging in Paris in 1896, which broke with convention and allegedly culminated in rioting. In consequence this performance has come to be regarded as the catalyst for a new movement. The account is factually incorrect, but illustrates how the history of modernist theatre tends to be construed, namely as a sequence of breaks with convention involving attacks on social mores.[1] Historians demonstrate their affinity with the way theatre professionals view themselves through this approach, characterising modernist theatre as a tradition of constant innovation. Their historical narratives turn upon the dynamic element of change, whereas continuity and stability are described pejoratively or else suppressed. It is remarkable how repeatedly the obstacle that needed to be overcome was the text-based theatre of illusion indebted to principles of mimesis. In actuality, it would be quite legitimate to turn this narrative around and describe the period, say, from 1870 to 1970 not as the 'century of innovation', but as the era of a great illusionist convention against which numerous modernist movements vainly rose up in arms. Why does such a historiographic project appear absurd? Perhaps because it is counterintuitive to describe the theories and practical endeavours of Edward Gordon Craig, Isadora Duncan and Antonin Artaud, for example, merely as counterpoints to the stability of a convention. The decades between 1890 and 1930 in particular were characterised by so many and such varied theatrical experiments and such intense debates about theatre that historians understandably find their *raison d'être* in discussing issues of performance that still seem relevant today. In my view, we cannot appreciate the significance of these theatrical innovations if we simply list exceptional performances and theories (event-based history) that serve to contextualise a series of innovations (history of trends).

For this reason I return to the starting point of my introduction: the relationship between modernity and modernism. The goal of this essay is to examine the central questions of modernist theatre from the perspective of modern theatre as it developed in the *longue durée* (i.e., the slow, contradictory, long-term processes since 1500). In my view this larger temporal perspective can create distance, which is relevant to historiography in two regards. First, it dissolves the problem encountered by the contemporary historian of modernist theatre who is unsure whether today (currently 2012) forms an ongoing part of this history, or whether it has now become possible to take stock of a finished process. Second, a theatre history fixed only upon events and trends will tend to explain changes according to the logic inherent in a closed set of oppositions. Unless we take a larger time-frame into consideration, connections will remain hidden. For example, when Symbolism is described as the antithesis of Naturalism, it is often forgotten that in Venice in the early 1760s the dispute between Carlo Gozzi and Carlo Goldoni turned upon much the same issue in theatre aesthetics.

Theatricalisation of theatre?

On the basis of these introductory remarks I will discuss modernist theatre through the lens of one catchphrase: 'Rethéâtraliser le théâtre' – the motto chosen by Georg Fuchs for his book *Revolution in the Theatre*, published in German in 1909. Many similar appeals to 're-theatricalise the theatre' were made during the first decades of the twentieth century, spanning multiple languages and aesthetic tendencies. We can understand these demands for theatricalisation simply as a formal means of distinguishing between productions that try to hide the mechanics of staging and productions that emphasise those mechanics. But this explanation does not suffice. Two different dynamics result from the reforming of theatrical norms between the sixteenth and the nineteenth centuries: on the one hand, a sprint to the finish for the bourgeois–humanist aspiration that theatre, via Naturalism, will have an impact upon society; on the other hand, a resolute rejection of the principle of truth or verisimilitude as a means to negotiate, through theatre, the realities of life. Only from a historical vantage point can we see in what sense a modern 'de-theatricalisation' of theatre has taken place and ultimately shaped the meaning of Fuchs's apparently tautological catchphrase.

A commitment to theatrical theatre can be understood in different ways. Three distinct aims are connected to Fuchs's formulation. The theatricalisation of theatre may entail demands for the rebirth of theatre as a collective spectacle, or demands for a new definition of theatre as Art. There is also a characteristic exploration of the boundary dividing popular culture from high culture, as in the crossover between theatre and the variety show or circus. This third definition of theatrical theatre raises questions about the perspective of the theatre historian.

The rebirth of theatre as collective spectacle

In his treatise *La Supplica* ('The Supplication', 1634), *commedia dell'arte* actor Nicolò Barbieri attempted to defend his profession against continuing accusations that theatre was tantamount to Satanism. Barbieri began his career around 1596 on the stage of a mountebank ('ciarlatano'), who was accused of practising necromancy. It is therefore no wonder that Barbieri complained of how actors ('istrioni') were often confused with magicians ('stregoni') and associated with supernatural powers like rain-making. Despite belonging to this group of highly suspect professional actors, Barbieri, like most playwright–actors of his day, sanitised his terminology by distinguishing sharply between the honest comedian and the shady 'buffoon' or 'charlatan'. François Hédelin d'Aubignac, as a scholar of French classicism, enjoyed a different social status from Barbieri, yet he also regarded the demarcation between theatre and religious ritual, whether pagan or Christian, as the precondition for the evolution of theatre. In his 'Projet pour le rétablissement du Théâtre François' (i.e., 'Plan for Reorganising the French Theatre'), 1657, he petitioned the king to declare once and for all that 'putting on a play is no longer, as it once was, to be regarded as a religious or idolatrous act', but 'solely as a public amusement'. Both Barbieri and d'Aubignac advocated perhaps the most momentous change in modern theatre history: namely, the exclusion of theatre from the domain of religion, and thus from public rituals and collective festivities that addressed existential questions via performance. This exclusion had the consequence of reducing the status of actors from mediators between earthly and divine spheres to mere players of roles. Ultimately, the Catholic Church's quarrel with actors was founded on the serious rivalry between priests and comedians as agents of spiritual matters. The development of a bourgeois–humanist theatre defused this competition by ceding existential matters to the Church and assigning to itself a worldly, rational realm. This reform sought to turn theatre into an institution, preferably with its own dedicated performance space, with actors who declaimed according to the prevailing laws of rhetoric and acted according to prevailing ideas of verisimilitude.

Scholars and practitioners of modernist theatre became intensely interested in this pivotal moment in modern theatre history. For them, the theatricalisation of theatre, and the attendant theoretical concept of 'theatricality', invalidated the standard model of a humanist and bourgeois theatre.

Theatricalisation involved the rejection of prevailing historical trends and a return to theatre as a collective spectacle, for which early and non-European forms of theatre served as reference point. Modernisers sought to ritualise the theatre in order to suspend the fundamental separation between actor and spectator and, instead, forge a theatrical union. Theatre's return to mythological subjects proved to be as important as the search for aesthetic principles conducive to collective imagination and ecstasy. The inherited architecture of the proscenium stage became the incarnation of everything that was wrong with theatre, and there was a quest for alternative spatial configurations, and even the complete abolition of traditional theatre institutions. Radically more far-reaching, however, was the aspiration to eliminate the boundaries between theatre and life. The creation of conditions that facilitated an alternative experience of the ontological relationship between the individual, society and the universe was an ideal diametrically opposed to a theatre committed to the mimetic representation of reality.

Russian theatre discourse proved a particularly fertile breeding ground in the search for a theatre that reassessed the relationship between theatre and life. Between 1904 and 1909, Vyacheslav Ivanov developed his ideas of a 'theatre of the future' under the influence of Friedrich Nietzsche's *The Birth of Tragedy out of the Spirit of Music* (1872) and concluded that 'the crowd of spectators must mingle in the choric body as in the mystical communion of the ancient orgy and mystery'. Central to his thought was the idea that everyone in the theatre would partake in a dynamic encounter, characterised by 'a great process of becoming'. Although he based his ideas upon ancient theatre practices, he foregrounds the plays of Henrik Ibsen as successful examples of modernist theatre, finding that in performance they behave like thunderstorms: their accumulated electrical energies respond to a suffocating heat and burst out in flashes of glowing language, but without clearing the atmosphere. He also saw a transformative power in the plays of Maurice Maeterlinck 'where we are led away into a labyrinth of mystery and abandoned before heavily locked doors'. And naturally for Ivanov, the Nietzsche devotee, Wagner's opera *Tristan and Isolde* falls into this category as well. Ivanov's 'theatre of the future' crossed the boundaries of genre, embracing both Naturalism and Symbolism. Influenced by the 1905 Russian Revolution, his ideas had a political dimension, as is clear when he declares that 'real political freedom' can only be guaranteed in theatre when 'the choric voice of the masses' can be held up as an 'authentic referendum of the true will of the people'.[2]

Ivanov sees the development of Western theatre as a path that led from a dynamic process of interaction between spectators and actors to the audience's passive contemplation of actors, and in 1907 Vsevolod Meyerhold examines this view in his remarks about *uslovnyi teatr* ('stylised theatre', a standard translation that loses the concept of a momentary interaction created through artifice). Meyerhold shared Ivanov's historical analysis and emphasised that experiments in modernist theatre are 'no coincidence, but a direct outcome of historical evolution'. In his opinion, the 'intimate theatre' of Naturalism is the end point of a process begun in antiquity and characterised by divisions and fragmentation, and he views it as an 'obstacle which is obstructing the rebirth of the universal theatre, the truly dramatic theatre, the festive theatre'. This is why he interprets Ivanov's focus on the collective spectacles of the ancient Greeks not as utopian nostalgia, but as a historically informed foundation for the theatre of the future, which will embrace 'tragedy, comedy, the mystery, the popular tale, the myth and the social drama' in equal measure. Further, according to Meyerhold, the Moscow Art Theatre with its naturalistic principles was able to master only the plays of Anton Chekhov, with Konstantin Stanislavski destined to fail when tackling Sophocles, Shakespeare, Ibsen and Maeterlinck.[3] The appeal for *uslovnost* included a return to 'the actor's creativity and the spectator's imagination' as the core of theatre, as well as a call to reinstitute those artistic methods whereby the actor, guided by the author and the director, activates the spectator as a 'fourth creator'.[4] For Meyerhold, the solution to his aesthetic quest lies with two related concepts – the Mask and the Grotesque. In his essay *The Fairground Booth* he explained that 'the rebirth of the festive theatre' requires a playful treatment of existential needs: 'In its search for the supernatural, the grotesque synthesises opposites, creates a picture of the incredible, and invites the spectator to solve the riddle of the inscrutable.' Once the grotesque has become the norm in theatre, the stage will become the locus of imagination and *joie de vivre*, helping to transcend the banality of everyday life.[5]

At the turn of the twentieth century, Meyerhold's historical analysis was echoed by numerous attempts to reconnect with early and non-European forms of theatre, in order to revitalise theatre's bond with and effect upon society. The modernist quest to theatricalise theatre – a counter to the effects of Barbieri's and d'Aubignac's efforts to appease the Church – sought to activate collective creativity in order to create an experience of the transcendental and universal. Experimenting with masks, the grotesque, pantomime, rhythm, dance, the chorus, distancing-effects and improvisation, theatre attempted to create situations where actors and audience could participate in equal measure. The more persistently such experiments were tried, the stronger was the need to escape the city and create utopian environments. In this light the activities of Rudolf von Laban on Monte Verità can be considered representative. Monte Verità, a hill near Ascona in Switzerland, had long served as the site for political, mystical, artistic and generally anti-modern utopias. During a conference of the 'Ordo Templis Orientis O. T. O.', in the summer of 1917, Laban organised a *Sonnenfest* (i.e., 'Celebration of the Sun') for dancers and other conference participants. The dance-hymn began in a meadow lined with trees, near the edge of a cliff, overlooking the mountains and the lake. As the sun was setting, a messenger approached the celebrants, was welcomed with a roundelay dance, and recited the 'Song of the Setting Sun', whereupon as darkness fell the women and children lit a bonfire. Following more dances, the celebrants set off with torches to another meadow, this one higher up the hillside, circular and dotted by five bonfires. Around midnight, 'witches and fiends', draped in natural materials, danced in the meadow accompanied by the drums and flutes of the 'demons of the night'. Eventually they ripped off their garments and burned them. Afterwards, the celebrants trekked back to the lower meadow, where they intoned the 'Song of the Conquering Sun', while women dressed in colourful silk costumes danced at dawn, their colours gaining intensity as the sun rose.[6] As the First World War was raging – eventually claiming the lives of seventeen million – the congregants on Monte Verità worshipped the sun as a symbol of the immortal soul and everlasting life.

The determination to return to theatre as a collective spectacle led in other instances to more pragmatic outcomes, such as the Bayreuth Festival, founded by Richard Wagner in 1876, and the Salzburg Festival, founded by Max Reinhardt in 1920. The primitivist tendencies in Vaslav Nijinski's ballet *L'Après-midi d'un faune* (1912) are just as much part of this story as the theoretical propositions of Antonin Artaud, who claimed that the elements of performance 'have to be taken not for what they represent but for what they really are'.[7] His words serve as a reminder that the theatricalisation of theatre, which may rapidly transform itself into a theatricalisation of life, remains a driving force, from Jerzy Grotowski to the 'Living Theatre', performance art, and happenings.

Theatre as art

In an essay entitled 'German Theatre' (1813), Johann Wolfgang von Goethe examined how theatre had integrated itself into a bourgeois-humanist lifestyle and concluded that an institution dedicated to sensuality had been passed off as a moral one. He claimed that theatre had been institutionalised on the basis of moral rather than artistic precepts. The insistence on verisimilitude, decreeing that everything theatrical in the theatre should be hidden, was a concession to anti-theatrical prejudice. While idealistic attempts were made to legitimise theatre by emphasising the production of meaning, the formal and material aspects of theatre remained suspect; as a result, the

possibility of understanding theatre as Art was accordingly limited, imprac-
ticable and even (because of the rejection of theatricality) paradoxical. The
bourgeois-humanist theatre sought to give primary artistic value to dramatic
content. Aristotle encouraged this way of thinking, for his *Poetics* gives very
little artistic credence to 'opsis' (the *mise-en-scène*), and in the nineteenth
century this position gained support from the philosopher G. W. Hegel's view
that theatre is the outward execution of a dramatic work of art. Meanwhile a
perception emerged that theatre should be understood as a synthesis of the
arts. This view sought to reduce the specifically theatrical qualities of theatre
by attributing them to traditional modes of high art – literature, painting,
sculpture and music – while pushing to the fore the synthesising or synaesthetic aspects of the performance. As early as 1598, Angelo Ingegneri, famous
for directing *Oedipus* at the Teatro Olimpico in Vicenza, analysed performance practices in his essay *Del modo di rappresentare le favole sceniche* (*On
the Manner of Representing Scenic Fables*) as a synthesis of distinct components: machinery, action and music. In the middle of the nineteenth century
Wagner developed his concept of the *Gesamtkunstwerk* ('total work of art'),
an idea that would attract controversy in modernist discussions. Meanwhile
professional acting troupes, whose craft was based upon the body, were
marginalised by the 'reformers' of theatre. While the latter claimed to regard
theatre as a 'liberal art', they denied the artistry of theatre with their insistence
upon theatre as the mimetic representation of dramatic works.

Modernist theatre practitioners reacted strongly to these problematic
claims made in the eighteenth and nineteenth centuries about the artistic
value of theatre, and Naturalism ignited the demand for a re-theatricalisation
of theatre. In a preface written in 1916 for his play *The Breasts of Tiresias*
(1903) Guillaume Apollinaire declared: 'Consequently, it is legitimate [...] to
bring to the theatre new and striking aesthetic principles which accentuate the
roles of the actors and increase the effect of the production. [...] Realism,
which is no doubt suited to the cinema is, I believe, as far removed as possible
from the art of drama.'[8] One can cite countless similar remarks that may be
interpreted in the broadest sense as expressing an anti-illusionist and anti-
naturalist aesthetic. However, they vary in their objectives and methodologies, so we need to highlight some fundamental differences. We have to
differentiate between ideals of synthesis, where there is an interplay of sign-
systems drawn from the fine arts and stage architecture, and ideals centred on
physical techniques and thus the creativity of actors. Furthermore, a theatre
committed to the harmonious synthesis of the arts must be distinguished from
avant-garde movements where the term 'synthesis' applies only loosely, since
the latter focus on a separation of the elements (Bertolt Brecht), with the

friction and confrontation of different sign-systems creating the basis for new ways of experiencing and perceiving theatre.

Naturalism is generally taken to mark the beginning of modernist theatre, for it represented the final radicalisation and perfection of the long drawn out modern reform of theatre. It was a radicalisation of both subject matter and dramaturgy. The bourgeois–humanist reform proposed from the very beginning that the subject matter of theatre should be social emancipation and social criticism. For political and economic reasons, theatre found no space to treat these topics in either court or commercial theatre. The German movement of 'Sturm und Drang' ('Storm and Stress') did indeed paint the individual as an embodiment of the ills of society driven to self-destruct, but most theatre institutions had no taste for these plays. Initially, Naturalism was only to be explored via an 'accident' of court theatre practice (at the Meiningen Court Theatre, 1866–1914), or through the creation of private club performances outside the reach of the court and commercial theatres with their attendant protocols and censorship (for example, at André Antoine's 'Théâtre Libre' in Paris 1887; Otto Brahm's 'Die Freie Bühne' 1889 in Berlin; Jacob Grein's 'Independent Theatre Society' 1891 in London[9]). In his essay 'Naturalism in the Theatre' (1881), Emile Zola formulated a manifesto: 'The movement of enquiry and analysis', he argued, has encompassed all the other arts and sciences in the course of the nineteenth century and must now finally also embrace theatre. Hitherto all styles of theatre found their basis in the 'manipulation and the systematic mutilation of the truth [. . .] on the pretext that nature has to be cleaned up and elevated. [. . .] But today the naturalists have come along, declaring that truth has no need for dressing up; it can walk naked.'[10] Zola believed that a scientifically exact representation of living conditions could serve as the outward manifestation of the moral condition of the individual and society. In 1887 August Strindberg sent his play *The Father* to Zola for appraisal. Strindberg regarded the play as a perfect example of naturalistic tragedy, but theatres refused to stage it. Zola responded by politely listing some of the play's merits and then came to the point: 'You know perhaps that I am not fond of abstraction. I like it when characters have a complete social identity, when one can rub shoulders with them, when they breathe the same air as we do. And your Captain who does not even have a name, and your other characters [. . .] do not give me the complete sense of life which I demand.'[11] The rejection of anything abstract and idealised in the representation of nature, and the substitution of predictable moral themes with the 'naked' truth and with socially conditioned characters, proved explosive – as illustrated by the turbulent performance history of Henrik Ibsen's *Ghosts* (1881).

Naturalism's aesthetic project was to perfect realist theatre. The Duke of Sachsen-Meiningen was the director of a court theatre who paid meticulous attention to his stagings and set out principles intended to create a perfect illusion of reality and historical authenticity in a synthesis of artistic elements. Still accepting the primacy of the dramatic text, he focused on creating the impression of stylistic coherence. For example, he worked to unite two-dimensional scenery with three-dimensional scenic objects. He thought about how to position actors and extras onstage in order to retain the illusion of perspective, while avoiding classical symmetry. Through intensive rehearsals he sought to eliminate any element of chance from his performances, and he banished stars prone to upstage the ensemble. When the Meininger ensemble started to tour in 1874, the idea of a director who sought stylistic unity in the service of illusion won wide acclaim, not least from theatre professionals such as Antoine and Stanislavski.

Once stylistic unity had been achieved through naturalistic illusion, the debate about theatre as Art became acute. While the unsparing social critique offered by Naturalist theatre provoked heated discussions in the public realm, many practitioners felt that the goal of perfect realism was absurd. Evreinov ironically criticised Stanislavski's 'ultra-naturalistic production' of *Three Sisters* for being 'still far too conventional and theatrical'. To serve the authentic ideal of Naturalism, Evreinov insisted with malicious glee, Stanislavski should have rented 'a small two-story house somewhere in the suburbs of Moscow' so that spectators could gather there and watch the action through keyholes and half-open doors at various times of the day.[12] Such remarks pointed out the aporias of Naturalism, whilst counter movements reflected a desire for transformation and abstraction in the stage picture as the key to a re-theatricalisation of theatre.

Adolphe Appia and Edward Gordon Craig were two modernists who developed their own visual and rhythmic aesthetics based upon a harmonious synthesising of the arts. Appia, a Wagner enthusiast, could not understand why perspective stage painting faked a three-dimensional space, when the stage itself was already three-dimensional, a fact made all the more obvious by actors moving across it, and he saw how Wagner's conventional set designs contradicted the new synthesis that Wagner had established between words and music. In his writings *The Staging of Wagnerian Drama* (1895) and *Music and Stage Setting* (1899), Appia set down his ideas on how to realise a word-tone drama. The production should be inspired by one central creative idea driving the play, and all artistic elements should serve that idea. His stage settings consisted of abstract three-dimensional spatial features that gained expressive power from the 'shaping of light'. In this way, Appia's atmospheric spaces allowed the actor to develop a high degree of expressivity. In *On the Art of the Theatre* (1905), Edward Gordon Craig writes that

> the Art of the Theatre is neither acting nor the play, it is not scene nor dance, but it consists of all the elements of which these things are composed: action, which is the very spirit of acting; words, which are the body of the play; line and colour, which are the very heart of the scene; rhythm, which is the very essence of dance.[13]

Consequently, he set out in great detail the responsibilities of a director who had to ensure the harmonious unity of the entire production. The skills of the director entailed craftsmanship, intellect and art in equal measure. Instead of allowing design elements to be created piecemeal and then integrated just as randomly into the rehearsal process, this concept demanded that the director should oversee every aspect of the production. And instead of invoking the presumptuous and, ultimately, impossible principle of imitating nature, the director should consider the concrete elements of a production from a formal point of view, so that nature is at most merely indicated. Such sweeping creative control reduced the status of actors to little more than living material that had to be disciplined by a solitary creative force – as indicated in Craig's theory of the 'Über-Marionette', a metaphor for the pliable actor necessary for a symbolist theatrical art form.

Seen in this context, the theatricalisation of theatre aimed at the formal abstraction of individual elements in a staging (e.g., stage design, costumes, acting, light), while still maintaining the goal of stylistic unity. It is telling that modernist theatrical concepts emphasising abstraction and symbolisation relied on a director for a harmonious synthesis of these elements, while actors constantly posed a problem. Maeterlinck, whose plays seduced many devotees of Naturalism to experiment with Symbolist staging, was convinced that the spiritual dimension of his literary text could never be reconciled with the materiality of theatre. Wagner and Appia felt compelled to stress the importance of actors in their later writings. It is clear, therefore, that those arguing for a synthesis of the arts or driven by architectural and visual obsessions had difficulties in reaching an understanding with actors. The rise of the director is linked to the decline of the actor as autonomous artist – a hallmark of modernist theatre that I will only touch on here to highlight the tension that characterised the search for theatre as Art: on the one hand, focus upon the actor as the vehicle of theatrical communication, and on the other hand, the wish to conjoin all the theatrical elements.

Familiar with the various aesthetic debates of his day and with ample directing experience behind him, Meyerhold decided to place at the centre of his theatre the actor and his power to move an audience. 'Above all, drama is the art of the actor', he writes, and then turns the traditionally derogatory meaning of the term 'cabotinage' ('ham acting') on its head: 'Perhaps it has always been so: if there is no cabotin, there is no theatre either; and, contrariwise, as soon as the theatre rejects the basic rules of theatricality it straightway imagines that it can dispense with the cabotin.'[14] Through acting on the forestage, use of the mask and the grotesque, Meyerhold advocates a renewed acquaintance with ancient theatre practices that 'transport the spectator to a world of make-believe, entertaining him on the way there with the brilliance of his technical skill'.[15] In this manner, the theatricalisation of theatre used physical techniques as the basis for a collective exploration of the world of the fantastical. This interpretation of modernist theatre, which decreed that 'words in the theatre are only embellishments on the design of movement', produced its own tradition of Western theatre, most notably in France and Italy (Étienne Decroux, Jacques Lecoq, Ariane Mnouchkine, Marcel Marceau, Dario Fo, Eugenio Barba).[16]

Another important tendency in twentieth-century theatre aesthetics was the rejection of synthesis. In his *Notes on 'The Rise and Fall of the City of Mahagonny'*, Brecht comments on Wagner's ideal of the *Gesamtkunstwerk* in order to distance his epic theatre from it.

> The great struggle for supremacy between words, music and production [...] can simply be by-passed by radically separating the elements. So long as the expression *Gesamtkunstwerk* means that the integration is a muddle, so long as the arts are supposed to be fused together, the various elements will all be equally degraded, and each will act as a mere feed to the rest.[17]

Here the theatricalisation of theatre is characterised by distance, differentiation and friction between individual sign-systems, which makes the spectator aware of the different production elements and requires active mental participation. One can regard this artistic confrontationalism as an appeal to the spectator to make connections between heterogeneous elements in order to construct a new sense of the real. We should also regard in this light not only the replacement of synthesis with epic techniques, but also the techniques of montage and collage, and in addition avant-garde movements such as Futurism, Dadaism and Surrealism. The Italian painter Giacomo Balla entitled his outline for a theatre project 'Disconcerted States of Mind' (1916), a piece intended to illustrate how one could experiment with a separation of elements. As no official performance record survives, we must rely on the outline to imagine it as follows. Four variously dressed performers stand in front of a white backdrop. In the first of four parts, separated by intermissions, each of the performers calls out a number twelve times (are they stockbrokers, calling out prices?). In the second part, still ignoring each other, the performers repeat a particular letter twelve times (an acoustic installation?). In the third part, they carry out everyday activities: one checks his watch; another raises his hat in greeting; the third blows his nose and the fourth reads a newspaper. In the fourth part they all emit sounds meant to indicate certain states of mind (distress, pleasure, quick-wittedness, stubbornness).[18] Compositions and studies of this type became important during the twentieth century in the fringe area of sound/installation/performance. These performance pieces did not seek to be considered as theatre in the conventional sense, for they rejected the principle of repetition and thus the possibility of commodification.

The boundary between popular culture and high culture

During the carnival of 1510, the banker Agostino Chigi invited a selection of guests to dine at his villa beside the Tiber in Rome in order to entertain them with a 'lovely, captivating and delightful comedy'. This early example of humanist theatre had the goal of reviving classical learning. The exclusivity of that evening is put into sharp relief by a guest who documented the event in a letter and shortly after describes a biblical play in St Peter's Square about the resurrection of Lazarus attended by 'twelve thousand people and more'.[19] There was an elitist tendency at the beginning of humanist theatre practice, which gained even more strength under absolutist and bourgeois regimes. The development of theatre within court society led architecturally to an auditorium structured by social distinctions. Inspired by the Enlightenment (see the next chapter), the theatre adopted educational principles in order to oust pleasurable aspects deemed obscene or hedonistic. These processes led perforce to the establishment of the three clear-cut categories of ballet and opera and an austere spoken drama as the basis of an elite culture. During the nineteenth century, such distinctions became ever more problematic: the majority of theatre institutions operated under the capitalist principles governing the 'entertainment industry', juxtaposing the 'classical' genres with popular ones. And while the forces of middle-class education never tired of lamenting this juxtaposition, with its implications for mixed theatrical programming, as a crisis of Western civilisation, more politicised practitioners of bourgeois theatre yearned for a true 'Volkstheater' ('Theatre of the People'). In 1874, Eduard Devrient concluded the last volume of his *History of the German Stage* with the weary remark: 'Only an independent national government can maintain the dramatic ideal at its true value; commercial dependence on audiences will drag it down to banality or grotesquerie.' Almost simultaneously, Wagner maintained in his *Actors and Singers* (1872) that 'only in the lowest of genres' is 'good theatre still performed in Germany'. With 'Shakespeare's primitive popular stage' in mind, he sees the beginnings of a new and popular German theatre germinating in fairground puppet shows.[20]

This contradiction, especially prevalent in German-speaking countries, gained in significance around 1900 and remains a challenge to this day when we try to understand modernist theatre. The vocabulary alone poses difficulties. Much of the terminology is pejorative when we speak of the 'entertainment industry', yet if we see commercialisation as part of the process of democratisation, then we must acknowledge all sorts of different theatrical forms as the rich offerings of a newly emerging metropolitan culture. The fact is that the bourgeois-humanist theatre, making more or less convincing attempts at aesthetic legitimisation, gained an entirely new context from the circus, the variety show, the music hall, the cinema, sporting events and every other kind of show. The sociological consequences of the industrial revolution and the demarcation of work from leisure time, ensured that the 'fourth estate' or working class became a driving force in determining the cultural events on offer.[21] Examining modernism through this lens, we can recognise the contradiction that ensues when historiographic constructs place mainstream art in opposition to modernism. This contradiction has been addressed in film studies and countered with the expression 'classical cinema as vernacular modernism'.[22]

In this context, the re-theatricalisation of theatre involved a blurring of the borders between elite and popular culture. Many examples could be cited, but a reference to Max Reinhardt's achievements will suffice here. These ranged from his Cabaret 'Schall und Rauch' ('Sound and Smoke'), satirising elite culture, to his 'theatre of the five thousand' in Berlin's Circus Schumann. The problem was that such efforts to create a 'People's Theatre' remained largely informed by ideas of the educated middle class. It would never have seemed logical to theatre professionals working in popular forms such as the operetta and the circus to demand a theatricalisation of theatre. The modernist Hugo von Hofmannsthal can serve here as an example of the ambiguities in play. As a literary figure, Hofmannsthal collaborated with Reinhardt on his production of *Oedipus* (1910) with its mass choreography, as well as Reinhardt's open-air staging of *Everyman* (1920) for the opening of the Salzburg Festival. Yet when he was sixteen, in 1890, Hofmannsthal witnessed the first demonstration of the labour movement on 1 May in Vienna and composed the following verse: 'If the mob is roaring in the streets, aye my child, so let it cry. / For its loves and hates are vulgar and mean! [...] Leave the mob in the streets: slogans, frenzy, lies and sham, / They disappear and fade – the beauty of truth lives alone!'[23] Such underlying attitudes permeated modernist theories and practical efforts to free theatre from the halo placed upon it by the elite.

If we want to place at the centre of modernist theatre popular forms of live entertainment that were a direct result of technological development and sociological upheaval, then we need a radical change of perspective. *The Merry Widow*, an operetta with music by Franz Lehár and libretto by Victor Léon, premiered in Vienna in 1905, and over the course of the next five years it was performed in Denmark, Russia, Hungary, Norway, Sweden, Great Britain, Spain, Australia, New Zealand, Cuba, Chile, the United States and several African colonies. By May 1909, 433 German, 135 English and 154 American cities had enjoyed over 18,000 performances.[24] *The Merry Widow* might thus, for example, become central to an interpretation of modernist theatre. Additionally, the circus, cabaret, variety shows, revues, popular dance shows, cinema and various newly founded workers' theatres would also move to the centre, and in consequence, women – hitherto marginalised – would also become central in their functions as animal trainers, trick riders, ring mistresses, singers and dancers. The case of *The Merry Widow* reminds us that theatre researchers need to rethink their terminology to describe the aesthetics and functions of modernist theatre. Dismissal of *The Merry Widow*'s success because of its affiliation with the entertainment industry would seem insufficient, because it is debatable whether Nora Helmer (main character of Ibsen's *A Doll's House*) or Hanna Glawari (eponymous main character in *The Merry Widow*) had a greater impact on the demand for female emancipation. To effect such a change of perspective, we need to undertake a careful examination of popular theatrical forms, their aesthetics and dramaturgical adaptations throughout the world. Concepts and terminology have to be developed to establish which aspects of popular culture were central to the development of modernist theatre, and which sat on the margins. In his 'Short Organum for the Theatre', Brecht voiced the crucial problematic in such an undertaking: 'Even when people speak of higher and lower degrees of pleasure, art stares back at them with an iron face; for it wishes to fly high and low and to be left in peace, so long as it can give pleasure to people.'[25] Whether we classify the opposing pairs as 'high' versus 'low' or 'elite' versus 'popular', or whether the helpful term 'vernacular modernism' is set up against 'sophisticated modernism', we cannot by means of such dichotomies solve the problem, as Brecht well knew. We have to remind ourselves of Art's 'iron face' if research on modernist theatre is to continue down this new road. Studies that trace and contextualise aesthetic trends like the cross-influences of theatre and film or theatre and circus as they circulate within popular culture will prove especially helpful in redefining modernist theatre.[26]

In retrospect

In this chapter, I have given a problem-oriented form to my account of modernist theatre. I have assumed like Meyerhold that modernist theatre is a 'direct outcome of historical evolution', in order to investigate the modernist position from the longer-term perspective of 'modernity'. And while I have devoted the greatest amount of attention to this task, the last section of my chapter suggested a different and less familiar approach: lateral and contextual exploration of the multiple theatre arts that emerged between 1890 and 1930, as a result of deep historical changes. This essay is both an attempt to introduce the problems associated with the historiography of modernist theatre and an invitation to question received understandings of modernism. It is an obvious fact that the experiments of this period are a meeting point and interface between the history of older Western theatre and what we call 'contemporary' theatre. Historiographically speaking, when we gaze back in the direction of modernist theatre, we are confronted with the theatre reforms of modernity, which mirrored both a modernist return to pre-modern traditions and a modernist search for a 'theatre of the future'. We cannot place these developments in a single timeline, because theatre wanders through time and space in a circular and erratic trajectory; only the standpoint of a particular historian can give it shape.

NOTES

1 See T. Postlewait, *The Cambridge Introduction to Theatre Historiography* (Cambridge: Cambridge University Press, 2009), pp. 60–85.
2 All the citations of Ivanov's 'Theatre of the Future' in C. Schumacher (ed.), *Naturalism and Symbolism in European Theatre 1850–1918* (Cambridge: Cambridge University Press, 1996), pp. 228–9.
3 All the citations in V. Meyerhold, *Meyerhold on Theatre*, trans. and ed. with a critical commentary by E. Braun (London: Methuen, 1969), p. 61.
4 V. Meyerhold, *Meyerhold on Theatre*, pp. 62–3.
5 *Ibid.*, p. 139.
6 E. Dörr, *Rudolf Laban: Das choreographische Theater* (Norderstedt: Books on Demand, 2004), pp. 98–103.
7 A. Artaud, *Selected Writings*, ed. S. Sontag, trans. H. Weaver (Berkeley: University of California Press, 1988), p. 160.
8 G. W. Brandt (ed.), *Modern Theories of Drama: A Selection of Writings on Drama and Theatre 1850–1990* (Oxford: Clarendon Press, 1998), p. 167.
9 D. Kennedy, *The Spectator and the Spectacle: Audiences in Modernity and Postmodernity* (Cambridge: Cambridge University Press, 2009), pp. 49–72.
10 Brandt (ed.), *Modern Theories of Drama*, pp. 85–6.
11 Schumacher (ed.), *Naturalism and Symbolism*, p. 303.
12 N. Evreinov, *The Theatre in Life* (London: George G. Harrap, 1927), pp. 137–8.

13 E. G. Craig, *On the Art of the Theatre*, ed. and introduced by F. Chamberlain (London: Routledge, 2009), p. 73.

14 V. Meyerhold, *Meyerhold on Theatre*, pp. 53 and 123.

15 *Ibid.*, p. 129.

16 *Ibid.*, p. 124. On Meyerhold's technique, see G. Baumbach, 'Meyerholds "Biomechanik": (Re-)Konstruktion der Schauspielkunst', in G. Baumbach (ed.), *Auf dem Weg nach Pomperlörel: Kritik 'des' Theaters* (Leipziger Universitätsverlag, 2010), pp. 297–351.

17 B. Brecht, 'Notes to the Opera *Aufstieg und Fall der Stadt Mahagonny*', in B. Brecht, *Brecht on Theatre*, ed. and trans. John Willett (London: Methuen Drama, 1964), pp. 37–8.

18 Balla sketched 'Sconcertazione di stati d'animo' on a sheet of paper by listing the numbers, terms and directions. How differently these sketches can be interpreted can be judged by the following two descriptions, where Berghaus arrives at a basically less abstract version. See M. Kirby and V. N. Kirby, *Futurist Performance* (New York: PAJ Publications, 1986), p. 63; G. Berghaus, *Italian Futurist Theatre 1909–1944* (Oxford: Clarendon Press, 1998), pp. 252–3.

19 The two events were reported in Italian by Alessando Picenardi, see F. Cruciani, *Teatro nel Rinascimento: Roma 1450–1550* (Rome: Bulzoni, 1983), p. 346.

20 E. Devrient, *Geschichte der deutschen Schauspielkunst* (Berlin: Henschelverlag, 1967), Vol. II, p. 390; R. Wagner, *Über Schauspieler und Sänger* (Leipzig: Fritzsch, 1872), pp. 29–30.

21 See K. Maase, *Grenzenloses Vergnügen: Der Aufstieg der Massenkultur 1850–1970* (Frankfurt on the Main: Fischer, 1997).

22 M. Hansen, 'The Mass Production of the Senses: Classical Cinema as Vernacular Modernism', *Modernism/Modernity*, 6 (April 1999), 59–77.

23 Quoted after D. Lorenz, *Wiener Moderne* (Stuttgart: J. B. Metzler, 2007), p. 21.

24 These figures were compiled by Barbara Denscher as part of a dissertation project at the University of Vienna which undertook the first basic research on the librettist Victor Léon. The publication of the thesis is planned.

25 B. Brecht, 'A Short Organum for the Theatre', in Brecht, *Brecht on Theatre*, p. 181. Translation modified.

26 Relevant studies include B. J. Faulk, *Music Hall and Modernity: The Late-Victorian Discovery of Popular Culture* (Athens, OH: Ohio University Press, 2004) and S. D. Charnow, *Theatre, Politics, and Markets in Fin-de-Siècle Paris: Staging Modernity* (New York: Palgrave Macmillan, 2005).

FURTHER READING

Brockett, O. G., and R. Findlay. *Century of Innovation: A History of European and American Theatre and Drama since 1870* (Englewood Cliffs, NJ: Prentice-Hall, 1973).

Gay, P. *Modernism: The Lure of Heresy from Baudelaire to Beckett and Beyond* (London: William Heinemann, 2007).

Lehmann, H.-T. *Postdramatic Theatre*. Translated and with an Introduction by K. Jürs-Munby (London: Routledge, 2006).

Pomerance, M., ed. *Cinema and Modernity* (New Brunswick, NJ and London: Rutgers University Press, 2006).

Schumacher, C., ed. *Naturalism and Symbolism in European Theatre 1850–1918* (Cambridge: Cambridge University Press, 1996).

Senelick, L., ed. *Russian Dramatic Theory from Pushkin to the Symbolists*, trans. and ed. L. Senelick (Austin, TX: University of Texas Press, 1981).

3

CHRISTOPHER BAUGH

Baroque to romantic theatre

The history of the theatre from the late sixteenth to late in the nineteenth century is usually framed around dominant periods of national dramatic literatures: theatre of the Spanish golden age; Shakespeare and his contemporaries; the classic theatre of France; the comedy of manners of the English Restoration; Weimar and the golden age of German theatre. Given the longevity, authenticity and the archaeological value of the printed play text, this framing is understandable and inevitable. Nevertheless, these histories with their focus upon 'great works' have the effect of identifying the written and spoken word as both the prime instigator and the most important archival souvenir of theatre. Inevitably such theatre histories have shaped our contemporary perception: what *we* consider to be 'good' dramatic literature. For example, beyond the small output of R. B. Sheridan and Oliver Goldsmith, the British eighteenth-century theatre produced few plays that are today considered to be 'good' dramatic literature, and yet in terms of audience popularity, famous actors and scenic developments, the period clearly produced great theatre. Likewise, during the period *c.* 1830–*c.* 1880, theatre throughout Europe was a hugely popular form that responded fully and widely to social and political events, and yet, in marked contrast to opera, few plays from the period have entered the canon of dramatic literature. There appear, therefore, to be distinctive periods of European theatre history when the co-existence of 'great' dramatic literature with 'great' theatre did not occur. It would therefore seem to be important to treat with caution modern judgements about what is great dramatic literature and to inflect the assumption that 'great plays' are a necessary ingredient of great theatre. Whilst dramatic literature is of considerable importance, it should serve as only *one* approach to the making of histories of theatre. This essay aims to use the framing of the baroque and the romantic in order to make *a* narrative of theatre as a spatial and visual phenomenon from the late sixteenth century to the modernist revolt against romantic and material realism, which began in the final decades of the nineteenth century.

The changes and developments within the visual arts that took place in Italy during the fifteenth and sixteenth centuries – a phenomenon known as the renaissance that the next chapter examines – travelled and mutated throughout the whole of Europe, blending with indigenous forms to generate new and distinctive variants during these and succeeding centuries. Thus the terms 'mannerism', 'baroque', 'rococo', 'neo-classicism' and 'romanticism' may be considered 'European' terms of art-historical classification. They have considerable value in making histories of theatre since they help us not only to understand the aesthetic concerns of theatre architecture and scenography, but also enable us to consider theatre outside and beyond the periodisation created by the historiography of dramatic literature. They help us to appreciate the way in which the social activity of theatre and its practices may be understood within broader cultural and artistic concerns alongside painting, sculpture, architecture and music.

Until theatre artists such as Georg, Duke of Sachsen-Meiningen [Saxe-Meiningen], in Germany and Henry Irving in London took the decision during the late nineteenth century to darken the auditorium to enhance the pictorial qualities of the picture-frame stage, visiting the theatre represented much more than being anonymously present, sitting in the dark, watching and listening to a carefully designed and harmoniously unified production. Because of the illumination provided by candle, oil and subsequently gas lighting, audience members were aware of themselves, their fellow spectators, their spatial arrangement within the theatre building and, for most of the seventeenth and eighteenth centuries, the reality of actors upon a forestage that overlapped their own architectonic space. The buildings constructed for performance can speak eloquently about the attitudes and theatrical values of their designers and builders, and they can tell us much about the expectations and assumptions of their audiences. Similarly, the iconography of scene and costume design can reveal through its style, manner and mode of graphic reproduction as much about the social and cultural values of theatrical performance as it can about the aesthetics and technologies of stage practice. Both may serve as indicators of the social base for the popularity of theatre and can suggest ways in which theatre and performance reflect the social and cultural ideologies of their age.

Juxtaposing the progression from the 'baroque' of the late sixteenth century to the 'romantic' of the nineteenth century and the intermediate tensions represented by the 'rococo' and 'neo-classicism' of the eighteenth century may therefore provide a framework for reflecting upon the changes and shifts that took place within theatre and its practices. These aesthetic changes parallel shifts from the cultures of monarchies wielding absolute political power over sovereign states and their subject peoples of the seventeenth and early eighteenth centuries towards the politics and cultures of the state, the nation and the people of the romantic period. For the purposes of making this narrative, I will exemplify the beginning of the baroque with the celebrations that accompanied the wedding of Grand Duke Ferdinando de' Medici to the French princess Christine of Lorraine in 1589. I will conclude with the challenges to romantic ambitions of performance towards the close of the nineteenth century, when electric lighting exposed the artificiality of the painted scene, and theatre could do little to adopt the visual aesthetics of contemporary art.

The word 'baroque' was not used by artists and commentators of the period to which it is usually applied; it is, as Gombrich cautions,[1] an invention of art historians, most notably Heinrich Wölfflin in *Renaissance und Barock* (1888). The term 'baroque' (Portuguese *barroco* = an irregular pearl) is generally used to describe the styles and artistic attitudes generated by a renewed Catholic fervour that arose following the Council of Trent (1564) in a desire to counter the Lutheran Reformation. It represents art forms of energy and passion, frequently breaking boundaries in order to make works of considerable emotional intensity using architecture, space, light, text and music. As a term of art history and criticism, 'baroque' is used primarily to describe the emotionally charged visual language of seventeenth-century Italian architecture and sculpture. Theatre historians commonly adopt the word to describe the scenographic revolution brought about by the development, in Italy, of techniques of painted visual perspective in the scenic presentation at court of spectacular entertainments known as *intermezzi*.

The Medici wedding was celebrated by a month of elaborate performances that used all the artistic, intellectual and administrative resources of Florence, still at the height of its wealth, power and cultural prestige.[2] This was theatre of political triumphalism combining with the emotionally charged iconography of a re-invigorated and increasingly militant Catholicism. Skills of perspective painting, modelling, costume and construction were used to make *intermezzi*, visual conceits and processions that took place in churches, palaces, theatres and courtyards, and site specifically in gardens, streets and city squares. These new technologies served to create the *meraviglie*, the marvels or wonders that seemed to push experience beyond the boundaries of the possible. Such performance was a powerful statement and assertion of absolute political and religious authority. '[R]epresentational culture ... within a palatial setting'[3] becomes a defining feature of baroque theatre practice.

Dukes and elite academies built spectacular theatres locked away inside frequently rather dour fortified palaces, and the court theatre became what Carlson calls the 'jewel in the casket'.[4] The absolute ruler required a *theatron* – a seeing place – where authority and triumphal power could be asserted and

1 Stage design by Bernardo Buontalenti for the wedding celebrations of Grand Duke Ferdinando de' Medici to the French princess Christine of Lorraine in 1589. A sorceress on an airborne chariot summons the spirits to sing a prophecy of the golden age.

exemplified through spectacle and performance. The magnificence of artistic display set within a jewel-like theatre served to confirm intellectual, religious and political supremacy. The auditorium of the theatre at Sabbioneta (1588), for example, became a physical metaphor of the universe, unifying political and religious authority. The architecture assigns proper place and degree to the classical gods, the ruling Gonzaga family and the audience who lived in the town, which was also designed and planned by its Gonzaga founder.

The attitudes, energy and recurring imagery of the baroque help to locate the scenographic values of courtly representational cultures and the theatre architectures that developed throughout Europe to facilitate these scenic strategies. In this context the baroque 'period', when applied to the theatre, may stretch from the *intermezzi* of the Italian courts of the late sixteenth century to include the stylistic dominance of Italian opera throughout Europe until the final decades of the eighteenth century. This understanding of the baroque is illustrated by the spread of a classically inspired architectural form and scenography throughout Europe during the late seventeenth and through most of the eighteenth century, by family generations of scenic artists travelling from court to court, creating spectacles and perpetuating a pan-European style of performance for royal weddings, court opera and theatre, funerals and other representations of absolute power. In addition, these artists acted as advisers on the design and construction of opera houses, so that by the end of the eighteenth century a network of remarkably unified and interchangeable theatres stretched throughout Europe. The baroque, therefore, not only applies to scenic styles and the design of courtly celebration and festivity, but also to the physical structure and, increasingly by the late eighteenth century, to the identity of theatre within urban societies.

One family may serve to exemplify the processes that created a unifying baroque aesthetic. The sons and grandsons of the Florentine painter Giovanni Maria Galli da Bibiena (1625–65) dominated baroque scenic spectacle throughout the period. In 1700, Francesco Galli Bibiena (1659–1739) designed a theatre in Vienna for Emperor Leopold I and was responsible for court scenic spectacle. He later designed theatres in Nancy, Verona and Rome. In 1708, his brother Ferdinando Galli Bibiena (1656–1743) organised the wedding festivities in Barcelona of Charles IV and then travelled with him to Vienna when he became Holy Roman Emperor, working on designs of scenery and decorations for court festivities and opera. Ferdinando's son Alessandro (1686–1748) designed the Court opera house at Mannheim. In 1717 Alessandro's brother Guiseppe (1696–1757) took over from his father as chief designer and organiser of court festivities in Vienna. In 1740, he published the influential *Architetture e prospettive*, which illustrated many of his designs for court staging, alongside designs for cathedrals, spectacular

2 Castle Theatre, Český Krumlov. This restored scene of c. 1766 extends the baroque world of the theatre architecture into the realm of performance.

funeral catafalques and monuments. With his younger brother Antonio (1700–74), he designed theatres, scenes and festivities in Linz, Graz, Dresden, Bayreuth and Prague; from 1753, he became permanently employed by Frederick the Great to design the imagery and emblems to represent and celebrate the Prussian state. Antonio Galli Bibiena (1700–74), Ferdinando's third son, designed the theatre in Bologna and also worked at the Hofburg court in Vienna. Francesco's son, Giovanni Carlo Galli Bibiena (1717–60), designed the Royal Opera House in Lisbon. The last scenic artist of this remarkable family, Carlo Galli Bibiena (1728–87), worked throughout Europe, including Germany, France, Austria and the Netherlands, from 1746–60; he also worked in London (1763), Naples (1772), Stockholm (1774) and St Petersburg (1778). Some of Carlo's scenes survive at the Swedish court theatre at Drottningholm, which opened in 1766. The scenery, costumes, theatres, illustrations and technical books of the Bibiena family and of other Italian and later German and French artists ensured the dominance and influence of this pan-European theatre style.

The application of the term 'baroque' to theatre in England usually refers to performance at the Stuart court during the period 1605–41 and is used to describe the masque designs of Inigo Jones (1573–1652). Jones made two trips to Italy, in 1599 and 1613/14, and the subsequent development of his scenic style and associated stage technologies are considered to represent imported Italian 'baroque' production values.[5] Masques, like the *intermezzo*, usually concluded with the triumphal appearance of the monarch heralding a golden age, and scenically presented as the spectacular solution to riddles posed by conflicts such as those between Love and Beauty, Youth and Wisdom, Virtue and Honour. Use of the baroque in the later historiography of English and British theatre is limited, typically referring to the use of extravagant scenic spectacle within the subscription opera seasons in eighteenth-century London, where theatre managers employed Italian scenic artists such as Nicolò Servandoni and Giovanni Battista Cipriani, who became a regular designer for Covent Garden Theatre during the 1770s. Like the Bibienas, they were also employed to design façades, decorative triumphs and extravagant 'machinery' for firework displays.

Although both were English, the theatre of Shakespeare and his contemporaries and the masques of Inigo Jones are frequently separated and considered as distinct worlds of performance: a paying public audience in open-air theatres on the one hand and private dance-based scenic spectacle at court for an elite, aristocratic audience on the other. Perhaps a puritan attraction for the reforming attempts of William Poel (1852–1934) to rid contemporary Shakespearean production of its extravagant, painted realism has directed the historian away from the powerfully spectacular, visual rhetoric of the public theatre. With his Elizabethan Stage Society, founded in 1895, Poel developed for Shakespearean production a scenically sparse performance practice that relied upon the visual potency of the dramatic text. However, George Kernodle[6] properly reminds us of the powerful iconography of painting, sculpture, stained glass, tapestry and *tableaux vivants* that informed the galleries, balconies, inner stages, curtains, side doors, canopies and heavens of sixteenth-century European open-air theatres, as well as the side wings and proscenium arches of the indoor Italian-style theatres. He argues that

> theatre is one of the visual arts. If it is an offspring of literature on one side of the family tree, it is no less a descendant of painting and sculpture on the other side … the Elizabethan stage was not an isolated invention but was, on the contrary, a logical result of the patterns and conventions of the visual arts of the Renaissance.[7]

Whilst it would probably stretch the term 'baroque' beyond its critical usefulness to suggest that it be applied fully to the public theatre in the reigns of Elizabeth I, James I and Charles I, Kernodle's argument offers an important corrective to the aesthetic and visual isolation that the literary achievement of the period has imposed upon its history. Experience of practice at the reconstructed Shakespeare's Globe in London suggests that performance was a visually rich, highly coloured and multi-media experience filled with scenographic gesture, rhetoric and spectacle. A visit to Shakespeare's Globe, even when no performance is underway, reveals both theatre and stage as powerfully representational visual forms already clothed with vivid and sophisticated associations.

As a 'new beginning', the licensing by Charles II of two playhouses in London after the restoration of the monarchy in 1660 has frequently been understood as representing an influx of European traditions and values – women actors and changeable scenery painted using Italian perspective techniques. However, the introduction of perspective scenery into regular professional theatre practice in 1660 should not be understood as a wholesale transformation of the stage, but rather a remarkably successful blending of the well-established acting traditions of Elizabethan and Jacobean theatres alongside the excitement and innovation represented by the painted scene. The large Elizabethan-style forestage and neutral doors of entrances placed at either side of the stage still dominated when theatre managers had the opportunity to build new theatres: Dorset Gardens Theatre (1671) and the Theatre Royal Drury Lane (1674). Perspective scenes served as spectacular, idealised and apposite backgrounds to the dramatic action taking place downstage. Their powerful aesthetic attraction lay in their ability to seemingly vanish and re-form before the eyes of the audience. The painted scenes were supported in

3 Christopher Wren's 'drawing for a playhouse', 1674. Wren's less exuberant, more Protestant, baroque theatre provides a place for the audience, a place for the actor and a place for scenic statement.

grooves upon the stage matched by corresponding grooves suspended above. Sliding the scenes off-stage to reveal fresh scenes behind provided the magic of transformation. Engravings representing Dorset Gardens Theatre illustrate a baroque external façade and a highly decorated proscenium and stage boxes, whereas a drawing by Christopher Wren presents the more stern qualities of a north European, more Protestant baroque, displaying less exuberance than its counterpart in the Catholic world.

The drawing's theatre building is a tripartite space, providing a place for the audience, a place for the actor and a place for scenic statement. There could be a close physical relationship between the actor and the scenic environment, for example through the creation of tableaux, but when it came to great moments of performance then the actor's place was, where it always had been, physically close to the audience and, in the auditorium chandeliers, sharing a common source of lighting. Although Wren's work is simply titled 'drawing for a playhouse', computer reconstruction shows that the Adam Brothers' design for the ceiling renovation of 1775 fits perfectly within the Wren drawing and offers a convincing argument that it represents the Theatre Royal Drury Lane of 1674.[8] The setting that backed and supported the actor might represent a city in the distance, a gorgeous palace, or stately garden which, as Kernodle suggests, 'led by undeviating mathematical progression to the infinite. Sometimes better even than such a palace as Versailles, the perspective setting could achieve a combination of sensual actuality, kingly glory, and divine magnitude'.[9]

In England, the 'Glorious Revolution' of 1688 dealt with the religious problems that had wracked the seventeenth century by tolerating nonconformists and suppressing Catholics. The heroes of the comedy of the restored monarchy – cavalier men and women of 'the town' – became the villains or objects of comedy, whilst restoration butts – the elderly, the hard-working and the sexually faithful – became the heroes of the developing Protestant, proto-romantic ethic, exemplified by Richard Steele's *The Conscious Lovers* (1722) and George Lillo's *The London Merchant* (1731).

The thirty years' religious war (1619–49) between Protestant and Catholic forces dominated continental Europe, and its lack of clear resolution assured the Catholic counter-reformation that, in one form or another, Protestant reform would remain and could not be eradicated by either evangelical or military force. European countries began to experience the slow shift from the absolute sovereignties of the Holy Roman Empire, the Hapsburg dynasty, the French monarchy, and the Stuart kings towards the eventual sovereignty of the people defined in terms of the nation or state. Values such as civilisation, enlightened and tolerant religion, benevolent monarchy, and a belief in scientific enquiry slowly banished the values of absolute royal authority:

rhetoric, debate, belief and opinion gave way to observation, experiment, and recording. Absolutist decadence and heartless morality were challenged by exemplary goodness, compassion, enlightened sensibility and concern for *humanitas* ('humanity'). Denis Diderot (1713–84), art critic, philosopher and editor of the multi-volume *Encyclopedia* that encapsulated the science and values of the 'Enlightenment', exclaimed in his *Discourse on Dramatic Poetry* (1758):

> Poet, do you have sensibility and tender feelings? Then pluck that note, and you will have it resound or tremble in every heart. ... Water, air, earth, fire, – everything in nature is good ... It is wretched conventionalities that pervert mankind.[10]

Opposing the Catholic concept of original sin, Diderot's Enlightenment values asserted the natural innocence of the newborn child: it was social pressure and subsequent 'conventionalities' that diverted the child along a sinful path. Concern for 'humanity' and a drama that was exemplary of moral behaviour proposed a new dramaturgy, and Diderot outlined the values of a related new scenography: 'If nature and truth once appear upon your stage, however modestly, you will soon realise how ridiculous and disgusting everything in contrast to them becomes.'[11] Although lacking in detail, Diderot is calling for a more intimate connection between actor and scenic environment. Whilst these connections were to become key features of late eighteenth and early nineteenth century scenography, the impact of Diderot's ideas on acting was more immediately apparent.

This impact may be seen in the contrast between the baroque extravagance and bombast of James Quin and the simpler, more 'natural' absorption of the young David Garrick. Richard Cumberland remembered in his 1806 *Memoirs*:

> heavens what a transition! – it seemed as though a whole century had been stept [*sic*] over in the transition of a single scene; old things were done away, and a new order at once brought forward, bright and luminous, and clearly destined to dispel the barbarisms and bigotry of a tasteless age ...[12]

However, the chronicler of theatre is frequently attracted to a seemingly natural puritan simplicity as opposed to courtly extravagance. Care should be taken when evaluating such evidence; invariably in welcoming new styles and approaches a contemporary eyewitness generally considers the earlier practice to be barbaric. In this way previous generations of actors are always considered to be unnatural and tasteless, whereas the 'new' actor of today is always thought to be natural and true to life.

Diderot's art criticism is contained in his accounts of the paintings displayed annually in the Paris Salon. Michael Fried suggests that in his *Salon de*

1765 Diderot sought a 'de-theatricalisation' of the relationship between the easel painter and the beholder. Fried argues that this new relationship entailed a conception of painting that established the 'fiction of the beholder's non-existence in and through the persuasive representation of figures wholly absorbed in their actions, passions, activities, feelings, states of mind'; the 'audience' for such painting appears to be ignored by its subjects, who appear to be completely engrossed and absorbed in their actions and feelings.[13] Although fundamentally a representative of Enlightenment values, in this account of a relationship between spectator and picture, and by implication audience and theatre event, Diderot may be understood as initiating the aesthetic ideology of the romantic stage, its audience and the eventual darkened auditorium.

During the latter half of the eighteenth century, the state, as a collective representation of an entire people with a conscious and developing sense of nationhood, starts to take over cultural patronage of the arts. Increasingly through the period, as John Brewer has shown,[14] cultural power begins to be transferred from the absolute power of the court towards the developing power of the state and to spheres of public consumption represented by coffee-houses, concert rooms, art galleries, pump rooms, pleasure gardens and *salons*. Notwithstanding this powerful drive, the surviving courts of Europe continued for much of the eighteenth century, but with varying timescales, to remain an inspiration for personal fashion, style and the decorative arts.

As a result, many of the forms and styles of the baroque persisted but with the underlying energy, passion and religious purpose removed. For example, the *commedia dell'arte*, which, in its forms, established itself during the latter half of the sixteenth century, was a theatre practice of great physical energy and passion. Its surviving iconography shows that it could adopt and modify the baroque perspective scene to serve as triumphal backing high up on a temporary platform stage in a north European market place as well as in a richly appointed Italian or French court theatre. Like the baroque scene and its architecture, the *commedia* and its performance practice spread, laying the foundation of a European comic dramaturgy. The *commedia* was especially fashionable at the French court, and by the 1680s the company of Tiberio Fiorilli were *comédiens italiens du roy*, performing in public at the Hotel de Bourgogne in Paris. The appearances and forms of *commedia* continued into the eighteenth century, where they provided, through the media of costume, fashion, easel painting and in porcelain figurines, iconic images of the rococo. The term rococo (*rocaille* = shell) evokes the attraction of external forms – the shell of the baroque. *Commedia* also survived as a dramaturgical impetus in the dance performance of John Rich as the harlequin 'Lun' at Covent Garden Theatre in London during the 1730s.

4 The style of Andrea Palladio provided a sober, neo-classical and patrician model for Georg Wenzeslaus von Knobelsdorff's Opera House on Unter den Linden in Berlin for Frederick the Great in 1741.

Thanks to architects such as the Bibienas and their courtly patrons, the baroque opera house remained the dominant form of theatre building, but important changes reflected the developing authority of the state. Enlightened rationalism began its rejection not only of 'the triumphalism of Versailles'[15] and the ecclesiastical art of the baroque, but also of the sensuous, decorative triviality of the rococo. Theatre buildings began to occupy important positions within the geography of the enlightened city. Frederick II commissioned the Opera House on Unter den Linden in Berlin when he came to the throne of Prussia in 1741. But instead of a glittering baroque court theatre, a 'jewel in the casket' belonging to the monarch, it became the first freestanding opera house in Europe.

The style of Andrea Palladio (1508–80) provided a sober, neo-classical and patrician model for the building that assumed the form of a classical temple. In opera houses built for the absolute monarch, the focus of attention was inevitably towards the royal box, but when Victor Louis designed the Opera House in Bordeaux in 1772–8 the focus of attention shifted towards the public sphere: the foyer and especially the great staircase. In his writings of the 1760s known collectively as *Hamburg Dramaturgy*, Gotthold Lessing (1729–81) conceived of the theatre as a public, civic arena and articulated the idea of a national theatre for the city-state of Hamburg. By the close of the century, when

Arthur Murphy wrote his biography of Garrick, he acknowledged the civic importance of the theatre building as a public space, saying that it 'engrossed the minds of men to such a degree ... that there existed in England a *fourth estate*, King, Lords, and Commons, and *Drury-Lane play-house*'.[16]

If the baroque was admired for its display of an achieved spectacle, then the romantic asked its audience to engage with its experience of presentation, each individual to be carried away emotionally by the act of performance. The audience for the baroque may have been transported with anger or delight, but to be transported so as to lose a sense of self-awareness would have been unthinkable. Whilst it may be possible to typify the baroque through its aesthetic and its forms of expression, the romantic should not be thought of as a distinctive visual style. For the theatre, the romantic was an attitude, an approach to the function of theatre and an expectation upon the part of the audience.

The period 1760–80 produced writings and events that may, collectively, help us to appreciate the growth and nature of this attitude. In 1761 Jean-Jacques Rousseau published *Julie, or the New Héloïse*, a novel about thwarted love in a rural setting that proved to be a remarkable popular success. For Rousseau, tilling the soil and living from its fruits seemed to be the only genuinely moral and natural activity, and a true relationship with nature became fundamental to the idea of romanticism.[17] Furthermore, while the rationalism of the Enlightenment sought to demystify religion, the Pietism of northern Protestant states emphasised the inward spirituality of a religion of the heart. This conviction was reflected in the work of German artists of the 1770s, known collectively as the 'Sturm und Drang' (storm and stress), who demanded that art should serve as an expression of intense personal feelings; Johann Wolfgang von Goethe's *The Sorrows of Young Werther* (1774) quickly became a model for art to express the anguish of sensitive, passionate, alienated youth. In revolt against dominant eighteenth-century operatic forms, Georg Benda's *Ariadne auf Naxos*, performed in Gotha in January 1775, was a musical drama of passion and excitement where the orchestra served as protagonist and foil to the intense *personal* emotion of the speaking characters. Mozart attended the production and saw this revolutionary form as a way of overturning the dominance of mannered Italian recitative.

In the baroque tradition of art training, young artists would visit Rome in order to appreciate the rules and to acquire the proper values and attitudes of art, but Philippe de Loutherbourg (1741–1812) rejected this practice: he was amongst the first to seek the 'picturesque' and to award artistic value to the northern European landscape. During the late 1760s, following his apprenticeship in Paris, he travelled through the Swiss Alps and along the route of the River Rhine, which became known as the Romantic Road, north from Bavaria through the heartland of the German states towards Frankfurt. His route continued to England in 1771–2 where he worked as scenic artist for Garrick and subsequently Sheridan at Drury Lane.[18] His ambition and practice in the London theatre exemplified many of the attitudes and values that would come to typify romantic theatre. He designed scenes both of wild nature and of considerable topographical accuracy and introduced new and developed scenic technologies. His ambition was to present a carefully constructed scene in which all elements (including the actors' costumes) achieved a visual harmony. When Loutherbourg negotiated his job description with Garrick in 1772, he outlined his desire for aesthetic control over all aspects of production:

> ... I must change the manner of lighting the stage so as to serve the effects of the painting ... Furthermore, I must make a small model of the settings and every-thing that is needed, to scale, painted and detailed so as to put the working painters and machinists and others on the right track by being able to faithfully copy my models ... I shall draw in colour the costumes for the actors and the dancers. I must discuss my work with the composer and the ballet-master ...[19]

Whilst the full effect of these ambitions was not achieved during Loutherbourg's lifetime, the implications of his work for romantic scenography are clear. The following table,[20] outlining changes in European theatrical presentation, indicates the extent of Loutherbourg's ambitions and may also serve to represent baroque and romantic modes of theatre.

c. 1650–1800	c. 1760–1900
• The actor was raised on a platform in the same architectonic space as the audience – a large forestage, a 'liminal space' set within the auditorium.	• The actor was raised on a platform in a different architectonic space from that of the audience – beyond a framing proscenium arch.
• Costume was codified, using emblems to indicate character and historical period and making no attempt at historical consistency.	• Costume was consciously researched and designed and tried to realise fully the dramatic character and the historical period.
• Actors and audience shared much of the same light that illuminated the entire theatre.	• Actors occupied a brightly illuminated acting space with a corresponding reduction in light on the audience – the darkened auditorium became a reality by the last decades of the nineteenth century.
• The spectator shared an intense awareness of her/his individuality and of a group membership.	• The spectator was invited to 'lose' his/her individuality in the act of public spectatorship.

- The actors demonstrated an intense awareness of the presence of the audience.

- Actors had less awareness of the audience – Diderot, and later Stanislavski, urged actors to perform as though the audience were not present.

- Scenery was drawn from stock – used over and over again – painted by artists as generic scenes.

- Scenery was custom designed and made for the production.

- Scenery was considered as a capital investment. Italian artists (the Bibienas, Cipriani, Servandoni etc.) toured Europe supplying theatres.

- Scenery was increasingly considered to be disposable when the production was removed from the repertory.

- Stage technologies were evident in the grooves and shutters – their operation was part of the spectacle – scene changes were visible.

- Technology was still enjoyed as part of the spectacle, but was hidden behind architecture and scenic illusion – scene-changes were hidden.

- Scenery served as a decorative background to the performance.

- Scenery aimed to provide an embracing environment for the dramatic action.

- The mode of theatre tended towards the presentational and rhetorical; an expressive audience participated in the performance: they admired, they wept, they laughed, and they applauded the display of consummate skill.

- The mode of theatre tended towards the representational; the audience witnessed a harmoniously conceived 'other' world and were invited to be transported, to become absorbed, anonymous spectators.

Romanticism saw the human being located within the environment and as integrated within the natural world. Hence dramatic characters became scenographically designed parts of the scenic environment. Scenery and costume that traditionally *showed* its audience an emblem of location, character or historical period now began the attempt to persuade an audience that they were observing an actuality or simulacrum – indeed, in some cases, to try to convince the audience that it was looking at the thing itself. This new aesthetic could no longer cope, for example, with the tokenistic costumes that had featured in the presentation of plays of the past. The baroque actor playing predominantly on the forestage in the same space as the audience could well appear in splendid 'street' clothes of the contemporary period but with the addition of formulaic emblems – a Roman breast-plate and plumed helmet for Coriolanus, or a lengthened coat and turban for a Turkish ruler and so forth. But when the actor moved upstage to become part of a designed and composed scenic environment, as Loutherbourg required, such costume strategies became inadequate.

When Loutherbourg left Drury Lane in 1781/2, he opened his own miniature theatre called the *Eidophusikon* in which he presented historical representations, disasters, the natural world, and meteorological phenomena such as storms alongside volcanoes and earthquakes. In miniature, he was able to combine new technologies of Argand lighting with sound and painting to generate the surprise and pleasure of recognisable topography, as well as awe and horror at the display of, for example, the tempest at sea that sank the East Indiaman *Halsewell* in 1785.[21]

The philosophical and ethical underpinnings of romanticism (and the dramaturgical forms of melodrama and grand opera) were in place by the early nineteenth century in most European countries. The French Revolution gave urgent and enhanced opportunity for reflection upon society, human progress and the past. By the 1820s, accurate topography and archaeologically detailed scenes and costumes enabled the theatre to become a space to encounter and celebrate history. Notwithstanding its passion for the natural, romantic theatre had a profound faith in new technologies and threw ever more resource at the challenge of representing realistic 'truth' on stage – Diderot's 'fiction'. Extensive use of the discoveries of the Industrial Revolution, such as new scenic pigments, cast iron structures, gas lighting and limelight,[22] helped project the theatre into the forefront of progress and metropolitan life. Although it is unlikely that the introduction of gas lighting by the early 1820s very significantly raised the brilliance of on-stage light, it gradually allowed light to be considered as colour and atmosphere and to combine with painted pigments, presenting the stage as a carefully composed picture. Limelight created an intense beam of light and, for the first time, enabled the individual actor to be picked out and isolated within stage space, which, by the middle of the century, could already be darkened by dimming the gas light. The isolation and loneliness of the individual within the natural world was a dominant theme of romanticism, and the spot-lit actor became a powerful and iconic emblem of romantic theatre.

The full flowering of this theatre may be seen in the growth of historical drama, grand opera and ballet and their associated scenographies. Alongside the historical plays of Goethe and Schiller in Germany and Alexandre Dumas *père* and Victor Hugo in France and the operas of Giuseppe Verdi in Italy, the plays of Shakespeare served as inspiration and were increasingly translated and revived. Through scenography and production, Shakespeare could satisfy the romantic desire for history, nature, horror and supernatural mystery, set alongside the deepest penetration and understanding of the human soul. The cultural and political values of Shakespeare could appeal powerfully to the romantic and the revolutionary. Furthermore, his plays represented longevity and stature and were believed to have emerged from the

5 Charles Kean's production of Shakespeare's *Macbeth*, Act II, Scene iv 'The Banquet', London, Princess's Theatre, 1853. The audience witness a harmoniously conceived 'other' world and are invited to be transported, to become absorbed, anonymous spectators.

pen of 'a man of the people'. He offered, within the history plays, themes and narratives that could be seen as key historical stepping-stones in the progress towards the civilised achievements of the nineteenth century. Charles Kean at the Princess's Theatre during the 1850s and Samuel Phelps at Sadler's Wells Theatre during the 1860s pursued that vision in ever more detailed and historically 'accurate' productions.

The productions of Henry Irving at the Lyceum Theatre during the 1880s and 1890s represent a culmination of romantic pictorial ambition. The technology of gas lighting and its control had developed sufficiently that the audience could sit in darkness to witness the stage picture. As director and artist-composer of the scene, Irving demanded control over every aspect of that picture. The collaborative contributions of art and technology are clearly indicated in Joseph and Elizabeth Pennell's 'Pictorial Successes of Mr. Irving's "Faust"', in *Century Magazine* (December 1887):

> One minute a wild shrieking, singing crowd of misty shapes, moving hither and thither, clambering over the rocks and up the trees, dancing and turning; the next, after one last shriek, wilder, shriller than the rest, a silent, storm-beaten mountain top deserted but for one flaming form.

Irving carefully composed his entrance as Mephistopheles, wearing a brilliant red costume to become the 'one flaming form' within the grey, hazy and wild atmosphere.

But this scenographic approach had within it the seeds of its own destruction. To achieve the degree of realism demanded, scenery had to become more three-dimensional, which meant that it could no longer benefit from the elegant, but fundamentally two-dimensional, groove-and-shutter scene-changing system of the traditional stage, where the flies, the wings and the below-stage were all predicated upon manoeuvring flat sections of scenery. Even more destructive was the rapid implementation of electric lighting (London, Savoy Theatre, 1888), which exposed the artificiality of painted effect: the three-dimensional actor was now seen to be absurd when performing within two-dimensional painted scenes. As early as 1881, as a result of the increase in illumination created by the invention of the gas mantle to compete with electricity, Percy Fitzgerald identified the problematic effect of such light: 'Under the strong glare, the flatness of such profiles, its hard edge, etc. is yet more revealed and the whole looks what it really is.'[23] This increase of light precipitated the use of even more built-up 'carpentered' scenery, which in turn necessitated long scene-change intervals, and, in the case of Shakespeare, for example, demanded wholesale re-arrangement of the plays.

During the last decades of the nineteenth century, the harsh gaze of mechanised industrialisation and scientific discovery further challenged the romantic imagination. Émile Zola wrote of the paintings in the Paris Salon of 1866 that when 'the wind blows in the direction of science, despite ourselves, we are pushed towards the exact study of facts and things'.[24] There was little that the theatre could do except fill the stage with more realistic 'things' and cumbersome attempts at three-dimensional scenery made yet more ridiculous in the revealing glare of electric lighting. But also, during the final decades of the century, the theatre could not maintain an aesthetic kinship with contemporary schools of art. Designers did not find a way, for example, to incorporate the visual style and language of impressionism within scenery or within stage costume. The romantic ambition for stage practice, initiated by artists such as Loutherbourg, was no longer tenable. Pictorial scenography and the architecture of the proscenium stage were challenged, and both collapsed in the face of the radical ideas of early modernity in the scenographic revolutions of, amongst others, Adolphe Appia, Edward Gordon Craig, Max Reinhardt and Vsevelod Meyerhold.

The history of theatre and performance from the sixteenth to late in the nineteenth century may be approached in many ways. It can benefit from histories of the actor, of the scenographer and the scenic space, of the architect and the semiotics of the playhouse, and of the playwright and dramatic literature. Equally it may benefit from narratives devoted to its economic, its political and its social histories. And, of course, these narratives will be inflected, and indeed directed, by contemporary approaches and our own theoretical concerns. Theatre is a complex social phenomenon, compounded of a wide range of tangible and less tangible qualities, which vanish as its audience leaves the place of performance, leaving no enduring trace. From imperfect archives of artefacts and iconography, published and unpublished playscripts, faded and empty theatres, narratives by practitioners and eyewitness accounts, the scholar will make a selection to suit their history. The attraction of making a micro-history is understandable since it avoids many of the difficulties and dangers of generalisation and over-simplification. But it is also of value to locate micro, national and regional activities within the trajectories of wider political and cultural events. This essay has undertaken the task of making a macro-history of the theatre, reflecting the transition between two powerful European movements of art – the baroque and the romantic. It has charted some of the changes that occurred in theatre and set them alongside the transition from the cultures of a dominant church and of political power that used performance as a representation of absolute authority, towards the pan-European growth of a romantic concern for the individual human soul located within the natural environment and represented through scenographic language in theatre and performance.

NOTES

1 See E. H. Gombrich, 'Norm and Form: The Stylistic Categories of Art History and their Origins in Renaissance Ideals' (1963), in Steve Edwardes (ed.), *Art and its Histories* (New Haven and London: Yale University Press with the Open University, 1999), p. 77.

2 For a full account of the Florentine wedding celebrations, see Alois Nagler, *Theatre Festivals of the Medici 1539–1637* (New Haven: Yale University Press, 1964); Roy Strong, *Art and Power: Renaissance Festivals 1450–1650* (Woodbridge: The Boydell Press, 1984); and James Saslow, *The Medici Wedding of 1589* (New Haven: Yale University Press, 1996).

3 Tim Blanning, *The Pursuit of Glory: Europe 1648–1815* (Harmondsworth: Penguin Books, 2008), p. 426.

4 Marvin Carlson, *Places of Performance: The Semiotics of Theatre Architecture* (Ithaca and London: Cornell University Press, 1989), p. 38.

5 See John Peacock, *The Stage Designs of Inigo Jones: the European Context* (Cambridge: Cambridge University Press, 1995).

6 George R. Kernodle, *From Art to Theatre: Form and Convention in the Renaissance* (Chicago: University of Chicago Press, 1944).

7 *Ibid.* p. 2.

8 Cat Fergusson's computer visualisations of the Theatre Royal, Drury Lane are at www.kvl.cch.kcl.ac.uk/THEATRON.

9 Kernodle, *From Art to Theatre*, p. 218.

10 Denis Diderot, *Oeuvres Complètes*, Vol. x, ed. Jacques and Anne-Marie Chouillet (Paris: Hermann, 1980), p. 337, my translation.

11 Denis Diderot, *Discours sur la Poésie Dramatique* (1758), trans. W. H. Pollock, London: 1883, cited in A. M. Nagler, *A Source Book in Theatrical History* (New York: Dover, 1959), pp. 325–6.

12 Richard Cumberland (1801), cited in Philip H. Highfill, Kalman A. Burnim, Edward A. Langhans, *Biographical Dictionary of Actors, Actresses, Musicians, Dancers, Managers and other Stage Personnel in London 1660–1800*, Vol. vi, Garrick to Gyngell, (Carbondale, IL: Southern Illinois University Press, 1978), p. 17.

13 Michael Fried, *Absorption and Theatricality: Painting and Beholder in the Age of Diderot* (London: University of Chicago Press, 1980), pp. 131–2. Fried's clarification of this 'fiction', which, Diderot suggests, should subsume characters in a 'unified compositional structure, thereby giving the painting as a whole the character of a closed and self sufficient system', anticipates the unifying scenography of Loutherbourg (discussed below).

14 See John Brewer, *The Pleasures of the Imagination* (London: HarperCollins, 1997).

15 Tim Blanning, *The Romantic Revolution* (London: Weidenfeld & Nicolson, 2010), p. 37.

16 Arthur Murphy, *The Life of David Garrick*, 2 vols., London, 1801, Vol. ii, p. 201.

17 The rural world, of course, had always been a subject for art. The clarity of the landscapes of Nicolas Poussin (1594–1665) had served as a significant movement away from the baroque, whilst his friend Claude Lorrain (*c.* 1604–82) fed the northern European 'picturesque' desire to transform the natural world through gardening into theatrically constructed landscapes.

18 For a detailed discussion and analysis of Loutherbourg's theatre practice, see Christopher Baugh, *Garrick and Loutherbourg* (Cambridge: Chadwyck-Healey, 1990).

19 Undated letter by Loutherbourg to Garrick, *c.* March 1772, Harvard Theatre Collection, my translation in *Garrick and Loutherbourg*, pp. 123–4.

20 A version of this table appears in Christopher Baugh, *Theatre, Performance and Technology: The Development of Scenography in the Twentieth Century* (Basingstoke: Palgrave Macmillan, 2005), p. 13.

21 Aimé Argand (1750–1803) effectively tripled the light that could be produced from an oil lamp by forming the wick into a cylinder, and intensifying the flame in the updraught created by placing a glass chimney over the burner.

22 Thomas Drummond (1797–1840) built a limelight lantern in 1826 to assist in military cartography. Burning oxygen and hydrogen is focused upon a stick of calcium oxide (lime), producing an intense white light. It was used in the theatre from the late 1830s.

23 Percy Fitzgerald, *The World Behind the Scenes* (London: 1881), p. 3.

24 Cited in Blanning, *The Romantic Revolution*, p. 179.

FURTHER READING

Baugh, Christopher. 'Scenography and Technology', in Jane Moody and Daniel O'Quinn, eds. *The Cambridge Companion to the British Theatre 1730–1830* (Cambridge: Cambridge University Press, 2007), pp. 43–56.

Bergman, G. M. *Lighting in the Theatre* (Stockholm: Almqvist & Wiksell, 1977).

Blanning, T. C. W. *The Culture of Power and the Power of Culture: Old Regime Europe 1660–1789* (Oxford: Oxford University Press, 2002).

Brewer, John. *The Pleasures of the Imagination: English Culture in the Eighteenth Century* (London: Harper Collins, 1997).

Brockett, Oscar G., Margaret Mitchell and Linda Hardberger. *Making the Scene: A History of Stage Design and Technology in Europe and the United States* (San Antonio, TX: Tobin Theatre Arts Fund, 2010).

Davis, Tracy C., and Peter Holland. *The Performing Century: Nineteenth-Century Theatre's History* (Basingstoke: Palgrave Macmillan, 2007).

Strong, Roy. *Art and Power: Renaissance Festivals, 1450–1650* (Berkeley and Los Angeles: University of California Press, 1984).

Worrall, David. *The Politics of Romantic Theatricality, 1787–1832* (Basingstoke: Palgrave Macmillan, 2007).

4

DAVID WILES

Medieval, renaissance and early modern theatre

All historians divide the past into periods, distinguishing moments of decisive change from times of relative stability. There is no other way to give the past a shape and thereby perceive it as something other than a random stream of events. Every label we put upon a historical period is already an interpretation and contains a story embedded within it. There is no escaping from this process into objectivity. Telling the story of the past in terms of centuries may appear to be a neutral process, but it is not, for the world flows on when centuries change. Italian theatre historians are relatively comfortable when framing books or essays around the *cinquecento*, the 1500s, because at the start of that century we find dramatists adapting Roman comedies into Italian in a decisive move into 'renaissance' drama, whilst at the end we find dramatists, again in imitation of antiquity, creating new forms of music-theatre that will later be defined as 'baroque opera'. English historians struggle harder to make 'sixteenth-century drama' work as a narrative frame and usually opt for 'Tudor drama', since the Tudor dynasty ruled from 1485–1603. Shakespeare's writing career straddled two centuries, not to mention two dynasties, and he has become the reference point for creating a sense of English theatre history. His mid-career *Hamlet* was probably written in 1601, while nothing remarkable seems to have happened in around 1500. The 'Sixteenth Century' works as an organising frame if the English historian wants to trace a process that culminated in the masterpieces of Shakespeare, but it yields a different kind of story to the Italian *cinquecento*.

The word 'medieval' (i.e., of the 'middle ages') has proved one of the most resilient of all period labels. The idea of a time *in the middle* emerged as early as the fifteenth century, when Italian intellectuals tried to emulate a lost classical civilisation, believing that the ten centuries since the fall of the Roman Empire had been a time of cultural darkness. With the ruins of ancient buildings littered about their cities, Italians sensed the importance of a vanished civilisation and wanted to recoup what they saw as their own past; in the Germanic world of central Europe, on the other hand, the institution of the Holy Roman Empire implied that a line of continuity joined the first pagan emperors of Rome to their Christian successors, so the concept of a 'middle' ages dividing then from now was slower to emerge. The word 'medieval' continues today to suggest a long hiatus before *our* world, modernity, gets under way. Medieval plays are not part of our theatrical repertory and with rare exceptions are performed only as academic experiments, religious community ventures or folkloric curiosities. They apparently belong to a period of hiatus, not to a period of development that culminates in what *we* do now.

The dominance of the Catholic Church is the most obvious feature of the 'medieval' age. In the first half of the second millennium, the nation-state was weak or non-existent, and Europeans gave their loyalties on the one hand to local communities and on the other to God, via his spiritual representatives. The Christian story provided the organising principle for almost all aspects of life, from the calendar of social events to moral debates about a just society. Tending to be secular creatures who pride themselves on their rationality, modern theatre historians usually find it hard to empathise with medieval theatre-makers who are on the one hand seen as significant ancestors, but on the other hand are seen as imbued in religion. It is hard to escape from the idea that there is something primitive about the religiosity of these ancestors.

The subordination of humanity to a divine scheme determined when dramas were performed in the Catholic world, whilst the eastern Orthodox Church, worshipping in ways that were inherently more theatrical, never spawned scripted dramatic works in the same manner. The solar calendar mapped out Christian festivals that commemorated saints and the events surrounding Christ's birth (Christ-Mass), while the lunar calendar mapped the Easter events around Christ's death and resurrection. Dramatic enactments brought to life stories embedded in the Christian calendar. Medieval audiences also enjoyed domestic farces about adultery and deception, but these too had their assigned place, at carnival time when people took leave of the flesh before a month of Lenten abstinence. Medieval drama was space-specific as well as time-specific. The most important spaces of everyday life were transformed into festive places to mark the importance of the moment, and certain sacred themes (like the resurrection) belonged to particular sacred places (like a stone tomb beside the church altar). There was no question of a special space being set aside for art and called a 'theatre'. Actors were amateurs not just because communities were too small to support full-time professionals, but also because, since every aspect of the external world had a symbolic meaning within the divine scheme, the job of the actor was to point up that symbolic meaning without needing sophisticated skills of delivery or impersonation.

Since Latin was the universal language of church services and the language used by all intellectuals, it makes sense to think of medieval theatre as a European rather than a national phenomenon. Most historians leave aside six classically inspired plays of the tenth century written by Hrosvitha, an aristocrat linked to the court of the Holy Roman Empire in Saxony. Since men were preoccupied by politics and warfare, women had more time for intellectual pursuits, but being female Hrosvitha is usually dismissed as a nun doing strange things in the privacy of her convent, even though she never belonged to an enclosed order.[1] Her attachment to a convent explains why her plays survived, and it is hard to tell how many other dramatists were at work in a courtly environment. Hrosvitha disrupts the standard historical narrative, which assumes that history equates with progress and makes European theatre reinvent itself from primitive ritual origins. Since service books survive, we know that in many monasteries in the decades around the first millennium an addition was made to the service before daylight on Easter morning: priests were required to represent three women approaching Christ's tomb with spices, an angel (singing in Latin) asks 'Whom do you seek?', and, when the women hear that Christ has risen, they turn and transmit this news to the congregation. Less remarkable when performed in a nunnery, the cross-gender transformation associated with this musical exchange has convinced most scholars that we see here a decisive tipping of ritual into something we can safely classify as 'theatre'.

Some historians speak of a 'twelfth-century renaissance' associated with a new 'humanism'. Though theatre scholars for the most part speak of *the* Renaissance as a later Italian phenomenon, a Europe-wide move to assert Christ's common humanity explains why, in the first half of the 1100s, in the Italian monastery where St Benedict established the principles of monasticism, we find our first surviving text of a 'passion play', where the story of Christ's 'passion' – his suffering, death and resurrection – is enacted. Stage directions refer to props, gestures and the manner of speaking. The lament of the Virgin Mary under the cross was sung in Italian rather than Latin, suggesting Mary had the power to mediate between ordinary people and the divine.[2] In the centuries that followed, the use of local languages became widespread in an effort to touch the hearts of popular audiences. The first play in this genre that seems to come from England is written in Norman French, an example of the complications of organising early theatre history on a national basis.[3] One of the major 'English' passion plays surviving from the fourteenth century is written in the Celtic language of Cornwall.

Most medieval drama documented outside the world of the monastery comes from the fifteenth and sixteenth centuries, usually classed as the *late* middle ages. Drama thrived in urban communities that were prosperous, free of plague and war, and proud of their autonomy. The well documented York pageants are often taken as the archetypal medieval drama: craft guilds here performed plays on wagons in sequence across the city over the course of a very long Corpus Christi day. Our impression of norms risks being shaped by a scholarly focus on English material, even though in France many more medieval plays survive, including plays about saints and miracles, and rustic farces sometimes performed by men in fool outfits, genres represented in England only by isolated examples. Vast French passion plays are unedited or printed in old and unobtainable editions. There are many good introductions to medieval English theatre, but few English-language introductions to medieval European theatre.[4] North Americans, often bringing their own cultural nostalgia to the task, have joined British scholars in searching for the world that Shakespeare knew in his youth and that informed his writing. In France, by contrast, passion plays have no obvious connection to a 'golden age' of French drama defined by Molière, Corneille and Racine. The French republican tradition, with its roots in the French Revolution, is militantly secular, its iconography classical, whereas in Britain the Queen remains head of the English Church and Parliament sits in a pseudo-medieval building. Present-day cultural differences shape patterns of scholarship that determine how the past is mapped. In Germany the situation is different again. Federalist impulses associated with the European Union encouraged the study of early plays written in German of which many were performed outside modern Germany in places such as Latvia and Hungary, Italy and Switzerland. The medieval world suggests how nationalism might be transcended.

As a descriptor of cultural life, 'Medieval' is often set in apposition to 'Renaissance', the French word for 'rebirth' used to characterise a period of creative engagement with Greek and Roman antiquity. Characteristic of this 'Renaissance' are 'humanist' accounts of the world that prefer to avoid Christian and other supernatural explanations. For theatre historians the term 'renaissance drama' is at its most clear-cut when we look at a play like Machiavelli's *Mandragola* ('The Mandrake', 1518–20), inspired by Roman comedy and ridiculing along with a corrupt priest the principles of Christian ethics. The end justifies the means in a Florence where there is no possibility of divine retribution. The play borrows the Roman conventions of five acts, a single set and action concentrated into twenty-four hours, creating a complete bounded world which the spectator grasps as a totality, and its elegant aesthetic form contradicts its moral anarchy. In terms of audience, the play reached out in two directions. A manuscript copy was presented to the unofficial ruler of Florence, Lorenzo de' Medici, and a performance was commissioned by the Pope, another member of the Medici family, but, circulated in a cheap printed edition, the play was also performed in Venice in the 1520s by amateur Florentine expatriates and by a semi-professional company to paying audiences.

The idea that the Renaissance was a distinct period owes much to the Swiss historian Jacob Burckhardt. In *The Civilization of the Renaissance in Italy* (1860), Burckhardt tied culture to politics with his concept of the state as a work of art, and he linked the Renaissance to modernity with his argument that here lay the birth of 'the individual'. If we accept his equation of the Renaissance with individualism, then we could say that *Mandragola* appealed both to the individual consumer exercising choice and to the individual as a ruler insisting on privilege.[5] For theatre historians, the continuing challenge of Burckhardt's book lies in the way it deflects attention from plays of this familiar kind to the visually extravagant interludes that punctuated them in performance, and to festivals and processions in the streets, where renaissance regimes employed theatrical artists in pursuit of their hold on power.[6] Let me take the example of *Calandria*, a Roman-style play written in the same Florentine idiom as *Mandragola* and performed at the ducal court of Urbino during the Carnival of 1513. A long letter sent by the producer to an absent courtier tells us nothing about the comic narrative, but goes into detail about the transformation of the palace throne room into an auditorium, about the set design and above all about the interludes that presented dancing and chariots with classical gods and monsters in a cumulative allegory about love and war.[7] Today historians of drama are interested in the scripted comedy, because it connects up with *our* world in what seems to be a continuous line: they may recognise from Shakespeare, for example, motifs in *Calandria* like the twins who engage in cross-gender disguise or the stooge who hides in a chest. The interludes seem of lesser interest because they reference a local political situation, because the language of ancient mythology is no longer part of today's culture, and because, unlike the words of the text, the visual spectacle has vanished. *Calandria* was part of a festive package constructed by a pair of consummate political operators. Whether we choose to home in on the script or investigate the package as a whole depends upon the academic discipline to which we adhere, and also upon national tastes. Continental theatre historians have often been less preoccupied by the dramatic script and quicker to look at the festival than English-speaking scholars.[8]

At stake is the question: what is theatre? Theatre historians have to decide whether to opt for tight definitions of their field or open themselves to fluid and uncontainable definitions of performative activity. In the medieval and renaissance world it is hard for historians to judge whether an event classified as a *ludus* (Latin for 'game' or 'play') should be deemed theatre or merely 'ritual': a Shrove Tuesday battle, for example, between a fat man representing

Carnival and a thin man representing Lent; the scripted speeches delivered by men in mythological costume who greeted kings as they entered city gates; or the mystic nun required by her convent to don a beard and carry a cross through the church.[9] The Renaissance offers a lifeline to scholars faced by this predicament because imitations of ancient comedy and tragedy are unambiguously 'theatre' and henceforth conveniently serve as the focus of the theatre historian's interest, making it easy to trace a line from Sophocles through Shakespeare to Pinter and Mamet. Other ludic activities are pushed to the margins as cultural phenomena better dealt with by colleagues in departments of history.

Theatre history is more commonly constructed in terms of texts brought to life than images brought to life, but this perception reflects patterns of scholarly interest rather than any absolute historical reality. As Christopher Baugh's chapter has demonstrated, there is no reason why we should not view theatre as essentially a visual phenomenon. Once we switch into the language of the art historian, however, we find the word 'Renaissance' being used with very different emphasis, because many 'Renaissance' paintings have religious subject matter, whilst it is axiomatic for historians of English drama that religious plays equate with 'medieval' plays. Let me give an example of the problem. Filippo Brunelleschi (1377–1446) is regarded as the great pioneer of Renaissance architecture, designing a dome for the cathedral of Florence that emulated the Roman Pantheon. Yet Vasari, in a book of 1568 much valued by art historians, describes how Brunelleschi used his engineering skills to create a rotating wooden dome that supported boys as dancing angels, and from which a beautifully lit angel descended to tell the Virgin Mary that she will give birth to Christ. Though recent research actually attributes the design to a goldsmith called Filippo, Vasari's anecdote forces us to recognise something important. A Florentine designer in 1447 created an animated renaissance painting to impress a crowd gathered before a church. The crowd in the piazza was looking at a moving image enriched with sound effects. There is no obvious reason why we should think of this event as 'medieval' theatre.[10] By the same token, many religious dramas written in Florence in the 1400s and known as *sacre rappresentazioni* can be regarded as renaissance plays that used writerly skills in a new way.

To escape this conundrum, it may be more helpful to think of medieval/renaissance as a spatial rather than a literary distinction. In medieval theatre, spectators typically inhabited an environment that contained multiple locations, and the action flowed between small booths each of which represented a different setting. The great renaissance innovation, pioneered by Brunelleschi and others, was perspective, which allowed the individual a position of detachment from which to survey a framed view of reality.

In the Florentine piazza, the stage designer was working towards a framed two-dimensional art-work, with an inner world animated by the magic of lighting. Part of the appeal of *Mandragola* was the excuse it provided for scenographers to create a huge perspectival painting of a street-scene in Florence, with actors placed in front of it to reveal the accurate nature of the painterly representation. This is what 'humanism' implies, a world that can be apprehended scientifically by the human eye, not a world where every material thing is a symbol of something spiritual. The spectators of *Calandria* enjoyed a renaissance mode of viewing when invited to look through a breach in painted city walls to see the buildings and streets of Rome laid out before them, but a medieval mode of viewing insofar as they themselves inhabited the fictional environment of a city moat.

We have a clear idea about medieval stagecraft from a number of diagrams that have survived. An East Anglian play of about 1420 involved throwing up a circular embankment around a mock castle with a roof. The audience sat on the embankment to watch a siege, and in amongst them were booths for actors representing God, the Devil, the World, the Flesh and Greed. The audience were not looking *at* the world: they were *in* the world represented schematically by the circular embankment.[11] Pictures are not always easy to interpret, as Barbara Hodgdon demonstrates in Chapter 16. One beautiful picture of medieval theatre depicts Hell on the right-hand side of a long frontal stage and Heaven on the left. In the centre, the gates of Jerusalem are framed by the temple and palace of Jerusalem, and two other doors stand beyond them. The image shows how one day of a twenty-five-day French performance was staged in 1547. The arrangement of doorways reflects the design of Roman theatres, and historians have to ask whether this picture reflects how the play was actually staged, or whether it reflects how the artist thirty years later thought it ought to be depicted.[12] The terms 'medieval' and 'renaissance' prove useful when we debate whether the original staging was environmental or frontal.

The spread of the Protestant religion across northern Europe in the early 1500s brought about a decisive break with multi-locational religious theatre, more rapidly in Protestant Europe than in Catholic heartlands. Old community solidarities broke down, and the new religion looked for truth in the words of the Bible, not in religious images, proving particularly hostile to dramatic representations of saints, of the Virgin Mary, and of God. In Paris, where the authority to mount plays had lain with one semi-professional 'confraternity', religious plays were banned in 1548. In English cities, once Queen Elizabeth had replaced her Catholic sister in 1558 and become supreme head of a Protestant national church, civic authorities withdrew their support from the remaining passion plays over the next thirty years. English historians are quick to see a new age dawning in 1567 when professional theatres begin to rise up in fields outside London. In Castilian (as distinct from Catalan) Spain, on the other hand, it is very hard to speak of a 'medieval' age coming to an end. The label is unhelpful. With a strong Jewish and Islamic presence, there is little evidence of Christian drama in cities or indeed in monasteries before the mid-1400s, whilst the best-known dramatists of the 1600s, in addition to plays for professional playhouses, wrote religious plays for performance on wagons on Corpus Christi day, a double role that continued until 1705. The celebrated dramatists Lope de Vega (1562–1635), Tirso de Molina (1571–1648) and Calderón de la Barca (1600–81) all entered the priesthood. For Spain, a different periodising language is required to take account of religious continuity.

In England, post-medieval terminology has been a source of much discussion. If a new age dawned with the coming of professional theatre, what are we to call it? To speak of the 'Shakespearean' period carries an all too obvious sense of priorities, yet Shakespeare is a focus of interest not only because of his place in the modern repertory but also because he is a reference point that allows dialogue amongst academics. Traditionally, scholars have talked of 'Elizabethan' drama to characterise the plays of Shakespeare and his contemporaries and of the 'Elizabethan' playhouse to characterise a purpose-built open-air theatre with a thrust stage and encircling audience of up to 3,000. The reign of Elizabeth I (1558–1603) is a poor chronological fit since we have few scripts from before the mid-1580s, Shakespeare did not cease writing until 1613, and such playhouses were still in use in the 1650s. The term 'Elizabethan' found favour because in English popular history Elizabeth has received a much better press than James, the homosexual Scot who succeeded her. The term sits comfortably with portrayals of Shakespeare as a creature of the establishment, a spokesman for national and hierarchical values. This slant is characteristic of period labels that borrow their names from monarchs, as when we talk of Georgian playhouses, Victorian melodrama and Yuan plays from the Chinese Yuan dynasty. Such terms imply that rulers are the drivers of historical change, which contradicts the great lesson of Marxism that important change happens from the bottom up through macro-economic processes. It has become intellectually unacceptable to think of history at large as something made by monarchs. The term 'Elizabethan' pre-empts an important debate about royal influence on the theatre. The Queen's Chamberlain and Steward were the two officers responsible for royal entertainments, and Shakespeare's company for most of the period 1594–1603 were formally servants to the Lord Chamberlain, while the rival company served the Lord Steward. How far plays were shaped by royal patronage and how far by early capitalism is unclear. What is clear is that, in a more democratic (or capitalistic) age, companies like the Royal Shakespeare Company and Shakespeare's Globe place themselves in a line of continuity by construing Shakespeare as a public dramatist rather than a servant of the Crown.

It used to be common to refer to Shakespeare as a 'renaissance' dramatist, but that term is no longer fashionable. The word 'renaissance' emphasised Shakespeare's use of classical genres called 'comedy' and 'tragedy', his penchant for Italian tales and settings, and his use of the Greek biographer Plutarch. Today the term has fallen from favour because it emphasises literary source material. Scholars today are less likely to have had a classical education and thus less likely to notice how the classical world is reflected in Shakespeare's writing. They have become less inclined to see circular Elizabethan playhouses as architectural allusions to the ancient world, preferring to see them as modified inn-yards or animal arenas. An interesting case study is the most famous of all illustrations of 'Elizabethan' theatre, a drawing of the Swan Theatre made by a Dutch traveller called Johannes de Witt and surviving in a copy made by a friend (see Fig. 6). De Witt commented on the wooden columns painted to look like marble, which supported his opinion that the theatre 'seems to represent the general notion of Roman work'.[13] The drawing gives prominence to these columns and is inscribed with labels in Latin that point up Roman equivalences. De Witt saw the Swan as a classical, which is to say a 'renaissance', building, but did his classical education and European perspective make him a typical spectator? The term 'renaissance' flags up a cultural interface between England and Europe in ways that the current default term 'early modern' does not.

'Early modern' found favour for many good reasons. It refused to privilege an educated social elite; it broke down what was seen as a false conceptual divide between the Middle Ages and the Renaissance; it sat comfortably with materialistic interpretations of history, helping to align literature with the work of mainstream historians describing socio-economic change; and it broke down aesthetic snobbery by reconfiguring the theatre in terms of its organisational structures. At the same time, however, emphasis upon Shakespeare's roots in his own English medieval past has obscured cross-cultural links to Europe. If we think of Shakespearean scholarship in geo-political terms as an institution sitting in the hands of a transatlantic alliance or a white Commonwealth, then we notice that there are vested intellectual interests in the idea of an indigenous Anglophone Shakespeare. To speak of Shakespeare as a 'renaissance' dramatist implies that England was slow in catching up with a more advanced European culture, whereas 'early modern' implies that Shakespeare sits on the threshold of modernity, the world that is *our* world. It is a feel-good term that helps us sense him in us and us in him.

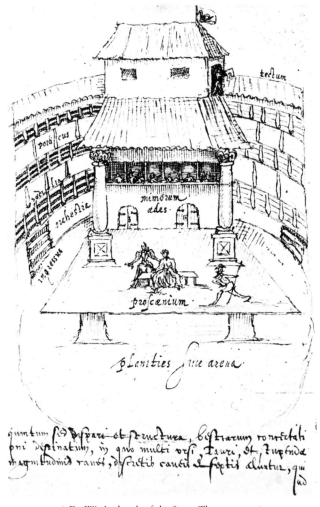

6 De Witt's sketch of the Swan Theatre, 1596.

The term 'early modern' was congenial to an important school of criticism known as 'new historicism' which had its heyday in the USA in the 1990s. Seeking to break down the interface between literary and historical study, this approach regarded the language people use as a key aspect of power within society. Although new historicists never found a satisfactory way of addressing the materiality of theatrical performance or the strategies of creative artists, they did open up questions about what it is to be a 'theatre historian', for they had no truck with the idea that you can split off the skill of studying texts from the down-to-earth task of establishing how plays were done, since meanings can never be separated from the social context of performance. Whilst the word 'renaissance' implied an engagement with aesthetics, 'early modern' relates to a politically inflected preoccupation with modernity, and modernity, as Stefan Hulfeld shows in Chapter 2, has been a key term in the analysis of how culture relates to deep political and economic change. In books like Peter Burke's *Popular Culture in Early Modern Europe* (1978) and Edward Muir's *Ritual in Early Modern Europe* (1997), cultural historians have found the concept of early modernity a helpful means of organising disparate material around changes wrought by the Protestant Reformation. Most theatre historians, however, have been wary of working on such a broad canvas in order to describe a society's way of life or, in a more French approach, the 'mentalities' of a given period.

Discussions of 'early modern' England are often used by mainstream historians to adduce a steady line of development to the modern British nation-state via the extension of parliamentary democracy and early industrialisation. The steady tradition of performing Shakespeare on the British stage sits comfortably with this model of continuous development. In Italy, which became a single nation-state in 1860, no such steady journey towards modernity can be traced, and different regions appear to have autonomous histories. One of the most striking achievements of Italian theatre was the so-called '*commedia dell'arte*', where the mix of characters reflected the cultural and linguistic diversity of Italy. The form has probably had more impact than Shakespeare upon subsequent theatre practice, and, although in the popular imagination '*commedia*' is a timeless tradition that somehow sits outside history, the artistry of the performers is thought by historians to have peaked in the time of Shakespeare. Before we can talk about transformations of the form through time, we must take apart the construct. '*Commedia*' refers to the classical genre of comedy, and aspiring Italian actors contemporary with Shakespeare were keen to establish a demarcation line between themselves as 'comedians' who performed plays based on classical plot structures in indoor spaces and mere 'buffoons' who performed on trestle stages in the piazza. Today the whole spectrum of improvised activity is subsumed under the eighteenth-century label '*commedia dell'arte*' (roughly equivalent to 'professional theatre') and classed as 'popular' theatre, and it is easy to forget that prestigious companies in the early 1600s performed fully scripted plays as well as improvised ones.

In this light, consider the parallels between William Shakespeare (1564–1616) and a celebrated actor–manager of the *commedia dell'arte*, Flaminio Scala (1547–*c.* 1620). Shakespeare came to London to be an actor, while Scala was known by his stage name of 'Flavio', the role of a young lover which he performed within many different troupes. Shakespeare was co-manager of the Chamberlain's Men, later known as the King's Men, while Scala from 1612 was the capocomico ('head actor') of a famous company called the Confidenti. Shakespeare had a shrewd sense of business and invested in property in Stratford, while Scala derived economic security from the perfume business that he ran in Venice. Both worked with commercial profit-sharing companies, but were reliant on aristocratic sponsorship to prosper, Scala's major patrons being a Mantuan duke and a Florentine cardinal. Aristocratic protection helped both men resist religious opposition. Both were keen to elevate the status of their art and sought out opportunities for indoor performance to a more select audience, though Shakespeare's company was for many years foiled in its endeavour to use the Blackfriars Playhouse. Both men relied on literature for their source material, but were not subservient to rules; Scala drew on literary texts as an actor, since lovers in the *commedia* were expected to have a fashionable poetic turn of phrase. And, finally, both had an ambivalent attitude to the printed text.

It is clear that Shakespeare thought of his plays as texts for the performer and not as literary works. His manuscripts were materials that became, like costumes, the property of the company. Some found their way into print in cheap and perfunctory editions, as did *Mandragola*, but there is no evidence that Shakespeare was much concerned about readers of his plays. The situation changed after his death when, in 1623, fellow actors published his complete works in a handsome and carefully edited Folio edition, thereby transforming Shakespeare from a maker of plays into an *author*, whose words must henceforth be read as the expression of a unique creative subject. Flaminio Scala in 1611, when it seemed that his career was drawing to a close, transformed himself into an author in an equally radical move.[14] His medium was not the fully scripted play but the scenario that served as a basis for improvisation, and he published a collection of fifty according to a literary model. Working up his material for publication, Scala shaped his scenarios as though they had been written for an ideal company comprising the most famous actors of the past thirty years. To judge from the prefatory matter, Scala's double aim was to leave behind a memorial to his distinguished career and to win status for the acting profession. He is ambivalent as to whether his publication is intended for the reader or for the amateur performer. Shakespeare's editors divided his plays between the three prestigious classical genres of comedy, history and tragedy, but they could as easily have followed Scala, whose title-page offered readers comedy, pastoral and tragedy.

To set Shakespeare's immortal verse alongside Scala's collection of plot-outlines may seem counter-intuitive, but if we reduce Shakespeare's *Tempest* of 1611 to the form of a scenario, we find that almost all its plot motifs are replicated in Scala's collection published in the same year: an island setting, a magician with unwilling spirits at his beck and call, the father–daughter relationship, plotting servants, feuds reconciled by marriage, magically vanishing food, and so forth. Both authors drew upon a common fund of classical plot structures and Italian romances, and one theatre historian has coined the term 'theatregrams' to characterise the units of action out of which both Shakespeare and Scala built up their plays.[15] We may be more struck by similarities than differences once we think of these two publications not as different types of text but as reflections of different approaches to acting. In Italy the actor was a creative artist who shaped his or her own text, whilst the English actor was more of a craftsman speaking the text of another. If the English audience benefited from better poetry, the Italian audience was treated to a more interactive and thus arguably a more 'live' experience.

Whilst English theatre relied on boys to play female roles, Italian theatre was animated by the presence of the actress, and the improvisatory format allowed women to demonstrate their intellectual skills as much as their sexuality, in what might be described as writing with the body. In Mantua in 1567, for example, we hear of a year-long battle for supremacy between two actress-led troupes that performed both to paying audiences and to the aristocracy. The most famous woman to break the gender barrier was Isabella Andreini (1562–1604), who entered the acting profession through marrying an actor and preserved her reputation for marital fidelity. To publish her poetry was a natural extension of Isabella's role as a performer, for the *innamorata* had to improvise her love scenes in high-flown poetic language. Scala in one of his scenarios depicts himself playing opposite her in a famous play about the madness of 'Isabella'. The actress was able to strew her clothes about her and utter obscenities in scenes of madness without damaging her public persona.[16] The use of boys to play women in English theatre, a custom retained on account of puritan sensibilities, encouraged the use of poetic language rather than the body to communicate eroticism.

The link between acting and authorship in improvised Italian *commedia* opened the door to acting being conceived as an art and therefore possessed of a history of sufficient status to merit historical investigation. Even though some manuscripts of Roman comedies transmitted sketches of gestures, Machiavelli showed no interest in the rediscovery of Roman acting. The old lawyer at the centre of *Mandragola* was played in Florence by a town crier, famous for his voice and his improvisational wit, not for his interest in antiquity. When Shakespeare's Hamlet gives advice to a company of actors visiting the Danish court, he urges them to imitate humanity and to avoid excessive gestures and shouting in the manner of Herod in the old passion plays. Historians have debated whether Hamlet delivers Shakespeare's own manifesto, or whether he is caricatured as a continental intellectual offering fashionable theory more relevant to his own state of mind than to the work of practising actors. Since Hamlet envisages a company with set roles reminiscent of the Italian tradition – king, soldier, lover, melancholic, clown and lady – it is at least clear that he does not have modern naturalism in mind. Each *commedia* role demanded its own technique, and artists were fascinated to draw or paint what they saw. This pictorial record makes it possible for historians to analyse *commedia* acting with a precision that eludes us when we try to imagine how Shakespeare's plays were first acted.

Locked into a slow process of economic and imperial decline, Spain lends itself no better than Italy to the forward-looking term 'early modern'. Spain was not torn apart by religious wars as Germany was, and professional theatre flourished in urban centres thanks to aristocratic protection. Spanish actors worked from scripts like English actors, but as in Italy actresses were at the centre of the theatrical experience. Purpose-built open-air playhouses were available as in London, though actors were prevented from settling in the capital. Lope de Vega theorised his playwriting in a way that Shakespeare never managed to do, explaining in 1609 how he understood the rules of dramaturgy set out by classically oriented French and Italian critics, but was obliged to follow a public taste conditioned by medieval passion cycles. Tragedy, moreover, should always be mixed with comedy because beauty lies in variety.[17] The parallels are striking, but rarely pursued by theatre historians because we have no vocabulary that allows us to speak of William Shakespeare, Flaminio Scala and Lope de Vega as creatures of a single historical period. Historians carve up time in different ways, in relation to where they see the golden age of playwriting in their own country.

English theatre historians tend to draw a line in 1642, when upon the fall of the monarchy public outdoor theatres were ordered to close. The commercial acting companies, formally constituted as servants of the royal family, fell with their masters, and this historical moment seems a natural break to historians preoccupied by organisational structures and the materiality of culture, a moment after which 'early modern' ceases to be a useful label to describe London theatre. In Italy and Spain, theatre historians commonly classify the 1600s as the 'baroque' era, using this word to depict a time when the 'Renaissance' transformed into something new. The term 'baroque', as Christopher Baugh has shown, evokes an ongoing engagement with classical antiquity, alongside a renewed spirituality that underpinned the authority of Church and Crown. In an age when religion had to coexist with knowledge that the earth was not the centre of the universe, these spiritual qualities were expressed through flamboyant and self-consciously theatrical works of art. In popular English usage the word 'baroque' has acquired negative overtones, much like the word 'Byzantine', and visitors to heritage sites are not often invited to admire 'baroque' architecture. For Anglophone scholars, Lope de Vega is a 'baroque' dramatist, Scala might be, but Shakespeare certainly is not, since the word 'baroque' has come to seem deeply un-British. Yet the great German critic Walter Benjamin, in the course of explicating the drama of his own country, had no hesitation in placing *Hamlet* as an archetypal 'baroque' tragedy on account of its melancholic mood and the way its royal protagonist becomes both martyr and tyrant.[18]

It would be very straightforward for a continental critic to define Shakespeare's *Tempest*, with its classical five-act structure and magical effects, as a 'baroque' play. The editors of the First Folio probably placed this play at the head of their collection because they wanted the magician Prospero to be read as a metaphor for the playwright of genius whom their volume created. Prospero's magic is more often interpreted today in terms of the court masque, which more than any other genre of English theatre cries out for the label 'baroque'. The scenography of the masque was developed by Inigo Jones (1573–1652), who explored Italy as a young painter and returned for a period of extended research in 1613–14 to consolidate his mastery of Italian stage technology. The 'Italian stage' deployed receding and movable flats to create a world of perspectival magic behind the proscenium, though human actors had to remain on the level forestage in order not to disrupt the scale. Such stagings were expensive, but flattered monarchs through their portrayal of an ideal world. King James I and his son Charles I commissioned Jones to design dance dramas for such temporary stages in order to position themselves as continental-style rulers. The playwright Ben Jonson, who in a successful collaboration wrote many of the texts for Jones's masques, came to lament the priority given to image over language, speaking in some sense for Protestant British values even though he was himself a Catholic.[19] When we use 1642 as a cut-off point in a history of English theatre, one of the consequences is to sideline the masque as an aberration on the part of a misguided royal family, rather than as the first step in the development of a stage technology that gradually became accessible to all.

It is a paradox that in an age of instant communications and globalisation, cultural exchange has in some ways become harder to achieve than it was in pre-modern Europe. Anglophone scholars tend not to read other languages, the knowledge explosion makes it hard for academics to stray beyond their own patch where they feel they can keep up with new publications, and schooling focuses on the study of national literatures. The level of cultural exchange characteristic of the era that I have examined in this chapter is often rendered invisible because of how scholars focus on their own national theatres. Exchange did not take place only amongst intellectuals capable of reading Latin or speaking Italian. In Spain, an Italian *commedia dell'arte* troupe embedded itself in the 1570s, winning a prize in Seville in 1575 for presenting the best Corpus Christi play on wagons.[20] In Germany, English actors toured extensively during and after the 'Shakespearean' period, mingling songs and acrobatics with abbreviated versions of plays once performed in London and incorporating an ever greater degree of German text.

In this chapter I have shown how time concepts tend to conceal space concepts because each nation maps the past in its own way. The historian cannot escape from the task of periodising, because otherwise we provide a mere chronicle of random events. Within the period covered by this chapter, very few historians fail to identify some sort of epochal change in or around the years 1500–50. In *Theatre Histories: An Introduction* (2006), seeking to escape the confines of national historiographies, the editors took the view that changes in the mode of human communication were a cross-cultural determinant of change, and the year 1500 serves as their convenient marker for the arrival of a culture based on print. It is a choice, and choices have to be made. Their choice invites a response from me as a fellow historian. In order to develop a counter-argument, I could challenge the detail, pointing out, for example, that in Italy the printing press assisted in the mushrooming of performances of passion plays.[21] Alternatively, I could embrace the argument and give it a different twist, emphasising literacy not publication as the key determinant of theatrical production. Or I could challenge the premise, maintaining that theatre is an autonomous mode of communication, in which case I am obliged to postulate another contender as the major driver of change: the emergence of professional actors, for example, or capitalism perhaps, or secularism, or colonisation. The world is infinitely complex, but as a historian I am required to map a route through the chaos according to my sense of priorities. Historians proceed through debate, seeking to understand why changes happen, and, unless they periodise, putting labels on eras and on phases, they have no way to conceptualise change. I have argued in this chapter that every period concept is already an interpretation. It is when historians take period concepts for granted, as though within the flow of time demarcated periods actually and objectively existed, that you need to be on your guard.

NOTES

1 See David Wiles, 'Hrosvitha of Gandersheim: The Performance of her Plays in the Tenth Century', *Theatre History Studies*, 19 (1999), 133–50.

2 Text of the Montecassino Passion Play in Sandro Sticca, *The Latin Passion Play: Its Origins and Development* (Albany, NY: State University of New York Press, c. 1970).

3 Text and translation of *La Seinte Resureccion* in David Bevington (ed.), *Medieval Drama* (Boston: Houghton Mifflin, 1975), pp. 122–36.

4 There has been no successor at the time of writing to William Tydeman, *The Theatre in the Middle Ages* (Cambridge: Cambridge University Press, 1978). For England, see for example Katie Normington, *Medieval English Drama* (Cambridge: Polity, 2009).

5 On the stage history, see David Wiles, *Theatre and Citizenship: The History of a Practice* (Cambridge: Cambridge University Press, 2011), pp. 63–9.

6 Jacob Burckhardt, *The Civilization of the Renaissance in Italy* (London: Phaidon, 1945), pp. 192–3, 245–60.

7 Castiglione's letter and a translation of the play by Bernardo Dovizi (Cardinal Bibbiena) can be found in Eric Bentley (ed.), *The Genius of the Italian Theater* (New York: New American Library, 1964), pp. 31–98, 511–15.

8 Particularly influential have been the three volumes of *Les fêtes de la Renaissance*, ed. Jean Jacquot and Elie Konigson (Paris: CNRS, 1956–75).

9 Edward Muir, *Ritual in Early Modern Europe* (Cambridge: Cambridge University Press, 1997), pp. 81–4; Gordon Kipling, *Enter the King: Theatre, Liturgy, and Ritual in the Medieval Civic Triumph* (Oxford: Clarendon Press, 1998) ; Richard C. Trexler, *Public Life in Renaissance Florence* (Ithaca, NY: Cornell University Press, 1991), pp. 191–2.

10 Vasari's description in William Tydeman (ed.), *The Medieval European Stage* (Cambridge: Cambridge University Press, 2001), pp. 451–3; reconstructions in Ludovico Zorzi, *Il teatro e la città: saggi sulla scena italiana* (Turin: Einaudi, 1977), plates 33–43. Nerida Newbigin establishes the facts in Joseph Farrell and Paolo Puppa (eds.), *A History of Italian Theatre* (Cambridge: Cambridge University Press, 2006), p. 23.

11 *The Castle of Perseverance*, in Bevington, *Medieval Drama*, pp. 796–900.

12 See Alan Knight's summary of the debate in Eckehard Simon (ed.), *The Theatre of Medieval Europe: New Research in Early Drama* (Cambridge: Cambridge University Press, 1991), pp. 153–4.

13 Glynne Wickham (ed.), *English Professional Theatre, 1530–1660* (Cambridge: Cambridge University Press, 2000), p. 441.

14 Translated by Henry F. Salerno as *Scenarios of the Commedia dell'arte: Flaminio Scala's 'Il teatro delle favole rappresentative'* (New York: New York University Press, 1967).

15 Louise George Clubb, *Italian Drama in Shakespeare's Time* (New Haven: Yale University Press, 1989).

16 See Robert Henke, *Performance and Literature in the Commedia dell'arte* (Cambridge: Cambridge University Press, 2002), pp. 86–94, 100–5; Clubb, *Italian Drama*, pp. 257–73.

17 *Arte nuevo di hacer comedias in esto tiempo* (1609), translated in Barrett H. Clark (ed.), *European Theories of the Drama* (New York: Crown, 1965), pp. 63–7.

18 *The Origin of German Tragic Drama* (London: Verso, 2003). First published in 1928.

19 On Jonson's 'Expostulation', see Stephen Orgel, *The Jonsonian Masque* (New York: Columbia University Press, 1981), pp. 195–6.

20 Melveena McKendrick, *Theatre in Spain 1490–1700* (Cambridge: Cambridge University Press, 1989), p. 241.

21 Farrell and Puppa, *History of Italian Theatre*, pp. 17, 19. *Theatre Histories: An Introduction* by Phillip B. Zarrilli, Bruce McConachie, Gary Jay Williams and Carol Fisher Sorgenfrei (London: Routledge, 2006).

FURTHER READING

Axton, Richard. *European Drama of the Early Middle Ages* (Pittsburgh: University of Pittsburgh Press, 1975).
Cox, John D., and David Scott Kaplan. *A New History of Early English Drama* (New York: Columbia University Press, 1997).
Dillon, Janette. *The Cambridge Introduction to Early English Theatre* (Cambridge: Cambridge University Press, 2006).
Farrell, Joseph, and Paolo Puppa, eds. *A History of Italian Theatre* (Cambridge: Cambridge University Press, 2006).
Fischer-Lichte, Erika. *History of European Drama and Theatre* (London: Routledge, 2002).
McKendrick, Melveena. *Theatre in Spain 1490–1700* (Cambridge: Cambridge University Press, 1989).
Normington, Katie. *Medieval English Drama* (Cambridge: Polity Press, 2009).

5

ERIKA FISCHER-LICHTE

Classical theatre

It is the traditionally held view that the history of all European theatre begins with ancient Greek theatre, which is regarded as the first and thus original form of theatre in Europe from which later forms evolved. This notion is underpinned by a linear concept of history, which implies that any phenomenon in history can be directly traced back to its 'roots'. This notion of history was dominant during the nineteenth century, but today history is no longer seen from within the narrow strictures of such a linear, even universalist, concept. We neither see Hegel's 'World Spirit' realising itself in history, nor recognise within history the law-governed inevitability of development from a primitive ur-community via class society to a Marxist classless society. We also no longer adhere to the modernisation theory of the eighteenth-century Enlightenment, according to which the course of history leads to the perfection of humanity. Such totalising and teleologically oriented constructions of history have long been overcome. In order to prevent the reader from walking into the trap of such a construct by blindly following a chronological order, it was decided to begin the historiographical section of this volume with modernist theatre, ending with ancient theatre.

Since belief in a single 'grand narrative' told by historians has been superseded today, the historian's task nowadays lies in writing multiple histories. Instead of macro-history – i.e. the grand narrative – we have to deal with many micro-histories. Theatre historiography constitutes a never-ending project, and historians of different eras will focus on different aspects of the past and follow varying traces and trajectories. This applies in particular to the historiography of classical theatre – and for good reason. If ancient Greek theatre is assumed to be the origin of European theatre, then in each epoch the need arises to link one's own contemporary theatre to that of ancient theatre – be it in agreement with or in opposition to it.

Another reason why we cannot construct a single grand narrative lies in the scarcity, randomness and fragmentariness of our sources. This is plainly the case in respect of Greek theatre. It is true that many theatre buildings have been excavated, among them the Theatre of Dionysus in Athens, where almost all of the extant tragedies and comedies were performed in the fifth century BCE. However, that theatre was rebuilt so many times that only a few stones from the original construction in the precinct of Dionysus' temple are left today, and the treatises on ancient theatre buildings that remain were written much later. Some inscriptions regarding the chronology and organisation of the festivals, which included performances, survive, while vase-paintings offer some evidence concerning masks and costumes. A few conclusions can be drawn from the works of Plato, Aristotle and other commentators, but no theoretical treatise on the art of acting or dancing has come down to us. The few plays that were preserved – mostly in special editions for educational purposes – are drawn from the wealth of tragedies written by Aeschylus (525–456 BCE), Sophocles (496–406 BCE) and Euripides (480–406 BCE) and of comedies penned by Aristophanes (450–388 BCE) and Menander (342–c. 290 BCE) and do not allow for any precise conclusions about acting or dancing. Regarding the music, only a few scattered fragments are known.

Whatever conclusions are drawn from such arbitrary sources will rely not only on interpretation but also on presuppositions that result from the particular perspectives and interests guiding the interpretation. That is to say that no historiography of ancient theatre will be able to tell us accurately what kind of theatre it was. Rather, each time, scholars and theatre practitioners will invent it anew by re-grouping and re-interpreting the known as well as the disputed facts in light of their own interests. As regards practitioners, they will select only those 'facts' that seemingly legitimise their own claim to a theatre of the future – aligning themselves with or contesting a model of antiquity. Theirs will be an act of creative appropriation based on whatever limited set of assumptions about ancient theatre prevails at the time. This appropriation will always be *partial* – at once incomplete and prejudiced.

In this chapter I shall examine some of the particular aspects of ancient theatre that were highlighted and exploited in those periods dealt with in the previous chapters: which of the 'facts' known at the time were taken into consideration, how they were used and, most importantly, what reasons were given for such a choice and how are these reasons to be evaluated in a larger context? I am asking and grappling with these questions from my own perspective, which, to a certain extent, is determined by my particular concept of history as well as my concept of theatre. As we will see, the knowledge and evaluation of classical theatre changes in each era, complementing or contradicting preceding ones. With this chapter, the historiographic section comes full circle.

It seems questionable that the end of the Roman Empire entailed the end of theatre, as standard theatre historiography from the nineteenth century onwards would have us believe. Against this view I would argue that the end of the Roman Empire marked the end only of those forms of theatre – along with other genres of cultural performance – that relied on state organisation and subsidies. These include the performance of scripted tragedies and comedies, which had already lost importance over time, as well as chariot and horse races, wild beast hunts and gladiator fights. In that sense, it could be argued that dramatic theatre came to an end. It was forgotten that tragedies and comedies, which were preserved and known as texts, had been written for the purpose of performance.

But what about theatrical genres that did not need state support, such as Atellan farce and 'mime'? The popularity of these informal and often improvised forms throughout the Roman Empire is well documented.[1] The question arises as to why the performers of the *atellana* and the *mimus* would simply stop performing, given that they were not dependent on the Roman state. It is more likely that they continued their business over the next centuries as wandering comedians, but due to the lack of surviving texts that could have borne witness to their trajectories, we lack evidence for the influence they may have exerted over medieval comic performances. Most theatre historians in the nineteenth and even some in the twentieth century adhered to a narrow concept of theatre that exclusively comprised performances of written texts. Performances of *mimus* and similar forms were not subsumed under it. As the particular concept of theatre guiding the respective studies did not allow theatre historians to consider these theatre forms, the argument was born that ancient theatre ended with the Roman Empire and that for approximately 500 years there was no theatre in Europe.

However, the influence of Roman theatre in early modern times, especially in Italy, is widely recognised by theatre scholars, since performances of plays by the Roman comedians Plautus (250–184 BCE) and Terence (190–159 BCE) are well documented. Already in 1487, Plautus' *Amphitruo* was performed at the court of Ferrara, followed in 1491 by a performance of Terence's *Andria*, both in Italian translation. In Rome, in the palace of the cardinals as well as before the Pope, comedies by Plautus and Terence were performed, alongside new plays, such as Bernardo Bibbiena's *La Calandria* (which premiered in 1513 at the ducal court of Urbino) and Niccolò Machiavelli's *La Mandragola* (which premiered in *c.* 1520 in Florence). Both of these followed the model set by Roman comedy.

Because of the frequent and continuous creative appropriation of Roman and Greek culture in various fields later on, this period was regarded as a special case and named the renaissance – the 'rebirth' of antiquity. The Italian word 'rinascita' was already used at the time. Such a 'rebirth' did not happen as an imitation but as a creative appropriation initiated by new interests and perspectives, as explained in the previous chapter.

Theatre concerns not only texts but also architecture. The first permanent modern theatre, the Teatro Olimpico in Vicenza, was built by drawing on the measurements of several ancient theatres in Rome and elsewhere as well as on Vitruvius' treatise *De architectura*. It was commissioned by the Accademia Olimpico, a society of humanist intellectuals, designed by Andrea Palladio, and modelled after Roman theatre buildings, but on a smaller scale and with significant alterations. The auditorium was shaped to form an ellipse. The rear part of the stage was closed off by the *scaenae frons*, a huge ornamented wall with three entrances, resembling that of a Roman theatre. While the Roman theatre was open-air, supplemented by awnings to shade the spectators, the Teatro Olimpico was covered by a painted ceiling that evoked the illusion of the sky. Regarding the *scaenae frons*, the middle opening was much broader than it had been in Roman theatres, and all three openings showed street views from a central perspective. These alterations pointed to the future of the so-called Italian stage, which dominated Western theatre from the seventeenth century until the end of the nineteenth. The significance of the Teatro Olimpico is largely to be found in this creative transformation of the Roman model, which in itself was a creative transformation of the model established by Greek theatre.

Sophocles' *Oedipus the King* was performed at the inauguration of the theatre in 1585. The tragedy was translated into Italian, and the music for the choruses composed by the Venetian Andrea Gabrieli. Since all that was known about Sophocles' original was that the chorus sang, though no example of the music had survived, Gabrieli had to compose an entirely new piece. This performance is interesting in our context not because it established a particular performance tradition – in fact, it did not. No other performances of Greek tragedies followed until the end of the eighteenth century, and then, the chorus was either left out or the songs were declaimed. Indeed it was not until Ludwig Tieck's production of Sophocles' *Antigone* in 1841 that a singing chorus appeared, with music composed by Felix Mendelssohn-Bartholdy. This performance took place in the amphitheatrically shaped court theatre of the New Palais in Potsdam. Performances of *Antigone* followed in Paris and London, using Mendelssohn's music.[2] Unlike the performance of *Oedipus the King* in 1585, here, in fact, a performance tradition *was* established.

The 1585 performance of *Oedipus* is interesting in terms of the historio-graphic problem of periodisation. To perform a Greek tragedy to inaugurate a theatre modelled after Roman theatre buildings suggests that *rinascita*, the renaissance, is a period shaped by Roman as well as Greek antiquity – that both together make up Graeco-Roman antiquity, marking the beginnings of a tradition that continues until today: the tradition of defining antiquity as a single period from the early Greek city-states to the end of the Roman Empire.

As far as theatre is concerned, such a view is debatable. The creative trans-formations of aspects and elements of Greek theatre undertaken by different forms of Roman theatre result in differences that, even if apparently only concerning detail, bear witness to quite new functions of theatre in Rome – a question that cannot be dealt with in the space of this chapter.

By 1800, it was a commonplace that the performances of tragedies and comedies in the Athens of the fifth century BCE took place as part of religious festivals, held annually in celebration of the god Dionysus: the Rural Dionysia (December/January), the Lenaea (January/February) and the City or Great Dionysia (March/April). The most important of these was the Great Dionysia, which the tyrant Peisistratos had expanded into an event of Panhellenic importance in the second half of the sixth century BCE. As performances of tragedies had not been part of the festival before his time, the ostensibly natural link between the ancient religious cult of Dionysus and the performance of tragedies is today regarded as false.

The Great Dionysia lasted for five days. On the eve of the festival, the statue of Dionysus was taken to a small temple outside the city walls and, in a festive procession amidst torch light, brought back to his temple in the holy precinct. During the course of the night, the news spread that the god had appeared and the festival could commence. It began with a procession, which wound its way through the city towards the temple of Dionysus. After the sacrifice, it moved into the theatre, where different ceremonies took place. This was followed in the afternoon by the competition – the so-called agon – of the dithyrambic chorus. The comic agon, in which five comedies were presented, took place the following day (from 486 BCE onwards). The festival was completed by the tragic agon, the most important part of the event. One tetralogy (three tragedies, originally linked thematically, and a satyr play) by a single poet was performed on each of the third, fourth and fifth days. Their order was decided by a lottery. With the announcement of the victor in the tragic agon, the Great Dionysia drew to a close. The following day, a public meeting was held in the theatre, in which the correctness of the procedure during the festival was debated.

It seems that for the archaeologists and philologists of the late eighteenth and early nineteenth centuries, the Greek festivals, with their roots in pagan religion, formed a shocking as well as fascinating subject of research. This knowledge, because of its appalling nature, did not exert any influence on the theatre of that time, and it was not until the middle of the nineteenth century that the idea of the Greek festival was taken up in order to make it productive for a new theatre.

In his early theoretical works *Art and Revolution* and *The Artwork of the Future* (1849) and *Opera and Drama* (1850/51), Richard Wagner (1813–83) based his idea of a new theatre of the future, the *Gesamtkunstwerk* ('total work of art'), on his knowledge of ancient Greek theatre as part of a festival. In his view, the Greek city-state, the polis, was an ideal, for in it everyone had the possibility to develop fully their potential both as individuals and as representatives of the human species. Wagner describes his idea of Greek tragic theatre as follows:

> This people, streaming in its thousands from the State-assembly, from the Agora, from land, from sea, from camps, from distant parts, – filled with its thirty thousand heads the amphitheatre. To see the most pregnant of all tragedies, the 'Prometheus', came they; in this Titanic masterpiece to see the image of themselves, to read the riddle of their own actions, to fuse their own being and their own communion with that of their god... For in the tragedy [man] found himself again, – nay, found the noblest part of his own nature united with the noblest characteristics of the whole nation.[3]

The festival Wagner envisioned and later established in Bayreuth in Bavaria, however, was not intended as part of a given religious and/or political festival. Rather, the performances of Wagner's operas in the Festspielhaus on the Green Hill in Bayreuth were themselves meant to embody the idea of festival: theatre as festival was declared the theatre of the future. This, however, was not intended as an imitation of Greek theatre. 'We do not wish to revert to Greekdom', Wagner writes in *Art and Revolution*, for 'only *Revolution* not slavish *Restoration*, can give us back the highest art work'.[4] Accordingly, the new theatre would be '*conservative* afresh' – looking back to ancient Greece and, at the same time, directed towards the future. Once a new, democratic society emerged, once theatre performances were no longer commodities available only to the rich but accessible to each and everyone, then will each person 'become in truth an artist'.[5] Returning to the Greeks here meant proclaiming a utopian vision of the future. In this respect, Wagner's music drama is to be regarded as another 'rebirth' of ancient Greek tragic theatre.

This is, in fact, what Friedrich Nietzsche (1844–1900) proclaimed as a kind of conclusion to his argument on the origin of Greek tragedy in *The Birth of Tragedy out of the Spirit of Music* (1872). While Wagner's political account of Greek culture did not question what the eighteenth-century art historian Johann Winckelmann described as its 'noble simplicity and quiet greatness', Nietzsche dwelt on those aspects that had shocked the classicists of the late eighteenth and early nineteenth centuries. He stated that ancient Greek theatre originated in the Dionysiac principle, which is manifested in and enacted by a chorus of satyrs, the original dithyrambic chorus. It is this principle that annuls individuation, transfers individuals into a state of ecstasy and transforms them into members of a dancing, singing community.

He concludes 'that dismemberment, the true Dionysiac *suffering*, amounts to a transformation into air, water, earth and fire and that we should therefore see the condition of individuation as the source and origin of all suffering ...'.[6] In the years to come, other classicists also highlighted the ritualistic aspect: Jane Ellen Harrison, for example, the leading spirit of the so-called Cambridge Ritualists, in *Themis: A Study of the Social Origin of Greek Religion* (1912), tried to offer evidence in support of her claim that the Dionysiac ritual was to be explained as an offshoot of the ancient sacrificial ritual to a universal Year-God.

In the last decades of the nineteenth century, as a consequence of industrialisation and urbanisation, anonymous masses flooded into the cities. On the other hand, there was a growing individualisation among the educated middle classes to the extent that 'the individual becomes the object of a sort of religion', as the French sociologist Emile Durkheim put it.[7] The problem was how the ability to form a community could come into being among competing members of societies characterised by the division of labour. In this context, the ritualistic dimension of Greek theatre, in particular the chorus as Nietzsche characterised it, attracted great interest.

Max Reinhardt (1873–1943) responded to this problem by creating his Theatre of Five Thousand, a new form of a people's theatre as a choric theatre. In 1910 and 1911, he staged Sophocles' *Oedipus the King* and Aeschylus' *Oresteia* in the Circus Schumann in Berlin. His *Oedipus* toured all over Europe with great success. In London, he restaged it, using the translation by Gilbert Murray, a member of the Cambridge Ritualists and close collaborator of Jane Ellen Harrison. It was the purpose of the Theatre of Five Thousand to unite actors and spectators into a community, even if this lasted only for the duration of the performance.

The choice of the Circus Schumann served two purposes. First of all, performing ancient Greek tragedies (the most precious 'possession' of the educated middle classes) in a circus (the venue of entertainment for the common people) bridged the gap between elite and popular culture. In it, all milieus, classes and strata could be united into a community. Second, the circus ring alluded to the orchestral circle or semi-circle of the ancient Greek theatre. Both orchestra and circus feature a round or oval arena lined with tiers of seats. In the same way that the *skene* (initially a tent or hut and later a proper building) was erected abutting the orchestra and facing the audience, so a kind of entrance to a palace reached by a flight of stairs arose in the circus. Such a spatial arrangement allowed the spectators not only to perceive the actors but also each other.

In ancient times, performances took place during the day, and the spectators – mostly men and citizens of Athens – were able to observe each other's particular behaviour and reactions. Therefore, they were affected not only by what the actors did, but also by the responses of their fellow spectators. Most likely, the actors, too, were affected by it. We have sufficient evidence that there was a lively interaction between actors and spectators, at least in the fourth century BCE. Demosthenes reports that if spectators did not like a certain actor, they pelted him with dried fruits and sweets. Moreover, spectators shouted comments, whistled, hissed, clicked their tongues and banged their feet on the wooden benches. It is very likely that such audience reactions exerted a certain influence over the judges. In this context, it is worth emphasising that the Greek word 'theatron', from which the Latin 'theatrum', the English 'theatre', the French 'théâtre', and the German 'Theater' derive, designates a space in which something is presented to the gaze of the people in order to be seen. It seems that the theatron itself proved to be a place for performance – a place where the city presented and negotiated its self-image and self-understanding before its own citizens and also before outsiders.

In Athens, the members of the chorus were not professionals. Dancing in the chorus was the duty and privilege of every Athenian citizen. They were chosen by the *choregos*, a wealthy Athenian who financed the chorus, supplying several months' provision for its members. Only those citizens were allowed as chorus members whose parents both hailed from Athens, emphasising the bond between the chorus, comprising twelve to twenty-four citizens who danced and sang in the orchestra, and the polis, the city of Athens, also represented by the majority of spectators surrounding the orchestra.

By the turn of the nineteenth into the twentieth century, even classicists who did not believe in Nietzsche's – or Harrison's – theory were well aware of the importance of the chorus with respect to the polis. So, besides incorporating a Greek-inspired spatial arrangement to foster community building, together with particular lighting and other staging devices, Reinhardt introduced choruses that consisted of hundreds of members. As one critic put it, he 'presents masses to the masses'.[8] These masses entered the circus ring through the auditorium in close proximity to the spectators, often triggering physical contact. The reviews suggest that this new form of choric theatre did indeed create an aesthetic community out of actors and spectators. Reinhardt's *Oedipus* and *Oresteia* became the models for different kinds of choric theatre between the wars, which relied heavily on masses but were very different from Reinhardt's, since they aimed at creating ideological communities, such as the Soviet mass spectacles of the early 1920s, the Nazi *Thingspiele* in the 1930s, and Zionist pageants in the USA between 1932 and 1946. These performances drew heavily on Reinhardt's productions of *Oedipus the King* and the *Oresteia*, without, however, referring to ancient Greek theatre.[9]

80

The new image of ancient Greek culture created by Reinhardt's productions was not well received everywhere. Gilbert Murray challenged the complaint that the production of *Oedipus the King* in London was not Greek:

> Professor Reinhardt was frankly pre-Hellenic (as is the Oedipus story itself), partly Cretan and Mycenaean, partly Oriental, partly – to my great admiration – merely savage. The half-naked torchbearers with loin-cloths and long black hair made my heart leap with joy. There was real early Greece about them, not the Greece of the schoolroom or the conventional art studio.[10]

However, Reinhardt's use of Greek theatre in his new people's theatre was not meant to disseminate this new historical image of ancient Greek culture, the battlefield on which many critics and classicists fought each other. Rather, it creatively appropriated both the spatial arrangement of Greek theatre and the chorus in order to open up a new function for theatre within a society threatened by disintegration. Carl Vollmoeller, who adapted the *Oresteia* for Reinhardt, praised this new theatre as

> an assembly for the peoples of today ... What the depoliticisation of our people during fifty years of imperial rule prevented is possible today: a gathering of thousands in a theatre space to build a community of active, enthusiastic, and sympathetic citizens ...[11]

A lasting community of participating citizens based on the model of Athenian democracy did not materialise, though this had been the hope at the beginning of the Weimar Republic when the Circus Schumann was rebuilt into an arena theatre, Reinhardt's Großes Schauspielhaus, which opened in 1919 with a revival of the 1911 *Oresteia*. The new people's theatre was able to realise its utopia only during the performance. The community that came into being in its course, uniting members of different classes and milieus, dissolved as soon as the performance ended.

In conclusion, I will briefly deal with three questions that arise from today's perspective. First, do performances of ancient drama constitute links of a chain designating an ongoing classical tradition, or does each represent a new beginning? The second question results from the enormous number of performances of Greek tragedies in the West since the 1960s, which begs for an explanation. Thirdly, we must discuss the reasons why, again since the 1960s, adaptations and performances of Greek tragedies are no longer limited to European/Western theatres.

Each recourse to ancient Greek or Roman theatre in different European cultures since early modern times has been based on a particular set of assumptions and concerned a limited number of elements. In the cases addressed here, they served to create a new theatre that would be able to cater to specific needs emerging at the time due to various aesthetic, cultural, social or political configurations. This raises the question of continuity or discontinuity. From a European perspective, one might be tempted to foreground continuity. Documented examples stretch from early modern times until the present, establishing a tradition of permanent encounter with antiquity and leading to the incorporation of specific elements that suited new ends and purposes. Within a national frame, however, differences are found. In German bourgeois culture, uninterrupted references to ancient Greek culture continue from the days of Winckelmann in the mid-eighteenth century through the era of National Socialism until today. In Poland, by contrast, no such tradition exists: only after the end of communism were Greek tragedies staged on a regular basis. Yet, within such a composite tradition as German culture, competing images of ancient Greek culture have led to completely different citations and uses. While Reinhardt drew on a Nietzschean image in order to bring into being aesthetic communities as an anticipation of potential social communities, the National Socialists hailed Winckelmann's image in order to proclaim Nazi Germany the genuine heir of and successor to ancient Greek culture. Despite a continuity of references to ancient Greece, discontinuities and ruptures remain, not necessarily caused by newly discovered sources but mostly by new interpretations of existing ones. The answer to my question about continuity depends for every case upon perspective, particular objectives, and context.

The second and third questions are often addressed in the same way. Since the 1960s performances of Greek tragedies have spread all over the world, so that between 1960 and today there have been far more performances of Greek plays than there were between 572 BCE and 1960.[12] It is therefore often argued, in particular by American scholars, that this is due to the universalism of Greek tragedy. However, such an explanation raises the question of why Greek tragedies, despite their 'universal truth', were not performed in the time immediately following the end of the Roman Empire. Against the thesis of universalism I would like to argue that the reasons can be found in the particular conditions emerging in the 1960s, when many Western cultures faced serious challenges to the political, social and moral order established or re-established after the Second World War. They witnessed various new cultural and artistic movements, and illusionistic, psychological–realistic theatre fell under attack. Performing Greek tragedies, in large part radically rewritten, served two different purposes in this context. First, they referred to an established tradition in order to break it; and, second, the tragedies were far removed from the demands of an illusionistic, realistic–psychological theatre.

It is not due to their ostensible universalism that Greek tragedies have spread beyond Western cultures and have been performed all over the globe since the 1960s. Let us consider two factors. The first refers to post-colonial countries. The emphasis in colonial education on Greek tragedies as the epitome of Western culture led many African writers to rewrite and adapt Greek tragedies for an African context after their countries gained independence. Among them were John Pepper Clark's *Song of a Goat*, reworking aspects of Aeschylus' *Agamemnon*, first performed in Nigeria in 1962, directed by Wole Soyinka; Efua Sutherland's *Edufa*, referring to Euripides' *Alcestis*, performed also in 1962 at the Drama Studio, University of Ghana; and Ola Rotimi's *The Gods are not to Blame*, rewriting Sophocles' *Oedipus the King*, first performed by Rotimi's own Olokun Acting Company in Nigeria in 1968. These were followed by a lively tradition of African dramatists rewriting Greek tragedies. Here, an act of creative appropriation critically explored the relationship between African traditions and colonial cultures. Another factor which helps account for the number of Greek tragedies now performed across the world can be found in the circuit of international theatre festivals, which have considerably increased in number since the 1980s. It is highly likely that the wish of international practitioners to be included in this circuit and present their work to worldwide audiences determines the choice of plays. This explains why Greek tragedies – alongside Shakespeare, Chekhov, Ibsen and Brecht – rank among the plays most frequently performed. It is not so much their 'universalism' but the familiarity of Western audiences with Greek tragedies that makes them a preference. Otherwise these audiences would most likely not take an interest.

Against this background, the argument for Greek tragedies' universalism offers a glimpse of the odious spectre of Western cultural imperialism: the 'others' will continue our tradition because it is universal and, therefore, 'superior' to theirs. This assumption rests on a false hypothesis. The history of the reception of ancient and in particular Greek theatre should not be regarded as the ultimate global triumph of a universally valid model, but as a contested field where diverse interests and agendas compete. To restate my opening point, there is no place for a definitive linear history here.

NOTES

1 See, for example, E. Fantham, 'Mime: The Missing Link in Roman Literary History', *Classical World*, 82 (1989), 153–63; R. Rieks, 'Mimus and Atellana', in E. Lefèvre (ed.), *Das römische Drama* (Darmstadt: Wissenschaftliche Buchgesellschaft, 1978), pp. 348–77. Allardyce Nicoll argued for the continuity of these forms in *Masks, Mimes and Miracles* (London: Harrap, 1931).

2 On the Potsdam *Antigone*, see E. Fischer-Lichte, 'Politicizing Antigone', in S. E. Wilmer and A. Zukauskaite (eds.), *Interrogating Antigone in Postmodern Philosophy and Criticism* (Oxford: Oxford University Press, 2010), pp. 329–52.

3 R. Wagner, *Richard Wagner's Prose Works*, trans. William Ashton Ellis, 8 Vols. (London, 1892–9), Vol. 1, p. 34.

4 *Ibid.*, p. 53.

5 *Ibid.*, p. 58.

6 F. Nietzsche, *The Birth of Tragedy out of the Spirit of Music*, trans. S. Whiteside (London: Penguin, 1995), p. 52.

7 E. Durkheim, *The Division of Labour in Society* (1898), trans. G. Simpson (New York: Free Press, 1933), p. 172.

8 Review by Fritz Engel, *Berliner Tageblatt* (8 November 1910).

9 Cf. Erika Fischer-Lichte, *Theatre, Sacrifice, Ritual, Exploring Forms of Political Theatre* (London and New York: Routledge, 2005), pp. 97–196.

10 Cited in J. Styan, *Max Reinhardt* (Cambridge: Cambridge University Press, 1982), p. 85.

11 Cited in Carl Vollmoeller, 'Zur Entwicklungsgeschichte des Großen Hauses', in *Das Große Schauspielhaus*, ed. Das Deutsche Theater (Berlin: Verlag der Bücher des Deutschen Theaters, 1910), pp. 15–21, p. 21.

12 See E. Hall, F. Macintosh and A. Wrigley (eds.), *Dionysus Since 69: Greek Tragedy at the Dawn of the Third Millennium* (Oxford: Oxford University Press, 2004), p. 2.

FURTHER READING

Csapo, Eric. *Actors and Icons of the Ancient Theatre* (London: Wiley-Blackwell, 2010).

Easterling, Pat, and Edith Hall, eds., *Greek and Roman Actors: Aspects of an Ancient Theatre* (Cambridge: Cambridge University Press, 2002).

Goldhill, Simon, and Robin Osborne, eds. *Performance Culture and Athenian Democracy* (Cambridge: Cambridge University Press, 1999).

Roselli, David Kawalko. *Theatre of the People: Spectators and Society in Ancient Athens* (Austin: University of Texas Press, 2011).

Wilson, Peter. *The Athenian Institution of the Khoregia: The Chorus, the City and the Stage* (Cambridge: Cambridge University Press, 2000).

Wilson, Peter, ed. *The Greek Theatre and Festivals: Documentary Studies*. Oxford Studies in Ancient Documents (Oxford: Oxford University Press, 2007).

PART THREE

Where?

History is constructed by the gaze of the beholder. To say this is not to deny the existence of hard historical data – to deny for example that a given number of real people suffered and died in Nazi-run gas chambers in the early 1940s. But as soon as bits of data are put together to form a story, the *historian* is at work, and the history that emerges reflects the perspective of whoever has assembled the story. There is no single authentic history out there to be recorded, although there are important disciplines by which the historian must abide, if she or he is to function as an ethical human being in search of truth.

Today the economic and political dominance of the 'West' is discernibly waning, which prompts a rethink about how we look back at cultural history. Ancient Greek maps placed Greece, often Delphi within Greece, at the centre of the world, while maps in medieval Christendom placed Jerusalem at the centre. In 1569 the Flemish map-maker Mercator used mathematical principles to render the globe as a flat surface, and he placed Europe in the centre because his map served the needs of European explorers who sailed north or south, east or west in search of new and profitable lands. Mercator's projection remains the basis of most modern maps of the world, and the same principle governs most works of theatre history. We describe the past from the perspective of where we stand. Though history is not necessarily organised around places, the drive to create a local and national history is particularly strong because of the interplay between history and community: to have a shared history is to have a shared identity. In this section we shall focus upon what happens when history is written from a different physical point of orientation, when one looks at the world from the perspective of communities that do not regard themselves as satellites of London or Paris or New York.

We offer the reader a series of representative case studies to indicate just how different the past looks from different points on the globe. The authors of these chapters will all function as mediators with feet in two worlds. They all have a long-standing personal experience of the world about which they write, but they also have experience of another world in order to communicate with the assumed reader of this book, who is certainly English-speaking, educated and wealthy enough to have access to this text.

We begin with the city of Liverpool, widely known and mytho-logised for an urban culture that spawned the Beatles. The importance of this chapter is twofold. First, it raises the question of how we see our collective identity: in terms of city, region or nation-state? To write the history of Liverpudlian theatre is to proclaim that 'Liverpool' is not just a geographical entity but a social entity. Second, it raises a question about power. Not only do politicians gravitate to London, but also journalists, actors and directors who wish to make a reputation for themselves, so should we accept that most accounts of English theatre are essentially accounts of what happens in London? From Liverpool, a city with just under half a million people, we move to Finland, a state with just over five million people, set physically though not politically on the outskirts of Europe. The major national language is famously difficult for foreigners to learn, so Finnish theatre is effectively closed to out-siders. What, therefore, is the role of a Finnish theatre historian? To reinforce national identity? To serve as cultural ambassador, talk-ing up the aesthetic merits of a home-grown product? To give a fresh inflection to European theatre history? Whilst nationalist impulses are generally deplored by English and US academics, who nevertheless frequently continue to work within national para-meters, academics in new and small nations are commonly less ambivalent about the moral value of nationhood.

From Finland we move outside Europe, only a small distance across the Mediterranean. Unlike many post-colonial states, Egypt has a long history of existence as a political entity, perhaps longer than anywhere else on earth. Here theatre matters in a way that it cannot possibly do in London or New York, for it is caught up in tensions between Islamic fundamentalism and the wish to be part of European or 'Western' modernity. Theatre-makers have long been answerable to a government enthusiastic about national identity but intolerant of free speech. This chapter was conceived before the abrupt ending of the Mubarak dictatorship in 2011, and the sensitivities involved in constructing a history seem all the more delicate today, within a nation engaged in some kind of self-reconstruction. From Egypt we move to Japan, likewise characterised by a tension between Western modernity and the antiquity of its own cultural inheritance. Japan possesses indigenous theatrical forms that owe nothing to Greece and Rome, and this chapter will concern itself with the tradition of Noh. What is the historian to do with 'traditional' theatre – to marginalise it as a folkloric curiosity, to place it as a remote point of origin and move on, to celebrate its influence upon modernist art-works, or to treat it as part of the fabric of the present? This chapter highlights a historiographic problem that confronts any historian seeking to operate in a diverse global community: the Greek-originated word 'theatre' embraces a spectrum of activities that cannot be caught by any comparable word in Japanese, or in Swahili. What is it, therefore, to be a 'theatre historian'?

This consideration complicates any attempt to write a history of world theatre that does full justice to the diversity of humankind. Is a global theatre history possible, when history always and inevitably seems to be written from the perspective of one person or a single community of scholars? In the final chapter of this section, we arrive at the logical alternative to the Euro-centric narrative structures explored in Part II, the internet. Does the internet open up radical new possibilities for comprehensive documentation assembled by a multiplicity of local experts, or is a covert power structure always at work, shaping the way we acquire political knowledge, for example defining the priorities of a search engine? Whose interests are served by an encyclopaedic accumulation of knowledge, and how many are disempowered by resultant feelings of inadequacy? We return to the principle that history is not simply *there* to be uncovered; it is an active process, something that historians *do* in order to have some impact on the world around them.

6

ROS MERKIN

Liverpool

In 2004, Marvin Carlson asked what was the single most important thing we could do to bring theatre history into the new millennium. His answer was simple: 'Become Less Provincial'.[1] His argument, that theatre history must broaden its remit both in terms of forms and of geographical reach, seems an obvious one in an increasingly global world, one in which perspectives have sometimes been very limited. But in lifting our heads upwards and outwards, there have been consequences. The local, never a very fashionable concept for mainstream historians, has become increasingly marginalised. It could be argued that we have found 'new locals', as the authors of *Theatre Histories* might claim in a book that covers not only performance from Western traditions (including late-Neolithic ritual pilgrimage), but also Bunraku from Japan, social drama from Kerala in India, and Gao Xingjian's *Wild Man* from post-Cultural Revolution China. Whilst this approach does allow for neglected areas of theatre and performance to be considered, there is also a danger that the 'old locals', i.e., Western 'provincial' theatre (in particular that based in theatre buildings), become increasingly marginalised. This neglect is further compounded by the increasing concerns to widen the events we encompass in our consideration of performance. Here, *Theatre Histories* includes cultural performances such as tourism and Times Square, shamanism and ritual and urban carnivals. At the same time, the old binary of the metropolitan and the local is still very much in evidence. Michael Billington's *The State of the Nation: British Theatre Since 1945*, for example, a book that claims to explore the pattern and shape of *British* theatre (my emphasis) since the end of the Second World War is in essence a book about theatre in the capital. He does include two short sections on regional theatre, one in a chapter called 'Scenes from an Execution', the very title of which sums up a pervading and sweeping perception of theatre outside of London: it is either in crisis or facing closure. The generalised view of the repertoire of regional theatre is summed up in another history that offers us very few real clues about the local outside of London, Simon Shepherd's *Modern British Theatre*, which talks about the sense of repertory theatres' staleness in the 1980s when 'a rash of musicals and modern classics followed like a nasty infection'.[2] If our perception of the local, like Shepherd's, is very generalised, matters are further complicated by an increasing concern to be cosmopolitan, as evidenced in a number of Palgrave's *Theatre &* series, where the books on globalisation, city and nation all champion cosmopolitanism, with its emphasis on the individual (rather than the corporation) as a citizen of everywhere, as an ideal preferable to globalisation.[3] In contrast to these cosmopolitan concerns, this chapter focuses on a specific place (Liverpool) and on a specific theatre (the Liverpool Royal Court). Even more particularly, it focuses on how the city presents itself on that stage. This is not to argue that the broadening and widening of theatre history that has taken place is not welcome, but to ask what we might be missing in what can become a stampede to follow fashions and trends in theatre history. If an inclusive history of world theatre is not to leave out Times Square or Bunraku, why exclude Liverpool? And if we do, what happens to our understanding of theatre history when we leave out that specific culture's history?

Liverpool is renowned for seeing itself as an exception. Bill Drummond, a member of the acid house band KLF, loved living in Liverpool because 'it never felt like you were living in England. The locals always considered themselves Liverpudlians above and beyond any nationality.'[4] The city has 'its sights set on the rest of the world and not on London', and it is on the edge, both of the country and of the culture of that country.[5] In the nineteenth century, it saw itself as the New York of Europe, a world-city rather than merely British provincial, and this sense of grandeur and separation continues today, as Paul du Noyer argues: as far as Liverpudlians (or Scousers[6]) are concerned, Liverpool is

> the Capital of itself. It's deeply insular, yet essentially outward-looking: it faces the sea and all lands beyond, but has its back turned on England. There were local men for whom Sierra Leone was a fact but London only a rumour... In his innermost heart, the Liverpudlian feels a little sorry for those born anywhere else. In his mental geography it's like that famous cartoon map of Manhattan. To the west there's Birkenhead, then Ireland and America. But look the other way and it's a vague place... where only the enemy football grounds have tangible existence.[7]

With such a strong sense of its own identity and isolation, it is no surprise that the city and its people appear on the city's stages, and nowhere more so in recent years than at the Liverpool Royal Court which, in 2000, was taken over by Kevin Fearon, executive director of Liverpool's Everyman Theatre in the 1990s and the instigator of the Rawhide Comedy Club. Without subsidy, he reinvented the 200-year-old theatre, which had become a crumbling and leaking rock venue, as the home of popular Liverpool comedy, complete with cabaret-style seating in the stalls and the possibility of dining prior to the show (at one time offering not *fruits de mers* but Fruit Dee Mersey, a dish using seafood from the local rivers Dee and Mersey). 'At The Heart of Great Liverpool Theatre', as its website proclaims (artfully and knowingly playing on Liverpool's penchant for the sentimental), the Royal Court has developed a pool of local writers. Its most successful show to date has so far played for four runs during the normally dead summer period and is due for a revival in summer 2011. Referred to as Liverpool's 'Scouse-trap', a pun on Agatha Christie's long-running London success, *The Mousetrap*, Dave Kirby and Nicky Allt's *Brick Up the Mersey Tunnels* is an anarchic and light-hearted comedy of class-war (a common theme in plays at the Royal Court). It is the story of the Kingsway Three who take their name from one of the two tunnels under the Mersey that they plan to block up, thus sealing off the Wirral on the other side of the river. It is unashamedly local in its storyline, based on the supposed tensions between the two sides of the Mersey in which the middle-class, aspirational Wirral residents, delighted to have been given a Cheshire postcode rather than being deemed Merseysiders, look down on the working-class residents of the city. In its themes, it reflects Andrew Cullen's earlier play, *Scouse*, staged at the Everyman in 1997, in which the Liverpool People's Party declare independence because, in Liverpool, they are nearer to space than they are to London. And it is unashamedly local in its references. Character names are drawn from local places; jokes rely on local knowledge. It is popular in its choice of music, offering the audience rewrites of famous songs, including 'The Blue-Rinse Mountains of the Wirral' and 'Like a Nine-Stone Cowboy'. Other new plays developed at the Court, including Len Pentin and Fred Lawless's *Slapheads and Slappers* (2003), Dave Kirby's *Lost Soul* (2007) and Drew Quayle's *The Salon* (2009), also work to a similar formula.

The popularity of Scouse comedy at the Court and the development of new writers have also led to 'spin-off' plays in larger venues. Nicky Allt has gone solo with a sequel to *Brick Up*, *The Wirral Strikes Back* (2010), preceded in 2009 with *One Night in Istanbul*, both performed at the Empire Theatre with its capacity of nearly 2,400. *One Night* is set in a grimy room of the Mamara hotel in Istanbul on the night in 2005 when Liverpool won the Champions League for the fifth time. A fictitious story (involving Adolf Hitler's cufflinks and counterfeit dollars) is secondary to the real issue of the football game and the story the audience already know – how Liverpool came back from being 3–0 down at half-time to beat AC Milan on penalties. The narrative of how they got to the final is told by a wandering minstrel between the scenes. More significantly, he is the front man for the finale when the audience are invited to join in the singing. On occasions, he is joined by footballing stars past and present including Rafa Benitez (former Liverpool manager), whose frenzied dancing, punching the air as he sings along, has developed legendary status and a huge following on YouTube. The finale, a mass celebration, is the whole point of the production, as the crowd take over from the actors, singing to the tune of 'A Horse With No Name':

> We went to Istanbul for a football game
> Where destiny called us again
> Three nil down the whole world had called it a day
> But they hadn't counted on the Liverpool way
> Na, Na, Na, Na, Na, Na, Na,
> Na, Na, Na, Na...

In full voice, the chorus becomes a taunt to the rest of the world, and the show is as much an event, a communal celebration, as a play.

Inevitably, such uncritical celebration lays itself open to the critique of re-enforcing stereotypes. It is, as Dominic Dromgoole has argued, an 'aggressive regionalism', inward looking and with an underlying suspicion of the wider world: an 'inverse snobbery tied up with a large-scale inferiority/superiority complex'.[8] Yet such an easy dismissal belies a more complex reality, both in understanding the content of some of these plays and the reasons for the Court's success. Some plays use the same formula, but step beyond and under it. Dave Kirby's *Council Depot Blues* (2008) is a comedy about the boys from the Excrement Eradication Department of Liverpool City Council and their discovery of a Gibson Mandolin worth £150,000 in a house they are clearing, drawing on Kirby's own experience of working for the 'corpy' (i.e., council or 'corporation'). But it is also a story of men living lives of quiet desperation and of lost dreams. From the outset, as we see Stan waking up in a lonely room that is all he has to look forward to after his last day at work, this is a comedy tinged with a deep sadness. The play might make jokes and sing songs (tellingly blues-based in this instance) about hating work and counting down the seconds until you can leave, but it realises that all one has is work, however menial, grim and boring, and the camaraderie that it brings (here developed through the characters' band, which rehearses in the houses they are clearing). Dreams of anything more, however narrow those dreams might be, seem destined to failure. The more Shorty, the wannabe drug baron, talks about wanting to open a bar in Ibiza, the more we know it will never happen; as the title song tells us, 'Lord knows I want so much more... but I don't get to choose'.

The appeal of all these shows lies in part in the laughter of recognition. The biggest responses from the audience are to the things they 'know': Widnes is a smelly city, Formby is posh, a radio report states that the capital of culture (or the England football team, depending on which year you saw the show) is officially 'shite'. The gangster landlord in Fred Lawless's dry-cleaning comedy *A Fistful of Collars* (2010) is Curtis, a nod to Toxteth-born drugs trafficker Curtis Warren. The sixty-six designer dresses that mistakenly end up in the dry cleaners belong to Coleen Rooney, wife of local (and now international) football star Wayne Rooney. There are jokes about former Liverpool Council leader Derek Hatton, nights out at the Grafton nightclub,[9] and, of course, Margaret Thatcher's dislike of the city. Familiarity now also allows characters from one play to reappear in another: Father O'Flaherty, for example, the intemperate priest who featured in the 2009 Christmas show *Merry Ding Dong*, reappeared in 2010 with his Sisters of Mersey in *Scouse Pacific*. There is also laughter at Liverpudlian stereotypes, from the workshy men of the council who, in the words of the title song of Kirby's play, 'get to work then f**k off at noon', to the feisty female characters who know how to keep a man in his place. The language and accent is familiar to those in the city but 'foreign' to everyone else; reviewer Lynne Walker, in a rare national review of a Royal Court play, advised *Independent* readers that they 'might need to brush up [their] Scouseology' if they were going to see *Council Depot Blues* (5 Nov. 2008), and *Scouse Pacific* makes great play of how the islanders were taught the fundamentals of the Scouse alphabet. The actors, too, are familiar and local. Andrew Schofield, Pauline Daniels, Eithne Brown and Paul Broughton (amongst others) turn up in a variety of guises. But more than the recognition, there is also a sense of ownership and participation. Liverpool audiences are encouraged to join in, to be active, to sing along and to shout out, to see themselves as the fifth Beatle or the twelfth man at Liverpool's Anfield football ground. The shows are also, despite frequent swearing and risqué jokes, safe and family-friendly; each show at the Royal Court is given marks on a 'Can I Bring My Gran-Ometer' for swearing, nudity and general rudeness. As Alfred Hickling comments about Fred Lawless's *Merry Ding Dong* (2009), another play about divisions, this time between Liverpool and Everton supporters:

> What is there not to like about the Liverpool Royal Court? It doesn't receive a penny of public subsidy, but packs itself out with a diet of unpretentious, popular drama. It also seems to have become the number one destination for work outings, which gives [this] comedy the atmosphere of a rollicking Christmas party.[10]

The success of the Royal Court's style of popular theatre, selling the myths of the city in a city that has an unequalled talent for self-mythologising, can on one level be seen as a response to a call made as early as 1875 by Philip

Rathbone, at a point when the city was re-imagining itself in the wake of the slave trade:

> It is for us, with our vast population, our enormous wealth (as a town), but without either politics or philosophy that the world will care to preserve, to decide whether we will take advantage of our almost unequalled opportunities for the cultivation of Art, or whether we shall be content to rot away, as Carthage, Antioch and Tyre have rotted away, leaving not a trace to show here a population of more than half a million souls once lived, loved, felt and thought.[11]

More pertinent here, however, than leaving a trace is Gary Younge's argument that, 'in the absence of any meaningful way to advance their interests as citizens, many retreat into laagers of place'.[12] The question is why are Liverpudlians retreating into their city?

Liverpool may have more reason than many cities to want to re-present itself both to the wider world and to itself, for it is probably the city with the worst reputation in the national consciousness. From the 1970s on, as Liverpool slid from being one of the country's richest cities to one with the highest unemployment, the images in the newspapers have been less than exemplary. It was a city that could boast the dubious claim of being a 'destination for those seeking urban blight' or of 'always setting new benchmarks for urban barbarity'. It had, as the *Financial Times* stated in 2008, 'reputational issues'.[13] It has been associated with riots, radical politics and economic meltdown, with gun crime, football violence and the kidnap and murder of two-year-old Jamie Bulger by two ten-year-olds in 1993. It stalked our television screens with images of inner-city Toxteth on fire during riots in 1981 and with Labour Party leader Neil Kinnock condemning the city council for the 'grotesque chaos' of a Labour council hiring taxis to hand out redundancy notices to its own workers in 1985. In the same year, pictures of rioting Liverpool football fans who caused a wall to collapse, killing thirty-nine Spanish supporters of Juventus at Heysel, were beamed into the nation's living rooms. It has filled pages of newspapers, most notoriously *The Sun*, which wrongly accused Liverpool fans of picking pockets of victims and urinating on the police when ninety-six football fans died at Hillsborough in 1989. If the images are bad, Liverpool is also a city seen to parade its status as victim. When Tory politician Boris Johnson wrote about the city's response to the murder of Liverpool-born Ken Bigley, kidnapped in Iraq and subsequently videoed being beheaded, he criticised the city for its tribal sense of community, its excessive predilection for welfarism and its wallowing in victim status. He was greeted with howls of outrage and forced to make a penitent pilgrimage (which he termed 'Operation Scouse-grovel').[14] So bad had matters become that *The Daily Mirror* famously pronounced: 'They should build a fence around and charge an admission fee. For sadly, it has become a show-case for everything that has gone wrong in Britain's major cities.'[15]

Popular television drama has also helped to enshrine these images. Carla Lane's sitcom *Bread* centred on a family abusing the welfare system. Tony Booth's Mike, in *Till Death Us Do Part*, might have been a sharp-witted Scouser, but he was also a left-wing layabout. Phil Redmond's *Brookside* (running for twenty-one years from 1982) brought social and class issues to soap opera, but its gritty social realism suggested a city beset with problems. Character comedian Harry Enfield's 'Scousers', with curly perms and bad moustaches, were pugnacious and pugilistic, (ironically) giving the country the all-pervasive and persistent 'calm down, calm down'. Current plans for *Mersey Shore*, a spin-off from the US reality show *Jersey Shore*, and *Desperate Scousewives*, a Merseyside twist on the US mega-hit *Desperate Housewives*, suggest such trading on stereotypes is set to continue. Most iconic of all has been Alan Bleasdale's drama series *Boys from the Blackstuff*, which came to speak for a nation under Thatcher. It too added catch phrases ('Gizza a job' and 'I can do that') to the national vocabulary and created a folk hero for the 1980s in the shape of Yosser Hughes. Yet, as a symbol of a city, Yosser is an uncomfortable hero, suggesting a city that is destroying itself as it slides into insanity. He is grim, helpless and desperate, painfully descending into madness and desolation as he loses his job, his family, his dignity and his self-respect, reduced to head-butting lamp-posts, confessional boxes, and policemen in an attempt to articulate his despair and take away the pain. Alongside him, the city slides into collective mania; in the final episode the pub is full of the desperate and despairing – a local character insistently whistling *If I were a Blackbird*, a glass-collector constantly calling time and drinking the slops, Shake-hands forcing everyone into a knuckle-crushing handshake and laid-off workers feverishly competing with each other to spend their redundancy pay. In contrast, Bleasdale's hero is Chrissie: decent, honest and placid, the ordinary man living an ordinary life until his job is taken away from him. He is left shipwrecked with nothing left to do except cause carnage, slaughtering the chickens and pigeons and the geese for Sundays in his back yard, as the dogs bark and a rabbit licks blood off its fur. As he walks off into the sunset down a derelict street at the end of the series, passing a demolition site with a warehouse bearing the sign 'Tate and Lyle 1922', a haunting reminder of Liverpool's long association with the sugar industry (the Tate and Lyle factory at Love Lane had closed in 1981), his final plea for a way out of the mess ('Beam me up, Scotty. Beam me up') was not the image remembered by the nation.

If the negative images in newspapers and on television are all-pervasive, it has taken a long time for the city to develop a school of theatre writers who might offer the city's own image of itself in response. As early as 1911, Ramsay Muir, a founding member of Liverpool Playhouse, a repertory theatre, was horrified that

> the great provincial cities were being drained of their vitality by the power of London, so that they had no intellectual life of their own…And I thought there was no more worthy aim that one could set oneself than that of trying to create an independent intellectual life in these great cities…It seemed merely intolerable that the theatres of a great city should be no more than booths for the entertainment of travelling companies from London. We must, if we were civilised, have our *own* theatre, in which we could produce plays that would affect and criticise our own life instead of being content with the drawing room (or bedroom) comedies of sophisticated London Society.[16]

However, Liverpool Playhouse, apart from occasional forays into local writing including James Sexton's *The Riot Act* in 1914, a play about the transport strikes of 1911 that provoked suffragist protest in the theatre, did not develop plays about the city. It drew instead on the Manchester school from The Gaiety, and it was not until the late 1970s, with the arrival of Alan Bleasdale as writer-in-residence, that things began to change, developing much more rapidly when the gang of four (Alan Bleasdale, Willy Russell, Bill Morrison and Chris Bond) took over the theatre in 1980. Then, the city did take to the stage through Jim Morris's *Blood on the Dole* (1981), Carol Ann Duffy's *Cavern of Dreams* (1984) and, most successfully for the theatre, Willy Russell's *Blood Brothers* (1983), now one of the longest-running musicals in London's West End and an example (one amongst many of Russell's plays) that suggests location-specific writing can also travel. The real roots of putting the city on stage can be found at The Everyman, which opened in 1964 and which, in the early 1970s, under the artistic direction of Alan Dossor, developed a tradition of local musical documentaries, including Stephen Fagan's *The Braddock's Time* (1970), Willy Russell's *John, Paul, George, Ringo … & Bert* (1974) and Chris Bond's *Under New Management* (1975). This tradition was developed under Chris Bond and later under Bob Eaton, whose play *Lennon* (1981) was revived at the Royal Court to mark the thirtieth anniversary of John Lennon's death and where Eaton now directs many of the shows. It is worth reminding ourselves of Kevin Fearon's links with the Everyman, so the connections between the two theatres are strong. In the 1980s, Eaton described the essential elements of the 'Everyman idea' of theatre as 'a firm local commitment and involvement with Liverpool issues both past and present; an abundant use of music; the encouragement of local writers and actors; an irreverent approach to the classics; an informal and lively style of presentation'.[17] These are the elements taken up by the Court.

Yet, things have changed in Liverpool since the bad days of the 1980s. Many date the resurgence to 2003 when it was awarded European Capital of Culture status, even though the announcement brought criticism and a BBC website full of apologies to the world for the city having been chosen. Others date the resurgence to a death – the shooting of John Lennon on the streets of New York in November 1980. This event offered the city a chance to rebrand itself, a need underlined by riots the following year, the arrival of Tory cabinet minister Michael Heseltine (to become known as the Minister for Merseyside) and the opening of the first urban development corporation. The Garden Festival of 1984 was the first step in rebranding the city, joined by the redevelopment of the city's derelict docklands from 1983, the opening of the Liverpool site of the Tate Gallery in 1988 and the awarding of UNESCO world heritage status to the waterfront in 2004. More importantly, the death of Lennon allowed the city to trade on its most significant legacy: the Beatles. It had been slow to do so, du Noyer noting in 1977 that there had been an almighty row when councillors had turned down a Beatles statue: 'They aren't worthy of a place in our history', said one. 'The Beatles couldn't sing for toffee', chimed another.[18] Five bullets from Mark Chapman's gun changed that view, and the legacy was now exploited. From the redevelopment of Cavern Walks (an arcaded shopping area) and the first section of the Mathew Street Cavern Quarter with the Beatles Cavern Club at its heart in 1984, through to the renaming of the airport as Liverpool John Lennon Airport in 2002 and the opening of the Beatles Museum in 2004, Liverpool has rebranded itself as a Beatles heritage city in the hope that tourism can compensate for all the economic life that has drained away.

All of this redevelopment and new-found confidence has meant that, theatrically, Liverpool could be having different kinds of conversations with itself and with others. In some places, this is happening. At the Everyman and Playhouse, joined as one operation in 2000, Gemma Bodinetz and Deborah Aydon have presided over more than twenty-three new plays by local writers since their arrival in 2003, many reflecting critically on the history and culture of Liverpool. Tagged 'Made in Liverpool', these have included Lizzie Nunnery's *Intemperance*, which juxtaposed the teeming poverty in nineteenth-century Liverpool with the building of a vast neo-classical edifice of civic pride that is St George's Hall, and the verbatim play *Unprotected*, which was staged after the murder of three street sex workers in the city and debated the issue of safe zones. While Phil Willmott's *Once Upon a Time at the Adelphi* might have championed Liverpool's fighting spirit (and produced a song that many thought should have been the anthem for Capital of

Culture, proclaiming as it did that 'it's Liverpool's time again'), Jonathan Larkin's *Paradise Bound* took a more critical look at redevelopment and the Capital of Culture. Asking if you can find happiness in your own backyard and if you can still belong if you are different, he went to the heart of arguments about who the Capital of Culture was really for, as one character explains:

> D'yer see any bastard throwin' us a bone? No, they threw us a bench. Then they said, 'Oh no, yer can't even 'ave that, yer can look at it through this nice bit of corrugated iron... Ann reckons they're gonna move that Chinatown arch across the middle of the road, then block it off so we can't get through... Can yer imagine? Keep the scum outta sight. Urban Splash, Beatles Museum and the Lambanana, that's what we need for 2008. Not scousers.[19]

As a body of work these plays have set up a far more complex and critical conversation with their audiences about what it is to be living in this city at this time, what it is to belong to this group or this tribe, than any of the new plays at the Royal Court.

But if the plays at the Everyman and Playhouse offer a different kind of perception of what it might mean to be a Liverpudlian, backs have not been turned on the past. The Royal Court has championed two of the writers most associated with the city, Willy Russell and Alan Bleasdale, and was the only theatre to produce their work during Capital of Culture Year. The key production here is the Liverpool homecoming of Bleasdale's 1993 play, *On the Ledge*, originally written for Nottingham Playhouse and the National Theatre. Set high above Liverpool, it is a play that sets before the city many of the issues confronting it today. The opening image of two disenfranchised boys, spitting angrily about how London hates us, as one holds the other upside down over the roof to write the misspelled graffiti 'ANACHRY RULES', sums up the mood of the play. It is a howl of uncontrollable rage, a dark look at the despair and self-hatred behind the easy phrase 'inner-city dereliction', in which a motley collection of misfits and criminals, the dispossessed and the displaced, cower on the outside ledges of a block of flats as those below set fire to the city and their own homes. The characters cling to the ledges as the only place of safety, both physically and emotionally, in a world that has gone truly mad and in which, in the words of the fireman sent to their rescue, 'the fuckin' community doesn't exist anymore'. As Shaun, the villainous property developer who has returned to his home town and made a dubious fortune out of rebuilding the city after earlier riots, shouts across the rooftops at the end of the play: 'Let them eat stale cakes, give them false dawns and broken dreams, shoddy goods and shitty lives, cheap gin and hard drugs. Let despair and squalor and disease be theirs...'[20] As a comment on the perils and pitfalls of regeneration, the arrival home of Bleasdale's play suggests that the Royal Court is willing to offer its audience more than celebration and stereotypes.

Although this summary of theatre in Liverpool is very tightly focused (and the city has a long and vibrant theatre history that can boast the opening of more than forty theatres and music halls during the nineteenth century), it suggests a more complex, more specific and more multi-layered picture of British theatre than the ones offered by Billington and Shepherd. Joseph A. Amato argues that local historians are 'judged to be the most myopic of all historians', seen as 'narrowly focused fact gatherers and eccentric story-tellers'.[21] Their fidelity to particularities can make them seem parochial, and they can fall prey to nostalgia and 'boosterism'. Yet, without the specifics, we have only generalities and, as Alexis de Tocqueville noted, general ideas 'enable the human mind to pass rapid judgement on a great many objects at once; but … the notions they convey are never other than incomplete'.[22] Instead, as Amato recognises,

> The need for a sense of place (as real and constructed) intensifies as impinging nations, economies, technologies and ideologies get larger, more complex, and increasingly abstract. In the last three to four decades in Europe, regionalism, despite moves towards overall unification, has exploded. Micro-regionalism does more than criticize centralization and excess taxes. It ignites passions, warms souls, and peddles politics.[23]

The current story of the Liverpool Royal Court is one particular story that starts to fill in the gaps left by generalities. There are many more, and a focus on these in our histories would allow for a more multi-layered, specific and complex understanding.

NOTES

1 Marvin Carlson, 'Become Less Provincial', *Theatre Survey*, 45:2 (November 2004), 177–80, p. 177.

2 Simon Shepherd, *Modern British Theatre* (Cambridge: Cambridge University Press, 2009), p. 68; Michael Billington, *The State of the Nation: British Theatre Since 1945* (London: Faber & Faber, 2007).

3 For a discussion of the differences between cosmopolitan and global see Dan Rebellato, *Theatre & Globalization* (Basingstoke: Palgrave Macmillan, 2009), pp. 59–71.

4 Paul du Noyer, *Liverpool: Wondrous Place* (London: Virgin, 2004), p. 5.

5 'Liverpool: Port, Docks and City', *Illustrated London News*, (15 May 1886), quoted in John Belchem, 'Celebrating Liverpool', in John Belchem (ed.), *Liverpool 800: Culture, Character and History* (Liverpool: Liverpool University Press, 2006), p. 9.

6 The term 'Scousers' has, since the 1970s, become the most common epithet for describing the citizens of Liverpool. For a discussion of the roots of the term see John Belchem, *Merseypride: Essays in Liverpool Exceptionalism* (Liverpool: Liverpool University Press, 2000), especially Chapter 2.

7 Paul du Noyer, *Liverpool: Wondrous Place* (London: Virgin, 2004), p. 5.

8 Dominic Dromgoole, *The Full Room* (London: Methuen, 2002), p. 105.

9 The Grafton, currently for sale, was an iconic Liverpool nightclub opened in 1924 for tea dances and big bands which had by the 1970s become better known for its 'grab-a-granny' nights frequented by older women supposedly on the lookout for casual sex. It came to some national recognition through the 1999 fly-on-the-wall documentary *Nightclub Tales from the Grafton* and is seen as the basis for 'The Palace' nightclub in Len Pentin and Fred Lawless's *Slapheads and Slappers*, which premiered at the Royal Court in 2003.

10 Alfred Hickling, 'Merry Ding Dong', *Guardian* (6 January 2010).

11 P. H. Rathbone, 'The Political Value of Arts in Municipal Life', quoted in John Belchem, 'Celebrating Liverpool', p. 18.

12 Gary Younge, *Who Are We – And Should It Matter in the 21st Century?* (London: Penguin, 2010), p. 8.

13 P. Jones and S. Wilks-Heeg, 'Capitalising Culture: Liverpool 2008', *Local Economy* 19:4 (2004), 344; Peter Popham: 'Gunfire Across the Mersey', *Independent* (23 April 1996); Paul du Noyer, 'Liverpool's Reputational Issues', www.pauldunoyer.com.

14 'Bigley's Fate', *The Spectator* (16 October 2004); Boris Johnson, 'What I Should Say Sorry For', *The Spectator* (23 October 2004).

15 Quoted in P. Boland, 'The Construction of Images of People and Place: Labelling Liverpool and Stereotyping Scousers', *Cities* 25:6 (2008), 363.

16 Quoted in Grace Wyndham Goldie, *The Liverpool Repertory Theatre 1911–1934* (Liverpool: Liverpool University Press, 1935), pp. 23–4.

17 Bob Eaton, quoted in Ros Merkin, *Liverpool's Third Cathedral: The Liverpool Everyman Theatre* (Liverpool and Merseyside Theatres Trust, 2004), p. 168.

18 Paul du Noyer, *Liverpool*, p. 15.

19 Jonathan Larkin, *Paradise Bound* (London: Methuen, 2006), pp. 104–5. The China Town Arch, built in 2000 by workmen from Shanghai with which Liverpool is twinned, is situated on Berry Street between the Dingle, where the play is set, and the city centre. Urban Splash is a development organisation associated in Liverpool with the regeneration of Ropewalks, an area of nineteenth century warehouses and merchants' houses where the narrow lanes were originally used to bind ropes. Derelict for many years, the area is now a centre for nightlife and the creative industries. Superlambanana is a statue by Taro Chiezo commissioned in 1998. It became an iconic symbol of the city during 2008, when 125 superlambananas were created by artists and communities and placed round the city – and beyond. One, Lovemedoodle, found its way to a platform at Euston Station in London.

20 Alan Bleasdale, *On the Ledge* (London: Faber and Faber, 1993), pp. 49 and 63.

21 Joseph A. Amato, *Rethinking Home: A Case For Writing Local History* (Berkeley: University of California Press, 2002), pp. 9, 12.

22 Alexis de Tocqueville, *Democracy in America*, quoted in Amato, *Rethinking Home*, p. 188.
23 Amato, *Rethinking Home*, p. 15.

FURTHER READING

Ackroyd, Harold. *The Liverpool Stage* (Erdington, West Midlands: Amber Valley, 1996).

Amato, Joseph A. *Rethinking Home: A Case For Writing Local History* (Berkeley and Los Angeles: University of California Press, 2002).

Belchem, John, ed. *Liverpool 800: Culture, Character and History* (Liverpool: Liverpool University Press, 2006).

Boland, Philip. 'The Construction of Images of People and Place: Labelling Liverpool and Stereotyping Scousers', *Cities* 25.6 (2008), 355–69.

Cochrane, Claire. *Twentieth-Century British Theatre: Industry, Art and Empire* (Cambridge: Cambridge University Press, 2011).

Dorney, Kate and Ros Merkin, eds. *The Glory of the Garden: English Regional Theatre and the Arts Council 1984–2009* (Newcastle: Cambridge Scholars Press, 2010)

du Noyer, Paul. *Liverpool: Wondrous Place. Music from the Cavern to the Coral*, 2nd edn (London: Virgin Books, 2004).

Goldie, Grace Wyndham. *The Liverpool Repertory Theatre 1911–1934* (Liverpool: Liverpool University Press, 1935).

Merkin, Ros, ed. *Liverpool's Third Cathedral: The Liverpool Everyman Theatre* (Liverpool and Merseyside Theatres Trust, 2004).

Robinson, Jo. 'Becoming More Provincial? The Global and the Local in Theatre History', *New Theatre Quarterly* 23.3 (August 2007), 229–40.

7

S. E. WILMER

Finland

Books on European theatre and world theatre have generally ignored Finnish theatre and Finnish theatre history. There are no world-famous dramatists or theatre directors as in other northern European countries, such as Henrik Ibsen in Norway, August Strindberg and Ingmar Bergman in Sweden, or Jerzy Grotowski and Tadeusz Kantor in Poland. Nevertheless, the theatre infrastructure is as impressive and the theatre audience as engaged as in any country in Europe. Is Finnish theatre then only for the Finns? What is the relevance of Finnish theatre and Finnish theatre history for an international audience today? While Finnish theatre is isolated by its language and its location and idiosyncratic in many of its features, it is representative of many European systems that emerged in the nationalist movements of the nineteenth century. Many parallels can be drawn between the development of Finnish theatre and, for example, Hungarian, Norwegian, Czech, and Irish theatre. As in other emerging nations in Europe in the late nineteenth century, the Finnish theatre became a force for cultural nationalism, using the local language, folk poetry and mythology to stress the distinctiveness of the nation and ultimately its right to political independence. Like Czechs and Norwegians, for example, Finnish cultural nationalists built an impressive National Theatre in a prominent location in their capital city as a focal point for Romantic nationalist cultural expression in advance of becoming a nation-state.

Situated between Sweden and Russia and subject successively to the rule of both countries, Finland emerged as an independent country after the Russian Revolution in 1917. For much of the twentieth century, Finland occupied a strategic position between eastern and western Europe. During the Cold War, it acted as a border state, associated more with the West while maintaining political and military neutrality in the shadow of the Soviet Union. Even today Finland continues to occupy a frontier position as the most eastern state of the European Union. Although the Cold War has ended, the Russian government continues to flex its muscles and intimidate neighbours, such as Ukraine,

Georgia and Estonia. Remembering the attempts by the Soviet Union to invade it during the Second World War, the Finnish population looks to the European Union for support but holds on to a semblance of neutrality by not joining NATO.

Despite being a small country in terms of population (just over 5 million inhabitants), Finland occupies a sizeable landmass near the Arctic Circle, larger than France and almost as large as Germany. Although the country has two national languages, Finnish and Swedish, the Swedish-speaking Finns have dwindled in number, with Swedish now being the first language of approximately five per cent of the population.[1] In addition, fewer than one per cent of the population are Lapps, who speak the Saami language and many of whom inhabit the most northern part of the country, herding reindeer.

The Finnish theatre scene contains some surprising features. It boasts an unusually large number of subsidised theatres per capita and an extremely loyal theatre audience, with approximately four million visitors per year. Other unusual features include the dominant voice of female playwrights since the nineteenth century, the strong history of workers' theatre, the importance of folk and amateur theatre, and the popularity of open-air theatre during the summer months. However, despite a very prolific theatrical environment, an impressive infrastructure, and an active engagement with European culture and politics, Finnish theatre remains largely isolated by its language. It is only in recent years that a corpus of plays translated into other languages has been disseminated abroad, helping to make contemporary authors such as Laura Ruohonen, Sofi Oksanen, Juha Jokela and Mika Myllyaho more widely known.[2]

Despite having a restricted market for their theatre productions because of linguistic inaccessibility, Finnish artists seek international visibility for their work, especially through international festivals in Finland and abroad. There are more than sixty arts festivals in Finland, many of them concentrating on music. The Helsinki Festival (which in the late 1960s replaced the Sibelius Festival held from 1951 to 1965) takes place in late August to early September. It is the biggest festival in Finland, exhibiting various forms of art including theatre, dance, classical music, circus, visual art, etc. In the past it has invited some major theatre companies such as the Berliner Volksbühne, directed by Frank Castorf, and the Schauspielhaus Zürich, directed by Christoph Marthaler. It also includes the 'Night of the Arts' when every performance is free of charge. Other summer festivals include the Jyväskylä Arts Festival, the Pori Jazz Festival, the Kaustinen Folk Music Festival, and the Kajaani Word and Music Festival. Dance festivals include the Kuopio Dance and Music Festival, Dance Arena Festival and Moving in November in

Helsinki, the Full Moon Dance Festival in Pyhäjärvi (which features modern dance groups), and the Tango Festival in Seinäjoki.

The Savonlinna Opera Festival, which was initiated by Aino Ackté in 1912 and occurred for several summers before disappearing, was reborn in 1967 and attracts a huge international audience in July each year to open-air performances in the courtyard of a medieval castle. In addition to Finnish operas (e.g., by Aulis Sallinen and Joonas Kokkonen), it presents performances of standard works by Wagner, Mozart, Puccini, etc., with visiting star singers. Since 1987 it has also featured a visit by a foreign opera company (such as the Mariinsky Theatre from St Petersburg) normally staging two operas. Generally it presents about six or seven operas in the season with a total of about twenty-five to thirty performances. The Tampere Theatre Festival, which started in 1968 as a festival of Finnish drama, is the major international theatre festival of Finland. It occupies various performance spaces in Tampere in the second week of August and regularly attracts performances from Russia, the Baltic States and numerous other countries. It also serves as a major platform for displaying some of the important Finnish productions of the year, as well as hosting a fringe festival of free performances. The Baltic Circle is a loose alliance of theatre groups and practitioners from around the Baltic Sea, hosted by the Q Theatre in Helsinki. Its occasional Theatre Festival has recently become an annual event in November, staging productions from various countries neighbouring on the Baltic Sea (for example, Poland, Russia, Germany, and the Nordic and Baltic countries), as well as Finland. The Baltic Circle also encourages and supports artistic co-productions for creating innovative work and functions as a meeting place and network for artists. Finnish theatre productions, such as from the National Theatre, also travel abroad to international festivals, particularly in neighbouring countries and to theatres within international networks. Moreover, Finnish plays are occasionally performed by foreign companies in translation, especially in Sweden, Estonia and Germany. Other forms of theatre that are not so linguistically bound, such as dance (e.g., by Tero Saarinen) and opera (e.g., by Sallinen, Kokkonen and Kaija Saariaho), have been more successful in achieving an international audience, and Finnish conductors (e.g., Esa Pekka Salonen and Sakari Oramo) lead some of the major orchestras worldwide.

Finnish theatre history

Finland was part of Sweden until 1809 when it became an autonomous Grand Duchy of Russia. Despite the majority of the inhabitants speaking Finnish, touring theatre companies performing in Swedish, German and

Russian were the predominant form of theatre in Finland in the eighteenth and early nineteenth centuries. One of the first proponents of Finnish-language theatre was Zachris Topelius, a prominent cultural nationalist and intellectual. At the end of 1847, in an article entitled 'The Future of Theatre in Finland', he put forward the idea of a permanent troupe in Finland with Swedish actors. He suggested that the company could gradually hire actors born in Finland and introduce extracts in the Finnish language into the programme. In a spirit of optimism he added,

> Then one would get used to hearing Finnish on stage. Instead of the songs and the various performances one would finally see smaller plays and maybe bigger plays performed in the Finnish language. And having come so far, then the time would have come to separate the Finnish and Swedish stages just as the Russian, French and German theatres are in St. Petersburg, under the same direction and in the same economic relationship with each other. Finland would then own a national theatre next to the Swedish one. Maybe it is only a hope that many would see as an illusion, but look at Hungary as an example where the German language was no less powerful than Swedish has been here. No friend of our fatherland considers the wish for the birth of Finnish literature as a vain dream. Why shouldn't we believe in Finnish drama? Bearing that in mind, the creation of a permanent theatre has an important meaning for both Finnish literature and Finnish drama.[3]

This essay by Topelius expresses the need to overcome cultural subservience to the dominant Swedish culture. A similar ideology can be seen in other emerging countries at the time: that the people were subjected to foreign rule and foreign culture, and that through a deliberate effort they could show that they were as good as those who dominated them. The development of the theatre was an important element in asserting national self-worth, and the telling of this history has become a salient feature in nationalist discourse.

In 1863 the Russian Tsar Alexander II set a challenge for Finnish-speaking people, hinting that if they could successfully show that the Finnish language was worthy of the highest level of poetry and discourse, then it, rather than Swedish, could be used for administrative and educational purposes. This challenge prompted the translation of plays and other literature into Finnish from Russian, German and ancient Greek to demonstrate that the Finnish language is capable of expressing high culture. When Finnish historians tell the story of such plays in translation, then in a sense they continue the same ideological project, demonstrating how the Finnish language gained respect by being able to represent the classic repertory of world theatre.[4]

As part of the response to this linguistic challenge, cultural nationalists founded the Finnish Theatre in 1872 with Kaarlo Bergbom as its artistic director. At first the Finnish Theatre co-habited the Arcadia Theatre in

Helsinki with a Russian theatre company, but after ten years the Russian company built its own theatre, leaving the Finnish Theatre on its own. After a slow beginning in which it experimented with producing opera as well as drama, the Finnish Theatre developed a repertory of Finnish-language plays, especially those by Aleksis Kivi and Minna Canth, and established a company of Finnish-speaking actors. The repertory grew increasingly nationalistic, using characters and stories from the *Kalevala*, the Finnish epic, as well as historic tales of Finnish battles against opposing forces and the depiction of Finnish rural lifestyle.

Following what was considered to be a successful battle in the 1870s and 1880s to demonstrate that Finnish-speaking people were capable of reproducing the finest literature and drama in their own language, Finnish language and culture encountered a new threat from a policy of Russification introduced by Tsar Nicholas II. His February Manifesto of 1899 threatened Finland's political autonomy, his Language Manifesto of 1900 announced that Russian would become the language of administration in Finland, and a new conscription law of 1901 made the Finnish army part of the Russian imperial army. Finnish resistance mobilised, leading to petitions, strikes, demonstrations, and ultimately in 1904 to the assassination of the Russian Governor General in Finland.

Finnish cultural nationalists seized the opportunity to assert their cultural independence by agreeing to build a massive granite temple to the art of theatre in the centre of Helsinki.[5] The foundation-laying ceremony in 1900 was scheduled amidst a three-day singing event organised by the Fennomanic Society of Popular Education. A photo of the ceremony shows a huge crowd with numerous large flags held in patriotic display. According to the Finnish theatre historian Eliel Aspelin-Haapkylä, 'The day started so that the celebration gathered at the Senate Square and filled it from corner to corner and the singers and orchestra organized themselves on the Nicholas Church steps and thousands of voices sang [the hymn] "A mighty fortress is our God"'. The celebration proceeded to the site of the new theatre for the laying of the foundation stone 'on that place where the Finnish National Theatre now stands as a great fortress to protect and guarantee the national theatre arts'.[6]

The opening of the new cultural fortress in 1902, on the 100th anniversary of the birth of Elias Lönnrot (the collector and compiler of the *Kalevala* epic poem), heightened the sense of Finnish cultural achievement and, in a symbolic event, linked the new theatre with Finnish mythology and folk poetry. Because a statue of Lönnrot had failed to arrive in time from France owing to poor weather conditions, it was particularly important that the building should be completed for Lönnrot's birthday. The labourers worked feverishly to finish the building, and despite governmental efforts to delay the opening by demanding a sprinkler system, the building was finally declared safe by the inspectors on the evening before the event. That the National Theatre is one of the most imposing buildings in Helsinki, designed in a grand National Romantic style reminiscent of other national theatres in the capitals of European countries seeking political autonomy, such as Oslo and Prague, is testimony to the efforts of the Finnish-speaking people to provide an impressive edifice to express great pride in their culture.

Despite the country having two national languages, the decisions of the Finnish Theatre in 1902 to rename itself as the National Theatre and to use only the Finnish language seem to go largely unquestioned today. This is understandable partly because the Swedish Theatre, a beautiful nineteenth-century building that predates the Finnish National Theatre and is situated in a prominent location in Helsinki, likewise uses only the Swedish language in its productions and is considered by many as the equivalent of the National Theatre for Swedish-speaking Finns. (At about the time of Independence the Swedish theatre transformed its company from Swedish actors to Swedish-speaking Finns, who pronounced Swedish differently.)

Another important factor in the struggle for linguistic hegemony is that, since the late nineteenth century, Finnish dramatists writing in Swedish have not gained as much recognition as Finnish-speaking authors. Up until the mid-nineteenth century Finnish intellectuals (such as Johan Ludvig Runeberg, Johan Vilhelm Snellman and Topelius) wrote in Swedish. A marked change occurred after 1860 with the advent of leading figures, such as the dramatist Aleksis Kivi, writing in Finnish. This pattern grew more pronounced by the end of the nineteenth century as writers and musicians (such as Jean Sibelius), influenced by the Romantic Nationalist movement, used characters, situations and lyrics from the *Kalevala*. Minna Canth, who was one of the most successful Finnish-speaking dramatists of the late nineteenth century (and indeed was recognised as the most important Finnish dramatist in the 1890s), caused great offence to her protégé Kaarlo Bergbom when in 1893 she wrote her play *Sylvi* in Swedish for the Swedish Theatre. But such a move by other writers was rare, and Canth returned to the Finnish language and the Finnish Theatre in 1895 with her final and most popular play *Anna Liisa*.

At the beginning of the twentieth century, the political power of women changed radically. From being a conservative country in which females were subjected to their fathers and their husbands under Lutheran doctrine and state laws, Finland (following the General Strike in 1905) became the first country in Europe to introduce universal adult suffrage. Not only did women vote for the first time in a general election, but many stood for office and won election to the new Congress of 1907, advancing more socially progressive legislation. In harmony with the political advancement of women, theatre helped to question and redefine the roles that women played in their public and private lives. In fact, the work of female Finnish dramatists has been surprisingly prominent by comparison with other countries: Minna Canth, Maria Jotuni and Hella Wuolijoki were amongst the most successful dramatists prior to the Second World War, while Hella Wuolijoki's *Niskavuori* series of plays, which feature female characters in a big farmhouse, was especially popular in the mid-twentieth century. Female dramatists continue to hold a strong position in Finnish theatre, led by Laura Ruohonen (*Olga* and *Queen C.*), Sofi Oksanen (*Purge*), Leea Klemola (*Kokkola*), Pirkko Saisio (*Insensitivity*), and Sirkku Peltola (*The Finnhorse*).

The contemporary Finnish theatre scene

According to Hanna-Leena Helavuori, Director of TINFO Theatre Info Finland, Finnish theatre has tended to be and continues to be issue-oriented.

> Theatre is perhaps the only truly popular form of art in Finland that still matters. Theatre here thrives. It has the ability to provoke public debates and stir the consciousness, whether it concerns school shootings, taking care of the elderly, the burnouts, the suicides, the decline of social security, or the increasing commodification of human beings. The themes tend to be rather heavy, even for a country noted for its gloomy songs that echo with carnival laughter.[7]

This is not to say that Finnish theatre is dour. Many Finnish playwrights create hilarious comedies out of topical concerns, such as Juha Jokela's *Mobile Horror*, on the mobile phone industry and its dominance by the Finnish company Nokia; Mika Myllyaho's *Panic*, about insecure and disoriented men seeking to find their way in a capitalist urban environment; and Sirkku Peltola's *Finnhorse*, on the effects of European Union regulations on Finnish farmers. Some of these plays evolve in small group theatres that devise their work with the writer and actors. A director who operates on a larger scale is Kristian Smeds, who has also worked in neighbouring countries during the last decade and was the first Nordic artist to receive the European Theatre Prize for New Theatrical Realities in 2011. Smeds's production of *The Unknown Soldier* for the National Theatre in 2007 was so elaborate that it could not tour, and when it was included in the programme of the St Petersburg Theatre Festival in 2008, the audience was offered a special coach to be bussed from St Petersburg to the National Theatre in Helsinki. Smeds regularly uses multi-media effects in his productions, mixing videoed scenes with live action, often cutting from one to the other or presenting them simultaneously, the video images either enhancing onstage action or upstaging it.

The Smeds production of *The Unknown Soldier* caused a major debate in Helsinki. Although the play is derived from a classic war-time novel by Väinö Linna and has become a perennial favourite of summer theatres, such as the Pyynikki Theatre in Tampere (which stages its battle scenes with explosions, army trucks, a tank and real horses), Smeds took a radical approach to it, undercutting the military heroism and ridiculing national icons. Even Marshall Mannerheim, the Finnish Commander-in-Chief and a great war hero for many Finns, was lampooned, with a video projection of him transformed into an image of Donald Duck. The final scene caused the greatest controversy with video projections of leading figures in Finnish society crackling and turning red, as if the soldiers were shooting them. Critics suggested that the anarchistic spirit of the production could spill out into the streets and result in copy-cat killings of leading figures in society, and the production continued to be discussed in the press for several months after it opened.

The production and the critical reaction demonstrated that national iconography and the portrayal of national character is still very much a key subject of Finnish theatre, especially in the National Theatre. Although the original novel is irreverent and pokes fun at military leaders while sympathising with front-line soldiers, its anarchic spirit is nonetheless set in a patriotic frame: defence of the motherland and loyalty to brothers-in-arms. The irreverence of the production, which emulated the general spirit of the novel, was criticised for going too far. Even leading politicians such as the Prime Minister and the Minister of Foreign Affairs voiced their opposition to the production without seeing it.[8]

Because Finnish is mainly spoken in only one country, one might conclude that Finnish playwrights aim at a domestic audience with a necessary knowledge of local idiomatic conditions, concerns and behaviours. This is only partly true. Kristian Smeds created multinational performances, for example, with his production of *Mental Finland*, which he wrote and directed. Pirkko Koski reported that 'the actors are Finnish and Estonian, the set and costume designer is Lithuanian, the sound designer and the musicians are Austrians, and the dancers come from different countries'.[9] Moreover, the production opened at the Royal Flemish Theatre in Brussels before being staged later at the Finnish National Theatre. Other plays by Finns such as Myllyaho's *Panic* and Ruohonen's *Olga* are so intimate in terms of their personal relations as to be universal. Thus *Panic*, which depicts the existential difficulties of three young men in an apartment, has been performed in Madrid, Copenhagen, St Petersburg, Budapest, Riga, Tartu and Moscow. *Olga*, which portrays the relationship between a lonely old woman and a young petty thief, has been performed in Edinburgh and Dublin and translated into many languages. Also, Sofi Oksanen's *Purge*, which evokes the dire experiences of Estonians under Soviet oppression during the war, has been staged in Tallinn, Stockholm, New York and Washington and translated into at least ten languages.

Finnish theatre historiography

Finnish-language drama has been regarded as an important medium for communicating aspects of national character, folklore and mythology. Likewise the recollection of this form of activity provides a strong aspect of national cultural history and myth-making. The back cover of the first comprehensive national theatre history (published in 2010) states: 'Finnish theatre has throughout almost all of its history fixed itself strongly in the society and has been a visible part of the development of the national identity.'[10] With two national languages, Finnish and Swedish, the competing linguistic groups have wanted to tell their own story in their own way. The history of the Swedish-speaking theatre was comprehensively written by Ester-Margaret von Frenckell in 1966, while a partial Finnish-speaking theatre history has been written several times.[11] The Finnish National Theatre, which was closely associated with the Finnish nationalist movement, has served as the focus for two of the Finnish theatre histories. As both of them were written by men who had worked in this theatre, the histories could be said to have been written with a certain bias and a nationalist agenda. Eliel Aspelin-Haapkylä, who was employed at the National Theatre at the beginning of the twentieth century, wrote a four-volume production history of its first years as the Finnish Theatre (1872 to 1902) and as the National Theatre from 1902 to 1910. It concentrated on the work of chief artists such as Kaarlo Bergbom, who was the founder and artistic director from 1872 to 1905, and his sister Emilie Bergbom who worked closely with him and took over the reins when he was abroad, as well as the important dramatists and leading actors in the early years of that theatre.[12] Rafael Koskimies, who was a member of the Board of the National Theatre for twenty-two years from 1938 to 1960, wrote the next significant history of the National Theatre in two volumes (from 1902 to 1917 and from 1917 to 1950). In addition to these two histories that concentrated on one institution and were written by people working within it, a number of other institutional histories and studies of artistic movements and theatre artists have been written. Timo Tiusanen, a professor at Helsinki University, published a more general history in 1969 that started from the seventeenth century. However, it again focused mainly on the early history of the National Theatre (and, to a limited extent, on the Swedish theatre), and ended with independence in 1917. This book was used as a standard textbook for the next thirty years.[13]

The history of the Finnish theatre has thus been a retelling of the story of national awakening, the threat to its culture by foreign imperialism and the eventual victory through political independence. It is perhaps significant that, like Koskimies's first volume on the National Theatre, Tiusanen's textbook on Finnish theatre history ends with political independence in 1917. Thus, political independence has been presented as a significant moment in Finnish theatre history. One of the implications of ending the story with Finnish independence is that it reinforces the triumph of the Finnish-speaking theatre in the language battle.

In the 1990s, Professor Pirkko Koski of Helsinki University, who had written a history of the Helsinki City Theatre, launched a more comprehensive approach to the study of Finnish theatre history, engaging many of her doctoral students in exploring previously under-researched topics, such as Eija Kurki's study of Sibelius's music for theatre. In an annual summer school that she organised from 1995 to 2005 with an international staff including Bruce McConachie, Janelle Reinelt, Freddie Rokem, Bill Worthen and me, these students presented new approaches to Finnish theatre history that in several cases grew into monographs. During this ten-year period Professor Koski and I also sought to make Finnish theatre more accessible to an international audience by co-writing *The Dynamic World of Finnish Theatre: An Introduction to its History, Structures and Aesthetics* and by co-editing three anthologies of Finnish drama in English translation (with Marja Wilmer, my Finnish wife, and me translating three of the anthologised plays).[14] These books, used in Finnish universities for international exchange students in MA and BA programmes and by universities abroad, have provided a major source for a new book on contemporary Finnish theatre in English by Jeff Johnson.

This developmental process has now borne fruit with the publication in 2010 of the first general Finnish theatre history, *Suomen teatteri ja drama* ('Finnish Theatre and Drama'). Edited by Mikko-Olavi Seppälä and Katri Tanskanen, two of Professor Koski's former doctoral students from the summer school, with sections written by them as well as other former and current doctoral students, including Professor Hanna Korsberg (Professor Koski's successor as Chair of the Theatre Department at the University of Helsinki), this Finnish theatre history is much more diverse than former histories. Rather than concentrating either on the Finnish National Theatre or on the history of Swedish-speaking theatre, this new history tries to give a wider overview of the many facets of Finland's theatre history from 1700 to 2010, as well as an insight into the nation's theatre infrastructure, providing chapters on Swedish-speaking as well as Finnish-speaking theatre. It also covers such topics as dance, musicals, children's theatre, amateur theatre, summer theatre, group theatres and the division in the early twentieth century between workers' theatres and bourgeois theatres. Although addressing a wide range of areas, it does not attempt to cover every area of Finnish theatre, omitting, for example, opera and ballet, whose histories have been published separately.

This history, like so many national histories in other countries in Europe, is part of the process of nation building: instantiating collective memories of past struggles and recording significant moments and achievements. By publishing the text in Finnish, the editors clearly have a Finnish audience in mind. Rather than emphasising Finland's links to the rest of Europe, the book, like many national theatre histories in other countries, concentrates on national events, movements and artistic expression, although more than half of the drama repertory comes from abroad. Just as European theatre history has ignored Finland, Finnish theatre history has not overemphasised its European connections.

Despite the efforts of the European Union to undermine it, national identity remains a powerful force in Europe. It is clear from this example of national theatre historiography that the countries of Europe continue to preserve and celebrate their cultural achievements and individuality. For the smaller countries of Europe, it is perhaps especially important to reassert what remains of their cultural as well as of their political independence. National theatres and cultural organisations as well as national theatre historiography naturally continue to emphasise the products of the nation.

NOTES

1 It was 8 per cent in the 1950s.
2 See Satu Rasila, 'The Finnish Play Today', in *Finnish Theatre*, 62 (2008), 4–8 and www.sofioksanen.com/theatre/purge , accessed 10 April 2011.
3 Valfried Vasenius, *Topelius om Teatern i Helsinfors 1842–1860* (Porvoo: Schildts, 1916), p. 80 (translated by Mikko-Olavi Seppälä).
4 See Kaarlo Bergbom, 'Muutamia sanoja nykyisistä teatterioloistamme', *Kaarlo Bergbomin kirjoitukset* (Helsinki: SKS, 1908), Vol. II, pp. 343–63.
5 Although the location was somewhat peripheral to Senate Square, it was located next to the central train station and across from the Atheneum art school and national gallery. For a discussion of the acquisition of the site, see Eliel Aspelin-Haapkylä, *Suomalaisen teatterin historia* (Helsinki: SKS, 1910), Vol. IV, pp. 148–9.
6 Aspelin-Haapkylä, *Suomalaisen teatterin historia*, Vol. IV, p. 135. Photos of the event call to mind the singing festivals in the Baltic countries when seeking independence from the Soviet Union ninety years later.
7 Hanna-Leena Helavuori, 'Foreword' in Jeff Johnson, *The New Finnish Theatre* (Jefferson, NC: McFarland, 2010), p. 1.
8 Jeff Johnson, *The New Finnish Theatre* (Jefferson, NC: McFarland, 2010), p. 129.

9 Pirkko Koski, 'Theatre with a Northern Edge', *UBU European Stages*, 48/49, (2010), 68.
10 Seppälä and Tanskanen (eds.), *Suomen teatteri ja drama*, back cover.
11 Ester-Margaret von Frenckell, *Om Teater* (Helsinki, 1966).
12 Eliel Aspelin-Haapkylä, *Suomalaisen teatterin historia* (Helsinki: SKS, 1906–10).
13 Timo Tiusanen, *Teatterimme Hahmottuu* (Helsinki: Kirjayhtymä, 1969).
14 S. E. Wilmer (ed.), *Portraits of Courage: Plays by Finnish Women* (Helsinki: Helsinki University Press, 1997). (An anthology of plays by Minna Canth, Maria Jotuni and Hella Wuolijoki, three Finnish female dramatists writing in the late nineteenth and early twentieth centuries.) Pirkko Koski and S. E. Wilmer, *Stages of Chaos: The Drama of Post-war Finland* (Helsinki: SKS, 2005). (An anthology of four Finnish plays from the 1950s to the 1990s.) S. E. Wilmer and Pirkko Koski (eds.), *Humour and Humanity: Contemporary Plays from Finland* (Helsinki: Like, 2006). (An anthology of five twenty-first-century Finnish plays.)

FURTHER READING

Johnson, Jeff. *The New Finnish Theatre* (Jefferson, NC: McFarland, 2010).
Korhonen, Kaisa, and Katri Tanskanen, eds. *Theatre People – People's Theatre: Finnish Theatre and Dance* (Helsinki: Like and Finnish Theatre Information Centre, 2006).
Kruger, Loren. *The National Stage: Theatre and Cultural Legitimation in England, France and America* (Chicago: Chicago University Press, 1992).
Mäkinen, Helka, S. E. Wilmer and W. B. Worthen, eds. *Theatre, History and National Identities* (Helsinki: Helsinki University Press, 2001).
Wilmer, S. E. *Writing and Rewriting National Theatre Histories* (Iowa City: Iowa University Press, 2004).
Wilmer, S. E., ed. *National Theatres in a Changing Europe* (London: Palgrave Macmillan, 2008).
Wilmer, S. E., and Pirkko Koski. *The Dynamic World of Finnish Theatre: An Introduction to its History, Structures and Aesthetics* (Helsinki: Like, 2006).

8

HAZEM AZMY

Egypt

On 25 January 2011, millions of predominantly young Egyptians staged a historic popular uprising to demand the immediate end of Hosni Mubarak's three-decade rule. Their action marked Egypt's most recent major appearance on the global stage, performed in the hail of worldwide acknowledgements of the country's history and civilisation. Holding that their homeland's past should have earned it a better present, many of the protestors proclaimed it as *umm al-dunnia* ('the mother of all the world'), a popular phrase that invokes a reminder of Egypt's distinction as, perhaps, the longest existing political entity on earth. A closer look at the case of Egypt may reveal more to this claim than mere euphoric exceptionalism.

To be sure, Egypt seems unique in its fabled defiance of time, having preserved its borders virtually intact since time immemorial. Located at the centre of the Arab world, it was once hailed by its neighbours as 'the beating heart of Arabness', a carry-over from Arab nationalist times when Egypt became the *de facto* capital of the region's culture and civilisation. Its Arab identity aside, however, the oft-invaded Mediterranean country has equally been shaped by its location at the intersection of different civilisations and continents, with each contributing a share to its makeup. As such, Egypt proudly bears the imprints of civilisations as diverse as the 'Pharaonic', Mediterranean/Graeco-Roman, Coptic Christian, Arabo-Islamic, Turco-Circassian and Nilotic/African. Yet this richly hybrid nature is but a facet of what gives meaning to the phrase 'mother of all the world', since today's Egypt is, perhaps, the sum total of its myriad historical constituents in a single, potentially conflictual composite whole.

Not all Egyptians are willing to talk up their country's immunity to change. Seeking to identify 'The character of Egypt' in a magnum opus with the same title, geographer and cultural theorist Gamal Hamdan (1928–93) argues that Egyptians' settled agrarian existence around a life-giving Nile, while a blessing in many respects, also gradually conditioned them to a system of political centralism, be it that of a central seat of power where all decisions are taken or, more oppressively still, that of an all-powerful, larger-than-life 'Pharaoh', at best a variant of the stereotypical 'oriental despot'. Writing in the aftermath of the 1967 military defeat, Hamdan further asserts that abandoning Egypt's time-honoured culture of 'Pharaonism' is a basic condition for any progress ever to be achieved; yet, he adds, Egyptians seem to have acquired across their history a certain debilitating fear of change. How else can one explain their proverbial patience in the face of injustices that elsewhere would have pre-cipitated a sweeping upheaval?

While recent events may have cast some doubt on Hamdan's pessimism, the more lasting relevance of his work resides in its highlighting of political power and its asymmetries as the vehicle around which Egyptians typically imagine the panoply of their life experiences. Indeed, enmeshed with the project of defining the nation, modern theatre in Egypt has always been an exemplary vehicle for expressing the same politically inspired imaginary. Writings about this theatre abound with testimonies to its political embed-dedness, even when not always discussed as a positive state of affairs. Mohamed Enani, one of Egypt's most respected literary critics as well as a published dramatist anxious for the integrity of his messages on stage, thus writes wearily in 1985 about 'a malaise from which very few people have recovered':

> The average theatre-goer, especially among the intelligentsia, often looks for the relevance of the play's incidents and characters to current events and public figures, and is often disappointed if he cannot find such 'projections' or oblique references. In fact, if serious, a play is expected to touch upon national issues, possibly the problem of government (with the Head of State thrown in for good measure)...[1]

Such statements confirm the centrality of politics to any historical account of Egyptian theatre, particularly if it is to do justice to local sensibilities and understandings. With this imperative in mind, the overview of Egyptian theatre that I present here purports to be neither comprehensive nor 'objec-tive'. Instead, it will simply offer snapshots of the way in which the Egyptian stage has historically evolved, almost invariably when negotiating its politi-cally charged energies, and especially when projecting 'extrinsic' realities on a performance so that they threatened to destabilise its other 'literary' or 'aesthetic' aims. At issue throughout this account is the tension that obtains when cultural producers – often armed with a Western, deceptively linear model of progress – are challenged in their endeavours by the entrenched heteroglossic realities of their local context. Given these potentially subversive dynamics, it is tempting to begin our discussion with pre-modern times, when indigenous performance forms claimed the status of *vox populi*, challenging the powers-that-be and implicitly upsetting the established order.[2] However, given my interest in issues of cultural transmission and negotiation, I will limit my discussion here to the time stretch from the nineteenth century onwards, roughly corresponding to the onset and subsequent career of Egyptian modernity. I am choosing to begin from this point in history since, as I will show, it was marked by a symbiotic moment – one in which all the cultural and theatrical currents now at play first entered into programmatic interaction with one another.

Snapshot one: staging Egypt on the modern world's stage

The reign of Khedive Ismail (1863–79), Egypt's viceroy under Ottoman rule, signalled what may be regarded as the country's full entry into modernity – as the ultimate conclusion of the reformist achievements initiated by Mohamed Ali Pasha (1805–48), Ismail's grandfather and founder of modern Egypt. A Paris-educated *bon vivant* endowed with boundless energy and imagination, a notorious penchant for lavish pomp and spectacle, and a mixed record in office that remains a bone of contention among historians, Ismail conceived of this modernisation project as a statement of Egypt's independence from the Turkish Ottoman Empire. In 1867, he famously announced that Egypt no longer existed in Africa: it was now 'a part of Europe'.

To realise this prophecy, he embarked on what was, arguably, the first attempt of its kind and scope to stage the Egyptian nation on the modern 'global' stage. Nowhere was this theatrical thinking more apparent than in Ismail's majestic scheme for the transformation of Cairo. Impressed with the 1867 *Exposition Universelle* held in Paris to mark Baron Haussmann's revolutionary reconstruction of the French capital, Ismail went back to Egypt determined to transform Cairo into another Paris on the banks of the Nile. Using the projected opening of the Suez Canal as an appropriate context for his plans, he conceived of a scene of national sovereignty whereby modern Egypt would make its debut before a captive audience of the world's most glamorous royals and dignitaries.

In both its euphoria and inherent contradictions, Ismail's vision appears with hindsight to have been paradigmatic of Egyptian modernity and of the cultural identities that this modernity imagined *vis-à-vis* its European models. Like its Western analogue, the Egyptian modern Self is of a nationalist character. Its natural concern with reflecting an independent and 'modern' enough image often leads Egyptian modernity to seek – and measure itself against – recognition of the Western Other. More ironically still, given the anxiety of influence that this emulatory relationship inevitably produces, it is

GOVERNMENT HOSPITALITY.

John Thomas (L—d D—r—y). "EGYPT! O—AR—YES! SORRY WE COULDN'T ACCOMMODATE YOU IN THE PALACE, BUT—AR—WE'D ORDERED A BED FOR YOU AT A DELIGHTFUL PUBLIC-HOUSE—AR—CLARIDGE'S, IN FACT; BUT THEY'LL TAKE YOU IN AT DUDLEY HOUSE."

7 'Kept at the Gate': A *Punch* cartoon dated 13 July 1867, commenting on Ismail's visit to London on his way back from Paris's *Exposition Universelle*.

precisely the hegemony of this Other that Egyptian modernity ultimately needs to shake off, if not totally combat and resist.

This contradictory impulse meant that, as part of his epic-scale scheme, Ismail gave instructions in 1869 to build the Khedivial (Royal) Opera House. Designed by Italian architects along the model of La Scala in Milan, the construction was completed in six months, just in time to be shown with pride to Ismail's distinguished guests. It was, after all, the first Opera House in Africa and the Middle East, located right at the heart of Ismail's European Cairo. Yet far from being impressed with the Khedive's refined Egypt, the disappointed foreign guests appeared to have set their fancies on a rawer exotic experience. As sociologist Janet Abu-Lughod puts it, citing Western accounts of the fêtes, while '[t]he guests at Ismail's grand reception at the Qasr al-Nil Palace were treated to a chamber concert and a performance of the Comédie Française, they had looked forward to an evening with Scheherazade'.[3]

It was not until a decade later that Ismail's vision of attaching Egypt to Europe came to its cruel realisation. The Khedive's radical development of the infrastructure (or his lavish spending, as his detractors routinely point out) necessitated more expenditure than Egypt's income and revenues could provide, a fact that led Ismail to contract unmanageable foreign debts. In 1875, he sold to the British Empire Egypt's shares in the Suez Canal. Claiming to protect their interests, European governments increasingly interfered in Ismail's government and finance. Finally, in 1879, the British and French governments prevailed on the Ottoman Sultan to depose Ismail. With tacit blessings from Tewfik, Ismail's more pliable son and successor, invading British troops defeated the Egyptian army in 1882, quelling the nationalist revolt led by peasant-born army officer Ahmed Urabi.

The quest for Egyptian national sovereignty thus ended perversely in a long and painful foreign occupation. Yet, culturally and socially, the nation's march towards modernity assumed a different life of its own. By 1895, when a broken Ismail died at his palace confinement on the bank of the Bosporus, the modern Egypt he once wished to display had become a staple of the cosmopolitan scene. Describing *belle époque* Egypt of the nineteenth-century *fin de siècle*, French writer Paul Ravisse summed up the contemporary received wisdom: 'politically a part of Europe, and to a certain extent the common property of all nations'.[4]

Snapshot two: an Egyptian theatre is born?

Diverging from its Western model, nationalist-oriented Egyptian modernity could never afford to claim a rupture with its immediate past. Instead, it has struggled over the years to make its founding, Western-imported world views coexist with its indigenous traditions. For Ismail's Egypt, this notion meant that old Cairo was to be kept almost intact, while a new city was to be constructed to the west of it. Underlying the act was a particular assumption that would remain predominant ever since, one which pre-supposed that in due course, and as if by virtue of mere juxtaposition, the (Western-imported) modern would rub off on the (autochthonous) old. Over the years, continuing attempts to resolve the contradictions inherent in such an assumption have become shorthand for the evolution of modern Egyptian theatre. This may explain why indigenous or 'pre-modern' Egyptian performance practices have never disappeared from the scene, even when relegated at times to the status of 'folklore', a realm popularly associated with the uneducated masses.

Such practices cannot be adequately discussed here. Still, it is tempting to take a brief look at the moment in which they first ran up against the influx of Western aesthetic ideals.

In tracing the birth moment of this creative collision, we need to go no further than the account written by journalist and playwright Yacub Sannu (1839–1912), an Egyptian-born Jewish polyglot of mixed ethnic origins. Originally a lecture delivered to a captive Parisian audience, this account was subsequently published in Sannu's 1912 book *Ma vie en vers et mon théâtre en prose* ('My Life in Verse and my Theatre in Prose'). The book's overall narrative establishes the Francophile author as a dedicated Egyptian nationalist, but also, in the same breath, as the founder of modern Egyptian theatrical practice. In 1870, we are told, Sannu decided to create the first Arabic-speaking Egyptian theatrical troupe, in reaction to the visiting French and Italian troupes then performing under the auspices of Ismail at the prestigious Ezbekiyeh theatre. Consciously emulating the Western model, he identified as his influences the dramatic works that formed the repertoire of foreign-language theatres close at hand: the comedies of Molière, Goldoni and Sheridan. He would subsequently refer to himself as 'The Molière of Egypt', a title that Sannu claims to have been given to him by a jubilant Ismail.

For all such European influences and official endorsements, Sannu's proclaimed interest in interacting with his Egyptian audience eventually led him to draw also upon the indigenous types of spectacle he found at his disposal – Karagoz, Shadow Theatre, and the strategies of improvisational street jesters known as *al-Muhabbizun*. In opting for such an unabashedly interactive model, he reports often being compelled to 'sacrifice' (as he puts it) many of the European theatrical traditions he initially held as sacrosanct. Actors' improvisations sanctioned by the audience routinely became part of the performance, while Sannu's active spectators took to commenting on the plot of the play while in progress, sometimes even dictating its ending. He cites a case in point:

> Having presented a number of farces and one-act comedies, I felt it was my duty at that point to start teaching good morals. As such, I wrote a play of two acts titled 'The Young Lady *à la Mode*'. At the centre of the play was a young coquette who flirts with several young men at once, only to end up deserted by all, like an old maid left pining for a husband on Saint Catherine's Day. As it happened, however, the play was booed by the audience who even called me on stage. 'In what way has my play offended your tastes?' I asked them.
>
> A young man answered back: 'You know full well, Molière, that Miss Safsaff who plays the young coquette is actually an honest and decent girl who has never flirted with anyone outside this theatre. She therefore deserves that you forgive her for all the inappropriate behaviour in which you have her engaged in

الشيخ أبو نظارة المصري

LE CHEIKH ABOU NADDARA (*)

(Reproduction du portrait paru dans les journaux illustrés d'Europe.)

8 Self-portrait of Yacub Sannu. Note Sannu's traditional attire and the use of his pen name, Abu Naddara (the man with the glasses) preceded by the Islamic title of Sheikh, two details which demonstrate his penchant for self-fashioning according to the sentiments of his audience.

your play. It is now incumbent upon you to find her a suitable husband worthy of her grace and beauty, and to make sure that the final scene of your comedy is duly dedicated to the conclusion of this marriage, for only then would we wholeheartedly applaud. Otherwise, we will never again set foot in your theatre.'

I was therefore obliged to add a new scene to the play, one in which the coquette realises the error of her ways, shows remorse, and then proceeds to acquire herself a husband at long last, much to the great exuberance of my spectators. Need I also add that the play was a huge success? Perhaps it will suffice to say that the play was performed one hundred consecutive times.[5]

Sannu's foregrounding of audience-interactive energies proved short-lived. His theatre was closed down in 1872 (when, according to him, the socio-political implications of his plays incurred the wrath of Ismail). The ongoing controversy around Sannu's pioneering role requires a separate discussion beyond my present scope. Suffice it to say that Sannu's painstaking presentation of himself as an ardent nationalist may have facilitated his subsequent 're-discovery' at the hands of historians and critics writing under the post-1952 order. As such, Sannu was practically reinvented as the ultimate initiator of truly 'Egyptian' theatre practice, but whose determination to speak truth to power eventually brought him into conflict with a despotic and decadent Ismail, himself the son of the much-reviled 'foreign' Mohamed Ali dynasty. Writers of that persuasion paid surprisingly scant attention to a number of contradictions and discrepancies attending Sannu's own, unverified account of his theatrical and public achievements. Such contradictions were meticulously detailed by theatre historian Sayed Ali Ismail in his 2001 book *Muhakamt masrah Yacub Sannu* ('The Trial of the Theatre of Yacub Sannu'), which painted a radically different picture of Sannu as a self-promoting charlatan.

Whatever his real contributions, the closure of Sannu's theatre ushered in the decline of the populist tradition in theatre. The subsequent influence of Levantine troupes, arriving in Egypt from 1876 onwards, consolidated the opposite text-oriented tradition, slowly but gradually leading up to a more didactic, bourgeois understanding of theatre – as 'the People's School' *par excellence*. Inextricably linked with this shift was the issue of language. In his enthusiasm for an interactive model, Sannu wrote and performed his plays in a multi-level *Ammeya* (colloquial Egyptian Arabic) that sought to reflect the different cultural and class backgrounds of each character. With the advent of Levantine troupes, however, *Fus'ha* (literary Standard Arabic) came to be regarded as the language of 'serious' theatre, which included, in addition to translated texts, plays with historical, epic and religious themes, as well as ones dealing with lofty or subtle ideas for the expression of which *Ammeya* was regarded as too limited and crude.

Snapshot three: 'Silence, you sheep!'

This shift in thinking about theatre and its socio-political function can best be illustrated by the divergent practices of three representative figures of pre-1952 theatre. The renegade scion of an aristocratic family, Youssef Wahbi (1898?–1982) fled to Italy where he reported receiving a theatrical apprenticeship of sorts, most detectable in his oratorical acting style (which, under plebeian post-monarchic times, he would successfully recycle into a tool for

9 Young Wahbi as the lone romantic genius.

self-parody). Returning to Egypt to receive his share of his father's inheritance, Wahbi created a theatrical troupe of his own in 1923, with the declared aim of 'salvaging' thespian art from the 'atrocities' of the day's two competing star vaudevillians: Ali al-Kassar (1887–1957) and Naguib al-Rihany (1892–1949). Seeking to endow the theatrical profession with a measure of the social respectability it then lacked, Wahbi paraded his aristocratic credentials, creating an aura around his Italianate Ramses theatre as a dignified place of cultural refinement. The regular fare of his theatre thus consisted of 'serious' plays that were either translated or adapted European texts, or original melodramas with morally laden social messages.

Occasionally writing his own plays, Wahbi preached in an elevated language that was either an outright *Fus'ha* or a sanitised form of *Ammeya* generously interlaced with *Fus'ha* diction and cadences. Both on and off the stage, Wahbi insisted on decorum, prohibiting any unwelcome noise from the auditorium. While on stage, theatre scholar Ali al-Rai reports, Wahbi often admonished misbehaving spectators with the words '*Silence*, ya ghanam!' – literally, 'Silence, you [unruly] sheep!' (with the word of command uttered in French, as if a reminder of Wahbi's elite station).

10 Al-Rihany as the petit bourgeois man in pre-Republican Egypt: a scene from *Ghazal al-Banat* (1949), the actor's last screen appearance.

A less top-down approach is to be found in the example of Naguib al-Rihany. An actor, manager and director, al-Rihany formed a creative partnership with playwright Badie Khairy (1893–1966), with the duo reworking French vaudevilles into imaginative and purely 'Egyptian' versions. Al-Rihany's early career thus saw him performing revues in which he played the *commedia*-like character he invented: Kish Kish Bey, a gullible country headman who is always caught up in misadventures thanks to his inability to cope with a cruelly modern Cairo. As M. M. Badawi describes this phase in the actor's career, al-Rihany 'continued to use Kish Kish Bey in one sketch after another as a symbol of the little man surrounded by a corrupt world whose falsehood, materialism and greed were brought into focus more sharply when set against the little man's basic goodness'.[6]

Although al-Rihany's identification with this little man figure became the hallmark of all his subsequent roles, the period after the First World War marked al-Rihany's gradual departure from folk comic style to playtexts characterised by distinct social messages, clearer literary boundaries, and a performing style that (albeit still betraying a measure of comic stylisation) may loosely be classified as Western representational acting. Still in collaboration with Khairy, the maturer al-Rihany refined an everyday *Ammeya* at once removed from the artificialities of Wahbi and

11 Al-Kassar in a photo dated 1917. Here, the 'blackie' is proving his Egyptian identity by fighting two British colonialists.

like-minded contemporaries, yet still capable of rendering deep emotions and subtle ideas.

Thanks to his stage and film interpretations of the petit bourgeois man of pre-Republican Egypt, al-Rihany secured himself the standing of the ultimate father of modern Egyptian comedy.[7] By contrast, al-Rihany's one-time rival, Ali al-Kassar, held on steadfastly to his improvisational folk comic style. On stage as well as in film, he continued to perform the stock character he invented and popularised: Osman Abdel-Basset, a kind-hearted Nubian *Barbari* ('blackie') who fused national and racial identities in an unprecedented and complicated way.[8] In 1935, however, al-Kassar's theatre closed down, due to financial losses. After a number of ever smaller roles in film, he died in 1957 – in virtual neglect and obscurity.

The same year that saw the closing down of al-Kassar's populist theatre marked another turning point in the opposite direction: the State's founding of the first National Troupe in 1935. Hosted at Al-Ezbekiyeh Theatre, the new troupe opened with a performance of *Ahl al-Kahf* ('The People of the Cave') by playwright Tawfik al-Hakim (1898–1987). Two years earlier, Taha Hussein, one of the most authoritative belle-lettrists of the day, had hailed the publication of al-Hakim's play-text as a watershed. For Hussein, the philosophically inspired work of his fellow Francophile was, indeed, the first dramatic text worthy of being described as Arabic literature.

The literary dramatist had finally arrived. With al-Hakim now upheld as a pace-setter, other playwrights would continue to see themselves as fully fledged men of letters – as intellectuals with a 'message'. They soon found a great ally in the Higher Institute of Theatre, established in 1944 under French-educated actor and director Zaki Tualymat (1894–1982). New generations of actors and directors were subsequently trained in the Western psychological paradigm, providing the infrastructure necessary to fulfil the aspirations of an emerging generation of playwrights and critics. Egyptian theatre was now prepared for what many Egyptian and Arab historians still regard as its 'lost golden period'. But therein hangs a complicated post-colonial tale.

Snapshot four: all hail the leader!

Following the end of British colonisation in the 1952 'revolution' and the Suez War of 1956, President Gamal Abdel Nasser (1956–70) sought to legitimise his own socialist-oriented, pan-Arabist nationalism. Historians and cultural producers of all types (but with theatre artists at the forefront) were immediately set to work. Past socio-political orders were vilified – or erased altogether – as either foreign or unpatriotic or both. Whatever the elitism and social injustice ascribed to such orders, they were now replaced with an 'alliance of all the working powers of the people', to recall one of the most oft-repeated official slogans of the times. Also, the junta of 'Free Officers' that toppled the Mohamed Ali dynasty predominantly hailed from peasant or middle-class backgrounds, a detail that helped promote a narrative of the new ruling class as quintessential Egyptians governing 'themselves' for the first time in centuries. Since they were still in their thirties, this also gave way to a companion narrative in which the young generation was now at the helm, shaping its own 'revolutionary' Egypt: for all intents and purposes, Egypt was now re-imagined as a forward-looking socialist utopia with an anti-colonial message to impart not only to its citizens but also to other Arab countries, as the latter presumably sought the guidance of the Egyptian 'elder sister'.

Within the same spirit of euphoria, the period saw the rise of a generation of directors with distinct artistic styles, most of them young talents just back from state-funded training abroad. Working in theatres funded and run by what seemed like a supportive state, these directors introduced modernist and predominantly avant-garde stage practices that helped shape the interpretations of the period's major dramatists. The latter, in turn, were either Egyptian or world-recognised foreign playwrights, their work rendered into Arabic by a new wave of dedicated dramatic translators. It did not take long for this creative bonanza to be proclaimed as a theatrical 'renaissance', so

12 A shaky alliance? Nasser decorating Tawfiq al-Hakim with the Order of the Republic in a picture dated 17 December 1958. Unlike many of his younger contemporaries, al-Hakim enjoyed uninterrupted official celebration throughout Nasser's life, with a prominent state theatre named after him and the president himself acknowledging al-Hakim's ideas as one of the main sources of his intellectual formation.

much so that the period's playwrights, directors, actors and critics continue to be regarded as the definitive generation in the history of modern Egyptian drama and theatre.

All the while, the impassioned but covertly sermonising soliloquy of a middle-class and often young visionary became all but obligatory on the Nasserist stage. The majority of dramatic writers and directors under Nasser apparently regarded themselves to be in some tacit alliance with him. As such, they celebrated the character (or mouthpiece?) of the middle-class intellectual as the seer of an emerging socialist order, while implicitly blaming the idolised Nasser for ignoring the advice of such a valuable 'voice of the people'.[9] In one indicative play after another, in a curious parallel to Nasser's populist rhetoric, the theatrical faction of the dominant ideological class in the 1960s continued to speak to their audience constituencies not only didactically but also empathetically – as if they were themselves speaking on behalf of the silent masses.

The paradoxes and dilemmas of this faction do not end here. As their imagined alliance with the state proved time and again dismal, and with the state continuing to use its repressive apparatus where the ideological apparatus seemed ineffectual, many theatre artists turned to historical and mythical settings to hide their politically subversive messages. These messages typically blamed the head of state for surrounding himself with corrupt advisers while alienating himself from his own people.[10] Such a depiction of the sitting ruler – whether Nasser or his successors – as a well-meaning but misguided autocrat has never since waned in Egyptian drama and culture. While often quickly dismissed as a perverse apologia, this tendency also invites wider questions about the contract between the ruler and the immobile masses and the latter's track history of surrendering their destiny to a single 'leader' figure. This lends credence to Hamdan's concept of 'Pharaonism', yet personality cult alone cannot explain the whole complex relationship between political power and cultural producers. Consider the more recent cases below.

Snapshot five: the curious case of 'Egyptian theatre martyrs'

On 5 September 2005, Egypt was two days away from its first-ever multi-candidate presidential elections, a long-awaited moment of cultural rejuvenation if one were to believe state media. Yet Hazem Shehata had no reason to feel any less disaffected. Like many of his generation, he was still in the midst of an uphill struggle – as a 50-year-old theatre critic and scholar whose eclectic assimilation of semiotic, Bakhtinian and deconstructive insights had earned him the respect of peers and mentees, but hardly the cultural standing or financial security commensurate with it. That hot summer evening found Shehata in the upper Egyptian city of Beni Suef, where he had been serving on the jury of a national competition for provincial theatre troupes – held, tellingly, at a makeshift theatre inside the local 'cultural palace'. Yet instead of the scheduled performance, an adaptation of Albee's *The Zoo Story*, he and all present were in for a much darker drama.

The flames of the candles used at the low-budget, amateur production caused the spray-painted scenery to catch fire. When finally put out, the blaze had claimed the lives of Shehata and thirty-four others, leaving sixty more either seriously or fatally injured. Such a high number of casualties, it soon became apparent, was due to the governmental building's lack of basic safety precautions, to say nothing of the inefficiency of the local fire brigade and medical amenities. The Minister of Culture made cryptic statements about an unaccepted resignation, while some officials were dismissed and eventually sent to trial. Held a few days later, the state-organised Cairo International Festival for Experimental Theatre (CIFET) was hastily dedicated to the 'Egyptian theatre martyrs' – an ironic word choice, cynics remarked, since it left those to blame suspiciously unspecified.

The immediate fallout of the incident is of less interest than its wider implications, for the Beni Suef 'holocaust' could scarcely be more emblematic of the State's liaison with successive generations of theatre/cultural producers, particularly the 'middle' one that Shehata and most other victims represented. This is the generation whose arrival in the early 1980s coincided with the beginning of the Mubarak era. Their story merits some unpacking.

It was, if anything, a limbo generation. Its members' late blooming or largely unrealised careers saw them, like their predecessors, 'speaking truth to power' from a marginal position within the official establishment – either as associates attached to government institutions or, more typically, as part of the public sector workforce. Unlike their predecessors, they also inherited the existential anxieties of their immediate antecedents, the overpowered radicals of the 1970s. Much of this anxiety was the outgrowth of the shift from the left-leaning populism of Nasser's times to the perceived espousal of traditionalist/Islamist voices by his successor, Anwar Sadat (1970–81). Equally disorienting was how the rightward political changes meshed with Sadat's version of *laissez-faire* capitalism, or what came to be called *Infitah* ('open-door' policy). An abrupt departure from Nasser's botched social welfarism, *Infitah* encouraged a mass exodus of professionals and intellectuals, as well as of peasants and workers, seeking greener pastures in the oil-rich Gulf Arab states. Affluent expatriates would return to Egypt with the consumerism and/or the more conservative mores of their host Gulf countries, but the period was also marked by brash and moneyed parvenus of all types as well as a new breed of capitalists with suspiciously acquired fortunes and a toxic, corrosive impact. Little wonder that *Infitah* came to be accused not only of shattering the middle class, with which cultural producers had traditionally been affiliated, but also of irrevocably upsetting the established structure of society.

No less murky was the theatre scene on which Shehata and his generation arrived. The 1967 military defeat at the hands of Israel had led to a re-examination of the top-down modernising project, gradually 're-awakening' seemingly dormant traditionalist/Islamist undercurrents. Only then was the literary model in the theatre seriously challenged, though never completely abandoned. For good or ill, far more forcefully than any earlier attempts,[11] indigenous traditions made their comeback as legitimate, even essential artistic alternatives, to be deployed from time to time experimentally, but also, far too often, appropriated commercially; hence, the rising consensus that Egyptian theatre was now 'in crisis'.

For critics of the day, the downward turn was thanks to the boom that private commercial theatres enjoyed since the 1970s, fuelled by the patronage of a new moneyed class as well as of indulgent Gulf Arab tourists on the hunt for easy summer diversions. Contrary to the literary dramatists' foregrounding of the text, the private theatres' fare tended, if anything, to shun clear narratives and sophisticated dialogues, making instead clever, often opportunistic use of indigenous popular comedy. For their part, the government-run theatres were left floundering, treated indifferently by the state and abandoned by an audience no longer beholden to modernising assumptions.

Sadat's peacemaking efforts with Israel transformed him into a celebrated figure on the world stage, yet the perceived volte-face in Egypt's positioning as the historic leader of Arab nationalism also eventually earned him an avowed opposition at home as well as across most of the Arab World. In September 1981, the embattled president ordered an unprecedented round-up of more than 1,500 of his critics, including Islamists as well as intellectuals and activists from all ideological and political stripes. When jihadists assassinated Sadat in October 1981, the coming to power of his Vice-President, Hosni Mubarak, occasioned an initial euphoria, inasmuch as the untested new ruler pledged a return to a more democratic atmosphere, including the relaxation of much official censorship. The period thus marked the state's warming up anew to art and culture as a means of combating the burgeoning Islamist threat, but also of projecting a more 'modern' image compatible with the drive for globalisation.

Yet for all the revived rhetoric of 'enlightenment', or perhaps because of it, the intelligentsia's old–new alliance with the state inspired scant rethinking of its assumptions. Writing as late as 1995, anthropologist Lila Abu-Lughod detected at work much of the same 'civilising' mandate:

> In Egypt, a concerned group of culture-industry professionals has constructed of ... women, youths, and rural people a subaltern object in need of enlightenment. Appropriating and inflecting Western discourses on development they construct themselves as guides of modernity and assume the responsibility of producing ... the virtuous modern citizen.[12]

As if complementing this outlook, the emergency powers declared after Sadat's assassination were to remain in place throughout the entirety of Mubarak's thirty-year rule. The top-down gift of a breathing space was always already retractable.

Snapshot six: 'free' at last?

From 1987 onwards, as if by sheer force of will, a group of practitioners, critics and scholars, including Shehata, directors Hassan al-Geretly and Saleh Saad (also a Beni Suef 'martyr'), UK-trained academic Nehad Selaiha, and critics Minha al-Batrawi and Maysa Zaki, came together as advocates of a new 'independent' theatre – a drive that was soon to challenge the period's age-old gerontocracy.

Consisting of young theatre enthusiasts with varying levels of training and artistic merit, the 'Free theatre movement' attempted an alternative model free, at least in principle, of state control and commercial theatre dictates. The state-run Al-Hanager Theatre, in operation since 1992 under the artistic directorship of Francophile academic and public intellectual Huda Wasfi (1992–2012), provided a home for the movement's artists, but also for the international artists and workshops recruited to nurture fledgling talents. Typically driven by an 'experimental' imagination that tested the limits of the written text or abandoned it in favour of physical forms, the movement produced some of the era's best younger talents, including a rare group of women directors and dramaturgs. To all appearances, a new generation was on course to take up the helm.[13]

Yet apart from the varying successes of a handful of members and the atypical relative stability of a small number of troupes with foreign funding-savvy directors (such as 'Al-Warsha' under Hassan al-Geretly and 'The Temple' under Ahmed al-Attar), the uneven career of the movement itself continued to pose troubling questions about the inevitability of containment – through either sponsorship or censorship, or, ever more often, a mixture of both.

It could be that the melange of money and power was fast becoming the order of the day. The low-turnout elections in September 2005 announced the 77-year-old Hosni Mubarak as the 'winner' of a fifth consecutive term with a platform that preached the usual rhetoric of passing on the torch to the nation's young and bright. Few could fail to see how the campaign slogans echoed the 'new thinking' within the ruling National Democratic Party: a rising inner circle, mostly businessmen-turned-politicians, had been setting the stage for a British passport-holding investment banker to 'inherit' office from the ever more distant Mubarak. Enter Gamal Mubarak (b. 1964), the president's younger son and, since 2002, the founding chair of the NDP's all-powerful Policies Secretariat.

Egypt was fast changing hands from the dysfunctional militaristic autocracy of the post-monarchic order to an unabashed hereditary plutocracy. Such, at least, was the sentiment against which obituaries for the Beni Suef dead were indignantly written. Inasmuch as the fire took place in the underdeveloped South, it joined a string of similar national tragedies, all products of the Mubarak era and thus lending new focus and urgency to the injustices long visited upon Egypt's 'subalterns'. More specifically, inasmuch as the incident took place at one of the state's dilapidated 'cultural palaces', it revealed the extent of the chasm between the aggressive neoliberalism of the new oligarchy and the socialist founding assumptions of the old public sector. Little wonder that many of the theatre artists and professionals picketing and running petition drives in September 2005 were at the forefront of the crowds in January 2011.

And hence we conclude where we started: Tahrir (Liberation) Square, the now-iconic site of the Egyptian revolution, but also the heart of Ismail's modern, tension-rife Cairo. This is where protestors staged an eighteen-day sit-in which, presumably, led to the toppling of the Mubarak dynasty and their top henchmen. At the time of writing in late 2011, many of these protestors are marking the first anniversary of the revolution by arguing 'the revolution must go on!' As such, they continue to battle a perceived 'counter-revolution' by the former regime's remnants and are entering ever more violent tests of will with the 'interim' supreme military council, demanding it hand over power to an elected *civilian* authority, practically the first of its kind since 1952. Many are no less wary of the triumphalism of some Islamists, who, emboldened by recent electoral gains, decry their opponents as 'infidels' and vengefully proclaim their agenda as the 'democratic' choice of a long-suppressed majority craving a 'return' to Egypt's 'Islamic' roots.

The implications for art and culture are far from certain. Whatever the future holds, these new–old conflictual dynamics remain perfectly in character and thus unlikely to go away in the foreseeable future. Time and again in tandem with the performance practices it has produced along its genesis, Ismail's theatrically inspired Cairo continues to act as the showcase of (post)modern Egypt, complete with its creative tensions and built-in contradictions: between the old and the new, between allochthonous models and local reconfigurations, between a hegemonic centre and sometimes freshly empowered peripheries, but also, above all, among the myriad voices and narratives that make up the nation, each staking a claim to the present by reconnecting with a version of Egypt's heterogeneous past.[14]

13 Actress Magda Mounir standing next to a poster for the 2011 "We shall forget you not", a commemoration held each 5 September in honour of the Beni Suef victims. The event culminated with post-Revolution minister of culture Emad Abu-Ghazi officially declaring the day 'Egyptian Theatre Day'.

NOTES

1 M. M. Enani, 'Introduction', *The Trial of an Unknown Man*, by Ezzeldin Ismail, trans. M. Enani (Cairo: General Egyptian Book Organization, 1985), p. 16.

2 See, for instance, Philip Sadgrove, 'Pre-modern Arabic Theatre', in Roger Allen and D. S. Richards (eds.), *The Cambridge History of Arabic Literature: Arabic Literature in the Post-Classical Period*, Vol. III (Cambridge: Cambridge University Press, 2006), pp. 369–83.

3 Janet Abu-Lughod, *Cairo: 1001 Years of the City Victorious* (Princeton: Princeton University Press, 1971), p. 112.

4 Qtd in Trevor Mostyn, *Egypt's Belle Epoque: Cairo and the Age of the Hedonists* (London and New York: Tauris Parke Paperbacks, 2006), p. 44.

5 Philip Sadgrove, *The Egyptian Theatre in the Nineteenth Century (1799–1882)* (Reading: Ithaca Press, 1996), p. 179; my translation.

6 M. M. Badawi, *Early Arabic Drama* (Cambridge: Cambridge University Press, 1988), p. 67.

7 A sample of al-Rihany's artistic style may currently be viewed on www.bit.ly/alrihany. The clip shows my English subtitling of a scene from al-Rihany's last screen appearance, the 1949 musical comedy *Ghazal al-Banat* ('When Girls Flirt').

8 See Eve M. Troutt Powell, *A Different Shade of Colonialism: Egypt, Great Britain, and the Mastery of the Sudan* (Berkeley: University of California Press, 2003).

9 I am indebted to the late Hazem Shehata for first alerting me to those defining aspects of the Nasserist stage (see Snapshot five).

10 See, for instance, Ali Salem's *The Comedy of Oedipus* (1970) and Mahmoud Diab's *Bāb al-Futūh* ('The Gateway to Conquest', 1971).

11 For an interesting discussion of these earlier experiments, see Marvin Carlson, 'Avant-Garde Drama in the Middle East', in James M. Harding and John Rouse (eds.), *Not the Other Avant-Garde: The Transnational Foundations of Avant-Garde Performance* (Ann Arbor: University of Michigan Press, 2006), pp. 125–44. Note the discussion of al-Hakim's 1962 *Ya Tali al-Shajara* and Youssef Idris's 1964 *Al-Farafir* as two of the most prominent pre-1967 efforts to revive indigenous traditions.

12 Lila Abu-Lughod, 'The Objects of Soap Opera: Egyptian Television and the Cultural Politics of Modernity', in Daniel Miller (ed.), *Worlds Apart: Modernity Through the Prism of the Local* (London and New York: Routledge, 1995), p. 191.

13 For an informative if slightly outdated collection of reviews and reflective accounts on the movement and its representative artists, see Nehad Selaiha, *The Egyptian Theatre: New Directions* (Cairo: General Egyptian Book Organization, 2003).

14 For an eloquent expression of these dynamics and how Egyptian artists of all stripes are responding to their emerging revolutionary *Zeitgeist*, see the 2011 documentary *The Noise of Cairo*, dir. Heiko Lange. Official trailer available at http://vimeo.com/28520129, alternatively accessible via http://bit.ly/noiseofcairo.

FURTHER READING

Rubin, Dan, ed. *The World Encyclopedia of Contemporary Theatre, Vol. IV: The Arab World* (London and New York: Routledge, 1999).

Sadgrove, Philip. *The Egyptian Theatre in the Nineteenth Century 1799–1882* (Reading: Ithaca Press, 2007).

Selaiha, Nehad. *The Egyptian Theatre: New Directions* (Cairo: General Egyptian Book Organization, 2003).

Selaiha, Nehad. *The Egyptian Theatre: Perspectives* (Cairo: General Egyptian Book Organization, 2004).

Selaiha, Nehad. *The Egyptian Theatre: Plays and Playwrights* (Cairo: General Egyptian Book Organization, 2003).

Zaki, Ahmed. 'Egypt', in Martin Banham, ed., *A History of Theatre in Africa* (Cambridge: Cambridge University Press, 2004), pp. 13–36.

9

DIEGO PELLECCHIA

Traditional theatre: the case of Japanese Noh

This chapter addresses the question of how we position 'traditional' theatre within a historical narrative that is likely to be constructed in linear terms and to be framed around the nation-state. Japanese Noh theatre offers a particularly interesting case study because it is self-evidently 'theatre' in terms of all normal Western definitions – Noh plays being based upon crafted literary scripts and offering the audience stories about distinctive characters – yet it sits outside the evolutionary narrative explored in Part II of this *Cambridge Companion*, which runs from twentieth-century modernist theatre back to the ancient Greeks.

In 1868, at the dawn of the Meiji restoration that overturned the military regime of the Tokugawa shogunate and restored the central position of the Emperor, Japan opened its borders to the outside world after more than two centuries of almost complete closure. It is during this period that notions of Noh theatre started to circulate in Europe and North America through the accounts of the few who visited Japan, mostly diplomats and literati. Noh performance was initially ridiculed because of its performative means, such as the use of masks and the melange of mime and dance, regarded as primitive by spectators used to the late nineteenth-century naturalistic stage. Noh was an antiquity seen through the lens of the archaeologist (see Fig. 14).

This initial reception was subverted by artists. Modernists such as W. B. Yeats and Jacques Copeau drew inspiration from Noh in order to reform what they considered the decadence of the bourgeois stage. They understood Noh as a model for 'total' theatre, bringing together masked drama, dance and music, genres that in the West reached the peak of their separation with late nineteenth-century naturalism. Yet for the majority of such artists, Noh was simply a vision built on the basis of a few descriptions and translations.

With the establishment of new diplomatic relations that followed the Second World War, exchanges between Japan and Western countries increased considerably, and more Western scholars and practitioners could experience Noh first-hand. Noh performance was deconstructed and analysed thanks to in-depth knowledge of the subject matter and new critical tools such as

14 Actor Udaka Michishige (Kongō School) as *shite* (main actor) for the Noh *Kurozuka* ('The Black Mound'). The old woman spins the thread of a cyclical time, signifying the impossibility of freeing herself from the feelings of solitude and wretchedness that keep her attached to this world.

anthropology. While European-style modernism had been characterised by an effort to bridge the gaps between genres and to return to 'total' forms of theatre, post-1945 experiments with crossing the boundaries of film, drama, fine arts and music drove a number of practitioners to look at Japan once more, in search of what was felt as the unbroken tradition of Noh. In addition, national organisations and international bodies like UNESCO sought to categorise and protect traditions such as Noh, 'threatened with disappearance due to insufficient means of safeguarding or to processes of rapid change'.[1]

All through the history of its reception in the West, Noh has been isolated as a discrete tradition, frozen in time. The process of defining cultural identity has involved two main players: on the one hand, a vaguely defined 'West', finding itself lost in the disintegration of its own tradition within the crisis of modernity; on the other hand, a sharply defined 'Japan', repository of pre-served and identifiable tradition. This 'West–Japan' dichotomy is a *topos* of the Orientalist discourse that has been fuelled both by Western (European and North American) scholarship and by the Japanese *nihonjinron* (lit. 'dis-course of Japaneseness'), which has sought to produce images of Japan as a unique and homogeneous country.

Within Japan, this process of categorisation of tradition has separated what in origin 'is Japanese' from what 'is not Japanese'. Within the field of perfor-mance, this has involved a rather clear-cut distinction between traditional performing arts (*dentōgeinō*) and other forms of theatre that have flourished in Japan since it began to import Western theatre, forms that are generally referred to by the word *engeki* ('drama'). Japanese traditional theatre consists of a number of genres, usually envisaged under the headings of Nōgaku, symbolic and refined, Kabuki, bombastic and popular, and Bunraku, the melodramatic puppet theatre.[2] Although historians often describe these three genres as 'still performed today', the emphasis is generally placed on their allegedly 'unbroken' tradition, that is, on their capacity to preserve the legacy of the past, rather than representing contemporaneity.[3]

Today, Noh, Kabuki and Bunraku have particular repertoires, performed in front of audiences that are by and large composed of aficionados well acquainted with their canon. Performers of the different genres belong to distinct groups, with no mobility among them, and no or little possibility of intermingling with other genres. In the case of Noh theatre, even the different role types (*shite* or main actor, *waki* or supporting actor, *kyōgen* or comic interlude player and musicians) belong to different stylistic schools and train separately, meeting only once before the performance. Their art is transmitted orally within kinship groups headed by a single master and measured accord-ing to degrees of difficulty and secrecy. Performers of these arts are expected to dedicate their lives to training and performing and to protect that tradition (*dentō wo mamoru*), to the extent that traditional practices are often dubbed as 'arts of the *way*' (*geidō*), where 'way' (*dō*, or *michi*) indicates a vision of artistic development as a path through life towards both aesthetic and 'spiri-tual' cultivation. As a consequence, deviation from the canon is forbidden, and in particularly strict environments, such as that of Noh theatre, results in the performer being ostracised from the community of practitioners.

The separation between genres and practitioners, however, has not always been this sharp. Noh developed by combining several pre-existent genres, and at the time of Zeami Motokiyo (1363–1443), the 'father of Noh' taken to personify the Noh tradition, there was no clear distinction between *shite* and *waki*, since performers of the same troupe would take various roles. Eighteenth-century Kabuki borrowed heavily from Noh, while Bunraku and Kabuki, which developed within the same cultural and commercial environment, continuously borrowed plays and expressive techniques from each other.

The regulation of 'ways' according to a rigid canon has its historical roots in the culture of the Tokugawa period (1603–1868) when, upon achieving peace after decades of civil wars that tore the country apart, the military regime sought to re-establish control by imposing strict regulations on every aspect of civil life, reducing social mobility and restricting travel across regions. All the arts – Noh, tea ceremony, calligraphy, etc. – crystallised into a mosaic of discrete traditions. When Noh theatre was designated as official entertainment of the court, Shōgun Tokugawa Iemitsu (1604–51) established a detailed code of performance and forbade deviation. The introduction of *katazuke* books and of printing technology provided new tools for the actors to fix tradition upon tangible objects and to claim the unique right to access it.[4] During this period the figure of the *iemoto*, the leader of each stylistic school, emerged as the only individual with the right to award licenses, authorise performances and publish texts. Embodying tradition, the figure of the *iemoto* has been both praised for the preservation and blamed for the fossilisation of the Noh tradition.

A second round of institutional rigidification came after the Meiji restoration, when Japan confronted the West for the first time and Noh was chosen as official entertainment for foreign guests, a counterpart to Western opera. At the same time European theatre started to be imported into Japan and precipitated a debate about the preservation or reform of the Japanese performing arts. Even today, the distinction between the 'traditional/indigenous' and the 'modern/foreign-influenced' in the arts is still very strong. Despite the many instances of 'modernisation' of traditional theatre, as in the case of Mishima Yukio's 'modern Noh plays', *dentōgeinō* remain confined within exclusive borders.

This fragmentation of cultural productions is reflected in the way academia treats *dentōgeinō* as opposed to *engeki*. The 2011 annual conference of the International Federation for Theatre Research (IFTR), entitled 'Tradition, Innovation and Community', was held in Osaka, Japan. It is interesting to notice how, despite location and theme, only four of the hundreds of papers presented discussed Japanese traditional theatre, and moreover none of their presenters was Japanese. This is because Japanese traditional performance does not lie within the remit of theatre departments, but of Japanese studies departments that focus on the study of history and literature rather than performance. This is ironic, given that, originally, Western theatre practitioners became interested in Noh because of its strong emphasis on body and movement at the expense of written text. It is as if Shakespeare and Aeschylus were the exclusive domain of English and Classics departments. The scenario was entirely different at the European Association for Japanese Studies (EAJS) conference in Tallinn, Estonia, held only a few days after the IFTR, where fifteen papers on Noh were presented.

This academic divide is not peculiar to Japan, but applies to most European/North American institutions: with the exception of programmes such as that of University of Hawai'i, Noh and other forms of traditional Japanese theatre are little taught and practised in theatre departments. Noh is typically associated with 'World Theatre' courses, touching on different Asian traditions (usually those of Japan, China, India and Indonesia), and echoing the typical positioning of Noh in theatre history books, often subsumed under a geographically as well as chronologically cluttered 'Oriental Theatre' category. Though recent theatre scholarship has occasionally challenged this categorisation, as in the Routledge *Theatre Histories*, which discusses *dentōgeinō* as case studies in different sections of the volume, most historical overviews relegate tradition to the pre-modern era.[5]

While 'comparative studies' have become unfashionable in the West because they tend to confine cultures within the boundaries of the nation-state in a manner that interculturalism contests, such studies are still common in Japan, as for example in Nakazato Toshiaki's excellent *Comparative Study on Culture in Drama* (2001), where the perspective of the author is expressed in terms of 'we, the Japanese'.[6] Books such as Miyao Jiryō's *Origins of Asian Theatre* (1998), one of the few in its genre, do not include Japan in the spectrum of the cultures discussed, strengthening the idea of Japan as unique and isolated from the rest of the world, including Asia.[7]

In a seminal inquiry into the concept of 'tradition', Edward Shils points out how, since the Enlightenment, the Western world has associated *tradition* with right-wing conservatism, in antithesis to liberal ideas of *progress*.[8] As Shils provocatively asserts, in the West 'it even appears untoward to say that some things should be left as they are or have been in the recent past. Once a situation is brought to attention, the presumption is that it ought to be changed.'[9] This condition is entirely different in Japan, where artistic objects incorporate elements belonging to different historical phases, which have been borrowed, mixed and remodelled into new shapes. This process is at odds with a Western tendency to 'discard the old for the new'.

According to historian Shmuel Eisenstadt, Japan underwent a process of 'alternative modernisation', characterised by a tendency to subsume change into the substratum of tradition and to legitimise elements of innovation as traditional.[10] Many of what are now considered as unique features of Noh, such as *kamae* (standing posture) and *suriashi* (sliding step), were not practices with which Zeami was familiar. The distinction between *tsuyogin* (dynamic chant) and *yowagin* (melodic chant), a principal characteristic of Noh vocal production, came into being only at the beginning of the seventeenth century (the Edo period), as Noh historian Yokomichi Mario points out, though the tendency of Edo actors was always to associate modifications of tradition with features that already existed during the Muromachi period, the time of Zeami.[11]

Despite the myth of its 'immaculate transmission', Noh theatre has undergone numerous changes that deeply affected its aesthetic form. Today, a Noh theatre is a modern hall containing the wooden structure that replicates the ancient outdoor stages, surmounted by a roof and circumscribed by a strip of white pebbles, around which are lined rows of modern chairs. The ancient masks and costumes treasured by Noh families are still used in performance because of their beauty and 'energy', but they are illuminated by electric lights.

Anthony Giddens has related tradition to Maurice Halbwachs's notion of 'collective memory', thus placing tradition as a fundamentally 'social' phenomenon.[12] In locations like Japan, where a culturally engrained collective identity projects a strong, albeit constructed, image of ethnic uniformity, tradition tends to be perceived as inherently value-laden because it symbolises the cultural heritage of the ancestors. It follows that, if tradition *qua* heritage is a tool for cultural identification, attempts by an individual to effect change will potentially jeopardise the cohesion of the cultural texture.

In her recent essay 'What Features Distinguish Nō from Other Performing Arts?', Noh scholar Yamanaka Reiko exemplifies the conservative attitude characteristic of the Noh establishment, describing how, in order 'to be called *nō*, a performance should consist of the traditional, well-known, existing units'.[13] Towards the end of her essay, Yamanaka raises questions about the association of the actor with a specific genre. It appears that the relationship between actor and genre is what most clearly distinguishes a Western conception of art, celebrating the genius and creativity of the individual artist, from the Japanese concept of the 'way' as a 'path through life' which appreciates the capacity of individuals to immerse themselves in the flow of tradition. Noh performers rarely talk about professional achievement as if it were the product of their own individual genius: rather, they relate individual endeavour to the legacy of an artistic school, or *ryū*, which in Japanese means 'flow', suggesting a continuous transmission of knowledge streaming along the same course. Similarly, newspapers reporting Noh theatre performances often omit the name of the actors, and give only the name of the *ryū*.

The case of Kabuki is different: not subdivided into *ryū*, but into families within which performance styles and a specific repertoire are transmitted. Kabuki actors are venerated as superstars: many of them appear in TV dramas, and their faces are visible on promotional posters. Yet, even in this case, the importance of family heritage is visible in the customary adoption of family names and generation numbers like Ichikawa Ebizō XI. A characteristic feature of Kabuki is the presence of 'professional shouters', who call out the names of the actors at critical moments of the performance. However, what is shouted is not their real name, but the *yago*, or 'house name', shared with other members of the same family.

Before entering the stage at the beginning of a Noh performance, the *shite* respectfully salutes the mask before donning it. Similarly, after appearing in front of the public via a revolving platform, the *tayu* or storyteller of Bunraku uses both hands to raise the script from which he will 'read' up to his forehead, as a sign of respect.[14] By saluting the totem of tradition, a performer establishes a relationship with a communal past. The Japanese verb used to translate the idea of 'acting in' or 'performing in' a play is *tsutomeru*, a word whose connotations include 'working', 'endeavouring', and also 'serving'.

I recently purchased a handbook of traditional performing arts at a Japanese convenience store.[15] It dedicates one third of its section on Kabuki to the description of stage families, including detailed genealogical tables, knowledge of which is supposed to make Kabuki 'even more interesting'. Manuals of this kind, available for most traditional arts, are meant to instruct the novice spectator on the correct 'way to watch' theatre. This represents a second 'way' typical of Japanese culture: the *kata*. Literally, *kata* means 'model', 'pattern' or 'form' and refers to any established 'way of' doing literally anything. *Kata* regulate all aspects of high and low culture, from the sophisticated movements of the tea ceremony to everyday actions like opening a packet of crackers. In the fragmentation that characterises Japanese traditional performance, different ways of executing *kata* identify different practice groups. For example, choreographed units in Noh are often referred to as *kata* – the most common of which consists in four steps forward while pointing with the fan held in the right hand, lifting the left hand to the same level as the right one, followed by three steps backwards while opening the arms and returning to the initial position. The five *ryū* of Noh have different ways of naming and performing this and other *kata* that build up the basic choreography of each play. The specificities of each school make each style so unique that it would be difficult for members belonging to different *ryū* to perform together.

Canonised according to rules that are often non-written and thus paradoxically prone to modification, the concept of *kata* as 'form', as opposed to 'content', stirred the interest of semiotician Roland Barthes (1915–80), who in his *Empire of Signs* (1970) described Japan as a place populated by 'empty signs'. Barthes saw Japanese culture as a set of perimeters deprived of a centre and associated this condition with the absence of the absolute god who governs the Judaeo-Christian cultural area. From this perspective, Japan can be said to lay emphasis on 'form', while Western culture privileges 'content'. Japanese tradition appears to be composed of ever-changing, 'empty' modules that preclude exact and unchanged definitions of their nature.[16]

Despite a manifest history of transformation, 'Japanese tradition' has often been fixed in a universalised, atemporal dimension and appropriated by political ideologies to serve a variety of agendas. In 1868, under pressure from Western powers, Japan opened its borders to the external world, thus putting an end to the period of closure that began with Shogun Tokugawa Iemitsu's Sakoku Edict (1635). For the first time in more than two centuries, confronted with the 'other', Japan was forced to reflect on its own tradition and delineate a national identity that could compete with those of the Western powers.

After an initial period of massive importation of all aspects of Western culture, during which Noh ran the risk of disappearing because it was identified with the deposed feudal regime, Japan embarked on a process of merging Western and Japanese thought, seeking to 'purify' foreign knowledge and transform it into something uniquely Japanese. In his best-selling book *Bushido: The Soul of Japan* (1899/1900), diplomat Inazo Nitobe reminded his compatriots 'that the change in those islands was entirely self-generated, that Europeans did not teach Japan, but that Japan of herself chose to learn from Europe methods of organization, civil and military, which have so far proved successful'.[17] In response to the strong image of the Western nation-state, Japan manufactured a self-image of strength and cohesion that originated in the 'native' genius.

Critics of *nihonjinron* discourses stress that such views of Japan are ideological constructs: underneath the appearance of solidity and uniformity is a continuous struggle between deviation and regularisation. This struggle has also characterised the performing arts. Recent studies have begun to debunk myths of Noh theatre's 'immaculate transmission' and have highlighted how political enterprises belonging to different historical periods have moulded Noh into forms that would suit specific cultural agendas.[18] Nationalist ideology often swept instances of deviation under the carpet of institutional orthodoxy. Many of the features of Noh, such as techniques of chant and dance, appearing to be part of an unbroken tradition and often marketed under the uniform 'Noh brand',[19] are in fact products of different historical periods.

During the modern period, Japanese tradition has been identified through being differentiated from its opposing 'other'. Noh was chosen as representative of the Japanese tradition and hence isolated as 'elite theatre', while Kabuki and other forms of 'popular' theatre became the subject of an extended debate about renewal. While Noh was expected to be frozen in time, attempts were made to infuse notions of European naturalism into Kabuki, giving birth to Shinpa ('new wave'), a hybrid between Kabuki and Western melodrama.

A drastic break with tradition was attempted by Shingeki ('new drama'), which adopted the texts and performance means of Western realism. One of the major representatives of the theatre reform straddling the nineteenth and twentieth centuries, playwright and critic Tsubouchi Shōyō, was aware of how influential the foreign gaze was in constituting Japanese identity in the arts and lamented that Orientalist perspectives on Japan encouraged the country to preserve its traditions, while Europe was free to advance.[20] Shingeki consti-tuted the Japanese theatrical avant-garde until the end of the Second World War, when its expressive means became a new orthodoxy, incapable of satisfy-ing the needs of a new generation. In a process of cross-influence characteristic of the post-modern period, new groups, such as Tadashi Suzuki's SCOT, returned to the ideal of an ethnically based and communal life training, an ideal shared by Western practitioners such as Jerzy Grotowski and Eugenio Barba, who claimed to be inspired by Asian practices.

In his presentation at the 10th International Symposium on the Conservation and Restoration of Cultural Property, held in Tokyo in 1991, James Brandon pointed out how Noh theatre has existed in isolation for centuries.[21] While originally constituted by elements imported from the performance traditions of China and Korea, Noh never made the return journey, unlike other Asian performing arts that have travelled from country to country. Only in recent times has the interest of foreign observers triggered a kind of self-recognition in the Noh establishment, and today there are many activities that seek to open up the knowledge of Noh to broader and more international audiences. From the progressive Western perspective, such knowledge is equated with a moral good: the more Noh is known, the better for humankind. However, this condition is in stark contrast to Zeami's precept of secrecy (*hisureba hana*), by which the 'flower' of performance blooms with the unexpected, the won-drous, the mysterious, the humanly ungraspable. This, I believe, is still one of Noh theatre's principal elements of charm for both its local and international audiences. Zeami's precept is not a celebration of ignorance, but an invitation to accept 'the unknown' as an existential condition, essential in any act of cognition and of artistic reception.

In a 2008 interview on the popular website the-noh.com, Haruo Nishino pointed out how today's excess of explanatory activities, such as opening dressing rooms to audiences and providing technical accounts of the perfor-mance process, endanger the 'unexpressed, hidden elements [that] make the

15 A scene from *Genshigumo* ('The Atomic Cloud'), written and performed by Udaka Michishige. Set in post-atomic Hiroshima, this *shinsaku-Noh* (new Noh play written according to canonical Noh dramaturgy) recounts the story of a mother in search of the spirit of her missing daughter, who died during the bombing. Tradition is re-invented in a conservative way and used to recount modernity.

expression of Noh vivid'.[22] Does this position simply signal that the sectarian nature of the Noh establishment has not changed, or does it actually focus on the preservation of the principle of 'indeterminacy' that Eisenstadt has identified as foundational of Japanese culture, and that allows tradition to morph even while conserving it, rather than erasing it in order to re-write?

As long as Noh is considered in terms of binary oppositions, a debate that places on the one hand conservation and sectarianism, and on the other innovation and dissemination, is unlikely to yield definitive solutions. The question I want to pose is: should we not now put an end to the debate? The energy that arises from friction between instances of secrecy and popularisation of Noh should prod us to re-evaluate tradition and progress in the performing arts. This reflection takes on a different cast and greater urgency when viewed from the perspective of practice. As Gilli Bush-Bailey demonstrates in her contribution to this volume, practice is an essential means of exploring history. In order to rescue Noh from institutional and academic isolation, one powerful answer is to *practise* Noh. In a world of theatre studies dominated by Anglo-Saxon academia, the presence of English-speaking, Noh-trained scholars is now a priority: Noh needs to be studied as a living organism, not a historical fossil.

This is not an easy solution. Noh is not something that only happened in the past: the tradition that has been transmitted is a continuous flux. If Noh is approached from outside its long-standing context and without awareness of its contemporaneity, the risk is to 're-enact Noh' through the commodification of its aesthetic elements. In this respect, secrecy and compartmentalisation prevent an all-too-quick and superficial appropriation of the aesthetics of Noh, which would otherwise lead to exoticised imitations. To do Noh is not 'to act doing Noh': to do Noh means first of all to follow its discipline and to reconsider the role of one's individuality in relation to the community of practitioners who comprise the past, present and future of tradition.

NOTES

1 UNESCO, 'Proclamation of Masterpieces of the Oral and Intangible Heritage of Humanity' (2006), p. 4. See www.unesco.org/culture/ich/index.php?pg=00103.
2 Nōgaku comprises Nō (here romanised as 'Noh') dance-drama and the Kyōgen farce, which is performed both as intermission between or within Noh performance and as an independent play.
3 A document issued by the Nippon Foundation divides traditional theatre into three main families, in turn subdivided into smaller genres, and provides a number of specific criteria that support this categorisation. Nippon Geinō Jitsuenka Dantai Kyōgikai, 'Dentōgeinō no genjō chōsa' (2008). See www.geidankyo.or.jp/o2shi/dentou.pdf.
4 E. Rath, *The Ethos of Noh: Actors and Their Art* (Cambridge, MA: Harvard University Press, 2004), pp. 190–214. *Katazuke* are books where choreography is

recorded along the lines of the lyrics of a Noh play. These notations are particularly vague and open to interpretation.

5 B. McConachie, G. J. Williams, C. F. Sorgenfrei and P. Zarrilli, *Theatre Histories: An Introduction* (London: Routledge, 2006).

6 T. Nakazato, *Engeki no hikaku bunkaron* (Yokohama: Oseania Shuppansha, 2001), p. 13.

7 J. Miyao, *Ajia engeki no genfūkei* (Tokyo: Sanichi Shobō, 1998).

8 E. Shils, *Tradition* (Chicago: University of Chicago Press, 1981), pp. 1–7.

9 *Ibid.*, p. 1.

10 S. N. Eisenstadt, *Japanese Civilization* (Chicago: University of Chicago Press, 1998), p. 313. This concept is akin to Eric Hobsbawm's notion of 'invented tradition'; see E. Hobsbawm, 'Introduction: Inventing Traditions', in E. Hobsbawm and T. Ranger (eds.), *The Invention of Tradition* (Cambridge University Press, 1983), pp. 1–14.

11 M. Yokomichi, 'Nihon geinō no denshō to saisei: nō wo chūshin to shite', in *International Symposium on the Conservation and Restoration of Cultural Property: Nô, its Transmission and Regeneration* (Tokyo National Research Institute of Cultural Properties, 1991), pp. 27–38, p. 32.

12 A. Giddens, 'Living in a Post-Traditional Society', in *Reflexive Modernization: Politics, Tradition and Aesthetics in the Modern Social Order* (Cambridge: Polity Press, 1994), p. 63.

13 R. Yamanaka, 'What Features Distinguish Nō from Other Performing Arts?' in S. Scholz-Cionca and C. Balme (eds.), *Nō Theatre Transversal* (Munich: Iudicium, 2008), pp. 78–85, p. 84.

14 The whole text is actually memorised beforehand.

15 H. Takahashi, *Nippon no Dentōgeinō*. Discover Japan (Tokyo: Ei, 2010).

16 Eisenstadt, *Japanese Civilization*, p. 313.

17 I. Nitobe, *Bushido: The Soul of Japan*, English translation (Tokyo: Teibi, 1904), pp. 159–60.

18 See, among others, Rath, *The Ethos of Noh*, N. Pinnington, 'Invented Origins: Muromachi Interpretations of "Okina Sarugaku"', *Bulletin of the School of Oriental and African Studies, University of London*, 61:3 (1998), 492–518, and G. Groemer, 'Elite Culture for Common Audiences: Machiiri Nō and Kanjin Nō in the City of Edo', *Asian Theatre Journal*, 15:2 (1998), 230–52.

19 'Establishing the Noh Brand', www.the-noh.com/en/zeami/brand.html.

20 S. Tsubouchi, 'The Drama in Japan', *The Mask: A Journal of the Art of the Theatre*, 4 (1911), 309–20, 309.

21 J. Brandon, 'The Place of Nō in World Theatre', in *International Symposium on the Conservation and Restoration of Cultural Property: Nô, its Transmission and Regeneration* (Tokyo National Research Institute of Cultural Properties, 1991), pp. 1–22, p. 4.

22 H. Nishino, 'Maintain the Courage to Leap', 2008, www.the-noh.com/en/people/sasaeru/002_haruonishino.html.

FURTHER READING

Komparu, K. *Noh Theater: Principles and Perspectives* (New York: Weatherill-Tankosha, 1983).

Leiter, S., ed. *A Kabuki Reader: History and Performance*. Japan in the Modern World (Armonk: M. E. Sharpe, 2002).

Ortolani, B. *The Japanese Theatre: From Shamanistic Ritual to Contemporary Pluralism* (Leiden and New York: Brill, 1990).

Powell, B. *Japan's Modern Theatre: A Century of Change and Continuity* (London: Japan Library, 2002).

Scholz-Cionca, S., and S. Leiter, eds. *Japanese Theatre and the International Stage* (Leiden and Boston: Brill, 2001).

10

MARVIN CARLSON

Reflections on a global theatre history

When theatre history was established as a field of study in the late nineteenth century, its focus, like that of political or social history, was upon the changes and developments in the object of study over time. A spatial understanding of this art was recognised as crucial by theatre historians from the beginning. Indeed one might argue that the essential feature that distinguished theatre history from the field of literary history out of which it generally developed was an interest in theatre as a spatial rather than as a textual phenomenon. Soon, however, this spatial interest expanded from a specific interest in the dynamics of the enacted literary text to a concern with theatre as a cultural event, embedded within a particular cultural space. The overall organisation of theatre history, from its creation as a discipline, has been geographical in nature, primarily concerned with tracing the development of theatre within a small and highly select number of modern, almost entirely Western European nation-states.

When Max Herrmann in Germany and scholars with similar concerns began developing the historical analysis of theatre,[1] the European nation-state was the major form of socio/cultural organisation with which they were familiar, dominant in Europe and widely and usually arbitrarily imposed throughout the rest of the globe by the European colonial powers. The major divisions within theatre history were the boundaries of these states. For most of its first century of development theatre history was not only essentially organised by nation-states but was extremely selective in its choice of which such states were considered worthy of study. Very soon an almost invariable and highly restricted narrative of so-called world theatre was developed, which may still be found in the majority of textbooks on this field of study. According to this narrative, after the obligatory introductory chapters on ritual drama in ancient Egypt and the theatres of classical Greece and Rome (in fact treated as modern unified nation-states – who noted where in the world Hellenistic theatres were actually located or observed that such 'Roman' church fathers as Augustine and Tertullian actually came from North Africa?), standard theatre went on to cover an only vaguely geographically designated 'middle ages' (in fact in its details largely English), and then settled more comfortably into individual narratives of the theatres within modern national boundaries, headed by England, France, Italy, Germany, Spain and the United States. In short, the field was based on an almost totally unacknowledged focus upon a very small part of the globe and a very few countries, essentially the major colonial powers. The close connection between the shape of modern theatre studies and the division of the globe by the major colonial powers is clearly indicated by the comparative attention paid to various centres of theatre activity. The history of theatre in London and Paris, the great international capitals of the colonial era, totally dominates theatre studies, within their own countries and abroad, and it was of course from these centres that the theatrical practices most studied and honoured were primarily disseminated (a situation that still exists in significant measure). The first major international history of theatre in English was Allardyce Nicoll's *The Development of the Theatre* (1927), which bore the ambitious subtitle 'A Study of Theatrical Art from the Beginnings to the Present Day'.[2] In fact, however, aside from classic Greece and Rome, Nicoll confined his study almost entirely to the four nations already mentioned, plus a few paragraphs on recent Russian theatre and passing references to major modern continental dramatists like Ibsen and Strindberg. Within the handful of European countries considered in some detail, the spatial range of interest was still quite restricted, almost entirely focused on theatre in a few central cities – London, Paris, Rome, Moscow. This orientation proved remarkably durable. A revised edition of Nicoll's book in 1966, when it was still considered a basic text in the field, had added only Spain (restricted to the golden age) and the United States, which from mid-century onward was generally accepted into the hitherto exclusively European private theatre club.

This orientation was in fact already well established in continental Europe before Nicoll's book appeared. Alphonse Royer's monumental *Histoire universelle du théâtre* (1869–78),[3] despite its pompous title, devoted almost the entirety of its six volumes to the major nations of Western Europe. Its claim to 'universality' was based on the fact that, aside from Western Europe, twenty pages of the first volume were devoted to classic drama in India and China and twelve pages in the final volume were devoted to the 'Orient', this 'Orient' being made up of Armenia, Romania and modern Greece! Although Royer was not translated into English, the next European multi-volume theatre history, *Skuespilkunstens Historie* (1897–1907) by the Danish actor and scholar Karl Mantzius, was translated almost as soon as it appeared[4] and did much to set the pattern of subsequent work in England and elsewhere. The first of its six volumes covered ancient India, Japan, China, Greece and Rome (the latter two of course dominating), and subsequent volumes, going up to the romantic period, were devoted almost entirely to France, England and Germany.

This spatial grounding of theatre studies may be clearly seen from the outset in the leading international organisation for such studies, The International Federation for Theatre Research, which was formally established in 1957. Its constitution called for the promotion 'in all countries' of 'international liaison between organizations and individuals devoted to theatre research'.[5] Such statements, and even the name of the organisation, expressed much more a hope than an actuality. Although theatre research as a field of study was at that time more than half a century old, it still was almost exclusively concentrated in Western Europe and the United States, both in the material studied and in the scholars involved in such study. The first conference of the organisation was held in Venice and was attended by representatives from seventeen countries.

Fifteen of these were from Europe, and eleven of those from Western Europe. The United States was the only country represented from North or South America and the entire rest of the world was represented by only one country, Japan. The original lack of global representation in an organisation devoted to theatre research 'in all countries' very much reflected the view of theatre history then prevalent. The most comprehensive history of the theatre at that time, first published in 1941 by George Freedley and John Reeves,[6] devoted fewer than 50 of its 772 pages to the world outside the US and Europe. There was not a single mention of any theatre in all of Africa or the Arab world. All of South America received only 8 pages and all of Asia only 30, almost entirely devoted to classic forms like the Sanskrit drama, Noh, and Kabuki. Typically, the brief section on China was entitled 'Incomprehensible China'. A decade later Nicoll published an even more monumental study, weighing in at a solid 1,000 pages, with the totalising title *World Drama*. Surely one might expect a volume of this size and with this title to encompass a much more ambitious geographical range than previous studies, but in fact this was not so. After the obligatory chapters on Greek and Roman theatre, Nicoll went on to the European middle ages and renaissance, with almost exclusive attention to England, France and Germany. The United States received substantial attention, but there was nothing else on any theatre in the Americas and the remainder of the non-European world was covered in a ghettoised 20-page section, 'The Drama of the Orient', subdivided into 'The Sanskrit Drama', 'The Drama of China', and 'The Japanese Drama'.[7] Surely the most ambitious theatre history project internationally at mid-century was the ten-volume

Theatergeschichte Europas by Heinz Kindermann (1957–74),[8] which, of course, did not consider any theatre outside that continent.

When Oscar Brockett's *History of the Theatre* first appeared in 1968, almost twenty years later, the landscape of theatre history had undergone almost no change.[9] Brockett devoted one chapter out of nineteen to what he called the Orient, primarily Japan, and offered nothing at all on Latin America, Africa, Australia, South-east Asia and the entire Arab world. Another candidate for a general theatre history that went so far as to call itself *World Theatre* was published this same year by amateur historian Bamber Gascoigne,[10] yet despite its title it reflected an almost identical geographical bias. Out of 335 pages, only 20 were devoted to material outside Europe and the United States. In this section, called 'The East', two pages were given to India, three to China and fifteen to Japan.

The subject matter of the chapters brought together in this book suggests how significantly this situation has changed in the new century. It is likely that only one of the other four essays in Part III, dealing with space, namely the chapter on Japanese tradition, embraces an area that would have been judged worthy of mention in any standard world history of a generation ago. Egypt is a particularly interesting case since, ironically, its ancient rituals were almost invariably considered in the opening chapter of traditional theatre histories, but then Egypt was never again mentioned, as though no theatre of any sort had existed there for the next 3,000 years.

Of the various twentieth-century so-called world histories of the theatre, only Brockett still remains widely read. Having established itself from the outset as the model for such a study, it maintained that dominance by appearing in new, steadily updated editions every three years or so. This updating allowed it to present a generally accurate ongoing summary of current attitudes toward theatre history. Geographically, what this approach meant during the late twentieth century was a gradually growing acknowledgement of theatrical traditions outside the traditional areas of Europe and the United States. As the European colonial era drew to a close, scholarly interest in non-European locations grew, regarding them not as colonial extensions of European influence and exploitation but as separate entities worthy of study in their own right and on their own terms.

This growing interest did not yet mean that significant numbers of non-European and non-American theatre scholars emerged to study the histories of their respective regions and cultures, but it did mean that more and more theatre research began to be undertaken by European and American scholars on non-European theatre. The profession of theatre history began to count among its numbers scholars specialising in Asian, African and Latin American theatre, and articles reporting this research began to appear not only in the already established leading scholarly journals in the field, such as *Theatre Journal* and *Theatre Survey*, but also in new journals established especially to focus on these new areas of investigation, such as *Latin American Theatre Review*, founded in 1967, and *Asian Theatre Review*, founded in 1984, and the *South African Theatre Journal*, founded in 1987. During the 1970s new editions of Brockett began to include more Asian material and then material from Latin America and Africa. By the middle of the 1980s theatre studies, with much more justification than thirty years before, regarded itself as a global discipline. Certainly great strides had been made in that direction, but very significant areas, such as the entire Arab world, from Morocco to Indonesia, still remained outside the spatial awareness of the discipline as the new century opened.

Very closely connected to the spatial expansion of theatre history was another significant change in theatre studies taking place at the same time: the rise of interest in what came to be called performance studies. Traditionally theatre studies had focused almost exclusively not only upon European–US theatre, but upon a particular part of that theatre, represented by the tradition of literary drama beginning with the Greeks and extending through such figures as Schiller, Shakespeare and Molière to Ibsen, Chekhov and their descendants. Other forms of theatre and of mimetic performance, such as much non-literary popular and folk entertainment, not to speak of storytelling, theatricalised dance, and puppetry, were generally considered outside the boundaries of traditional theatre history. Opening theatre studies to these other performance genres meant that theatre historians no longer needed to confine themselves to studying theatre in the traditional Western model, and since in most of the world this model was imposed on indigenous performance traditions by colonialism, this expansion allowed and indeed encouraged a much richer and more comprehensive historical study of the new areas of investigation outside the European and North American continents. This reorientation centrally involved space in two ways: both geographically, in the opening to theatre studies of parts of the globe hitherto ignored by theatre historians, and phenomenologically, in moving from a text-based discipline to one concerned with the spatial conditions of the performative act.

The most significant attempt to date to reflect these new concerns and to attempt a break with the orientation, geographically, thematically and discursively, of traditional theatre history was the 2006 volume *Theatre Histories*, whose dedication to pluralism was reflected not only in its title, but in the fact that in acknowledgement of the growing complexity and diversity of the field, it was created by four authors.[11] Its preface claims it as a 'fresh approach' to the subject, offering a 'global perspective'. Brian Singleton, president of the

International Federation for Theatre Research, emphasised the revolutionary quality of the book, which 'finally' conceived theatre history in world terms, a book which 'breaks down the Euro-American boundaries that have marginalized the theatres of other cultures for so long'.[12]

There is no question that this new project offers a more contemporary perspective, opening with a useful section on oral cultures and concluding with an equally useful section on interculturalism and hybridity. Between these two sections, however, we are on basically long-familiar terrain, even though the volume claims to be concerned with theatre, drama and performance from many cultures 'not in the margins of western theatre but in and of themselves'.[13] A simple tabulation of material is quite revealing. The opening and closing theoretical sections make up 85 of the 520 pages of the text. The rest moves through the traditional European-based history from ritual drama in Egypt (as always, the only example of performance from the entire Arab world), through the middle ages, the renaissance, the romantic period and the avant-garde, to contemporary international theatre. Fewer than 70 pages of the 435 that chart this course in fact move outside what Singleton calls the Euro-American axis, and about 50 of these are devoted to the long accepted pillars of the Orient – Japan, India and China; the Mayan drama gets 5 pages, and all the rest of Latin America and the African continent (aside from Egyptian rituals) another 3. In fact, spatially, both in terms of content and geography, this new 'world theatre' text is not nearly so radically different from its predecessors as it claims. It is surely not without significance that although the work boasts four authors, all distinguished theatre historians, the geographical range they represent is remarkably narrow – three are US professors and one British (though originally from the USA). The second edition (2009), which one would expect to improve this traditional narrow Euro-American perspective, and which in fact claims to do so in its introduction, actually on this point offers surprisingly little change, as is clearly illustrated by the twenty-nine 'case studies', specific analyses that provide arguably the book's best opportunity to expand its coverage outside the basically traditional narrative of the main text. Although the preface to the new edition boasts 'We have added new case studies – on African, Asian, and Western subjects',[14] again, huge traditionally neglected areas like Latin America and the Arab world are not considered, but more seriously, even the very modest claim of new, significantly broadened case studies is not in fact carried out. Two case studies have been dropped, one on Beckett and one on niche marketing, and two added – neither in fact on Asia, but one on the white English-speaking South African dramatist Athol Fugard and the other on Schiller and the rise of the German national theatre, a completely traditional subject.

It is certainly not my intention to offer a kind of negative review of a book that I in fact admire a good deal and one that makes the most serious attempt so far to deal seriously with global theatre history. I do think it important, however, to point out its shortcomings, which can be largely traced to its reluctance to shift from traditional paradigms in both subject matter and presentational mode. The challenges of contemporary global theatre history call both of these into question. I have been primarily considering the geographical challenges of the subject matter and the response of modern theatre history to an increasing global awareness, which has been to keep adding new countries to these already in the history canon. As the range of required countries, cultures and language traditions has continued to expand, the project of writing a widely acceptable world or global theatre history has become more and more unwieldy, especially for the sort of single scholar who created the standard one-volume world theatre histories of the last century. Thus the four authors of *Theatre Histories* frankly and reasonably admit in the preface to their first edition that they will not 'attempt the impossible task of covering the entire history of theatre and drama in the world',[15] and I think most theatre historians would now agree with their assessment of such a project, confidently undertaken by scholars of earlier generations, as impossible today.

The problems presented by dealing with global theatre history, however, go far beyond the mere proliferation of possible countries to consider, difficult as that has become. An even greater problem is posed by the growing awareness of the many important dimensions of theatre, past and present, that cannot be studied or understood within the traditional nation-state model. To begin with one of the most straightforward examples, one must acknowledge the growing awareness of performance traditions reflecting the activities of various ethnic groups, like the Kurds of central Asia and the Berbers of North Africa, who do not fit comfortably into the traditional nation-states created during the colonial era and who as a result have been forgotten or ignored, often by the dominant ethnic groups in the states involved and certainly by theatre historians. All over the world there are ethnic groups of varying sizes contained within or shared among traditional nation-states whose performance traditions merit attention but who have been forgotten in the emphasis on national traditions. These include not only long-established cultural enclaves like the Berbers and the much better known and established theatrical traditions of Flanders, and Catalonia, and Quebec, but also the theatre and performance created in constantly evolving and shifting communities created by populations voluntarily or involuntarily moved from their original locations to establish new communities, such as immigrant enclaves and refugee camps. Until recently, theatre history, focused on the nation-state, paid very little attention to such exceptions to this system as emigrant theatre, refugee theatre, and colonial theatre, or even to such clear and important examples as British theatre in India and French theatre in North Africa. Today, inspired in part by the rise of the field of Francophone studies, especially in Africa and the Caribbean, and of post-colonial studies, which has as a central concern the mixing and negotiation of different cultures, more and more attention is being paid to theatre of the former European colonies. There is still nothing like a comparable interest in theatre and performance in immigrant or refugee communities, although obviously such communities are becoming a more and more visible and influential part of the emerging global experience. Once again, any serious attempt at tracing global theatre history today should surely have to come to terms with the activities and negations of rapidly changing communities like these.

A closely related problem is the difficulty of imposing a European nation-based model of multiple national traditions upon theatre and performance activities in those many parts of the globe, such as Africa and the Middle East, where European colonialism created largely arbitrary nation-states whose performance tradition is multiple, hybrid and almost totally incompatible with the standard European model. Take, for example, the African Maghreb: Morocco, Tunisia, Algeria, and, somewhat more marginally, Libya. These four modern nations, managed in very different ways during the colonial period (protectorate, colony and actual part of the parent country) by different colonial powers (France, Spain and Italy) have during and since the colonial period been considered primarily as separate nations in terms of theatre and performance, while all sorts of performance traditions are completely independent of these European-imposed borders. Among these are many pre-colonial ritual and tribal practices, particularly those of the indigenous Berber peoples, the performative practices connected with Islam, and the remnants of the Turkish puppet tradition left by the earlier Ottoman occupation. The picture has been much further confused by the attempts of the colonial powers, or subsequent governments, to create 'national' traditions for these new, often arbitrary states, by selectively forgetting and remembering historical material, quite frequently in the most arbitrary fashion. Evan Winet's recent *Indonesian Postcolonial Theatre* suggests the complexity of this dynamic in a complex multi-cultural and multi-linguistic 'country', created by colonialism, whose performance history mixes practices from all over South-east Asia, not to mention China, India, Europe and the Arab world.[16] Even putting aside the problem of somehow representing the vast body of different performance traditions that make up global theatre, the even more formidable problem of dealing with the constantly shifting interplay between these traditions, historically and geographically, would seem to make a global theatre history, if conceived of along traditional lines, an impossible dream.

A global theatre history project would have to find a way to approach complex melting pots of traditional material like Indonesia, and in my opinion, the best critical approach currently available for approaching the challenge of dealing with global theatre history on these terms is to embrace a paradigm shift that replaces the narrative model of the European nation-state with the more flexible and open-ended intellectual model that has recently been widely applied in cultural and social studies, the model of the rhizome, as developed by Gilles Deleuze and Félix Guattari. In their book *A Thousand Plateaus*, they oppose a 'rhizomic' mode of theory and research to traditional 'arborescent' knowledge, which is dualist and based on linear connections, in the manner of traditional theatre history.[17] The rhizome, on the other hand, moves freely across phenomena, making connections potentially in all directions, without seeking fixed structures or linear narratives. It allows for fluid multiple connections without privileging any controlling models of either representation or interpretation. Such an approach recognises that theatre both past and present is best understood not as a series of such linear narratives but as an ever-shifting web of cultural interweaving.

Even if one resisted this rhizomatic approach and simply attempted to preserve a more traditional historical approach while continually expanding the geographical coverage, the enormous challenge presented by the recognition of cultural interweaving would remain. This has always been an important, if generally ignored, part of theatre history,[18] and today it has become more evident, more significant and more complex than ever, with highly mobile performances and audiences, within shifting populations created by all manner of voluntary or forced movement of linguistic, ethnic and cultural communities. Theatre history has always been far more rhizomatic than theatre historians have admitted, but the ever-increasing inter-relatedness of the contemporary world is forcing an acknowledgement of this reality for theatre activity of both the present and the past.

Let me briefly illustrate this situation with a case study of my own, suggesting some of the implications of attempting to add a single almost universally omitted small country, Bangladesh, to the narrative of global theatre history. One discovers almost at once that this neglected region has important interconnections everywhere. Geographically located at the crossroads of India, China and South-east Asia, it has witnessed the moving among these areas of live theatre, dance and puppet drama for untold centuries. Sufi masters contributed to this mixture more than 1,000 years ago, among the eventual results being an important living tradition in Bangladesh of the Islamic passion play, the Ta'zieh, which theatre historians, if they mention it at all, associate only with Iran. Bangladesh considers Rabindranath Tagore its national dramatist, though in fact this country did not even exist in his lifetime, when India was united under British occupation. All that complex colonial and post-colonial history is thus part of the story. Tagore (not mentioned in *Theatre Histories*) takes us in many other directions. He was the first non-European to win the Nobel Prize in literature, opening the vast subject of East–West literary recognition and negotiation. He was admired and translated by William Butler Yeats and Ludwig Wittgenstein, each of whom opens major perspectives into other cultural spheres. Tagore's *The Post Office* was famously performed by children of the Warsaw Ghetto just before they were sent to Treblinka: consider the connections that opens. Moving on, the best known theatre organisation in Bangladesh today is the so-called Centre for Asian Theatre, which despite the title opened with Ibsen's *Ghosts* and has made a speciality of the works of that dramatist, including hosting a major international Ibsen conference and festival of Ibsen productions from around the world in 2006. Consider the implications of this festival for the interweaving of current theatrical activity. And on it goes.

Obviously, one might follow this same process with any much more familiar and traditional examples from standard theatre history, such as Schiller at Weimar or British pantomime (two case studies from *Theatre Histories*), and in fact very limited explorations of these possibilities have been occasionally undertaken, but the dominant context for most events of theatre history remains their position in an evolving national tradition. A rhizomatic approach allows one to deal with this phenomenon in a very different manner. Wherever one takes hold of a thread in the tapestry of theatre and performance, one is there led quickly not into a linear narrative, but into an ever-more complex inter-relationship of political and cultural activity that can be pursued justifiably and productively in an infinite variety of directions.

The obvious and most accessible tool for such an approach today is of course the internet, which at least theoretically offers exactly the sort of rhizomatic presentation of material that allows an investigator to follow whatever threads of theatre history she finds of interest, building up whatever webs of associations and interactions are most useful to her in the project she is pursuing. No one researcher will ever be able to cover global theatre through the web, but of course no one researcher was ever able to do that in traditional theatre history either. What the web offers is the potential to pursue material and to connect material in a way that non-rhizomatic sources, such as traditional histories of world theatre, could never make possible, and in a way that much more accurately and honestly offers access to the actual workings of theatre and performance both at present and in the past. In the Bangladesh example cited earlier, for example, a researcher might enter the network through any of the subjects I mentioned – Tagore, Bangladesh, Yeats, the Centre for Asian Theatre, Ibsen festivals, the Ta'zieh, and so on, each of which would open the possibility of making further connections and a richer web of associations opening a wealth of possibilities impossible to lay out or to anticipate in any normal linear discursive work.

While encouraging readers to make use of web resources, the authors of *Theatre Histories* also evidence an understandable caution, and one must admit the validity of their concerns. Indeed their second edition includes a section specifically entitled 'A caveat on using resources on the World Wide Web'.[19] They make the essential point that anyone can post data on the web, and so the user is not protected by the normal review by experts that traditional scholarly publications must undergo. Of course this caveat is essential, but it means only that the web user must exercise more extensively the same caution always involved in research. There have always been accessible many sources of information, and their reliability has varied widely. The researcher must continue to test the trustworthiness of sources and to exercise great caution when the sources are suspect. With the far greater amount of material of every sort offered by the web and the far greater ease of access to it comes a far greater need for the user to employ the same critical judgement that has always been necessary in assessing and utilizing accessed material of every kind. This is a major challenge, but the fact is that at present the web offers the closest thing to the rhizomatic organization that I am convinced is the only way to deal with the concept of global theatre history, and so one must either give up that project or accept the challenges the web presents. The brief caveat in *Theatre Histories* distinctly implies that the web, used with proper caution, can be an extremely useful supplement to the 'scholarly books and articles' within the network that includes this text itself. Adding the web as an epicycle to this paradigm merely attempts to enrich the traditional linear narrative of theatre history, while I am arguing that global theatre history requires a reversal of this priority, moving the rhizome to the centre with the continued possibility of the web leading to and being constantly expanded both by traditional scholarly linear research and by new structures of investigations inspired by and made possible by the operations of the web itself.

To date, the only aspect of globalisation that theatre historians have generally considered is the most straightforward, circumscribed, and highly publicised aspect of this phenomenon, and that is the growing importance of international theatrical productions, international directors and stars, international festivals, and a few highly publicised 'culturally mixed' productions such as those of Ariane Mnouchkine, Tadashi Suzuki and Peter Brook. Obviously this work represents only a very tiny part of what would be involved in a truly global view of theatre and its history. The current preference for the term 'global' instead of 'world' seems particularly concerned with drawing attention to a much greater consciousness in recent decades of the interconnectedness of cultures and the ever-increasing flow and mixing of material, including performance, from different parts of the world. Whether that interconnectedness will become steadily further developed in the decades ahead or whether local counter-forces will create an even more complex pattern of connection and resistance, so long as the current interest in trying to pursue a global theatre history remains, then at the most basic level, analytic strategies must be developed that will acknowledge and truly reflect the constant flow and interaction in global phenomena like theatre and performance.

NOTES

1 Michael Quinn traces this process in '*Theaterwissenschaft* in the History of Theatre Study', *Theatre Survey*, 30:2 (1991), 123–36.
2 (London: G. G. Harrap, 1927).
3 (Paris: Ollendorf, 1869–78).
4 (Copenhagen: Gyldendal, 1897–1907); *A History of Theatrical Art in Ancient and Modern Times*, trans. L. von Cossel (London: Duckworth, 1903–21).
5 Article II. The Constitution may be found at www.firt-iftr.organization/constitution.
6 (New York: Crown Publishers, 1941)
7 Allardyce Nicoll, *World Drama: From Aeschylus to Anouilh* (London: George Harrap, 1949; New York: Harcourt, Brace and Company, 1950).
8 (Salzburg: O. Müller, 1957–74).
9 (Boston: Allyn and Bacon, 1968).
10 (London: Ebury Press, 1968).
11 Phillip B. Zarrilli, Bruce McConachie, Gary Jay Williams, Carol Fisher Sorgenfrei, *Theatre Histories: An Introduction* (London: Routledge, 2006).
12 Quoted in *ibid.*, back cover.
13 *Ibid.*, xvii.
14 Zarrilli *et al.*, *Theatre Histories*, 2nd edn (2009), p. xvii.
15 Zarrilli *et al*, *Theatre Histories* (2006), p. xvii.
16 (New York: Palgrave Macmillan, 2010).
17 Gilles Deleuze and Félix Guattari, *A Thousand Plateaus: Capitalism and Schizophrenia*, trans. and foreword Brian Massumi (London: Athlone Press, 1988), original French publication 1980.
18 However, theatre histories dealing with flows and exchanges of cultural material have in recent years begun to appear, headed by Joseph Roach's seminal *Cities of the Dead* (New York: Columbia University, 1996).
19 Zarilli *et al.*, *Theatre Histories*, 2nd edn (2009), p. xxxv.

FURTHER READING

Brockett, Oscar. *History of the Theatre* (Boston: Allyn and Bacon, 1968).
Canning, Charlotte M., and Thomas Postlewait, eds. *Representing the Past: Essays in Performance Historiography* (Iowa City: University of Iowa, 2010).

Chambers, Jonathan, ed. *Re-Imagining History in the Theatre Arts Curriculum.* Special issue of *Theatre Topics*, 17.1 (March 2007).

Freedley, George, and John Reeves. *History of the Theatre* (New York: Crown, 1941).

Nicoll, Allardyce. *The Development of the Theatre* (Harcourt, Brace and World, 1927).

Postlewait, Thomas. *The Cambridge Introduction to Theatre Historiography* (Cambridge: Cambridge University Press, 2009).

Quinn, Michael. '*Theaterwissenschaft* in the History of Theatre Study', *Theatre Survey*, 30.2 (November 1991), 123–36.

Zarrilli, Phillip B., Bruce McConachie, Gary Jay Williams and Carol Fisher Sorgenfrei. *Theatre Histories: An Introduction* (London: Routledge, 2006).

PART FOUR

What?

In order to write a history of the theatre, one has to determine what 'theatre' is. As became increasingly clear in the last section, this is a political question. We had originally hoped that Part III would include a chapter on South African theatre. In his proposal for that chapter, Temple Hauptfleisch planned to address

> the pervasive Western tendency to maintain an artificial distinction between art and life, between fine art, applied arts and social forms and practices – in brief between 'art' and 'non-art' – and the accompanying Western need to talk about, define, categorise and evaluate art forms in terms of such dichotomies. Largely the creation of a book-culture, not a performance culture, this kind of thinking led to the idea that any performance could only be 'legitimised' when it could be recorded and 'placed' somehow in terms of a Western concept of theatre, or at least a recognisable concept of performance... So the obvious strategy in the past has been to leave anything that does not fall into the clear-cut categories out of the reckoning. Hence festivals, street theatre, ritual dances, communal performances of all kinds were ignored and never recorded with tools or in ways that would make them meaningful to the theatre historian.

The issues that concerned Hauptfleisch in his aim to write theatre history for a democratised South Africa necessarily concern us all. In Britain, lower status forms like music hall, not honoured by the label 'theatre', allowed groups disadvantaged in society by class and gender to flourish. Part IV opens up a series of case studies in order to show how definitions of theatre that we often take for granted are but the product of convention.

We begin with a question of first principle: should a historian be concerned primarily with what happens on stage, or with the experience of the audience? Of course a play is more than a dramatic script, and the birth of theatre studies as an academic discipline stems from that recognition. But can we be content to define the play as an activity that takes place on stage, or should we rather define it as an interactive encounter between two groups of people: performers – who watch each other as well as the audience – and spectators – who interact with each other as they play out their social roles? If we grant the premise that the play is essentially an event, then many standard source materials used by the historian become problematic, because they obliterate the active spectator from the historian's field of vision. From spectators we turn to actors, often considered less important than playwrights and directors who today have more cultural authority and seem to make the decisive artistic decisions. Biographies of actors are two-a-penny, but a history of the art of acting is much harder to pin down because performances are ephemeral. Knowledge of acting is transmitted more naturally and effectively through the body than through words, and trained actors, in the process of honing their skills, acquire a sense of how their own technique differs from that of earlier generations. Chapter 12 therefore explores the historical knowledge and intelligence that are embedded in the work of actors and teachers of actors. Attempting to write a history of acting involves confronting the nature of historical knowledge, which may be embodied rather than enshrined in documents.

Chapter 13 relates to the development of a specific modern skill-set, that of the actor–musician. We could regard the actor–musician as a curious hybrid, but from another perspective the historian can equally well argue that the separation of acting from music-making, or the hiving off of 'opera' from 'theatre', is a far odder historical phenomenon. A historian specialising in African or Asian 'theatre', or a historian of popular European forms like variety, is more likely to question the received common-sense that takes acting and music-making to be distinct disciplines. There are institutional reasons why historians so often focus upon activity conceived as avant-garde and thus progressive, rather than upon forms like the musical, which are conceived to be commercial and thus retrogressive. From music-theatre we pass to circus, where performers use many of the same skills as actors, tell stories in their own way, and assume roles. Although circus borrows a spatial form from classical antiquity, normally a sign of high cultural status, circus has been excluded from most histories of the theatre, taken implicitly to be a low status form unworthy of serious consideration. The development of 'Cultural History' and 'Performance Studies' within the academic world has allowed theatre historians to widen the scope of their enquiries without being constrained by the anxiety that real plays need storylines. Whether the lens of theatre offers the most productive way to look at circus is an open question.

11

WILLMAR SAUTER

The audience

When in 1908 George Bernard Shaw was shown the new Royal Dramatic Theatre in Stockholm, he exclaimed that it looked like a palatial bank, though Shaw may not have been aware that in fact the building was financed by a private consortium of bankers and industrial leaders. The recently completed edifice looked like a palace: white with gilded details on the outside, white marble and colourful paintings in the foyer, and turquoise seats in the auditorium – all inspired by the fashionable art deco style of the time. The building was a manifestation of modernity and marked the beginning of European modernism in Swedish theatre. Furthermore, the Royal Dramatic Theatre was from now on organised as a joint-stock company, in which the state owned all the shares. How did these changes in an institution established in 1788 affect the audience of the new era?

Some days before the opening of the Marble Palace – as the citizens of Stockholm dubbed the building – a short announcement from the new management of the theatre appeared in newspapers. In a few lines the public was urged to refrain from the traditional end-of-scene applause and to restrict their clapping to the end of an act. What were the implications of this appeal?

The far-reaching significance of this insignificant little announcement, rarely observed in theatre histories, becomes obvious only in the light of audience behaviour in a wider perspective. I see this change of attitude towards the spectator around 1900 as a historical watershed at the rise of theatre modernism. I will briefly describe the spectators' participation in performances of the nineteenth century and August Strindberg's harsh opinion of the audiences of his day, before looking at the nature of spectatorship in some pre-modern performances. In the modernist era the audience was silenced, and its integral function as part of a public event was effaced, but theatre nevertheless continues to remain dependent on the close relationship between actors on stage and spectators in the auditorium.

Let me recall the situation in a commercial European theatre of the nineteenth century. When the star actress – be it Sarah Bernhardt on her extensive tours or just a local celebrity[1] – entered the stage, she would immediately be welcomed with long, warm applause. Even when the applause faded, there were still whispers in the audience, one spectator telling another when she saw the actress last, a father explaining to his daughter who she was, and so forth. The actress waited for complete silence before she spoke her first lines. The excitement in the audience was tangible, and when she finished her monologue, a gratifying applause would accompany her exit and, depending on its length, she would return to the stage, approach the footlights and bow deeply to the crowd. A dialogue might provoke similar reactions and, in this case, all the actors would come forward and express their gratitude at the front of the stage before the action of the play resumed. For the audience, mid-scene and end-of-scene applause confirmed that they were attending a marvellous

16 An early nineteenth-century theatre audience in Sweden.

performance and that it had been worth bringing family and friends to such an occasion.

This interactive behaviour was common not only in performances of spoken drama, but also in opera and ballet. Here the music was composed in such a way that it invited or provoked applause at the end of an aria or ensemble scene. The conductor would halt the music, as indicated in the score, to allow for the 'spontaneous' response of the audience, and this is still the case today in many opera houses, when works from the last century are performed. The Swedish opera star Elisabet Söderström, who has sung all over the world, once remarked that an ageing singer has to be careful that the entry-applause does not become longer than the exit-applause. If the audience remained silent after 'Nessun Dorma' in *Turandot* or after the thirty-two fouettés in the ballet *Swan Lake*, it would be considered a complete failure.

The practice that lingers today in the world of opera and ballet is a reminder of the historical behaviour of audiences in all theatrical genres. Today such reactions on the part of audiences may seem exceptional, but they serve as a reminder to the historian of behaviour patterns that were once normal. The dominant interest of historians in innovations and modernisation makes this easy to forget. What we take as normal today only became normal at the point when modernism became the leading aesthetic principle of drama productions.

So when did modernism arrive in theatre, bringing with it its silent audience intent on viewing art? Was it, for example, when Adolphe Lemoine Montigny put a table in the middle of the stage and thus created a recognisable bourgeois environment for French audiences of the 1850s?[2] Or was it when electricity revolutionised stage design? There are many opinions about the advent of modernism, as Stefan Hulfeld's essay in this volume indicates. A number of writers from the margins of Europe were clearly influential in propagating a new form of dramatic writing. Anton Chekhov from Russia, Henrik Ibsen from Norway, Minna Canth from Finland, Maurice Maeterlinck from Belgium, and Gabriele D'Annunzio from Italy deserve mention, as well as August Strindberg from my own country of Sweden. This last not only trumpeted his own view of the modern stage, but, like Émile Zola in France, fiercely attacked the traditions of the nineteenth century.

Inspired by his European colleagues, Strindberg had succeeded in establishing his own Intimate Theatre in Stockholm just a few months before the Royal Dramatic Theatre's 'Marble Palace' opened in February 1908 with his popular five-act history play *Master Olof*, written in the 1870s. By now, however, Strindberg did not want to write any more long plays, preferring short chamber plays in one act. He explained his reasons in his *Memorandum to the Personnel of the Intimate Theatre*, written in 1908 as a manifesto.[3] In his new plays he would henceforth avoid all 'glamour, calculated effects, applause markers, star roles, solo numbers' – in other words, everything that audiences enjoyed in traditional performances. He wished the auditorium to be fully concentrated on the actions on stage. Not even an intermission should break the attention of the spectator. He was especially opposed to the habit of serving alcoholic beverages between the acts, although the sale of liquor would have paid half the rent of the theatre. The prospect of having an even slightly intoxicated audience in the second act horrified him: 'The combination of scenic art and alcohol causes the lengthy intermissions, the length of which is determined by the proprietor of the restaurant', he furiously exclaimed.

Strindberg's view of theatre is linear, conceived from the standpoint of producing a script. In the beginning there is the author, who writes the play-text. The text is given over to the actor–manager or (later) director, who instructs the actors, for 'in aesthetics the art of acting is not considered an independent art, but a subsidiary one', Strindberg declares, because the actor needs the author's text, while the author's drama can stand without the actor. The staging of the play aims at presenting the words of the dramatist to the spectators, who must give their entire attention to the drama on stage and to nothing else. Strindberg's audiences were expected to have an aesthetic and moral experience, with aspects of entertainment and leisure banned from his theatre.

Strindberg represents a typical approach to modernist theatre. Focus upon the drama on stage – on its content as well as its aesthetic values – was paramount, and the nascent profession of the director had the task of presenting plays in such a way that the audience became fully involved in the dramatic action. The art of acting as the primary component of performance was reduced and marginalised. Theatre critics eventually accepted this tendency which, in due course, was also taken up by the majority of theatre scholars. Research on stage directors is much more plentiful than studies of individual actors, as any theatre shelf in an academic book store reveals.

In my discussion of Strindberg's modernism, a few keywords have surfaced: aesthetics, entertainment, morality, leisure. I regard these as functions of theatre. For Strindberg, these functions were produced by the dramatist and, hopefully, grasped by the spectator, in accordance with his linear perspective. He expected the audience to acquire from the play certain values important to the producer: a certain moral standard proffered, via serious and coherent content, as an aesthetic experience in accordance with the social and artistic ambitions of the dramatist. Since Strindberg was a dramatist and since the Intimate Theatre presented only plays written by him during its few years of existence (1907–10), his attitude is understandably personal, but it also has broader implications for the function of theatre.

Theatrical performances would not exist unless there were members of society who wished to attend them. Why would anybody want to go to the theatre if they had no expectations that they wanted the performance to match? In other words, despite Strindberg's idea of a one-way transaction, the relationship between stage and auditorium is based on a mutual exchange, which means that the functions of theatre cannot be understood solely from the aspect of its production: the functions have to be conceptualised as a two-sided, interactive process of communication.

The question of aesthetics provides an example. Theatre critics as well as theatre historians tend to accord the highest aesthetic values to productions of an innovative character. This attitude justifies the copious number of books published about the beginnings of theatre modernism in around 1900, and subsequent attention given to the theatrical avant-garde in the wake of this modernist movement.[4] Yet any theatrical performance displays aesthetic values, be it a commercial Broadway musical, a traditional Shakespeare production, an amateur performance and even children acting as spring flowers on the stage of a school hall. There is always an artistic aspect to be considered: otherwise the audience would not even recognise the performance as being 'theatre'. The problem is that aesthetic principles are evaluated quite differently by scholars and by those frequenting such performances. The variety shows of the nineteenth century, for instance, enjoyed a high degree of popularity, but are rarely dealt with by theatre historians from an aesthetic point of view.[5] How could their artistic principles be described? As a mixture of performance practices, as loans from other genres? The singing, dancing, juggling, talking and other expressive modes of entertainment were certainly not invented by the producers of variety shows, but they combined them into a specific conglomerate that constituted a particular aesthetic ideal. It is my claim that there is an aesthetic function involved in any theatrical performance, and the question is, how are we as theatre historians to deal with it?

If the spectator is not reduced to a consumer of theatrical productions, but is seen as an active participant in a theatrical event, then the relationship between the agent on stage and the beholder in the auditorium can be understood as reciprocal. On the one side, the actor, singer, dancer, mime or puppeteer exhibit themselves on stage in order to be watched, demanding attention from those who sit or stand in the auditorium. The spectators, on the other side, have come to the performance in order to watch those appearing on stage. Neither performers nor spectators would gather in the theatre were it not for the presence of the other. Those on stage are very much aware of the audience – their number, their mood, their attention, their enthusiasm, but also their neglect or boredom; at the same time, the spectators have come to be attracted and involved by the personalities or presence of performers in the flesh. This basic, sensory contact between agent and beholder involves a ritualistic element: both sides agree to keep to certain rules, knowing that the performance lasts a limited time and expecting actions that are different from everyday life. In genres such as naturalism these actions may resemble everyday life in some respects, but the positioning on stage, the seating arrangement, the intermission as well as the projection of the actors' voices remain very much ritualised. The spectators not only watch persons acting in front of them, but are also aware of the other members of the audience around them. Personal experience becomes embedded in a triangular relationship between oneself, the other spectators and the performers.

While responding to a stage personality, the spectator also recognises the actor as an artist, who employs expressive means to present actions that exceed everyday experience. Particular skills are displayed: the performers speak, sing and/or dance according to the genre in which they are placed. The spectator expects these skills, for seeing and hearing such skills was the purpose of buying the tickets. What reactions does the display of artistry trigger in the audience? In the best of cases, the spectators will feel pleasure and be well entertained. Experienced spectators will also judge the quality of artistic expression, compare it to earlier experiences and feel satisfied (or not) with what they hear and see. These feelings can be described as an aesthetic experience, related to but not entirely dependent on the skills of the performers. Even amateurs with minimal skills can arouse aesthetic pleasure.

The frame of the ritual encounter between performer and spectator and the stimulus of the artistic appearance invite the audience to interpret stage actions. The stage personality and performing artist is transformed into a fictional or, depending on the genre, into a more or less symbolic figure. This fictional or symbolic figure is displayed in actions that imitate serious or comic situations related to human behaviour. Certain moral conclusions can be drawn, since stage actions ultimately reference human actions outside the performative event. In other words, all fictional and symbolic actions on stage have an ethical dimension, which ultimately has a didactic function: the spectators learn something about themselves, about their history, about their world.

Last but not least there is an economic aspect to every theatrical experience. In most periods of theatre history, the spectators have contributed to the costs of performances. The box office or the hat passed around are sites of monetary exchange between performers and spectators. Even when theatrical enterprises are financed by external public or private resources, the patrons seek performances that will please the taste of their audiences. Theatre, whether in the market place or as a market place, allows the audience, by attending or spurning the performance, to influence its course.

17 Checking for payments. Danish travelling actors are performing a French comedy in the attic of the old city council of Ystad, Sweden. Early nineteenth century.

The functions that I have outlined are relevant to all theatrical enterprises, but may be foregrounded in particular ways depending on the particular genre and historical moment. To summarise, the gathering in the theatre has been compared to a *ritual*, with a ritualistic frame placed around the artwork. The performance demonstrates *aesthetic* values, but provides at the same time *entertainment*. These aspects are complementary rather than competing components of the theatrical event. The performance as a symbolic representation implies a world-view that I have called its *morality* or ethics, and in this sense it has a *didactic* function, no matter whether this constitutes its primary purpose. Finally, there is the matter of *economics*. These functions are mutual, inter-communicating elements, which can be realised only through the simultaneous presence of performer and spectator.

Are these functions applicable to every epoch of theatre history? And if such functions can be traced in diverse historical periods, what will they reveal about theatre audiences? A few examples will illustrate the advantages of a functional analysis of audiences, for I wish to demonstrate how such analysis can alter our view of historical audiences. My argument invites a critical review of existing historiography, especially of books that offer an overview of the history of (Western) theatre. Generally speaking, such studies focus their attention on the stage, whereas the auditorium is, so to speak, left in the dark, even when performances have taken place in bright daylight.

I shall take as my first example the theatres of the Roman Empire. Whoever has climbed up the steps of a Greek theatre to the top of the auditorium is stunned by the magnificent view over the surrounding landscape, for the Greeks often located their theatres on the edge of town, resting the *theatron* (the seating area for the audience) on a sloping hill. The Romans, however, built their theatres in the middle of the city as free-standing structures, not dependent on the natural environment. The Roman stone theatre was a closed building with walls all around the space, and the entire area could be covered with *vela*, awnings that protected the spectators from the sun.

The auditorium or *cavea* of the Roman theatre was divided into horizontal sections or circles, which replicated the social hierarchy of society. In the semicircular 'orchestra' closest to the stage, the highest-ranking senators and associates of the Emperor were seated. In the first section of raised seating, the knights and other nobles had their seats, followed by wealthy citizens, until finally the lowest-ranking members of society found their places on the top circle of the *cavea*. Each horizontal section was clearly separated from the others by a wall that prevented access to the rest of the auditorium. The separation of the spectators took place outside of the theatre, at street entrances that indicated to which sections the various doors would lead. By way of a skilfully designed system of corridors and staircases underneath the seating area, the visitors reached their designated seats. Under the emperors, the Romans opened their theatres to all who wanted to enjoy the performances, including women in contrast to the Greek world, but they prevented a mixing of the social classes. Class distinction was built into the architectural structure of the building. Although no plays survive from this era, we have ample documentation of how audiences expressed political opinions through their noisy responses, and some examples of how actors responded.[6]

The Roman social segregation of audiences was echoed in many theatre auditoria of later periods. Although the Teatro Olimpico in Vicenza in Italy

(1585) was intended as a replica of a Roman theatre, its auditorium with simple wooden benches actually reproduced Greek seating arrangements appropriate to the men who built it, members of the Olympic Academy amongst whom no differences of rank applied. Only when the theatre buildings of the Renaissance and Baroque were opened to the public did the Roman separation of classes make sense. Alongside the creation of social hierarchy, the economic aspect grew in importance. When patrons had to pay for tickets, unlike the Roman world theatre where admission was normally free, then the price a person could afford created new distinctions in the space of the auditorium. The process of substituting class stratification with a purely economic stratification would extend over centuries, from the Elizabethan playhouse to today's Broadway.

My second example addresses the relation between theatre and religious worship. The idea that medieval theatre began as a 'Bible for the poor' – a visual display of biblical stories for a non-reading congregation – is a scholarly fabrication, as theatre historians have known since O. B. Hardison's book on the liturgical drama in early medieval Europe.[7] The 'liturgy' is the order of prayers and other acts during church services. Within the Easter liturgy, the dramatisation of the visit of the three Marys to find that Christ's tomb was empty is sometimes still wrongly interpreted as a theatrical device to teach illiterate Christians the wonderful fact that Christ rose from the dead, suggesting that the overall purpose of medieval drama was didactic.

Of course there was a didactic aspect to the liturgical drama, but those who were supposed to learn from it were not visiting peasants from nearby farms. Young novices in the monastery were taught to sing in Latin, to perform publicly in front of their elders and also to entertain the congregation of monks by their skilful rendering of this well-known biblical scene. The tenth-century manuscript of Bishop Ethelwold in Winchester called *Regularis Concordia* requires explicitly that the three Marys turn to the 'choir' rather than to the congregation to proclaim that Christ is risen.[8] In symbolic form, the theatrical presentation of this central element in Christian belief made the resurrected Christ *present* in the middle of the monastic community. On a spiritual level, both those performing and those witnessing this elevated moment could perceive the historical event as happening right in front of them. The only function apparently missing in this context is the economic one, for the costs and effects of the performance could not be measured in money – though we should not underestimate the extent to which performance enhanced the prestige of economically powerful monasteries.

Such an interpretation of liturgical drama is dependent on the definition of the audience. The ancient manuscripts rarely mention spectators other than the 'clergy' and 'choir' that feature in Ethelwold's description, so these have to be imagined by the scholar, a task that requires our assessment of tenth-century Europe where cities were practically non-existent. Cultural life was concentrated in fortified monasteries, where theatrical presentations were used to celebrate the significant moments of the church year. The celebrants were the monks who acted and the monks who watched, a rare convergence of performers and spectators in theatre history.

Many of these Easter texts remained in use during the following centuries – one copy, for example, found in Linköping, Sweden, was dated 1280. An interesting change in the audience gradually took place. There were still the monks or nuns in the abbeys watching their novices acting, but in addition the audience might include a community of lay people from the nearby town. David Wiles emphasises the presence of such a congregation in his contribution to this volume. For these worshippers, there was only a thin line between those monks playing the Marys and the rest of the monks singing the anthems of the Easter liturgy, for both were performing in some way. In other words, there were now three groups – performers, participants and spectators, all united by faith and place. Questioning the supposed educational function of these performances as vehicles for imparting the biblical story, I prefer to underline the creation of presence – the very moment at which the angel announces Christ's resurrection: 'surrexit dominus, sicut ipse dixit' ('arisen is the Lord as he himself predicted!'). The mysterious cornerstone of Christian faith was re-enacted for all present in the church: the monks, the novices and the non-Latin speakers of the congregation. The 'as-if' of the participants oscillated between representation of a historical event and participation in a ritual.

While the medieval manuscripts and their related iconography contain almost no information about the audiences of these theatrical events, pictorial evidence can be obtained from many other periods. I shall consider as my third example the famous painting of the so-called *Boerenkermis*, which is usually attributed to Pieter Brueghel the Younger, but seems to be a replica of an earlier sixteenth-century original by Pieter Balten.[9] At the centre of Balten's picture stands a booth stage with a back curtain, the action on stage attracting the attention of several of the many figures populating the canvas. The spectators surround the elevated stage, and some have climbed onto the roof of an adjoining tavern. Just as interesting to me are all the personages in the painting who do not care about the ongoing performance. They are busy talking, dancing, playing cards, eating, buying merchandise, kissing and so forth, for the theatre performance is taking place in the middle of a marketplace that offers multiple entertainments.

In this particular painting, a few figures deserve special attention. One woman, standing next to the stage, interacts with a stage-hand behind the

18a Performance of a farce during a Flemish *kermis* in the sixteenth century.

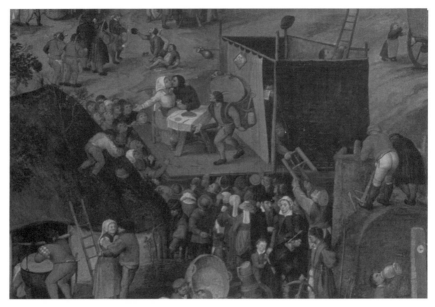

18b Detail of Fig. 18a.

curtain who is lifting or lowering a stool – is she part of the theatre company, or is this a casual encounter? Close to the stage, some people stand with their backs to the action, and at least one of them is dressed as a Protestant priest. Are they protesting at the performance? This is difficult to say, but later copies of the painting omit this group of overt non-spectators. Without going into further details of Balten's painting, the variety of spectators indicates a familiar feature of historical theatre audiences. Not everybody close to a spectacle is necessarily watching it, and all kinds of reactions from participation to protest are possible. This is not only true of open-air performances: even in indoor theatres, reactions to the perceived entertainment, ideologies, aesthetics and rituals extend far beyond the intentions of the performers. Thus it is often difficult to speak of the meaning of a theatrical performance – one has to ask, meaning for whom?

My second observation relates this performance to the festival of a *kermis*, usually celebrated in honour of the patron saint of a local church, which constitutes the larger ritual framing of the event. This religious occasion allows for more worldly pleasures, and the theatre performance in Balten's painting is surrounded by a profane celebration that provides facilities for the bodily and spiritual recreation of the local population. A further ritualistic frame is created by the performance itself. To become a spectator who focuses on stage actions and participates in the creation of a fictive story, thus adhering to rules of play, may be seen as ritualised behaviour, repeated in performance after performance.

Balten's picture is a reminder of the major environment for theatrical events throughout most of theatre history, namely festival. Today theatre is essentially a product, available in major cities on almost any day of the week at a variety of venues. Up to the eighteenth century, and setting aside certain metropolitan centres, I would argue that most theatrical performances took place as part of festivals held to celebrate gods and goddesses, weddings and funerals, seasons and anniversaries.[10]

The traces of past audiences can be found in many sources available to theatre scholars once the centrality of their presence is recognised. Most easily accessible are newspaper reviews, which represent an informed and privileged spectator's view of a performance. In most European countries, this type of source goes back as far as the eighteenth century. Often, especially during the nineteenth century, critics include some account of the reactions of the general audience, and it is a reasonable assumption that critics shared their broad value judgements with the majority of the audience. Although critics have often been bewildered by modernist innovations, and plays pronounced to be flops by the critics have sometimes gone on to win the hearts of audiences and to enjoy long runs, these are exceptions. In the 1980s I conducted a number of audience surveys in Stockholm, where the evaluations of spectators were compared to the judgements of theatre critics; the performances were graded in very similar ways, although there were deviations within single reviews or among particular groups of spectators.[11]

Reviews provide the historian with qualitative information, whereas quantitative information can be retrieved from the archives: for example, how many performances were given of a particular production, were they sold out, do we know how many tickets were sold in different price categories? Sometimes, this monetary information is available before the age of printed newspapers, as in the famous Henslowe Papers of the Elizabethan era, where the costs and profits of each performance at the Rose Theatre were registered. Medieval records sometimes tell us what spectators had to contribute to the cost of occupying a seat, as in the passion plays at York, and the twenty-five day epic performed in 1547 at Valenciennes in France. Memoirs and diaries are also valuable for historical audience research. For example, the Swedish princess Hedvig Eleonora Charlotta jotted down detailed reports on the court theatre of Gustav III in the late eighteenth century, and the famous diaries of Samuel Pepys from the English Restoration period record visits to London theatres. Many actors and actresses have described their careers in memoirs, although the reliability of these retrospective accounts is often questionable. Finally, as

I mentioned in the context of the Roman theatre, buildings, including ruins and blueprints, represent a major source for audience and reception studies.

Who saw the performances? This question has for a long time been of primary interest to audience historians, followed by *what* exactly audiences had access to in terms of the repertoire available, and then most problematically *how* spectators perceived performances. Qualitative questions have usually proved the most difficult for the historian to answer. I have proposed a number of functions as key terms in order to bring together the who–what–how questions that we need to ask of historical audiences. The functions discussed here allow for a cross-disciplinary approach to available evidence and tighten our focus on the performer–spectator relationship. In my view, historical audience research is impeded less by a lack of source materials, than by sufficient theoretical and empirical procedures through which to integrate the spectator in the theatrical event.

NOTES

1 On audience response, see, for example, Cornelia Otis Skinner, *Madame Sarah* (1962; rpt New York: Paragon House Publishers, 1988), and Bruce A. McConachie, *Melodramatic Formations: American Theatre and Society 1820–1870* (Iowa City: University of Iowa Press, 1992).

2 Montigny's table, described in a Swedish publication by Gösta M. Bergman, is mentioned also in Oscar G. Brockett, *History of the Theatre* (Boston: Allyn and Bacon; 9th edn rev. F. J. Hildy, 1999), p. 377, citing the dramatists Victorien Sardou and Alexandre Dumas *fils* as sources.

3 Published in Swedish in 1908 by Björk & Börjeson, Stockholm. English translation in E. Törnqvist and B. Steene (eds.), *Strindberg on Drama and Theatre* (Amsterdam: Amsterdam University Press, 2008), pp. 45–68.

4 See, for instance, Erika Fischer-Lichte (ed.), *TheaterAvantgarde. Wahrnehmung–Körper–Sprache* (Tübingen, Basel: Francke, 1995), to which I have contributed, and Christopher Innes, *Avant-garde Theatre 1892–1992* (London: Routledge, 1993).

5 An exception worth mentioning is Tracy C. Davis, *Actresses as Working Women: Their Social Identity in Victorian Culture* (London: Routledge, 1991).

6 David Wiles, *A Short History of Western Performance Space* (Cambridge: Cambridge University Press, 2003), pp. 174–5.

7 O. B. Hardison, *Christian Rite and Christian Drama in the Middle Ages: Essays in the Origin and Early History of Modern Drama* (Baltimore: Johns Hopkins University Press, 1963).

8 E. K. Chambers, *The Medieval Stage*, 4 vols. (Oxford: Oxford University Press, 1903), Vol. II, p. 14.

9 These paintings are variously attributed to Pieter Brueghel the Younger, copying his father's painting or, more likely, copying Pieter Balten's painting; for more details, see, for instance, www.oxfordartonline.com. In Brueghel's version, the spectators are to the right of the stage, with some omitted; in Balten's, they are to the left.

10 Cf. Temple Hauptfleisch *et al.*, *Festivalising! Theatrical Events, Politics and Culture* (Amsterdam and New York: Rodopi, 2007).
11 A brief discussion of the relationship between spectators and critics can be found in Willmar Sauter, *The Theatrical Event: Dynamics of Performance and Perception* (Iowa City: University of Iowa Press, 2000), p. 184.

FURTHER READING

Beacham, Richard C. *The Roman Theatre and its Audience* (London: Routledge, 1991).
Bennett, Susan. *Theatre Audiences: A Theory of Production and Perception*, 2nd edn (London and New York: Routledge, 1997).
Gurr, Andrew. *Playgoing in Shakespeare's London*, 3rd edn (Cambridge: Cambridge University Press, 2004).
Lough, John. *Paris Theatre Audiences in the Seventeenth and Eighteenth Centuries* (London: Oxford University Press, 1957).
Nicoll, Allardyce. *The Garrick Stage: Theatres and Audience in the Eighteenth Century*, ed. Sybil Rosenfeld (Manchester: Manchester University Press, 1980).
Sauter, Willmar. *The Theatrical Event: Dynamics of Performance and Perception* (Iowa City: University of Iowa Press, 2000).

12

JOSETTE FÉRAL*

The art of acting

'an awareness of history...'[1]

How can we construct a history of the art of acting? Acting is an evanescent art form that leaves few visual traces behind, while the creative work leading up to a performance is soon effaced from memory. What approach should we adopt in order to trace the evolution of the actor's art? Should we study key dates, or should we instead concentrate on the talent of particular actors whose art assumed a distinctive form?

The history of performance can be written in different ways, depending on which of these two approaches is chosen. In the first, the sum total of past events generates a developmental sequence that today we dismiss as a utopian vision – merely the reflection of the researcher's selective gaze upon moments that have been privileged over other moments. In the second approach, focusing on individual artists and their performance skills, the picture seems to disintegrate, since an impressionistic overview, brought into close-up, cannot capture the overall reality of an art.

Beyond this fundamental question about how to create the history of the actor's art lies a much more crucial question – one that arises in critical discourse and in acting schools – concerning the very necessity of this history. Can a better understanding of history really shed light on the present of a theatre characterised by its urgent need to get on with the show, to illuminate the text, or to stage a collective work? These questions are fundamental to any historical inquiry. They are questions that the historians of the 'Annales' School[2] addressed by creating a history of ideas and attitudes rather than a history of facts and events, a history that places events in their contexts and geographic settings and, crucially, examines the bearing these events have on the present. In what follows, my thoughts will be guided by the responses of three directors to the question 'What place do you accord to history?' These directors are Jacques Delcuvellerie, Jerzy Grotowski and Antoine Vitez.

In his 1997 book on the training of actors, Jacques Delcuvellerie, founder of Groupov in Belgium, notes that one of the greatest handicaps an actor faces is that he cannot project himself directly into history because he is situated in

---

* This chapter was translated from the French by Roxie Lapidus.

the here-and-now of the performance and leaves no trace behind him.[3] Where writers and painters can turn to a long heritage of models and other works for inspiration, the art of actors disappears with them and, even in the most ideal scenario, only a few tens of thousands of people may have seen them perform. While cinema gets around this problem, it is only intermittently mitigated for the theatre when certain performances are filmed. Acting remains essentially an archaic phenomenon that depends upon direct, unmediated experience, which is nevertheless elusive in its actual effect.[4]

This being so, is it relevant to talk about the necessity for actors to know the history of acting to enrich their own performance skills? Delcuvellerie's reply is that it is indispensable, not only on the cognitive level, but because it allows an artist to inscribe himself within a tradition. Moreover, knowing one's place in history can make all the difference between an actor who has an impact on the traditions of performance, and one who is content to practise his craft – however skilfully – without contributing to the science of the profession:

> There are very popular actors who are good actors; they generally portray specific social types and their success stems from the audience's recognition of this typology. Take Bourvil, for example. If an actor lacks an awareness of history, if he leaves the tools of expression in the state in which he found them, his 'art' cannot inspire. His characters die with him, and that is for the best … One can admire Bourvil, but one is not inspired. The actor before him or after him is no different. He is not a necessary link to anyone following in the same genre … The same cannot be said of Karl Valentin, at least not entirely. An awareness of history… Likewise, the same cannot be said of Dario Fo, Julian Beck, Helene Weigel or Ryszard Cieslak.[5]

The difference established here between artists who practise their art skilfully, but without historical influence and thus without posterity, and those whose work has an impact on the evolution of their art, is crucial. Thus, an actor's awareness of history takes the form of 'pondering the general conditions of producing his art', of recognising what is 'not intrinsic to it' – that is, knowing the practices and forms that preceded it. Through this process, the artist participates in 'a foundational adventure' and finds his place in history.[6]

The foundational theatrical adventure evoked here is identified in the West with the workshops fostered by Antoine, Jacques Rouyer, Stanislavski and Meyerhold in the late nineteenth and early twentieth centuries. Also in this lineage are all of the modernist reformers of the art of acting – the 'creators of traditions'[7] who shaped current theatre: Vakhtangov, Artaud, Appia, Copeau, Jouvet and Dullin, as well as Chekhov, Meisner, and Spolin. More recently we have Living Theatre, Grotowski, Barba, Strehler, Brook,

Mnouchkine, Vassiliev and many others. The strength of each lay in their claim to establish a true science of acting and performance. Beyond differences in teaching and technique, their quest is the same: to rethink theatre on new ethical and professional bases by recognising its heritage and striving to go further.

From Stanislavski to Vassiliev, and including Meyerhold, Appia, Copeau, Baty, Dullin, Jouvet, Grotowski, Vitez, Brook and Mnouchkine to name but a few, many have sought out the traditions of the past and attempted to understand their predecessors in order to draw upon them and eventually surpass them. Thus Meyerhold drew upon Wagner's historical theories and Appia's texts; he studied the Noh theatre and found inspiration in the grotesque style and in popular forms (fairground theatre, *commedia dell'arte*, pantomime, masks, puppetry). Like Brecht, in his own way Copeau also drew inspiration from popular forms of theatre (circus, clowns, cabaret) and sought to understand their success. Dullin was inspired by melodrama, where 'there lay the secrets of a genuine acting tradition',[8] as well as Japanese theatre, where he found a particular way of using the body, the voice and gesture. The Parisian 'Cartel' of Baty, Pitoeff, Dullin and Jouvet, wanting as Copeau put it to 'deham [*décabotiniser*] the actor' so the theatre might become a quasi-metaphysical place, emphasised the need to regain an inherited 'continuous or rediscovered tradition',[9] a living tradition that had sustained the golden ages of theatre. More recently, Vitez resurrected the old verse form of the alexandrine, and like Craig the world of puppetry. Kantor found his 'little room of memory'[10] and the history that filled it an inexhaustible source for performances. Mnouchkine plumbed the Greeks and the texts of Shakespeare to find the forms she needed to render the present. Grotowski had a huge interest in forgotten traditions: ceremony and ritual, Eastern theatre, African dance, and Voodoo practices. Barba also emphasised the importance of historical perspective:

> The history of theatre was my source of consolation, my magic carpet, my El Dorado. In it, I found the essential: Stanislavski's solitude and Artaud's isolation; the exile and the loss of language of Mikhaïl Chekhov, Reinhardt, Piscator, and Helene Weigel; the importance that Vakhtangov, Brecht, and Lorca accord to amateur theatre; Stanislavski and Meyerhold's persistent research into the *life* of an actor; Sulerjitski's laboratory of shared life, and the first Moscow Art Theatre studio. Theatrical history was my Talmud, my Bible, and my Koran. I had only to read and decipher the anecdotes, events, and details neglected by historians. An Atlantis of information emerged, clarifying my hesitations and doubts, revealing the desperate examples and clever solutions of those who preceded me... Theatre became the place where the living meet the non-living, the dead, the ancestral reformers who had crossed the desert.[11]

This luminous reflection on the importance of the past and history, history understood as the study of attitudes and influences affecting current practices, is echoed in Barba's observation that there are two forces guiding work performed by his Odin Theatre: 'memory of the past, and nostalgia for the future'.[12] The method used by Odin's actors stems from this duality. The actor becomes the intersection of these two elements, rich in the influences of the past that shape the course of the future.

However, this relationship to the past takes different forms, according to the person. For Grotowski and Kantor, it is memory – the memory of forms and traditions, but also personal memory. Moreover, an individual's relationship to memory differs according to the culture from whence he sprang. Marc Fumaroli's account of a workshop conducted by Grotowski in the 1960s illustrates such cross-cultural differences. Over the course of this workshop, a marked difference divided the young Americans from the young Europeans, which Fumaroli describes as

> symptomatic of what, mentally, still in 1968, separated Europe and the U.S.A. On the one side, memory and the potential to call on its creative energy; on the other, atrophy of memory coupled with the mechanical exploitation of superficial vitality – erotic or cerebral – disconnected from memory. It was clear that for Grotowski, the theatre was the place where the profound life of memory could be substituted for the mechanics of life without memory.[13]

For Barba, working with the past begins with training exercises that convey this history – exercises conceived as privileged vehicles of transmission. The actor must first bend with the exercises; then, as he acquires expertise, he can modify the exercises as part of his own particular training. 'Today we recognise that the exercises were one of the most extreme adventures in the Golden Age that was the twentieth century... Exercise is a mnemonic amulet that allows the actor to incorporate the knowledge that is fundamental to constructing organic forms of acting.' The word 'mnemonic' is key. If the first exercises employed at the Odin Theatre are really the bearers of history and borrowed from classical ballet, acrobatics, rhythmic dance and Grotowski, those that follow correspond to other phases in the actor's training. These are the second phase, where the actor assumes responsibility for his own training, and the third, where his own personal dramaturgy is born. For Barba, this evolution in the exercises and in the role they play in the actor's training is the sign of an anthropological shift that can only be achieved through a thorough knowledge of history.[14]

Barba goes even farther, claiming that although the great reformers rejected past forms, they first studied them and imbibed their spirit. This is how they were able to contest them so effectively. According to Barba, tradition entails an act of refusal, because 'it is our retrospective gaze on human beings, on the profession, on all of the History that has preceded us and from which we choose to distance ourselves through the continuity of our work ... Personal tradition is an echo from afar' – an echo fed by that past which we have entered the better to separate ourselves from it. And bear in mind, he says, that all the great reformers 'had needs that went against the grain of their times'; they were 'exploring uncharted land, alone and vulnerable, abandoning contemporary practices before replacing them with new practices whose prestige could protect them'.[15]

Restoring to actors the memory of time

Antoine Vitez (1930–90) is one of the great teachers passionate about conveying to actors the memory of their profession. 'The artistry of an actor's performance does not lie in the simple, spontaneous unspeakability of emotion. It is an art with a history, modes, and a system of codes that are difficult to identify because, of course, the actor's performance disappears, due to its very nature, which is ephemeral.'[16] Hence the importance that he ascribes to memory – which is another form of history – in his work with young students.

> I realised that I was trying to restore several kinds of memories to the actors. First the literary, philosophical and political memory of objects, of the written traces upon which they were working. It seems to me important for the actor to be able to integrate into his performance, into tiny, practical, and concrete details – like the way he picks up an object, greets another character, or questions him – the allegorical characters or great figures of myth, history and politics that underlie the texts he is playing. As a director and teacher, my task is to restore the memory of Time to the actors. By practicing their art they are also bearing witness to past centuries. They are rescuing from oblivion the great causes of times past, which remain inherently those of our own times, even if they take different forms.[17]

This relationship to memory cultivated by Vitez comes from his conviction that 'if the actor is profoundly informed by this memory, if he can recover it, he will find the true roots of his emotion, which precede even the plot of the play itself'. This memory will allow the actor to better situate the roots of his art and to know his place in time. The role of the director and the teacher is specifically to assist the artist in reviving this memory that is indispensable to moving beyond the self, to 'induce that state of openness, of divination – a trance-like state that gets in touch with buried memories, unspeakable memories, and inadmissible memories. Only thus can actors achieve extraordinary things.'[18]

Paradoxically, Grotowski does not refute these comments, which close the gap between him and Vitez, although everything else about these two men's approaches puts them at opposite poles. The two converge upon the place they accord to history and memory, borne by the actor like stigmata.

The actor as both vessel of memory and creative agent

The past that was in question in the age of art theatre was a remembrance of forms based not on texts, but on bodies and oral and stage tradition – hence the importance of a history of the body. Up to this point, the prevailing vision of performance techniques focused exclusively on great individual actors, masters of their art, whose trade secrets remained unknown to their successors. (Famous French examples include tragedienne Adrienne Lecouvreur (1692–1730); Mlle Clarion (1723–1803) who revolutionised costume and declamatory technique; Lekain (1729–78) who starred in the neo-classical plays of Voltaire; the romantic theatre's Marie Dorval (1798–1849).[19] By rejecting the prevailing practices, modernist reformers, following Stanislavski, transformed the actor's role and gave it its current form: that of a creator at the heart of the theatre. They called for actors not simply to be interpreters, but to imagine their acting as organic, through a study of the tools of acting, and also through recourse to physical and mental resources that the actor himself would supply. Actors became the indispensable partners of directors, with the responsibility of perfecting their instrument in order to express more powerfully the reality of the stage:

> One of the defining qualities of the actor in contemporary society is that he has established himself as a *creator* on the same level as poets and painters: he is no longer only an interpreter, he is an inventor who creates the forms of a living collaboration.[20]

We must grasp the impact of this profound shift in the actor's role at the end of the nineteenth century in order to better understand not only the role he is called upon to play on the contemporary stage, but also the means he must seek out to fulfil these new functions. Thus, again following Stanislavski's lead, the reformers sought the organic processes that would trigger an actor's inspiration and lead him to surpass himself. Hence the work required of the actor is as much physical as mental.

This is the vision of all the reforms rocking the theatrical world at the beginning of the twentieth century. Their goal was to completely reinvent the actor. He must become an entirely different person, endowed with expertise, but whose technique does not erase his sensitivity. Exercise, dance lessons, gymnastics, fencing, elocution, voice lessons, techniques of muscular relaxation and of concentration all aimed at making the actor the master of his instrument, able to reflect the laws of theatre subsequently pursued with such determination by Mnouchkine and Brook in the last part of the century. Unity with these laws could only be attained at the end of a path of discovery unique to each actor, touching the most profound aspects of his being. This path also includes a thorough knowledge of theatre's place in history.

Knowing one's place in history

The recourse to history that Delcuvellerie, Grotowski, Barba and Vitez invoke in different ways is not necessarily sequential or genealogical, although it can be. It is a memorial history, and as such it opens up our understanding of the possibilities of contemporary training, a crucial component of acting as a profession. Memorial history helps both the researcher and the practitioner to find direction in the present.

For the actor, these learning methods offer a way of entering into past practices, to better absorb them and to discern earlier artists' links to current practices. For researchers, the benefits are similar, providing an aesthetic answer to how current practices are related to past ones. In both cases, the process is cognitive – a matter of better understanding – but for the artist, the trajectory is a double one, with empathy accompanying cognition. This claim can be found in the writings of Peter Brook, and even Grotowski and Barba. For his part, Vitez illustrates a different understanding of history – history as a mode of intervening upon the real, another way of telling the story of the past – as his productions always demonstrated. The staging of his Molières (*Tartuffe*, *Dom Juan* and *Le Misanthrope*) in 1978 proved a major breakthrough in this regard. He was among the first ones in France to deal with great texts in a disrespectful and at the same time very respectful manner, using them as old myths, almost archaic but revealing the present. 'Their relative but real place in History is what I explain to my students and try to teach actors. Whatever we do, wherever the place, their tiniest gesture is located in History.'[21]

New paradigms for considering the training of actors

'Knowing one's place in History' is also Delcuvellerie's goal. Whether or not one believes in the 'grand narratives' whose demise Lyotard proclaimed,[22] whether or not one believes that all history told from a single point of view is necessarily hegemonic, no one would disagree that there was a profound shift in aspirations and attitudes surrounding acting at the beginning of the twentieth century.

The twentieth century saw a paradigmatic and qualitative change that affected the entire field of Western performance. It was the moment of new, emerging performance imperatives, with performance becoming an autonomous field of exploration. Heretofore an intrinsic part of spectacle, tied to the art of actors who refused to reveal their secrets, acting now becomes a matter of training, of development, and of self-perfecting work. Actors become the repositories of this art, charged with keeping it alive and tending its flame. Thus they became not just the indispensable partners of directors, but the pivot of the entire theatrical creation.

Stanislavski was the first to embrace this shift in his Art Theatre. The movement continues today, passed on by a lineage that extends from Meyerhold to Vassiliev and Mnouchkine. The last seeks to provide actors with training that culminates not in a performance, but in the development of the artist – a development subsequently viewed as an art as much as a science.

It is not surprising that this shift is necessarily accompanied by a radical modification in the nature and the function of theatre in society. Theatre has become a way of being – this was already Dullin's, Copeau's and Jouvet's claim – and not only of doing. Theatre has to do with a way of life. As such, it invokes ethical principles that may take priority over aesthetic aims. Now subject to such intense demands, theatre lends itself to a certain asceticism that is 'legitimised' by the actor's vocation. One is initiated into acting's mysteries only by great effort and self-sacrifice, through rigorous work habits that develop the body as well as the spirit.

Paradoxically, the reforms that have left their mark on all current theatre involved a return to the past, whether drawing upon the forms of popular (*commedia dell'arte*, cabaret, circus, music hall, puppetry) or Asian traditions (primarily Japanese theatre). These reforms are rooted in a sense of history that requires us to rethink the theatrical stage from a global perspective, driven by socio-political goals.

These different aspirations (aesthetic, social and event-driven) are linked to a history of mentalities that must be clarified in order to create a true history of acting. Moreover, this history of mentalities is dependent on the progress of knowledge in the period, particularly in two fields that would have a powerful impact on the theatre: the development of science and of society's perception of the body at the end of the nineteenth century.

A history of acting in dialogue with the history of the body

At the end of the nineteenth century, the relationship to the body shifted, with repercussions throughout society. In the early twentieth century, the body's place in all discussion of the arts sheds light on the establishment of theatre laboratories that radically influenced performance practice in subsequent generations, and the last two decades have seen a burgeoning of publications on the history of the body.[23] Following Nietzsche, one of the first to centre philosophical discourse upon the body, current writings emphasise the importance of the body as a mark of our identity. Made visible and accessible by medical technology, the body in which the subject's identity resides is no longer imagined or representational, but entirely real. It is through this real body that representations of the world are possible. The body is the interface between outside and inside, allowing apprehension of the world by means of sensations and perceptions.

The evolution of acting techniques is inextricably linked to this history, as can be seen in the matter of sports. The social importance the body assumed at the end of the nineteenth century was reflected in the public's increasing participation in sports, and echoed in the training actors received in this era (Dalcroze, Copeau, *et al.*), a practice that persists today. Participation in sports was perceived as a sign of health and a means to return to nature and authenticity, as well as a path to personal liberty. The same was true of the theatre. It called for a body freed from its sartorial straitjacket, much like the athlete's body, and placed on a stage – Copeau's 'bare boards' – where the actor's body was valorised.

This privileging of the external body at the beginning of the twentieth century was compounded by the influence of Freud and his idea that emotions and feelings tangibly manifest themselves in and upon the body. This vision of the body as the totality of all our experiences and physical sensations, where our experiences are integrated thanks to associations established over the course of our experiences, conveys a historical understanding of the tradition within which today's theatre is located.

A scientific aspiration

This place accorded the body also reflects scientific aspirations manifested at the end of the nineteenth century and persisting into the early twentieth century. Science was on the rise during this era, and the new sciences (physics, thermodynamics, physiology) played a driving role in the transformation affecting the theatre of the period. Research at this time was centred, amongst other things, upon mechanics. Thus we see the human body likened to a machine that burns resources to produce heat, energy and waste. Doctors and scientists sought to measure the body's performance and to determine when and how it surpassed its apparent limits. The body began to be seen as susceptible to transformation under the effects of exercise. An individual's potential increased. Performance became something that was measurable. There was a slow shift from a biomechanical concept of the body to a bioenergetic one.[24]

This analogy did not confine itself to the external body. According to Vigarello, it extended to the 'motor' – i.e., respiration – the core of the actor's work. Henceforth, 'the criterion is output. Work is viewed on the basis of receipts and expenditures.'[25] We see here a reversal from the cultural to the biological, with the latter taking precedence. This historical view of science's role, rarely invoked in studies of theatre, sheds light on the position of actor training today. We see how these forms of training came to be imposed at a moment when the founders of traditions sought scientific bases for their beliefs.

A contextual and transversal reading

Understanding this scientific approach to the body sheds light on the complex relations between art and science and on the context in which these different reforms took place. Without an understanding of these contextual and lateral connections, our vision of performance today remains truncated, fragmented and imprecise. We cannot understand its meaning outside of this frame. Furthermore, we would not be able to foresee the future development of acting, in its different phases that are to come.

One might argue that this analysis of connections applies exclusively to Western performance history. It is perhaps the only one to have changed so much over the course of the centuries, while other traditions – Asian and African – have tended to remain constant. Even if this criticism were fair, it does not prevent my argument from shedding light on the kind of theatre that has now become the norm. Without a deep understanding of these historical links, it is difficult for actors to grasp their precise place in history, to trace their line of descent, and to recognise patterns of change and variation brought about by culture or aesthetics.

The vision I am presenting here cuts across Western performance practices, independent of local and artistic variations. Should we speak of a hegemonic model that breaks with more fragmented and geographically limited perspectives? I believe so, despite the prevailing view that privileges the diversity of local practices. As I see it, the existence of so many constants in the evolution of Western performance techniques cannot be pure chance. They are responses to changes in mentalities and in the state of knowledge. That these changes are determined by social developments that ascribe a new meaning to the body's capacities is apparent. This, of course, in no way contradicts the fact that other cultures may have a different history and a different relationship to the body.

The role of the researcher is to shed light on this interplay of relationships, influences and determinisms, while stressing the way each individual artist exploits this totality of knowledges and discoveries. The challenge of research is to navigate between individual activity and larger historical forces, to consider the whole when crafting a narrative, and to generalise without imposing rigidity. However, there are always dangers.

While this return to history is essential, as Barba justly notes, we must also prevent the past from becoming 'a wall that protects us and, at the same time, is a prison'. It is important to know how to extract ourselves from our history, and to dissent. Yet no dissent is possible if we do not know what in the past was at stake. As artists acknowledge, performance practices are fuelled by 'dissent from the commonplaces of professional thought and practice', but the issues must be identified, the history and stakes understood. Vitez agrees with Barba that artists must invent their own traditions, but adds in the same breath that in order to do so they must also know the traditions of others.[26]

During a conference in 2000 on the ideas of pedagogues,[27] Peter Brook described how Stanislavski on one hand and Grotowski on the other understood how to push actors to surpass themselves. In their quest for a veritable science of theatre, the duo are linked to others who also set themselves on the quest to surpass: Craig, Meyerhold, Brecht and Artaud. By making such connections and emphasising lineage, Brook not only appeals to a sense of history, but attempts to show that this inscription within history is indispensable to understanding the current state of performance. In his own words: 'What is our relationship to all their magnificent endeavours? Where do they lead us? What can we draw from them? How can we profit from them while knowing that the worst thing is imitation?' He later adds: 'The question is this: how can we give welcome to... all that is traditional, how can we accept the flow that comes down from the past without thereby causing it to run dry?' Brook points to the paradox in the reconciliation attempted by all the great theatre reformers, between the ephemeral nature of theatre and the longevity of traditions that must keep being rediscovered lest they become deadening. He adds that one must know, contemplate, and employ these traditions, using them as sounding boards (as one can feed off the texts of the Greeks or Shakespeare): 'These ancient works remind us that a certain level of quality was attained and can still be attempted. Thus the lesson of the past becomes concrete... If you look to the skies, you learn where to steer.'[28]

NOTES

1 My epigraph is borrowed from Jacques Delcuvellerie, who mentions the necessity for the actor to have such an *'intelligence historique'* in his *Le Jardinier... (...et avec lui la vie d'un homme): le Groupov et la formation de l'acteur* (Liège: Cahiers Groupov no. 2, 1997), p. 22.

2 The École des Annales, founded by Lucien Febvre (1878–1956) and Marc Bloch (1886–1944), dominated French historiography of the twentieth century.

3 Throughout this essay, 'he' is used to mean 'he/she' in accordance with normal French usage.

4 Delcuvellerie, *Le jardinier*, p. 17.

5 *Ibid.*, p. 22. André Bourvil, born André Robert Raimbourg (1917–70) was a French actor and singer best known for his roles in comedy. On screen, his naive and funny characters seemed inspired by his intimate sensitivity. Karl Valentin, born Valentin Ludwig Fey (1882–1948), was a German artist, author and clown. He performed in Munich theatres, juggling and struggling with Bavarian dialect and leaving a heritage of comic and biting texts, films and audio recordings.

6 *Ibid.*, p. 23.

7 E. Barba, 'L'essence du théâtre', in J. Féral (ed.), *Les chemins de l'acteur: former pour jouer* (Montréal: Québec Amérique, 2001), pp. 21–60, p. 31.

8 C. Dullin, *Souvenirs et notes de travail d'un acteur* (Paris: Librairie théâtrale, 1985), p. 3.

9 J. Copeau, in M. H. Dasté and S. Maistre (eds.), *Jacques Copeau / Registres I: Appel* (Paris: Gallimard, 1974), pp. 28, 295.

10 See T. Kantor, 'The Quest for the Other: Space/Memory', in Michal Kobialka (ed. and trans.), *A Journey Through Other Spaces: Essays and Manifestos,1944–1990* (Berkeley: University of California Press, 1993), pp. 311–64.

11 Barba, 'L'essence', pp. 55–6.

12 *Ibid.*, p. 25.

13 M. Fumaroli, 'Grotowski ou le passeur de frontières', in *Alternatives Théâtrales*, 70–1 (2001), 11–18, p. 12.

14 Cited in Barba, 'L'essence', pp. 37–8; 46–8.

15 *Ibid.*, pp. 24, 26, 32.

16 A. Vitez, 'Une entente', in *Théâtre/Public*, 64–5 (1985), 25–8, 26.

17 *Ibid.*, 25.

18 *Ibid.*, 26.

19 The voices of many other such actors are preserved by T. Cole and H. Krich Chinoy in their anthology *Actors on Acting: The Theories, Techniques, and Practices of the World's Great Actors, Told in Their Own Words* (New York: Crown, 1970).

20 J. Duvignaud, *L'acteur* (Paris: L'Archipel, 1993), p. 182.

21 Vitez, 'Une entente', 28.

22 J. F. Lyotard, *La condition postmoderne: rapport sur le savoir* (Montréal: Éditions de Minuit, 1979).

23 Examples include M. Feher, R. Naddaff and N. Tazzi (eds.), *Fragments for a History of the Human Body*, 3 vols. (New York: Urzone, Collection Zone, 1989); D. Le Breton, *Anthropologie du Corps et Modernité*, new edn (Paris: Presses Universitaires de France, 2005); G. Vigarello, A. Corbin and J. J. Courtine (eds.), *Histoire du*

Corps, 3 vols. (Paris: Éditions du Seuil, Collection L'Univers historique, 2005–6); M. Foucault, *Le gouvernement de soi et des autres* (Paris: Gallimard, 2008).

24 Etymologically, biomechanics is the study of mechanical laws and their application to living organisms, especially the human body and its locomotive system. In theatre, the notion is linked to Meyerhold's acting theory relying on a set of very precise exercises which help determine the actions on stage according to rules and steps.

25 G. Vigarello, *Le corps redressé: histoire d'un pouvoir pédagogique* (Paris: Jean-Pierre Delarge, 1978), p. 207.

26 Barba, 'L'essence', pp. 25, 24.

27 Organised by the Académie Expérimentale des Théâtres and the Théâtre l'Odéon in Paris.

28 P. Brook, 'Qualité et artisanat', in *Alternatives Théâtrales*, 70–1 (2001), 6–10, p. 8.

FURTHER READING

Barba, Eugenio, and Nicola Savarese. *A Dictionary of Theatre Anthropology: The Secret Art of the Performer* (London: Routledge, 1991).

Cole, Toby, and Helen Krich Chinoy. *Actors on Acting: The Theories, Techniques, and Practices of the World's Great Actors, Told in their Own Words* (New York: Crown Trade Paperbacks, [1970] 1995).

Copeau, Jacques. *Copeau on the Theatre*, ed. and trans. John Rudlin and Norman H. Paul (London: Routledge, 1990).

Dullin, Charles. *An Actor's Notes*, trans. Donald I. Cairns (New Haven: Yale University Press, 1963). Translated from *Souvenirs et notes de travail d'un acteur* (Paris: Odette Lieutier, 1946).

Feher, Michel, Ramona Naddaff and Nadia Tazi, eds. *Fragments for a History of the Human Body* (Cambridge, MA: MIT Press, 1989).

Hodge, Alison, ed. *Twentieth-Century Actor Training* (London: Routledge, 2000).

Richards, Thomas. *Heart of Practice* (London: Routledge, 2008).

13

ZACHARY DUNBAR

Music theatre and musical theatre

Music theatre is a complex subject. We often find ourselves adrift in trying to conceptualise two interlocking art forms, our task complicated by the need to order and investigate music theatre's rudimentary elements such as song, dance and dramatic text. These simple terms carry unfixed meanings because, throughout history, different traditions and practices have conceived them in various ways. The concept of music theatre covers not only twentieth-century avant-garde theatre, examples being Stravinsky's *The Soldier's Tale*, Philip Glass's minimalist opera *Einstein on the Beach*, and a Meredith Monk piece of movement/vocal theatre, but also a spectrum of commercial work popularly known as 'musical theatre', such as West End and Broadway productions of *Legally Blonde* or *Chicago*. The blurry meaning of music theatre is further complicated by recent scholarly work in nineteenth-century popular theatre, which illustrates the difficulty of distinguishing theatre *with* musical elements from entertainments labelled as music hall. The figure of the actor–musician has always occupied the space between music-making and theatre-making. Such an apparently hybrid performer trained and worked in fifth-century BCE Greek tragedy, in Zeami's fifteenth-century Noh theatre, in Sanskrit and Jingxi theatre, and in a John Doyle staging of a Stephen Sondheim musical.

To write music theatre history is to make sense of its complexity, establishing webs of transmissions and shared genealogies that join the worlds of music and of theatre together. To this end we have to accept the history of music theatre as more than the sum of its musical and theatrical parts; in other words, this history is inherently interdisciplinary. With this is mind, I will identify and describe key historical landmarks and developments in music theatre under the categories of 'hybrid', 'collaborative', and 'totalising'. These three descriptors equate with the three notions of convergence, permeability and integration and offer a means of conceptualising the ways in which disciplines engage. They elucidate processes in music theatre that explode or reformulate boundaries in the arts. To some extent, most if not all works of music theatre possess all three attributes: that is, they are overtly cross-bred with past and contemporaneous styles, idioms and practices (hybrid); they combine music and theatre practices to produce innovations in form and content (collaborative); and they fuse both art forms so that our ways of hearing and seeing are redefined (totalising).

In this chapter, 'music theatre' and 'musical theatre' will be discussed as separate topics, but not because they indicate a clear fork in the road: the genre takes over-layered and often undifferentiated paths. Music theatre as currently defined and taught tends to exclude high opera, which is studied and its traditions imparted within a different sphere of contemporary culture; for this reason, opera sits on the margins rather than at the centre of this account of 'music theatre' within a volume dedicated to theatre history. We need, however, to set out the invention of opera as an interdisciplinary process in order to account for the heredity of music theatre.

Origins and modern formulations

The invention of opera by Renaissance humanists is considered to be the earliest formal attempt in modern European history to combine music and poetry in theatre. The attempt was fuelled by a need to validate the humanist worldview within the trajectory of classical knowledge and practice, a process described by Erika Fischer-Lichte in Chapter 5 and David Wiles in Chapter 4 in this volume. The basis of such an experiment was predicated on a totalising view of the arts in ancient Greek drama, and the main players in the invention of drama-in-music (or what we today call 'opera') were the distinguished poets, musicians and artists of the day, who convened in humanist academies, such as the Florentine Camerata, and were motivated to put theory into practice.

A leading patron of the Camerata from 1573, Count Giovanni Bardi di Vernio, conferred with Vincenzo Galilei, a leading music theorist of the day, who in turn consulted with Girolamo Mei, a classical scholar of Greek music and poetry. After Bardi went to Rome, the musician Jacopo Corsi continued the Camerata's collaborative efforts and worked with Jacopo Peri, an accomplished instrumentalist and singer, who in turn developed dramatic recitative in a tragicomic pastoral by the poet, Ottavio Rinuccini. The result was the first prototype opera, *Dafne* (1598), music theatre that combined music and poetic speech through musical recitatives and arias. The ongoing legacy of early opera in music-theatre manner is exemplified by works where spoken dialogue is interspersed with sung passages, such as Mozart's 1791 *Singspiel* (song-play) opera *The Magic Flute*, and by later works where music and libretto are suffused with elements borrowed from high opera and populist culture, such as George Gershwin's *Porgy and Bess* (1935) or Kurt Weill's *Street Scene* (1947).

The early formation of music theatre is also exemplified by the singing and playing of music within the staging of a classical drama. Such an interdisciplinary experiment was first witnessed in the Republic of Venice: in the city of Vicenza, the Accademia Olimpica, a humanist academy established in 1555, witnessed a musicalised version of Sophocles' *Oedipus Tyrannus* (1585). Staged in accordance with classical principles, the resulting spectacle harmonised the poetic text of Orsatto Giustiniani and the rich homophonic choral writing of Andrea Gabrieli.

These two examples of music theatre from the Italian Renaissance, *Dafne* and *Oedipus*, serve to punctuate an uninterrupted history of engagements between music and theatre: from the ancient Athenian Theatre of Dionysus to Roman pantomime, from medieval Passion plays to Tudor masques, the ideal of unifying poetry and music is found repeatedly. Take, for example, the multimedia spectacle of the 'Queen's Comic Ballet' created for Catherine de' Medici in 1581: Bal de Beaul recalled his hope that this event would manage 'to diversify the music with poetry; to interlace the poetry with music; and most often to intermingle the two, even as the ancients never recited poetry without music and Orpheus played only with verse'.[1]

The close dialogue of music and theatre, foregrounded by the late-nineteenth-century rhetoric of modernism, entered a new phase at the turn of the twentieth century. Conventionally the period between 1890 and 1910 is identified as the beginning of *modern* music theatre, when avant-garde composers and artists tapped into the synergistic impulses associated with the breakdown of conventional boundaries imposed on music and theatre by previous centuries.[2] For instance, Wassily Kandinsky dramatised the synaesthetic correlation of colour and music, Émile Jacques-Dalcroze developed a methodology that reinforced musicality through movement, and Adolphe Appia designed lighting according to the affective principles of music rather than representational scenography.

Inescapable components of the avant-garde were the 'modernist' tendencies associated with radical individualism, a reflexive engagement with the medium, and an anti-authoritarian attitude towards political or cultural institutions. One of the institutions targeted for demolition was nineteenth-century opera. From the interwar neo-classicism of Paris, to the experimental happenings of the 1960s and onwards, modern music theatre sought to deconstruct the conventional *mise-en-scène* of opera, by which I mean its naturalistic story-telling principles, in order to create a more porous relationship between spectator and performer, blur the different significations of theatre and concert hall, and incorporate new techniques for notating and producing sound. A recent definition of music theatre treats music and theatre as coefficients in this process:

Music theatre is theatre that is music driven [. . . A]t the very least, music, language, vocalization, and physical movement exist, interact, or stand side by side in some kind of equality but performed by different performers and in a different social ambiance than works normally categorized as opera (performed by opera singers in opera houses) or musical (performed by theatre singers in 'legitimate' theatres).[3]

Music theatre: hybrid forms

Both Arnold Schoenberg (1874–1951) and Igor Stravinsky (1882–1971) were fascinated by the relationship between composition and the theatre stage. The physical and acoustical properties of voice and character particularly constituted an area of music theatre subject to experimentation. In *The Hand of Fate* (1913), a 'drama with music', Schoenberg orchestrated lighting effects with the music and also used a hybridised kind of speech-singing, or *Sprechstimme*. The impulse to bring musical and theatrical elements together also operates within his seminal composition of the twentieth century, the song cycle *Pierrot lunaire* (1912). Schoenberg appropriated seventeenth- and early eighteenth-century music structures in his composition. At the same time a modern atonal system decentralises harmonic keys, *Sprechstimme* breaks down the hierarchy of speech and song, instrumentalists represent musical dramatis personae, and the gender-bending protagonist, Pierrot, is a male character played by a female performer.

When Stravinsky wrote *Renard* (1916), *The Soldier's Tale* (1918), *The Wedding* (1922) and *Oedipus Rex* (1927), he used distancing techniques such as mime to create a disjunction between the actor's role and the sound or text s/he is meant to enact. In *The Soldier's Tale* particularly, Stravinsky was interested in reorganising the way that text, music and the actor were configured in theatre space. This process influenced especially the new music theatre of the sixties and seventies, which turned the visual and auditory aspects of music-making into a form of theatre performance. Stravinsky was also eclectic in the way that he incorporated past and present music styles: the clear-textured classicism of eighteenth-century French music, the melodiousness of Italian opera and Russian folk elements, and the raucous vitality of popular jazz.

Music theatre: collaborative forms

The boulevard theatre of Jean Cocteau (1889–1963) belonged to the era of interwar neoclassicism, a loosely defined movement that generated eclectic collaborations among the avant-garde artists of Paris. Music theatre underwent a process similar to form and representation in cubist and surreal art.

There was a rejection of the turgid romanticism of Wagnerian music and any form of naturalism in theatre, in favour of crudely juxtaposed genres, pared down and at times commonplace music, and a patchwork of performance styles. In *Parade* (1917), Cocteau presented a set of bizarre scenarios, in which the high jinks style of the circus arts reflected early modernism's irreverence for dogma and high art. The production, given its premiere by the ground-breaking dance troupe, the Ballets Russes, under Serge Diaghilev's direction, was choreographed by Léonide Massine, designed with cubist décor by Picasso, and provided with music by the early minimalist Eric Satie. *Parade* was followed by *The Wedding on the Eiffel Tower* (1921), a riotous pastiche combining Cocteau's text with music by five contemporary composers. For this work Cocteau claimed a ground zero for his collaborative music theatre, mentioning in his preface how

> we see developing in France, little by little, a theatrical genre which is not properly speaking ballet, which has no place in the Opéra, nor at the Opéra-Comique, nor in any of the fashionable theatres. [...] The new generation will continue its experiments in which the fantastic, the dance, acrobatics, mime, drama, satire, music, and the spoken word combine to produce a new form.[4]

During the 1920s and 1930s in America, we witness in the Harlem Renaissance a similar cultural awakening, a response to the continuous oppression of blacks and a rejection of racism and stereotypes in nineteenth-century popular entertainment such as minstrelsy. Among the New York City milieu of emerging literary artists, musicians and painters, the multitalented Langston Hughes (1902–67) used new jazz poetry, traditional spirituals, and a gospel church choir in his socially motivated music dramas, such as *Don't You Want to Be Free?* (1938).

Music theatre: totalising forms

The nineteenth-century aesthetic ideal of *Gesamtkunstwerk* (the 'total art-work') was expounded by the composer and music theorist Richard Wagner (1813–83) and provides the twentieth century with a reference point for the formal synthetic vision of the arts. Wagner characterised it as a complete immersion of music and drama in a theatre space. Like the Renaissance humanists, Wagner was interested in the way Greek tragedy expressed a unity of myth (drama) and the arts (music).

In the early part of the twentieth century, the notion of totality was shaped by institutions such as the Bauhaus school, founded in 1919 by Walter Gropius at Weimar. By fostering an all-encompassing view of the various arts, including architecture, the institution inspired artists of the day to find new ways to organise and amalgamate elements such as form, space, movement and light. At the same time, an anti-art sentiment led by the Dadaists celebrated 'total' chaos and purposeful ambiguity in the making of art. After the Second World War, aesthetic notions of holism and disorder were channelled in the musical works of two composers, Karlheinz Stockhausen (1928–2007) and John Cage (1912–92), who each explored determinacy (predictability) and indeterminacy (chance).

In America, Cage focused on the sensation of chance by manipulating conventional structures, methods and materials of music. Nowhere was 'chance' more celebrated than in a landmark piece of music called 4'33″ (1952). The score instructs a pianist *not* to play the piano over the time period of exactly four minutes and thirty-three seconds. By 'silencing' formally composed music, Cage re-sensitised the human listener instead to the musicality of noise, which randomly occurs in the performance space, and also challenged preconceived ways in which we listen to music and see images in relation to it.

In the same year, a totalising mixed-media 'Happening', *Untitled Event*, took place at Black Mountain College in North Carolina, an art school founded on the principles of American liberal arts studies. Cage laid out a geometrically configured space that merged performers and the audience. Cage, while on a ladder, gave a lecture on the relationship of music to Zen Buddhism, his co-creator David Tudor played a piece for prepared piano, choreographer Merce Cunningham danced, and Robert Rauschenberg's *White Paintings* were displayed alongside slide-and-film projections. Although Cage bracketed the participants' performances in more or less discrete time-frames, the net effect of randomised images, sounds and performances was to liberate the sense of hearing and seeing from preconceived modes of reception.

Stockhausen's experiment in serialism generated a compositional process that induced in the listener a holistic sense of musical order and structure, and in seminal works such as *Song of the Youths* (1956) and *Groups for Three Orchestras* (1957) he erased differentiations of sound that divided individual parts from the whole. A few years later Stockhausen extended the principles of holism and indeterminacy in a piece of music theatre entitled *Originale* (1961). The score-script requires a motley collection of performers, from a poet and painter to a newspaper vendor, each of whom has a precise time structure within which to perform actions and music, but Stockhausen randomly varied these directions and their duration during the performance.

Music theatre today encompasses a wide range of experimentations that not only develop the seminal work of Cage and Stockhausen but also apply musical processes, materials and aesthetics as part of music theatre-making:

crosshatching the sonic nature of speech and the human voice (new vocal theatre), probing the function of musical instruments and of musical actions in concert performance (instrumental theatre), infusing multimedia elements (or intermedial theatre), and re-inscribing the composer as theatre-maker (composed theatre). Leading makers of totalising music theatre include Fluxus Happenings, Luigi Nono, Josef Anton Riedl, Dieter Schnebel, Manos Tsangaris, Mauricio Kagel, Heiner Goebbels, Christoph Marthaler, Philip Glass, Pierre Boulez, Robert Wilson and Meredith Monk.

Musical theatre

The twentieth-century commercial American musical, alongside its British counterpart, has been such an influential form throughout the world that it merits a separate discussion. As a subspecies of music theatre, musicals may be differentiated by the degree to which a show absorbs and reconfigures past and present styles and forms. For instance, *In Dahomey* (1903), the successful early African-American Broadway musical, evidenced the influence of nineteenth-century vaudeville, comic opera, and minstrelsy, as well as relatively modern ragtime.[5] One hundred years later, choral oratorio singing can be heard alongside the raucous strains of ballad opera and burlesque in a show such as Stewart Lee and Richard Thomas's *Jerry Springer, The Opera* (2003).

As the complex sum of its parts, musical theatre is defined on the basis of its integrated-ness: that is, the degree and frequency with which song flows from dialogue, or music combines with story-telling plots. Historians trace an increasing co-operation in the working relations of song, dance, and plot in emerging forms. For instance, eighteenth- and nineteenth-century ballad operas and operettas positioned song at the forefront of musicalised dramas. In nineteenth-century melodramas, music increasingly conveyed dramatic meaning: for instance, a trembling diminished chord might shadow a villainous character in a play, jaunty rhythms signify buffoonery, and plangent strings underscore romantic scenes. The advent of the Hollywood cinema industry reinforced for a growing movie-going public the power of music to underscore action and to enhance the drama.

We may place the history of musicals onto overlapping spectrums: from the structured story-telling drama, to shows formed into a whole by a unifying theme or style. Musical comedies such as *Very Good Eddie* (1915), *Oh, Boy!* (1917), and *Oh, Lady! Lady!!* (1918), produced at Broadway's Princess Theatre, may be construed as prototypes of the integrated form of American musical because of the way songs are made to interrelate with plot. During the mid- to late-1900s an increasing drive toward a unity between storyline, song and dance succeeded mainly where a musical was based on a pre-existing work of literature or a film, such as Jerome Kern and Oscar Hammerstein II's *Show Boat* (1927), Richard Rodgers and Hammerstein II's *Oklahoma!* (1943), Jule Styne and Stephen Sondheim's *Gypsy* (1959), and the Disney corporation's *The Lion King* (1997; film 1994). The seamless integration of dance, song and drama in *West Side Story* (1957) is often considered paradigmatic of the integrated musical. Although integrated-ness implies a unity between the structure and function of music and drama, disjunctive and distancing devices often come into play: the use of a narrator or chorus stepping out of dramatic time, meta-theatrical lyrics or dance sequences may eliminate the otherwise invisible coherence of a show.[6]

The cobbled format of nineteenth-century music hall, burlesque, vaudeville and revue influenced a kind of twentieth-century musical in which the constituent elements of the show amalgamate around a loose story or theme. Ira and George Gershwin's Pulitzer Prize-winning *Of Thee I Sing* (1931), with book by George S. Kaufman and Morrie Ryskind, is in essence a political revue. Kurt Weill, Ira Gershwin and Moss Hart's *Lady in the Dark* (1941) juxtaposes largely dialogue-filled scenes and musical dreamscapes to evoke its psychoanalytical theme. Stephen Sondheim's dystopian view of love and marriage in *Company* (1970), Michael Bennett's dance-based musical *A Chorus Line* (1975), Richard Maltby and David Shire's 'bookless' revue *Closer Than Ever* (1989), and works that sit between song-cycle and musical theatre, such as Bill Russell's *Elegies for Angels, Punks and Raging Queens* (1989), Jason Robert Brown's *Songs for a New World* (1995), and William Finn's *Elegies* (2003), all inherited a legacy that blended variety acts, singing and story-telling.

Musical theatre: hybrid musicals

John Gay's ballad opera, *The Beggar's Opera* (1728), the operettas of Arthur Sullivan and William S. Gilbert in the Victorian era, and two twentieth-century political musicals will serve as my examples of hybrid musicals.

The invention of the ballad opera resulted from a conscious lampooning of 'serious' eighteenth-century Italian opera. *Opera seria* was known for its plot-interrupting aria, which purposefully called attention to itself with its fiendishly difficult vocal writing, a staple for the celebrated castrati and virtuoso female singers and for the bourgeoisie who came to hear them. In the innovative ballad operas, the popular 'ballad' song became a central element, but, unlike the elaborate arias of *opera seria*, these ballad songs, often from popular sources, used short stanzas and simple tuneful refrains, with new words sometimes inserted into popular songs to suit the satirical flavour of the story. Despite its subversive nature, the ballad opera catered to the tastes of the London upper middle class that mingled with aristocrats, keeping its lowbrow tone suitably inlaid with highbrow wit and sharp local commentary.

Like the hybrid ballad opera, nineteenth-century musical burlesques featured songs that absorbed tunes from well-known operas or popular ditties, and operetta in turn absorbed the world of burlesque. In the operettas of Jacques Offenbach (1819–80), the thematic content owed much to a playful grotesquery of political life, while the music drew on the sophisticated Italian bel canto style of singing (characterised by smooth phrasing, clarity and a sweetness of sound) and upon the well-known tunes of early nineteenth-century Italian composers such as Bellini, Donizetti and Rossini. The operettas by Gilbert (librettist) and Sullivan (composer) followed the lead of ballad opera by making fun of the ennobled themes celebrated in *opera seria*. In shows like *H. M. S. Pinafore* (1878) and *The Pirates of Penzance* (1879), the parodic mode, similar to that of popularly attended burlesques, subverted classical learning and middle-class habits, while relishing savvy political asides and social commentary. In America, *Pinafore* influenced the development of the form and content of American musical theatre not least because the operetta was widely burlesqued and spoofed before its first official performance in New York in 1879. The European model of operetta, which included the genteel Viennese style represented by Franz Lehár (1870–1948), influenced the American operettas of Victor Herbert (1859–1924) and Sigmund Romberg (1887–1951) and the formation of light-hearted American musical comedy at the start of the twentieth century.

The hybrid musical also gave theatrical voice to expressions of the twentieth century's politically turbulent histories. In *The Threepenny Opera* (1928), inspired by Gay's *The Beggar's Opera*, Bertolt Brecht and Kurt Weill eschewed the melodramatic theatre of the German bourgeoisie, but unlike Gilbert and Sullivan, they fostered a political ideology that gave voice to the struggle of the working class and promulgated a functionalist view of the arts. As a composer, Weill was influenced both by cabaret and the modernising style of the composer Ferruccio Busoni (1866–1924). His music, as in *The Threepenny Opera*, intentionally blurs high and low art by mixing jazz, ragtime and contemporary harmonies. In 1963, *Oh What a Lovely War*, developed by Joan Littlewood's ensemble-based Theatre Workshop and rooted in the politically charged theatre of Brecht, established a sense of identity with its audience by using popular music-hall style songs (specifically parodies of songs and hymns from the First World War) and fostered a collectivist style of theatre through its collaborative-devised methods. This hybrid musical, according to historian Derek Paget, was a 'Trojan horse through which anti-naturalistic, political theatre gained a significant foothold in Britain',[7] though Unity Theatre's political pantomime *Babes in the Wood*

(1938) could be claimed as the true precursor of politically-motivated hybrid music theatre.

Musical theatre: collaborative musicals

During the early 1900s, song- and book-writers such as Ira and George Gershwin, Cole Porter, Irving Berlin, Jerome Kern and Guy Bolton, alongside their British counterparts including Noel Coward, Ivor Novello and P. G. Wodehouse, used the song as a vehicle for story-telling. Innovation seems to have been a by-product of mass production as musical theatre songwriting grew alongside the music-publishing culture of New York's Tin Pan Alley – a conveyor-belt song culture that flourished from about 1885 to the 1930s. The growth industry of Broadway productions included Florenz Ziegfield's *Follies*, which featured a new revue every year from 1907 to 1931.

The classical paradigm of the 'integrated' book-based musical is represented by the output of Richard Rodgers and Oscar Hammerstein during what is considered the golden era of Broadway musicals in the 1940s and 1950s. *Oklahoma!* (1943) stands out as a landmark work that fulfils the principles of an integrated 'book' musical because of the way dancing, acting, and singing are interwoven and connected to a storyline, itself constructed from a stage play by Lynn Riggs called *Green Grow the Lilacs*. The long afterlife of this work can be attributed to a successful collaborative partnership that included Agnes de Mille's individualised choreography, Rodgers's dramatically expressive music, and Hammerstein's memorable lyrics.

Stephen Sondheim, building on the legacy of Hammerstein's book-writing and craftsmanship as a lyricist, is primarily responsible for the development of contemporary American musical theatre in the latter half of the twentieth century. Through his collaborations with experienced figures in the Broadway industry such as producer Harold Prince and writers such as Arthur Laurents and James Lapine, Sondheim privileged dramaturgical rigour and stagecraft over purely populist entertainment. Moreover, he transformed the genre by experimenting with non-linear story-telling devices that are often shaped by a concept or theme. The resulting innovations in song writing, scenography and book are exemplified in shows such as *Company* (1970), *Follies* (1971), *A Little Night Music* (1973), *Pacific Overtures* (1976), *Sweeney Todd* (1979) and *Sunday in the Park with George* (1984).

Musical theatre: totalising musicals

Totalising aspects of musical theatre focus our attention once more on the *Gesamtkunstwerk* principle and the exceptional degree to which song, dance and drama may be perceived as interconnected processes. We might discern this 'exceptionality' in two areas: the multifaceted creativity of practitioners involved in the making of a musical, and the manner in which a show aspires to 'spectacle', an experience that results from an aggregating sum (or overkill, as some might argue) of visual and auditory elements.

The Broadway musical *West Side Story* involved an exceptional integration of the arts. The dramatic story, a modern 1950s gangland version of Shakespeare's *Romeo and Juliet* set in New York, seems to be conveyed equally through text, dance, music and song. It is unsurprising that the creative team included Stephen Sondheim (lyricist, but elsewhere a composer), Leonard Bernstein (composer, but also a conductor/educator), Jerome Robbins (choreographer, but elsewhere a director), and Arthur Laurents (librettist, but elsewhere a playwright). Bernstein in particular, like his musical theatre predecessors George Gershwin and Frank Loesser, knew how to cross the boundaries of theatre- and music-making. While following the principles of commercial musical theatre, Bernstein was able to 'vernacularise' classical styles and contemporary compositional techniques.

The something-for-everyone spectacle with simple stories, an ideal sought by present-day blockbuster musicals, has its roots in the late nineteenth century. Henry C. Jarrett and Harry Palmer's *The Black Crook* (1866) was a five-hour long extravaganza that featured elements of melodrama, German romantic fantasy, French-style balletic chorus, spectacular scenery, a large cast, and music by several composers that represented popular styles of the day. The show was performed in the 3,200-seat Niblo's Garden on Broadway for a record number of performances. During the American Depression, such extravagance was toned down in Broadway stage productions but was recreated through the magic of film, especially those by the choreographer–director Busby Berkeley (1895–1976).

Spectacle remains a characteristic of today's musical blockbusters, or so-called 'megamusicals'. In tune with 1980s monetarism in the UK and the corporate culture of the Disney industry, Andrew Lloyd-Webber's The Really Useful Theatre Company and producer Cameron Macintosh deployed aggressive global merchandising to create the new brand of musical, in a commodifying process often nicknamed the McDonaldisation of theatre. According to the theatre historian Dan Rebellato, McDonaldised musicals guarantee worldwide a standardization of expectation, an 'imitation of the metropolitan original' (complete with 'spectacle'), and a reduction of the workers' control over their conditions of work.[8] Such musicals at the time of writing in 2011 include *Mamma Mia!*, *The Phantom of the Opera*, *Les Misérables* and *The Lion King*. Like their forebears in the late 1900s, the essential qualities of commercial musical theatre – direct and instant gratification, simple stories, catchy tunes and immediate connection with popular culture – are ingrained in the creation of megamusicals.

Global perspectives

Intercultural research, ethnomusicology fieldwork, and voice and movement studies raise questions about prevailing historical discourses built around the terms 'music' and 'theatre'. Musicalised media-supported performance events, such as MTV productions, reality-television dramas such as *X Factor* and *Pop Idol*, on-line flash-mob productions (http://improveverywhere.com), and karaoke performance, encompass ever-expanding subgenres and therefore new emerging music theatre histories. This *Cambridge Companion to Theatre History* addresses the problem of global inclusivity, something that my structuring of the field, rooted as it is in an Anglo-American and European sphere of theatre history, should at least broach.

Given the way music theatre and musical theatre developed as a result of cross-breeding between 'high' operatic shows and 'low' popular music theatre, we might want to ask similar questions as to whether contemporary forms, such as in Asian dance theatre, evidence infusions of 'elite', 'folk' and 'urban' theatre practices and styles.[9] In a more specific example, contemporary musical theatre in the Philippines may be understood as a by-product of American and Spanish colonialism, which accounts for hybrid forms such as *Komedya*, influenced by the Spanish *Zarzuela*, and *Bodabil*, which derives from American-style vaudeville.[10]

From whatever centres our historical traditions stem, one might consider music theatre, both in the past and in the present, as a continuously emergent form of theatre, with degrees of resistance to, and tolerances of, transmissions between 'high' and 'low' forms of art. Contributing to the frequency and intensity of exchange are any number of interwoven socio-political and aesthetic conditions, as well as the narrative of production relations. The word 'transmission' deserves interrogation, yielding too easily the impression of universality and suggesting that music enjoys a unique permeability and adaptability through all cultures. Exploring the history of music theatre nevertheless forces one to engage with an apparent universality in the cross-over between music-making and theatre-making, as well as with the ways in which such cross-overs adapt themselves to global and local settings.

NOTES

1 S. J. Cohen (ed.), *Dance as Theatre Art: Source Readings in Dance History from 1851 to the Present* (London: Dance Books, 1974), p. 19.

2 Previous to this period, 'music theatre' is not part of the academic discourse applied to performance events, but historians might choose to challenge this boundary, pointing, for example, to the late eighteenth- and early nineteenth-century *Musiktheater* of Goethe's Weimar period.

3 E. Salzman and T. Desi, *The New Music Theater: Seeing the Voice, Hearing the Body* (New York and Oxford: Oxford University Press, 2008), p. 5.

4 M. Benedikt and G. E. Wellwarth (eds. and trans.), *Modern French Theatre* (New York: Dutton, 1966), p. 98.

5 T. Postlewait 'The Hieroglyphic Stage: American Theatre and Society, Post-Civil War to 1945', in D. Wilmeth and C. Bigsby (eds.), *The Cambridge History of American Theatre*, Vol. II: *1870–1945* (Cambridge: Cambridge University Press, 1999), pp. 107–95.

6 M. Taylor, 'Integration and Distance in Musical Theatre: The Case of Sweeney Todd', in *Contemporary Theatre Review*, 19:1 (2009), 74–86.

7 D. Paget, 'Case Study: Theatre Workshop's *Oh What a Lovely War, 1963*', in Baz Kershaw (ed.), *The Cambridge History of British Theatre*, Vol. III: *Since 1895* (Cambridge: Cambridge University Press, 2004), pp. 397–411, p. 399.

8 D. Rebellato, *Theatre & Globalization* (London: Palgrave Macmillan, 2009), pp. 40–6.

9 J. R. Brandon (ed.), *The Cambridge Guide to Asian Theatre* (Cambridge: Cambridge University Press, 1993), pp. 2–3.

10 *Ibid.*, pp. 214–21.

FURTHER READING

Bradby, David, Maria Delgado, and Henry Little, eds. *Adventures in Music Theatre.* Special issue of *Contemporary Theatre Review*, 14.1 (2004).

Brown, Peter, and Suzana Ograjenšek, eds. *Ancient Drama in Music for the Modern Stage* (Oxford: Oxford University Press, 2010).

Everett, William A., and Paul R. Laird, eds. *The Cambridge Companion to the Musical*, 2nd edn (Cambridge: Cambridge University Press, 2008).

Hischak, Thomas S., ed. *The Oxford Companion to the American Musical: Theatre, Film, and Television* (Oxford: Oxford University Press, 2008).

Rebstock, Matthias, and David Roesner, eds. *Composed Theatre: Aesthetics, Practices, Processes* (Bristol: Intellect Ltd, 2012).

Studies in Musical Theatre, 1– (2007–).

Symonds, Dominic, and Dan Rebellato, eds. *The Broadway Musical: New Approaches.* Special issue of *Contemporary Theatre Review*, 19.1 (2009).

14

MARIUS KWINT

Circus

The circus might not at first glance appear to have much to do with either theatre or history. It mainly shows actual physical feats, not theatrical make-believe, story-telling or play-acting. It seems to inhabit a time of its own, separate from the course of events, ever the stuff of family outings and child-hood nostalgia. Hasn't the circus always been there? Even in the wake of the animal-free New Circus movement of the 1990s, and the advent of stylishly choreographed and expensive metropolitan shows such as the Montreal-based Cirque du Soleil, the great majority of the world's circuses still peddle candy-floss and clowns, parping horns and miniature bikes, and sometimes sorry menageries. Nell Stroud, writer, performer and director of the success-ful neo-Edwardian-style Gifford's Circus in England (see Fig. 19), has authored a children's book on circus history, but assures me that, for the most part, circus people are not very interested in the subject.[1] An honours degree in Circus Studies has for some years now been offered by Circus Space in London, but students receive only one lecture on circus history, with the theoretical emphasis firmly on the critical analysis of performance. By con-trast, in art schools, the history of art and design has long been a mainstay of the classroom and indeed serves as the benchmark for progress and moder-nisation in these fields. It is my view that most circuses fail to engage in a conscious dialogue with their own past and so risk becoming slaves to a dwindling repertoire of hackneyed traditions. Attempting to rectify this situa-tion, the journalist Tony Montague is, at the time of writing, currently work-ing on a production for another Canadian company that draws upon key episodes of early circus in North America, but feels that this is quite a solitary and pioneering task.

So why bother? What can circus history do for the circus? More impor-tantly, I want to ask, what should the place of circus history be within a history of the theatre? For the performer or producer of circus or of theatre, as for any creative arts practitioner, the past offers an inexhaustible supply of refreshing source-material to inform and inspire contemporary practice.

19 Gifford's Circus's 2011 rendition of Tolstoy's epic novel *War and Peace*, reviving the nineteenth-century Romantic circus tradition of swashbuckling narratives performed on horseback, or 'hippodramas'.

For those with a more theoretical interest in the nature of performance, the very existence of circus as not-quite-theatre, not-quite-sport reveals the processes of refinement, exclusion and contestation by which particular genres came to be elaborated and legitimised as institutions, each with their associated buildings, organisations and practices. For the field of cultural studies, the circus offers some insights into the construction and refraction of class hierarchies, and the representation of race, ethnicity and sexuality, through mass cultural forms. And for those in search of stories, the circus boasts plenty of derring-do and picaresque characters, as might be expected of a business that pushed the boundaries not only of physical possibility, but also of the law, respectability and economic viability.

Early patterns in circus history

The modern circus is, in essence, the theatre of various physical feats and marvels, usually taking place in a ring approximately 13 metres (42 feet) in diameter. It is, in this form, an invention of the late eighteenth century and is not a direct descendant of the Roman circus, although in some respects it bears comparison with its ancient forebear. The most famous of these was the

Circus Maximus in Rome, a huge stadium accommodating some 150,000 spectators around a track in an elongated oval measuring 621 metres long by 118 metres in diameter. This stadium served as a model for the building of circuses throughout the empire and remains in impressive ruins to this day. From the sixth century BCE it was the principal site of games including chariot and horse-racing, athletics and, before the completion of the Colosseum in 80 CE, it was also used for gladiatorial combats and ritual hunts of exotic wild animals. Most of these games were sponsored by local worthies keen to curry favour with both the gods, for whom several shrines were built around the circus, and the populace. Roland Auguet has argued that its fundamental logic was to demonstrate the politico-cosmic order by testing the limits of its governing categories (the distinction between slave and citizen, human and animal, etc.).[2] The circus became synonymous with the calculated distraction of the plebs, whence the catchphrase 'bread and circuses'.

Circus legend and circus scholars alike attribute its modern re-invention to Philip Astley (1742–1814), a handsome former sergeant-major in the light dragoons, with a distinguished service record from the Seven Years' War.[3] Accompanied by his wife Patty, his infant son John, a fine white charger that his commander gave him upon demobilisation, and a nag called Billy that he picked up for five pounds at Smithfield, he first set up a ring for his displays of trick riding supplemented with acrobatics, tumbling and clowning, in a field near the present site of London's Waterloo Station in 1768. Trick riding, pioneered in the previous decade by the Irish groom Thomas Johnston, had proved fashionable in pleasure-gardens, fairgrounds and race-courses around London, often performed by riding-instructors as a means of advertising their more bread-and-butter teaching work. Their routines would include standing astride up to three trotting horses, doing headstands on a pint pot balanced on the saddle, dancing on horseback, picking up handkerchiefs from the ground at a canter and shooting pistols with military flourish. Styling himself 'The English Hussar', and referring to the celebrated general John Manners, Marquess of Granby, Astley, in one of his early routines, had Billy the horse lying down motionless while he bellowed

> My horse lies dead, apparent at your sight,
> But I'm the man can set this thing to right ...
> But first pray give me leave to move his foot
> That he is dead, is quite beyond dispute ...
> This shows how brutes by heaven were design'd
> To be in full subjection to mankind,
> Rise, young Bill, & be a little Handy
> To serve that warlike Hero, Granby.[4]

In a time when the horse was a commonplace but widely appreciated animal, such acts showed that men and a few women of modest backgrounds could shine and even make their fortune in the elitist world of equestrian pursuits. Astley became something of a celebrity, and he was soon reported to be making the astronomical sum of 40 guineas a day from his shows, which attracted, as his advertisements on the front of *The Times* newspaper boasted, the 'Nobility and Gentry', as well as many more ordinary Londoners and tourists who could afford the basic sixpence for standing-room.

Though a talented horseman, Astley was more of an impresario and famous curmudgeon than an innovator, and, as is so often the case with accredited inventions, the trend for trick riding was well under way before Astley established it in a commercially enduring and metropolitan form. By 1768, competing riding masters, including the dashing cosmopolites Mr and Mrs Charles Hughes and, more locally, Mr and Mrs Wolton at the Dog and Duck pub, had already begun to mix some traditional popular entertainments into their show, partly to provide a break from their exhausting routines – and indeed Astley himself had to contend with an old war-wound in his leg. Astley and his wife Patty were nevertheless the first to introduce clowning, re-enacting the recent urban myth of a foppish London tailor who attempted to ride to Brentford to vote for the radical upstart John Wilkes and ended up being chased home by his horse. Political narratives, of a distinctly reactionary kind, were in at the start.

Astley's so-called 'Riding School' (Fig. 20) flourished to attract a socially diverse audience, some influential patrons, and intense competition, most notably in the form of the more innovative and luxurious Royal Circus, founded nearby in 1782. This, the project of Charles Dibdin, an unemployed actor from Covent Garden Theatre, coined a distinctive name for the genre but also turned it into a hybrid of theatre by introducing a mixed programme of pantomimes on stage and feats in the ring. By the late 1780s, Astley had toured much of the British Isles and continental Europe and had established a permanent covered 'Amphitheatre' at the foot of Westminster Bridge, a second base in the Rue Faubourg du Temple in Paris, and another in Dublin. The Paris Amphitheatre, which had been built on land reportedly donated by a fashionably Anglophile Queen Marie-Antoinette, was confiscated during the Revolution but later passed into the hands of Antonio Franconi, who set up a comparably dominant circus dynasty in France. Thereafter the idea of the circus spread rapidly across the globe, often thanks to the enterprising travels of the leading English 'riding masters'. It took firm root in the United States in the 1790s; there, in the conditions of the frontier, it developed powerful marketing and touring techniques, among them the big top tent, with which the first visiting American company, Richard Sands' Circus, returned triumphantly to Europe in 1842.

20 Astley's Amphitheatre in 1777. Circuses developed from performances of trick riding outdoors or in riding school arenas in the late 1750s and 1760s. The image stresses the civilised nature of the amusement and the commodious seating available, segregated according to price. The elements of the ringmaster, clown and equestrian performer are present.

British circuses, including many small companies of less than a dozen staff, continued in their own idiosyncratic, melodramatic style, adapting themselves to existing entertainment infrastructures, as well as setting up temporary wooden buildings or more permanent quarters in regional towns and cities. They perpetuated a branch of 'illegitimate' theatre (a term to which I shall return) where physical feats were presented within robust narratives frequently derived from current news, folklore or classical mythology. Astley's Amphitheatre retained its name after the family had died out, continued its off-season tours to the provinces, and survived under several famous managers, including the great equestrian Andrew Ducrow (Fig. 20), to become a fountainhead of popular Romanticism. 'We saw Lord Byron's story of Mazeppa acted for the 104th time', recorded the 18-year-old Mary Nichols, daughter of a successful publisher, in her diary in 1827, after one of her family's biannual trips to Astley's.[5] *Mazeppa* was Astley's most famous hippodrama, based upon Byron's stirring poem whose eponymous hero was sentenced to be stripped and bound to the back of a wild horse ('Who looked as though the speed of thought / Were in his limbs') and sent galloping off across the steppe to his presumed death. Nichols's description of the event was clearly informed by the playbill for that week, announcing the '104th Night of Mazeppa' in fat red type around a lurid picture of Mazeppa and his

21 Early hybrid circus performances took up to five hours and had three parts: hippodrama using both stage and ring, scenes in the circle, and pantomime. It was customary to admit audiences for half price after the initial hippodrama had taken place; holders of those tickets would first assemble on the stage for the 'scenes in the circle', and move into the ring to watch the final pantomime on stage.

unbroken steed being pursued by wolves.[6] Then as now, circus playbills and posters, with their exuberant, eclectic typography and bold images produced using the latest printing techniques, conveyed much of the bold, graphic and tableau-like visual appeal of the genre.[7]

The circus had quickly prospered to become one of the chief entertainment forms of the industrial era, but in England this took place in the teeth of repeated opposition both from jealous managers of rival attractions and also the forces of law and order. Numerous historians[8] have debated the apparent alienation of the ruling classes from 'popular culture' during the early modern period, and their attempts to discipline the behaviour of the workers. The circus proved a difficult thing to tackle with existing laws partly because of its cross-class appeal, and partly because of its hybrid form which combined theatre with equestrian sport. These aspects made it difficult to capture with laws that were designed either to censor an articulate drama on the one hand, or to suppress disorderly proletarian amusements on the other. Moreover, the early circus proprietors, Astley among them, proved exceptionally wily and resourceful characters, well capable of marshalling public opinion to their cause and of exploiting legal loopholes. In one infamous instance whilst in Paris in 1786, John Astley, Philip Astley's raffish and brilliant son, invented a

Par Permission du ROI, & de Monseigneur le Lieutenant-Général de Police.

EXERCICES

SURPRENANS

DES SIEURS

ASTLEY,

RUE ET FAUXBOURG DU TEMPLE,

Aujuourd'hui MERCREDI 27 Décembre 1786.

[*To face p.* 44.

22 The '*pont equestre*' (equestrian bridge) for tumblers was a ruse designed by Philip Astley's son John to circumvent the strict terms of his licence in the city of Paris, which only permitted his company to perform on horseback, not on stage.

horse-borne stage so that acrobats could perform while complying strictly with the terms of their licence that permitted them only to present displays on horseback (Fig. 22). In order to understand such strategies and ruses, and their longer-term artistic effects, it is first necessary to consider the legal predicament in which circus managers found themselves.

Legislation on the performing arts was prompted by fears about the general crime and disorder associated with crowds, and the seditious, heretical or immoral material to which they might be exposed. Both England and France operated a hierarchical distinction between spoken drama and mimed or musical genres. This distinction was not formalised in England until 1662, when the restored monarch Charles II granted exclusive patents for the performance of stage plays to the managers of two theatres in what is today the West End. As with most apparatuses of suppression and censorship, a constant stream of imaginatively shifting genres would always find ways to evade the letter of the law. There persisted, in the suburbs of London especially, many forms of commercial entertainment that enjoyed a strong theatrical element, but studiously avoided uttering the spoken word on stage. These included burlesque operas based on currently fashionable plays and topical issues, known as 'burlettas', as well as pantomimes and puppet shows, most of which could be seen at fairground booths.

A trio of statutes governing commercial entertainment – the notorious Theatre Licensing Act of 1737, the Vagrancy Act and the Disorderly Houses Acts – would provide a legal maze for circus practitioners once they began to establish their own premises with such traditional elements as clowns and acrobats. Circus men and women had little time for the law, its officers, or the jealously guarded monopoly of the 'legitimate' theatres across the river in Westminster. Astley himself, for example, successfully pleaded that horsemanship did not constitute an 'Entertainment of the Stage' and that as local householders, neither he nor his performers could be considered vagabonds. He also bribed the witnesses at his trial and threatened to sue the magistrates for abuse of process. Thanks to their commercial potency, shrewd dealings and cultivation of respectable friends, circus proprietors were to help undermine and reform this hastily constructed and leaky raft of theatrical laws, with considerable effects on the nature and politics of British theatrical culture in the nineteenth century.

A climax was reached in 1782 when the petulant dramatist and songwriter Charles Dibdin opened the Royal Circus with the backing of a group of sporting financiers. Dibdin's plan was to build a venue for his highminded patriotic extravaganzas and musical pantomimes, which would be made commercially viable by the interspersing of displays of horsemanship, for which he personally held little regard. The Royal Circus was to operate under the guise of a theatrical academy for juveniles, which would nevertheless attract an audience paying premium prices. With a splendid neoclassical building and sumptuous auditorium boasting a proscenium stage next to the ring, it looked altogether too much like a regular theatre for the patent theatre managers in Westminster to bear (see Fig. 23). They rallied the immediate opposition of local informers and magistrates alike when it opened, without any kind of licence, in 1782. After some considerable

23 The circus hordes rout the muses of art, poetry and drama and trample Shakespeare's and Pope's works. The cartoon was probably commissioned by jealous West End theatre managers. The human and animal performers are caricatures of actual acts appearing at either Astley's or the Royal Circus, including John Astley on horseback.

skulduggery and the closure of both houses, one of the more irregular justices forced a settlement after a celebrated trial. Licences were issued on condition that the circuses did not infringe the season of the legitimate theatres and ceased to utter the spoken word on stage. The two circuses had now been brought into the legal fold and would henceforth be regulated, rather than suppressed.

Astley's went on to further triumphs and disasters, including twice burning down, and with various alterations to its structure was managed by the successful dramatist Dion Boucicault among others, before being finally demolished in 1893 as the taste for equestrian theatre gave way to musical halls and cinemas. Circus was by then well established as a travelling genre, however, and became perhaps the pre-eminent mass entertainment of the twentieth century, next to cinema and football. Big tenting companies in the UK such as Bertram Mills and Billy Smart's were modelled on late nineteenth-century American predecessors such as Ringling, Barnum and Bailey's, not to mention the various Wild West Shows that toured the eastern United States and Europe, thrilling audiences with exaggerated representations of the American colonial frontier and propagating the racist myth of 'Cowboys and Indians' well before Hollywood stepped in. In continental Europe, a large number of smaller touring companies were supported throughout the twentieth century and into the twenty-first. In the more rural context of much of mainland Europe, popular revulsion at the exploitation of captive animals may not have been as pronounced as it was in the UK, where Parliament enacted anti-cruelty legislation as early as the 1820s, motivated chiefly by bourgeois sympathy for the plight of working horses. Accusations of cruelty towards animals and sometimes humans have remained a sporadic problem for the circus community since the nineteenth century.

Genre, nation and imagination

Having noted that the present-day circus often underestimates the richness of its own past, it would be wrong to give the impression that the circus has always been neglectful of history. In some respects, the sense of history is at the root of the circus's self-definition as a genre. An important tactic by which the circus managed to survive the suspicions of both the magistrates and moralistic opinion-formers was to hitch its fortunes to the established reputation of the classical past. The term 'circus' had respectably antique overtones, invoked by Charles Dibdin in 1782 when he coined the term and established the Royal Circus next to a five-way intersection of new roads, already called St George's Circus, on the notoriously uncivilised Southwark marshes of south London, and only a mile away from what Astley later called his

'Amphitheatre'. Alluding to the glories of imperial Rome, these two key establishments were situated among the so-called 'metropolitan improvements' that also included a classical obelisk at St George's Circus.

By the early nineteenth century, classical ideals were being challenged by a more popular narrative of Merrie England and the Olden Time. This, as Peter Mandler has argued, was the nostalgic fantasy of a somewhat Tudor Golden Age that served to legitimise popular discontent with the current parliamentary order.[9] These notions affected the content of performances as well as publicity: as ring-master, Philip Astley would banter grandiloquently with his clown whom he called 'Master Merryman', aping a Shakespearean style, while playbills and songs would be littered with references to the Roast Beef of Old England and the imagined plenty of the Elizabethan banqueting-table. Such rhetoric persuaded some commentators, too: in 1801 Joseph Strutt noted the circus as the true descendant of the sort of robustly Anglo-Saxon 'popular antiquities' that were the birthright of all free Englishmen and stood the nation in good stead for continued martial prowess.[10] Popular antiquarianism fed a lively genre of publishing. Sympathisers with the culture of the people such as William Hone and Thomas Frost celebrated the festivities of the modern city, the latter writing what was the first history of the circus in English in 1875.[11] Journalistic history-writing in this vein continued until the 1930s, and the publication of Maurice Willson Disher's nostalgic evocation of Astley's, *Greatest Show on Earth*. Willson Disher was a fringe member of the Bloomsbury group, and his book was aimed at older readers who might just have remembered the final days of the Amphitheatre, and 'romance that tumbles and smells of oranges'.[12]

The post-war years brought about a re-evaluation of Britain's cultural heritage, foremost amid which stood theatre. A broad-based mainly amateur movement arose, seeking to wrest the study of theatre from the hands of literary scholars who concentrated entirely on the dramatic text. The Society for Theatre Research championed document-based scholarship devoted to the organisational, scenographic and architectural substance of the theatre world. Prominent in this group was the historian George Speaight, who wrote a thoroughgoing international history of the circus,[13] in addition to publishing on the history of conjuring, puppetry and playing cards. Speaight and his fellow amateur historians did not have much time for academic interpretations, but helped to set a standard of accurate factual detail and the discovery of new sources that subsequent scholars have been hard pushed to emulate. Scholarship of this kind, focused on institutions rather than on the dramatic canon, depicted a continuum that linked circus with popular theatre and other 'illegitimate' forms. Very much in this spirit was the work of Raymond Toole Stott in compiling a four-volume bibliography entitled

Circus and Allied Arts.[14] The success of commercial circuses like Billy Smart's in the mid-twentieth century also prompted some purist accounts like that of Antony Hippisley Coxe. His book, *A Seat at the Circus*, incorporated some of the key points of circus history into a pioneering critical appreciation of circus performance that strove to legitimise circus in aesthetic terms.[15] Meanwhile, inside the universities, the new social history movement was beginning to champion the warm-hearted customs of the English working class. Much of the historiography within this tradition tended to regard circus as a meretricious commercial imposition upon the natural home-grown traditions of the people, understanding it as part of the industrialisation of leisure.[16]

The history of circus has been bound up with a class-inflected history of national identity. Astley sits within this account as a particular national type, strongly related to the popular stereotype of John Bull. Even in his own lifetime Astley became a figure of London legend, partly thanks to his vigorous self-publicity. Bluff, rotund and overbearing, but philanthropic and genial to some, he was rapidly absorbed into the capital's parade of memorable characters that Dickens, who as a young journalist wrote about Astley's, would fictionalise in his novels. Although his role as an innovator is questionable, Astley is widely acknowledged among French historians to be the primary exporter of the genre to Paris and thence to the European continent. During the years of the French Revolution at the end of 1700s, Astley's amphitheatre in Paris also served as a conduit that allowed French fashions in melodrama and dance to percolate into London, though this aspect has not been stressed by English historians. After Astley lost control of his amphitheatre in Paris, his circus was taken over by the Franconi family, Italian in origin, who tend to be regarded as the founding figures of French circus.[17] The patronage of Astley by Marie-Antoinette prepared the way for French circus to be regarded as an authentic art form with grand permanent quarters in the Cirque d'Hiver and the Cirque Olympique. In the 19th century, these became sites for huge equestrian spectacles celebrating the glories of the Napoleonic Empire. As a recognised art form, circus to this day continues to enjoy a significant measure of state support in France, comparable only to Russia and China.

French circus history did not have to hide under the umbrella of theatre history. Partly inspired by Henry Thetard's *La merveilleuse histoire du cirque* of 1947, Tristan Rémy formed the Union des Historiens du Cirque (UHC), which acquired an international membership and took and circulated a total of eighty-five papers by twenty-one contributors across Europe and the USA between 1957 and 1967.[18] Stemming from its history of state support, French circus has long had a high level of intellectual and aesthetic credibility, evident in its treatment by artists such as Seurat and Degas. To French historians, circus seems self-evidently significant and worthy of historical study without needing to be rationalised as part of popular culture. The current renown of French-Canadian theatre companies like Cirque du Soleil arises from the French tradition of regarding circus as a respectable branch of the arts – though the positioning of that company in Las Vegas and in other major cities around the world is part of a nevertheless ruthlessly commercial strategy of global branding.

The case is different in the USA, where broadly speaking circus has been regarded as an industry rather than an art form. The story goes that American circus was started up in the 1790s by an Englishman by the name of John Bill Ricketts, who learned his trade under Charles Hughes at the Royal Circus in London. George Washington attended Ricketts's circus four times and sold his white horse, named Jack, to him. His fine, unfinished portrait by society painter Gilbert Stuart, from around 1795, resides in the National Gallery in Washington, DC. American circus is notable for the extraordinarily efficient system of distribution that allowed it to travel the large distances between towns using the railroad with performances given under the big top, accompanied by extensive sideshows and sometimes menageries. For American historians, questions of cultural hierarchy have been of less concern. Networks of enthusiastic aficionados hold annual conferences on circus history. They are supported by numerous local archives and rich collections (including much material on European circuses) held in universities, not least at the Harvard Theatre Collection. The Ringling Museum in Sarasota, Florida, holds the world's largest collection of circus memorabilia, endowed by a famous circus family. The interpenetration of circus and theatre characteristic of Astley's era in England was brought about by a system of licensing that had no equivalent in the USA, and therefore American historians have seen no need to make links between the two genres.

Historians of whatever kind tend to write about something they value in order to validate it in the public mind. We have seen how the circus has acquired different values in different international settings. There nevertheless seem to be important similarities between circuses in different countries, to which novelists and painters have often responded. It has been represented as a redemptive space for social misfits and outsiders and those with something to hide or escape: an accepting environment that can accommodate anyone. From Dickens's *Hard Times* (1854), to Thomas Hardy's *Far From the Madding Crowd* (1874), to Australian Katharine Susannah Prichard's *Haxby's Circus* (1930), to Angela Carter's *Nights at the Circus* (1984), the circus has represented a space of alterity and a critique of mainstream society. Whereas the aspiration of the literate might be the theatre, those who had only their physical capabilities to sell would seek out the circus. In novels from the time of Dickens onwards, the circus became a kind of emblem of forlorn human hope and dreams in the context of a merciless capitalist structure.

This romantic nineteenth-century mythology that has accrued around the circus does not sit altogether comfortably with what we know of Astley's, which was as hard-nosed an operation as any other successful form of popular entertainment. Although a few stars flourished there, the Amphitheatre was adept in suppressing the wages and aspirations of most of its dozens of performers and musicians, writers, scenic artists, carpenters and stable-hands. The myth was, however, effective, and woven into its marketing strategy. Ostensibly, Astley's equestrian techniques incorporated much of the ethos of the European Enlightenment. Circus riding masters claimed the advantages of literate and even scientific methods in the training and cultivation of both human and horse. The horse, of course, was the totemic animal of the time, as George Stubbs's paintings of glossy thoroughbred stallions so eloquently testify.[19] The circus made entertainment out of those who might otherwise turn their muscular frames against their masters, people as much as horses. Like the military with which it was originally associated in Britain, the early circus was an organisation that purported to bind those who possessed little more than their bodies into a web of social and national obligation, bestowing on them a sense of continuity and the prospect of useful employment. This mythology helped it survive the hostile attentions of magistrates and the movement for the reformation of manners.

For me, the job of the historian today is to unpick these myths while grasping how and when they emerged. It would be too simple to debunk them, for myths made the circus what it is and assured its power. My own strategy has been to locate these myths in the socio-economic realities of the time. The strategy of others has been to attend to the courage of circus people, their diversity and their resourcefulness. There are, for example, absorbing and inspiring stories such as that of Pablo Fanque (born William Darby, 1796–1871), the Black English circus proprietor mentioned by the Beatles in their Sergeant Pepper album, whose name John Lennon got from an old circus bill.[20] However, this work has so far done little to inform the artistry of current circus practitioners. Perhaps if circus took a stronger interest in its own history, it would be better equipped to play a more decisive part in contemporary culture.

NOTES

1 Nell Stroud, *Who was . . .? Philip Astley – the Inventor of the Circus* (London: Short Books, 2003).

2 Roland Auguet, *Cruelty and Civilization: The Roman Games* (London: George Allen & Unwin Ltd., 1972); see also John H. Humphrey, *Roman Circuses: Arenas for Chariot Racing* (Berkeley: University of California Press, 1986).

3 See, for example, Jacob Decastro, *The Memoirs of J. Decastro, Comedian*, ed. R. Humphries (London, 1824); Edward Wedlake Brayley, *Historical and Descriptive Accounts of the Theatres of London* (London, 1827), pp. 58–66; Maurice Willson Disher, *Greatest Show on Earth: Astley's (afterwards Sanger's) Royal Amphitheatre of Arts* (London: Bell, 1937); George Speaight, *A History of the Circus* (London: Tantivy, 1980), ch. 6; Marius Kwint, 'The Legitimization of the Circus in Late Georgian England', *Past and Present*, 174 (February 2002), 72–115; Stroud, *Philip Astley*.

4 Transcript of newspaper advertisement, *Gazetteer*, 11 June 1768: British Library, London, Th. Cts. 35 (Astley's Cuttings from Newspapers), item 14.

5 Mary Nichols (1813–70), diary, 25 July 1827, 14 July 1829 and 2 August 1831. Thanks to the diary's editor Julian Pooley for this source.

6 The playbill for the week of the Nichols family visit, 1 August 1831, with the well known engraving by A. Bowen, is in Victoria and Albert Museum Theatre and Performance Department, Blythe House, London.

7 Broadside bills and circus posters are a prime source for the circus, and communicate much of its visual, demonstrative style: in the UK, notable collections are at the V&A Museum, the National Fairground Archive in Sheffield, and the John Johnson Collection at the Bodleian Library, Oxford; in the USA at the Harvard Theatre Collection and the Ringling Museum, Sarasota; in Canada at the Collection Pascal Jacob at the École Nationale du Cirque in Montréal; and in France at the Musée Carnavalet, Paris.

8 See, for example, Robert Malcolmson, *Popular Recreations in English Society, 1700–1850* (Cambridge: Cambridge University Press, 1973). This field is much influenced by E. P. Thompson's Marxian concepts of cultural resistance among the working class during the industrial revolution. See also Hugh Cunningham, *Leisure in the Industrial Revolution* (London: Palgrave Macmillan, 1980), p. 32; J. M. Golby and A. W. Purdue, *The Civilization of the Crowd: Popular Culture in England, 1750–1900* (London: Batsford, 1984); on broader European patterns see Peter Burke, *Popular Culture in Early Modern Europe* (London: Temple Smith, 1978).

9 See Peter Mandler, 'The Wand of Fancy: The Historical Imagination of the Victorian Tourist', in Marius Kwint, Christopher Breward and Jeremy Aynsley (eds.), *Material Memories: Design and Evocation* (Oxford: Berg, 1999), pp. 125–42.

10 Joseph Strutt, *Glig-Gamena Angel-Deod: The Sports and Pastimes of the People of England* (London, 1801), pp. 185–6.

11 Thomas Frost, *Circus Life and Circus Celebrities* (London, 1875).

12 Willson Disher, *Greatest Show on Earth* (the title is of American coinage, from Barnum, and would not have been used by Astley's); see also Samuel McKechnie, *Popular Entertainments through the Ages* (London: Low, Marston, 1931).

13 Speaight, *History of the Circus*.

14 Raymond Toole Stott, *Circus and Allied Arts: A World Bibliography*, 4 vols. (Derby: Harpur, 1958–71).

15 Antony Hippisley Coxe, *A Seat at the Circus* (London: Macmillan, 1951).

16 See note 8 above.

17 See Caroline Hodak, 'Du théâtre équestre au cirque: commercialisation des loisirs, diffusion des savoirs et théâtralisation de l'histoire en France et en Angleterre, 1760–1860', 2 vols. (Ecole des Hautes Etudes en Sciences Sociales, Paris, Ph.D. thesis, 2004).

18 Giancarlo Pretini (ed.), *Thesaurus Circensis*, 2 vols. (Udine, Italy: Trapezio, 1990).

19 On George Stubbs (1724–1806), see Stephen Deuchar, *Sporting Art in Eighteenth-century England: A Social and Political History* (New Haven: Yale University Press, 1988).

20 See John M. Turner, 'Pablo Fanque: Black Circus Proprietor', www.100great blackbritons.com/bios/Pablo_Fanque.htm.

FURTHER READING

Assael, Brenda. *The Circus and Victorian Society* (Charlottesville, VA: University of Virginia Press, 2005).

Chevalier, Tracy. *Burning Bright* (London: Harper Collins, 2007).

Russell, Gillian. *The Theatres of War: Performance, Politics and Society, 1793–1815* (Oxford: Oxford University Press, 1995).

Saxon, Arthur H. *Enter Foot and Horse: A History of Hippodrama in England and France* (New Haven: Yale University Press, 1968).

The Life and Art of Andrew Ducrow and the Romantic Age of the English Circus (Hamden, CT: Archon, 1978).

P. T. Barnum: The Legend and the Man, 2nd edn (New York: Columbia University Press, 1995).

St Leon, Mark. *Circus: The Australian Story* (Melbourne: Melbourne Books, 2011).

Stoddart, Helen. *Rings of Desire: Circus History and Representation* (Manchester: Manchester University Press, 2000).

Stroud, Nell. *Josser: Days and Nights in the Circus* (London: Virago, 2000).

PART FIVE

How?

It is an illusion to think that history exists and that historians subsequently choose how to study it. Rather, the method of historical study defines the outcome, the history that is created. Historians work from sources, and sources tend to be gathered together in libraries, museums, databases and other forms of archive because somebody has anticipated that researchers in the future may find this material useful, while judging that other material can be discarded. Thus the present does much to determine how the past will be regarded by future historians, even though the best will characteristically work across the grain and use sources in ways that could never have been anticipated.

Documents, often loosely conceptualised as 'facts', sit at the heart of the historian's work. The first chapter in this section, Chapter 15, takes up one particular constellation of documents in order to address a specific historical problem. This chapter is concerned with the nature of historical argument and the discipline of responsibility to facts that governs all historical work. Decisions to be made usually involve trust. We consider the difficulty of knowing anything for sure, when so many 'primary' source materials derive ultimately from word of mouth. Most of us think that what we see with our own eyes is more reliable than what we are simply told. Chapter 16 considers one particular category of evidence that might be found in an archive, pictures, which often create the impression that, unlike words, they are unmediated records of how the play was actually done. The truth is that the historian needs a high level of visual literacy in order to determine how and why a given image was created, and how, in a different historical environment with a different mode of seeing, that image might once have been interpreted. Chapter 17 is concerned with the way documentary material has been collected into archives, for the use of future scholars and practitioners. We see how the gathering of data is increasingly regarded not as a hoarding of wealth but as an intervention upon the present, involving communication and distribution as much as accumulation.

Our penultimate chapter, Chapter 18, considers how the historian is but a flesh-and-blood human being. Through their own physical engagement with spaces, costumes or words, historians may acquire forms of knowledge that may or may not be transmissible through language. Is dressing up and re-enacting the past an amateurish activity that no serious historian should contemplate, or is there much to be said for engaging in the flesh with the material practices of the past, as distinct from engaging with reproduced documents? We live in an increasingly virtual world, and within the very recent past the internet has emerged as an astonishingly rich source of historical information, information that is heterogeneous and of mixed reliability. Our final chapter, Chapter 19, looks at the possibilities and pitfalls of the internet, exploring the new avenues of research that have opened up. Since the internet offers a multiplicity of voices, this chapter is framed as a debate, reminding you incidentally how any assumed body of knowledge is bound up with the authority of whosoever holds that knowledge.

The contributors to this *Companion* form a diverse group, and each has written from a point of personal engagement with their material, making no claim to legislative authority. What we all claim in our different ways is a strong professional and ethical commitment to the task of being a historian.

15

THOMAS POSTLEWAIT

The nature of historical evidence: a case study

i

What do theatre historians do? How do they do it? Two simple questions, but the answers are complex, as I wish to demonstrate in this chapter on historical evidence. In order to provide some useful answers to these two questions, especially the *how* question, I will feature an event in theatre history that continues to generate controversy among theatre historians: the sudden death of the English playwright Christopher Marlowe (1564–93), who was killed on 30 May 1593. Marlowe's death is a mystery to be solved. How and why did he die? How was the event understood at the time, and how has it been reconstructed in our own time? What does the evidence reveal or conceal? As this last question implies, I want to conduct an investigation of not only the historical event itself but also the interpretive methods that are used to reconstruct the event. I will therefore consider the relative value of several kinds of evidence (e.g., written versus oral sources, official versus unofficial statements, eyewitness versus hearsay reports). I will also identify some of the challenges and problems that theatre historians face in their methods of research and analysis.

I recognise, of course, that no single event can offer a full perspective on the wide range of topics and research methods in theatre studies. Theatre historians investigate all kinds of performance events that have occurred throughout human time and across the whole globe. This rich heritage of human entertainment is not limited to the performance of plays, but also includes festivals, parades, circuses, animal acts, cabarets, puppetry, variety and magic shows, and political spectacles. Moreover, besides these many kinds of performance events, theatre historians and biographers also study the lives, communities and social worlds of the people who create and participate in these events. Despite this great diversity of possible topics, there are still some basic methods of inquiry that guide historical research. For example, those two questions at the beginning of this chapter provide a vital clue to the fundamental procedures that theatre historians share with all historians. One sentence begins with the word 'what', the other with the word 'how'. Those two interrogatives launch this chapter, and most historical inquiries. Looking back at historical events, we want to know *what* happened and *how*. In turn, we are also guided by four additional interrogatives: *who*, *when*, *where* and *why*.

Together, these six interrogatives generate our search for historical sources and clues. They organise human actions and motives into their basic aspects. Similar to Aristotle's four causes (efficient, material, formal and final), which name the causal factors that constitute objects and events, or Kenneth Burke's dramatist pentad (act, scene, agent, agency and purpose), which provides a grammar of action, these interrogatives identify an event's basic attributes.[1] Aristotle taught us to divide objects and actions into what they are made of (material cause), the form they take (formal cause), the force or forces that produce or animate them (efficient cause), and their ends or purposes (final cause). Somewhat differently, Burke identified acts or actions by their agents, their methods of agency, the scenes or settings in which the acts are performed, and their purposes. At this initial level of investigation, the interrogatives, like the four causes and the dramatist pentad, provide both a check-off list for naming the parts of an event and a method for distinguishing the parts from one another. For the historian, the significance and meaning of the events or actions emerge out of these distributions.

ii

So, what do we know about Christopher Marlowe's life and death, and how should we interpret the available evidence? Marlowe was twenty-nine years old at the time of his death. He had already written half a dozen plays, including *Tamburlaine* (Parts I and II), *Dr Faustus*, *The Jew of Malta*, *The Massacre at Paris* and *Edward II*. His well-crafted plays, immediately popular with the London audiences, revealed a genius for playwriting. The plays quickly influenced other playwrights, including Thomas Kyd, Robert Greene, Thomas Nashe, and a young playwright by the name of William Shakespeare. We can identify a small number of performance dates, playhouses and theatre companies for the staging of Marlowe's plays, but we know almost nothing about his professional and personal relationships with the other playwrights, the players, the playing companies, and their patrons.

Likewise, we know very little about his activities beyond the theatre. Did any of them contribute to his death? How so? Why? A few documents have survived on his birth, family and schooling in Canterbury (1564–79); a few others exist for his years at Corpus Christi College, Cambridge (1580–7). But for his non-theatrical activities between July 1587 and March 1593, only four sources have been discovered: one from 1589, three from 1592. All four are tied to court cases,[2] which reveal that, besides playwriting, he had a talent for initiating confrontations.

As is the case with the life of Shakespeare, the documentary record on Marlowe is slight.[3] But in addition to the four sources from 1589 and 1592, half a dozen documents exist from the last few weeks before his death on 30 May 1593. This limited evidence suggests that during his last few months he had gained a reputation for putting forward controversial ideas on religion. Then, subsequent to his death, well over a dozen documents have survived. Because it is not possible in this short essay to cover the full documentary record and historical debates on Marlowe's life and death, I will limit my comments to those sources that refer directly to his death. Even this one event introduces us to several kinds of evidence. It also reveals some recurring problems in historical study.[4]

According to popular legend, Marlowe was killed on 30 May 1593 in a street or tavern brawl, which supposedly was caused by some kind of grudge or love rivalry. Although an official investigation took place two days after Marlowe's death, the governmental report was not made available to the public.[5] Only a handful of people knew about this inquest. The report and related documents remained buried in governmental archives until they were discovered in 1925. Thus, in the months and years after Marlowe's death, public knowledge was limited to bits and pieces of hearsay information – gossip and innuendoes – that circulated in London. This unofficial public discourse generated two types of published statements: (1) miscellaneous tributes and evasive references to Marlowe from fellow playwrights, including Shakespeare; (2) several slanderous anecdotes written by people who blamed Marlowe's death on his supposedly heretical views on religion or his sexual behaviour. Until 1925 these two types of statements, positive and negative, served as the historical record on Marlowe's death. What can we learn from these sources?

In the decade after Marlowe's death, several fellow writers, including George Peele, Ben Jonson, Thomas Nashe, Michael Drayton, and Shakespeare, published their tributes and laments. For example, in *As You Like It* (1599) Shakespeare provided some indirect references to Marlowe and also quotes from Marlowe's poem *Hero and Leander*, which was published posthumously in 1598: 'Who ever loved that loved not at first sight?'[6] In these indirect references, Shakespeare paid homage to Marlowe. Like most of Marlowe's colleagues, Shakespeare admired Marlowe's writings and wished to portray him as a talented and honourable man. Yet none of these writers described the actual killing or any specific reasons for it.

By contrast, there was nothing evasive about three slanderous statements that were published between 1597 and 1600. These reports, by people outside the theatre community, accused Marlowe of immoral beliefs and actions and represented him as a brawler who, having started a fight, received his just punishment. The first of these statements appeared in Thomas Beard's *The Theatre of God's Judgements* (London, 1597). In his patchwork pamphlet that catalogued examples of God's punishment of sinners, Beard proclaimed that 'Marlin,[7] by profession a scholler, . . .by practice a playmaker, and a Poet of scurrilitie, . . .denied God and his sonne Christ, and not only in word blasphemed the trinitie, but also (as it is credibly reported) wrote books against it, affirming our Saviour to be but a deceiver, and *Moses* to be but a conjurer and seducer of the people, and the holy Bible to be but vaine and idle stories, and all religion but a device of pollicie.' Beard then described the death: 'It so fell out, that in London streets as he purposed to stab one whom hee ought [owed] a grudge unto with his dagger, the other party perceiving so avoided the stroke, that withall catching hold of his wrest [wrist], he stabbed his owne dagger into his owne head. . . .' Marlowe 'shortly died thereof. . . ,' but not before 'hee even cursed and blasphemed to the last gaspe. . . .' The death, Beard proclaimed, was 'a manifest sign of Gods judgement. . . .'[8] Beard's statement was derived from secondary, unofficial sources, based most likely on hearsay reports.

A year later Francis Meres claimed that 'Christopher Marlow was stabd to death by a bawdy Serving man, a rivall of his in his lewde love.'[9] And two years later William Vaughan, drawing partially on Beard, located the stabbing 'at Detford, a little village about three miles distant from London'. Marlowe 'meant to stab with his ponyard [dagger] one named Ingram, that had invited him thither to a feast, and was then playing at tables [backgammon?]'. This Ingram 'quickly perceyving it, so avoyded the thrust, that withall drawing out his dagger for his defence, hee stabd this Marlow into the eye, in such sort, that his braines coming out at the daggers point, hee shortlie after dyed. Thus did God, the true executioner of divine justice, worke the ende of impious Atheists.'[10]

Several additional negative statements on Marlowe and his death, similar to those of Beard, were published in the seventeenth century. As far as we can determine, none of these people, including Beard, Meres and Vaughan, knew Marlowe personally.

Our historical understanding changed radically in 1925 when J. Leslie Hotson published the report on the inquest, which took place on 1 June 1593, two days after the killing. The inquest was convened by William Danby, the coroner of the Queen's court. His short report, written in Latin, required only about 650–700 words. After paying homage to Queen

Elizabeth, Danby listed the names of the sixteen jurors. He explained that the jurors viewed 'the body of Christopher Morley, there lying dead & slain'. As part of his responsibility, Danby measured and described the fatal knife wound 'above the right eye' (*super dexterum oculum sum*). The inquest was apparently held at the scene of the killing, the residence of Widow Eleanor Bull who lived in the town of Deptford, at the eastern edge of London on the river Thames. This location was close to the Queen's residence at Greenwich Palace.[11] In his report Danby does not identify Widow Bull's place as a public inn, but she served lunch and dinner to the four men – Marlowe, Ingram Frizer, Nicholas Skeres and Robert Poley – who spent the day together in conversation.

In the main, the inquest report provides the eyewitness testimony of Frizer, Skeres, and Poley. According to Danby's summary, the three men (whom he identifies as gentlemen) and Marlowe (who does not warrant this designation) arrived at Widow Bull's place at 'around the tenth hour before the noon'. They 'passed the time together and lunched and after lunch kept company quietly and walked in the garden ...until the sixth hour after noon of the same day, and then returned from the aforesaid garden to the room aforesaid and there together and in company dined'. After dinner Frizer and Marlowe 'exchanged divers malicious words because they could not concur nor agree on the payment of the sum of pence, that is *le recknynge*' (the bill) for the food. Marlowe was resting on a bed in the room; Frizer was sitting at the table, with Skeres and Poley on each side of him. 'Christopher Morley suddenly & of malice aforethought towards the same Ingram [Frizer], then & there maliciously drew the dagger of the said Ingram, which was visible at his back, and with the same dagger the said Christopher Morley then & there maliciously gave the aforesaid Ingram two wounds on his head....' Initially pinned in by Skeres and Poley, Frizer quickly got clear of them, and then 'in his own defence & for the saving of his life, ...[he] struggled with the said Christopher Morley to get back from him his dagger...' Frizer grabbed the dagger and 'gave the said Christopher then & there a mortal wound over his right eye of the depth of two inches & the width of one inch; of which mortal wound the aforesaid Christopher Morley then and there instantly died'. The report states that Frizer 'neither fled nor withdrew himself' after the killing. It does not describe any actions or reactions by Skeres and Poley during or after the struggle. Only Frizer was charged with the killing. The report concludes with a statement that the jurors, on their oaths, judged the killing to be an act of self-defence. They then 'set their seals'.[12] Less than a month later, the Queen pardoned Frizer.

In contrast to the public rumours on Marlowe's death, the inquest report seemed quite reliable. This was the untroubled judgement of G. L. Kittredge, a well-respected Renaissance scholar, who wrote a short introduction for Hotson's book: 'The mystery of Marlowe's death, heretofore involved in a cloud of contradictory gossip and irresponsible guess-work, is now cleared up for good and all on the authority of public records of complete authenticity and gratifying fullness. Every detail of the strange affair is vividly set forth on the testimony of eyewitnesses.'[13] From Kittredge's perspective, the 'authority of public records' and the 'testimony of eyewitnesses' delivered the historical truth.

Kittredge's judgement accords with the guidelines in research manuals for historical scholarship.[14] These manuals advise historians to depend upon primary sources, such as eyewitness testimony, rather than secondary sources, such as gossip. The best evidence usually derives from those who were present at the event, not from those who offer second-hand commentary, picked up from other sources. Likewise, the guidebooks encourage historians to prefer written sources over oral ones. A careful historian needs to be sceptical of oral sources because they may depend upon 'hearsay' anecdotes that charm, seduce and mislead us.

Given this distinction between primary and secondary sources, the unofficial gossip put forward by Beard, Meres and Vaughan is quite suspect. Their statements, based upon religious convictions and rumours (as Beard states), lack credibility. There is no evidence, for example, that Marlowe was killed in the 'London streets', that he 'cursed and blasphemed to the last gaspe', that Frizer was a 'Serving man', or that Marlowe engaged in a dispute over 'lewde love' (male or female).

Yet before we divide the documents into two opposing groups, thereby neatly separating the reliable sources from unreliable ones, we should recognise that secondary sources, though dependent upon hearsay, may prove to be reliable in some matters. For example, a few details reported by Beard and Vaughan are in accord with the inquest report, including the struggle between the two men and death by a dagger. And Vaughan not only located the killing in Deptford but also correctly identified Frizer's first name of 'Ingram'. Indeed, this identification, which corrected the misnaming of 'ffrancis ffrezer' in the burial report, provided the crucial clue that set Leslie Hotson on the right path for his discovery of the coroner's report. Thus, despite several inaccuracies, the statements by Beard and Vaughan cannot be dismissed. The two men apparently had access to someone (perhaps a juror?) who was familiar with the inquest proceedings or had access to the report. Whatever the case, their statements illustrate how bits and pieces of information, spread haphazardly by the oral networks of a community, can deliver some reliable facts into written records.

What should we conclude, by contrast, about the inquest report, which has the authority of a legal document? Prepared by a respected court official, signed by sixteen jurors who were members of the community, and based upon eyewitness testimony, the report would seem to be a most reliable document. And yet questions and doubts developed soon after its publication. At first the concerns focused on a technical matter: would Marlowe have died instantly from the depth and angle of the knife wound, as reported by Danby? In the following years doubts were expressed about the testimony of the eyewitnesses. Then some scholars questioned the thoroughness of the inquest investigation. Scepticism grew, and by the end of the century a full scale critique had been mounted.

Danby may have been a respected and competent coroner, but he defined his task narrowly and ignored many issues. He failed to explain why these four men met at Widow Bull's house or what was discussed. Nor did he clarify what the relationship was between Marlowe and these men. Who were Frizer, Skeres and Poley? Why should we trust their testimony? Perhaps Danby decided that such information was irrelevant to his task. Whatever the case, the absence of these details in the historical records of the event has hindered investigations of Marlowe's death since 1925.

Also, as we evaluate the report, we need to see that the standard distinction between written and oral evidence collapses. Despite being an official written document, the report depends on oral statements by Frizer, Skeres and Poley, the eyewitnesses to the murder. Yet because we lack their individual statements – if indeed they were even taken and transcribed – the report does not provide a direct record of testimony. Danby did not quote directly from any of the men. Instead, he crafted whatever the three 'gentlemen' may have reported into a condensed general statement – a hearsay summary – with a single perspective on the events. Thus, the written report, which has the apparent authority of a primary document, is actually a secondary document based on oral sources.

Frizer, Skeres and Poley had the ability to tell the truth – one of the key requirements for credible testimony – but were they willing to do so?[15] Because we do not know what each of them reported to Danby, we cannot test the credibility of their statements. Nor do we know how competent Danby's interrogation of them was. Apparently the three men agreed with one another in their testimony. If so, they may have told the truth about a brawl. But they may have agreed among themselves to tell a lie. We cannot prove this, one way or the other. Even if we had in writing the signed testimonies of the three men, we still would have to determine, if we could, that their statements were trustworthy. Eyewitness testimony has the status of primary evidence, but quite often it is unreliable.

Basically, we have to take the report on trust, despite our many questions. Because too many questions remain unanswered, our uncertainties and doubts have opened the door to speculations. In recent years, ever since Charles Nicholl published *The Reckoning: The Murder of Christopher Marlowe* (1992),[16] several theatre historians and biographers have developed elaborate narratives for what might have happened. Some speculations focus on Marlowe's controversial views on religion. Others focus on the possibility that Marlowe participated in espionage for the government, uncovering Catholic plots against the government. Was he killed because of his controversial views on religion? Or was he eliminated because he had become an untrustworthy spy? Who ordered the murder? Were Frizer, Skeres and Poley hired assassins? Why did the Queen pardon Frizer?[17] What if the inquest was part of a governmental cover-up for a planned murder of Marlowe? If so, who arranged the cover-up operation? All of these questions imply, sooner or later, that Marlowe's death resulted from some kind of conspiracy.

These hypotheses offer fascinating 'what if' narratives, but there is one problem: no direct evidence exists for a planned murder. Nor is there any proof that Marlowe was a governmental spy.[18] Consequently, though lacking facts, the speculators must develop their narratives by means of *arguments by analogy* (e.g., Robert Poley was a governmental courier and informant; perhaps, then, Marlowe, who knew Poley, did similar work), *guilt by association* (e.g., Frizer, Skeres and Poley were devious men; by meeting with them, Marlowe joined them in devious matters), and *fallacious reasoning* (e.g., on 20 May Marlowe was called before the Privy Council; ten days later he was dead; thus, one or more members of the Privy Council hired Frizer to murder Marlowe). At best, the arguments rely on a clever gathering of circumstantial evidence; at worst, they depend upon false syllogisms and the suspect logic of *post hoc, ergo propter hoc* ('after this; therefore, because of this'). In this short chapter I do not have the opportunity to examine and argue against each of these conspiratorial speculations. I note, though, that these fanciful hypotheses, like all conspiracy theories, are based upon a series of propositions that have to be supported by rhetorical phrases such as 'it seems likely', 'quite possibly', 'one would think', etc. Even when no evidence is available, the arguments continue (e.g., claims that Lord Essex, Lord Burghley, or perhaps even Queen Elizabeth ordered Marlowe's death). The absence of any documentary evidence is taken as proof of secret activities because the authorities cunningly covered their tracks. In this way, counter-factual claims substitute for actual evidence.

iii

There are many questions about Marlowe's death – all of which quite appropriately raise doubts about the reliability of the inquest report. We need to recognise, however, that all of these doubts and uncertainties depend upon a fundamental question that applies to all historical research: *what is the nature of the available evidence?* Of course, all historical investigations require and benefit from conjectures and hypotheses. Besides the six basic interrogatives, historians can also ask 'what if' questions that play out possible explanations. But unlike detectives in mystery novels, historians, including theatre historians, lack the good fortune of always discovering a sterling piece of evidence that answers the riddles of an investigation. We must honour the constraints imposed by the available evidence. The authority of our historical arguments depends upon how we identify, describe and analyse the available evidence.

Although the six interrogatives help to initiate an investigation, there is no formula for how to use sources as evidence. Nor is there a single or correct way to carry out the analysis. The primary control on interpretation depends upon the historical rigour and judgement of each historian. There are, however, two basic models of historical analysis prevalent today, which can be identified as *microhistory* and *macrohistory*.

The *microhistorian* burrows deep into an event in order to find the particular pieces of evidence often buried at its centre. Interrogating each document, each statement, each piece of evidence, this historian seeks the inner sanctum of an event, its endogenous features. Space and time are often narrowed to a sharp focus, a specific location and moment. Where exactly did the event occur? When? Who was there? Not until all of the sources are identified and displayed for analysis do the clues begin to reveal what actually happened, how it occurred, and why. Perhaps, then, a small piece of evidence emerges that solves the investigation. This is the method, for example, of forensic science in criminology.

Countering this approach, the *macrohistorian* tends to search the margins of an event in order to discover the framing factors and issues that contribute to the event's definitive features. This method focuses on the contextual conditions, such as possible social, economic, political, religious, moral and/or geographical factors. The investigation seeks the manifest identity of the event in its encompassing or exogenous conditions. Sometimes a reigning and powerful idea in a community or society controls human actions and aims. Perhaps the historian is able to identify determining factors of which the participants themselves may not have been conscious. In order to encompass broad and general conditions, the macrohistorian expands the spatial and temporal parameters of the event under investigation. The search is for those shaping forces that push at the event and hold it together. They influence, even determine, its identity.[19]

Whether delving inward or expanding outward, historians must contend with certain abiding challenges and dangers. For the *microhistorian* the challenge is to find and identify the significant details and motivations within the event that will constitute its identity and meaning. The search may depend upon the historian's cunning analysis of a missing or misidentified piece of evidence that reveals what happened. The danger, however, is that the historian, by placing too much significance in a single source, misinterprets the event. Too much credit is given to one document or a single eyewitness report. The moment of discovery – of proclaiming 'eureka' – may not withstand critical analysis. Gold turns into fool's gold.

For the *macrohistorian* the challenge is to identify, among the many possible external conditions that may contribute to the event, the primary factor that shaped, directed and perhaps controlled the actions and thoughts of the participants in the event. The full meaning of an event emerges when the historian is capable of identifying the external force or forces that underlie the event and caused it to happen – as it did, where it did, and when it did. The danger, though, is that the historian may be drawn to a grand theory of causality (e.g., a theory of human behaviour or a single social condition), which is then imposed on the event. Modern scholarship has shown how tempting certain consuming ideas, such as Marxism, Freudianism and post-colonialism, have been. The historian, seeking an underlying cause, is tempted to embrace an expansive idea or supposition that imposes a grand interpretation. But this explanation, instead of doing justice to the possible contextual conditions, delivers a reductive proposition that ignores other contributory factors (and contradictory evidence).

It should be apparent that historical research usually requires both a trip into the interior and an exploration of the exterior. Instead of committing to a single method, the accomplished historian weaves together the internal and external aspects of an event. The analysis is both inductive and deductive. Such approaches are both practical and necessary because a full explanation of who, what, where, when, how and why usually requires the ability not only to identify both the internal and external factors but also to determine the relative importance of each factor in the make-up of the event. Finding sources is a vital skill for the historian (e.g., Hotson's discovery of the inquest report), but calibrating their importance is the real test for historical understanding.

Yet even when the savvy historian is capable of offering an insightful interpretation of an event, the explanation is often partial and incomplete.

It is based upon possibilities, not certainties. An effective historical investigation often fails to reach a decisive and final conclusion. Unlike clues in a mystery story, historical sources seldom constitute a well-made plot with a revealing conclusion (though some literary biographers are compelled to discover speculative evidence for a total design – with a villain). Of course, it is often possible to identify the basic factors of *who*, *what*, *where* and *when* in an event. But answering the interrogatives of *how* and *why* is more difficult. Indeed, in the majority of historical investigations, especially of events before the modern age, the best explanation that a historian can deliver is one built carefully out of a set of possibilities and probabilities. Even then, because the evidence is usually partial, the analysis is open to challenge. Other historians will likely disagree on how to order, rank, describe and interpret the existing evidence. By shifting the relative values and priorities for pieces of evidence, we also shift their possible meanings. And because the evidence is partial, other historians will feel compelled to search for additional information at the microhistory level and to offer other interpretive ideas at the macrohistorical level. To be expected, then, the major events of history, including those in theatre history, have often been studied by many scholars. Just as any great artistic work – play, opera, poem, novel, painting, symphony – invites and deserves many possible interpretations, so too do complex historical events.

Moreover, whatever the event, the method of investigation, and the interpretive strategy, historians often discover that there are significant gaps in the extant record. Unlike most art-works, which have attained a definitive text and complete design that invites interpretation, historical events are usually incomplete, for we lack some of their definitive details. Vital records are absent. Some documents were destroyed, some were modified, some were lost or misplaced, and some were never created in the first place. Nonetheless, analysis is required. Ignoring the gaps is seldom wise. But historians need to proceed carefully. The emptiness invites acts of interpretation, but it only rewards those explanations that do justice to all factors, present and absent.

Some historians are capable of intuitive leaps of interpretation. They possess a talent, like a spider, for spinning connecting threads. And like a spider they are capable of leaping across the empty spaces, landing gently on the available historical nodes. Weaving the strands across the emptiness, they create a connecting web that transforms the emptiness into a unified design. In this way, the historical imagination connects what is unknown to what is known. If, for instance, we can identify who destroyed certain documents, we may be able to figure out the possible reasons; then, out of the motivations, we conjure some of the possible details. We can then reconstruct what a person attempted to hide. Some gaps can be closed, at least partially. In a similar way, an archeologist is capable of reconstructing a whole community out of the partial remains of buildings. Or a world of dinosaurs is reconstituted out of miscellaneous bones. This talent for reconstructing a presence out of an absence is crucial to all historical disciplines.

But it takes a special talent to tease a hidden presence out of an apparent absence. Sometimes, though, despite the search for connecting clues, one needs the discipline to accept uncertainties. Many gaps cannot be closed. Unfortunately, some historians lack the ability to live with the empty spaces in the records. They prescribe instead of discover meanings. All too often, their speculations lack the care and restraints that the available evidence calls for. In such cases historians need to resist the temptation to compose a unified narrative for the events. They impose a false order and authority onto the uncertainties of the past. Quite often these historians also have trouble living with ambiguities, contradictions and paradoxes. They lack the ability to accommodate themselves to historical silences.

iv

What, then, should we conclude about Marlowe's death? We can be certain about some factual information. We know *when* and *where* he died; we know *who* was with him. We even know *how* he died: a knife above the right eye. So we have preliminary answers to when, where, who and how. We do not know, though, *what* the four men were discussing that day, nor do we know *why* they were meeting: big, unanswered questions. It may be the case that Marlowe started a knife fight in which he then lost his life. This is a possible explanation, and given the record of his previous conflicts, it may even be a probable explanation.[20] Still, many uncertainties remain. The coroner's report leaves too many issues and concerns in the dark. But the flaws in the report do not require an explanation based upon either God's punishment of sinners or governmental conspiracies. Both deductions not only exceed the available evidence but also require an acceptance of principles of causality that in the final analysis have to be taken on faith. Both explanations express a believer's mentality in hidden, invisible forces that punished Marlowe, yet operated without leaving even one piece of direct evidence. A leap of faith is required.

Historical study requires a less ambitious and less totalising explanation for human activities. As a discipline, historical study is a this-world practice; it requires and rewards the mundane task of immersing oneself in what can be known. The search for grand and secret powers, hidden behind all available evidence, may allow one to create a total and unified narrative, but human actions are seldom so neat. Our records, in accord with our motivations and actions, are messy, incomplete, contradictory – a mixture of reliable and unreliable testimony. As we attempt to take the measure of historical documents, such as the inquest report, we should keep in mind the warning from the eminent historian Marc Bloch: 'There is no reliable witness in the absolute sense. There is only more or less reliable testimony.'[21] Absolute answers are beyond us. Consequently, we should assume, as a general guideline, that all sources – written and oral, official and unofficial, primary and secondary – must be investigated for their credibility and reliability. Scepticism is required. But that scepticism needs to be directed not only at the historical sources but also at our own hypotheses and speculations. Conjectures are quite easy to fabricate, but they can quickly mislead us. Most troubling, they can convince an investigator to accept, without question, a set of unwarranted assumptions and fanciful interpretations. Historical research then becomes fictional narrative, a self-deceiving practice with little or no credibility.

NOTES

1 For an overview on Burke and Aristotle, see Thomas Postlewait's *Cambridge Introduction to Theatre Historiography* (Cambridge: Cambridge University Press, 2009), pp. 104–5, 229–30.

2 For these documents, see Constance Brown Kuriyama's *Christopher Marlowe: A Renaissance Life* (Ithaca, NY: Cornell University Press, 2002), pp. 203–6, 209–10, 210–11 and 211–14. Three of these court cases arose out of street altercations involving Marlowe, one of which resulted in a death. The other case was tied to charges of counterfeiting by Marlowe and two other men. In all four cases the charges against Marlowe were dropped.

3 Most of the pertinent documents on Marlowe are reproduced by Kuriyama.

4 In an essay to be published subsequently, I will consider the full documentary record and offer a critique of the historical methods of the modern historians, critics and biographers who have written about Marlowe. Among other documents, I will examine those by Thomas Kyd and Richard Baines.

5 The inquest report, written in Latin (except for a few words), was discovered, transcribed and translated in 1925 by J. Leslie Hotson, *The Death of Christopher Marlowe* (London: Nonesuch Press, 1925), pp. 28–34.

6 See III. v. 81. Touchstone's line, 'it strikes a man more dead than a great reckoning in a little room' (III.iii. 13–14), echoes Marlowe's phrase 'infinite riches in a little room' in *The Jew of Malta*. Shakespeare also seems to take up the word 'reckoning' from the coroner's report, yet how would he have obtained access to the document? Pure coincidence? Perhaps someone involved in the inquest gossiped about the fight over the reckoning of the bill, but this improbable conjecture lacks any supporting evidence.

7 In the documents on Marlowe, his name is spelled in various ways – Marlowe, Marlin, Marlow, Marley, Morley, Marly, Marlye. This variety reflects not only the

elastic options for spelling in the era but also the shifting patterns of pronunciation from person to person. As David Wiles noted to me, the several spellings of Marlowe's name suggest possible pronunciations, and thus the influence of the oral traditions on written documents.

8 Hotson, *Death*, pp. 11–13. Here and in following quotations I have silently changed the Elizabethan 'u' to 'v' in a few words.

9 *Palladis Tamia* (London, 1598), a miscellany of information on Elizabethan writers. Hotson, *Death*, pp. 13–14.

10 *The Golden Grove* (London, 1600). Hotson, *Death*, pp. 14–17.

11 Apparently the Queen's coroner oversaw investigations of deaths that occurred close to the Queen's residence.

12 Hotson, *Death*, pp. 28–34.

13 G. L. Kittredge, 'Introduction' to Leslie Hotson, *The Death of Christopher Marlowe*, p. 7.

14 See, for example, Louis Gottschalk, *Understanding History: A Primer of Historical Method*, 2nd edn (New York: Alfred A. Knopf, 1969).

15 On these matters of eyewitness testimony, see Gottschalk's *Understanding History* (pp. 150–5) on six tests of credibility: ability to tell the truth, competence, degree of attention, leading questions, reasoning in a circle, and egocentrism.

16 London: Jonathan Cape; New York: Harcourt Brace & Co., 1992. See, also, David Riggs, *The World of Christopher Marlowe* (London: Faber & Faber, 2004), and Park Honan, *Christopher Marlowe: Poet and Spy* (Oxford: Oxford University Press, 2005). Given their open-ended speculations, it is not surprising that they disagree on the causes for his death and the identity of the governmental person supposedly responsible.

17 The Queen's pardon, discovered by Hotson, accompanied the inquest report. Latin and English texts are reproduced in Hotson, *Death*, pp. 34–7.

18 All we know is that in 1587, while still a student at Corpus Christi College, Cambridge, he provided some kind of service for the government. For all we know, that service was nothing more than delivering messages for a few weeks within England. See Kuriyama, *Christopher Marlowe*, pp. 69–73.

19 On both endogenous and exogenous factors, see cruxes 1 and 2 in Postlewait's *Cambridge Introduction to Theatre Historiography*, pp. 226–36. See, also, Carlo Ginzburg on microhistory and Fernand Braudel on macrohistory.

20 In her biography Kuriyama accepts this explanation, despite the limitations of the inquest.

21 Marc Bloch, *The Historian's Craft*, trans. Peter Putnam (New York: Alfred A. Knopf, 1953), p. 101.

FURTHER READING

Braudel, Fernand. *On History*, trans. Sarah Matthews (Chicago: University of Chicago Press, 1980).

Canning, Charlotte, and Thomas Postlewait, eds. *Representing the Past: Essays on Performance Historiography* (Iowa City: University of Iowa Press, 2010).

Collingwood, R. G. *The Idea of History*, revised edition, ed. Jan van der Dussen (Oxford: Oxford University Press, 1994).

Ginzburg, Carlo. *Clues, Myths, and the Historical Method*, trans. John and Anne Tedeschi (Baltimore: Johns Hopkins University Press, 1989).

Johnson, Stephen. *A Tyranny of Documents: The Performing Arts Historian as Film Noir Detective.* Performing Arts Resources, Vol. xxviii (New York: Theatre Library Association, 2011).

Postlewait, Thomas. *The Cambridge Introduction to Theatre Historiography* (Cambridge: Cambridge University Press, 2009).

Postlewait, Thomas, and Bruce McConachie, eds. *Interpreting the Theatrical Past* (Iowa City: University of Iowa Press, 1989).

16

BARBARA HODGDON

The visual record: the case of *Hamlet*

'Look ... upon this picture, and on this'
(*Hamlet*, III.iv.53)[1]

Like Hamlet, confronting his mother with portraits of his father and of the brother who murdered him, theatre historians work within a realm of loss, attempting to re-member who (and what) has disappeared. Yet visual traces of performance – engravings, paintings, drawings, cartoons and photographs – persist: ghosted images return to haunt us. Also like Hamlet, mapping one portrait's features against another, inauthentic and authentic images of a father, what theatre historians most desire is a visual image that preserves the paradox of a 'theatrical real'. For Shakespeareans, that ideal image might show costumed players at work in a 1590s theatre space, performing a moment recognisable as deriving from a particular play – even, perhaps, including spectators. In 1925, E. K. Chambers introduced a pen-and-ink drawing purporting to show just such a scene: since then, the 'Peacham drawing' – and the forty lines from *Titus Andronicus* transcribed below it – have undergone numerous interpretive changes.

Resembling an early modern version of Victorian toy theatres, the drawing reveals striking varieties of costuming: Titus as an ancient Roman, Goths dressed like Romans but bearing Tudor weapons, Tamora wearing a sixteenth-century loose gown with puffed, embroidered sleeves – a medley that may or may not represent an early modern company's wardrobe stock. Whoever transcribed the passage (Peacham's hand; another's?) below the drawing attempted to link this image to text. Yet no connection pertains between the signed and dated passage (1595?), the drawing and an endorsement on the opposing page, now discounted as a nineteenth-century forgery. Did Henry Peacham make the drawing? He described himself as addicted to drawing people's faces but whether he also was addicted to theatre-going or to sketching *dramatis personae* as he imagined them from reading is unknown. What purpose did the drawing serve? What purposes have historians' narratives and counter-narratives made it serve? Does the drawing reference Shakespeare's play or *A Very Lamentable Tragedy of Titus Andronicus and the Haughty Empress*, performed in Germany by English actors? If it does allude to an early staging of *Titus*, might it be understood through conventions of simultaneous representation prevalent in medieval and early modern painting, as in *The Spanish Tragedy*'s 1590 title-page woodcut? Does it represent an emblematic reading, symbolising rather than depicting Titus' tragedy? Or might it be an aide-memoire combining several episodes, highlighting what the artist thought most significant?

Similar questions trace through the images in this chapter's mini-archive of *Hamlet*'s visual record. In the archive, the materiality of an image is less factual than textual: the historian holds an engraving, drawing or photograph in her hand like a page, attempts to discern its meanings. Of what, exactly, does an image constitute evidence? What relationships pertain between the image and the facts of performance? In what contexts? What if any ancillary documentation supports such relationships? What power structures lie behind the production and archiving of images used as evidence? What narratives and counter-narratives burr onto the image, make it speak its secrets, connect it to cultural history? Despite the adage that one picture is worth a thousand words, a theatrical image often speaks through its caption, usually a Shakespearean citation. Yet captioning does not exhaust an image's meanings, for, like beauty, meanings reside in the eye of the beholder. And that eye / I, when engaging with a 'Shakespearean' gaze, always looks through a cultural poetics that changes over time and according to the assumptions of whatever critical agendas hold sway within the profession. Here, I oscillate between close looking and close reading, between a perhaps affective reading and one that, touching on theatrical culture, encompasses particular institutional politics. I search for an edge that will re-animate the theatrical event, steal its images back towards performance. Theatrical culture, argues Joseph Roach, reproduces and re-creates itself through processes of surrogation[2]: extended to the visual record, such processes of repetition and substitution reveal that particular key scenes, moments, lines and gestures feature prominently and consistently in *Hamlet*'s long iconographic history. Yet whatever relationship the images reproduced here bear to performance, whether representing it more or less directly or merely gesturing towards it, they cannot be subsumed under a unitary visual epistemology.

First beginners

Perhaps the closest connection to Shakespeare (who, according to legend, was the player of Old Hamlet's Ghost) is the figure of Sir Thomas Betterton or, more properly, a likeness resembling his 'personation' of Hamlet that constitutes the frontispiece to Nicolas Rowe's 1709 edition of *Hamlet*, for which Rowe acknowledged Betterton's help (Fig. 24). Representing the Ghost's appearance to Hamlet in the so-called closet scene (III.iv), the image resembles

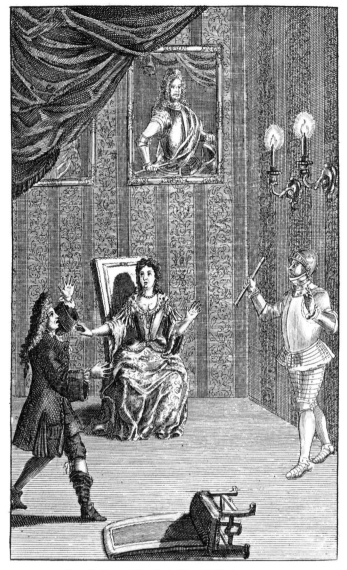

24 Frontispiece to *Hamlet* in Rowe's *Shakespeare*, 1709.

a little perspective box populated with wooden figures in wooden poses: far from naturalistic, it relies on a visual tradition in which 'design and emblem convey narrative and concept through composition and allusion'.[3] At left, Hamlet faces the Ghost, who apparently has materialised through the right wall: dressed in full armour, he extends a truncheon, as though to block

Gertrude's look. Seated upstage centre below two portraits – one festooned with a curtain (a theatrical metaphor?), the other resembling the Ghost – Gertrude is between Hamlet and the Ghost: her arms and legs widespread in amazement, she looks only at Hamlet, who stands with legs wide apart, one with a stocking 'foul'd, / Ungarter'd and down-gyved' (II.i.79–80). His position and gestures – both arms extended, his palms open, his partially open mouth registering shock or awe – recall Betterton's famous 'start' upon first seeing the Ghost (I.iv), praised by eyewitnesses for effecting a kinaesthetic response 'felt so strongly by the Audience, that … they in some Measure partook of the Astonishment and Horror … this excellent Actor affected'.[4]

What does this image reveal about eighteenth-century stage practice? For one thing, the tall chair at near foreground (presumably overturned by Hamlet) remembers a bit of stage business Betterton inherited from Richard Burbage via Joseph Taylor and Sir William Davenant and (so legend claims) suggested by Shakespeare himself. Such anecdotes, of course, are one way in which theatre tells its history. Yet although this frontispiece may allude to Italian Renaissance theories of perspectival staging later popularised in England by Inigo Jones, or exemplify rhetorical gestures mentioned in contemporary treatises influencing performance (and painting), this image does not *record* the experience of watching a performance event. Consider, however, another trace of Betterton's Hamlet-body. Speaking of 'all regular Gestures of the Hand', Betterton commented how Hamlet's fright at the Ghost's appearance was 'spoke with Arms and Hands extended, and expressing his Concern … [with] his Eyes, and Whole Face…'.[5] Although his comment does not offer 'proof of performance', it supports the conjecture that Rowe's frontispiece *alludes* to Betterton's Hamlet: for an eighteenth-century reader who had seen Betterton perform, the image might serve as a stilled mnemonic. The relationship among the figures, suggesting how Gertrude, seated below both her husbands' portraits, is trapped between the Ghost of her former husband and her son, not only references the moment's psychological scenarios but also draws together (through the 'down-gyved' stocking) Hamlet's appearance to Ophelia in *her* closet (II.i) and (through gestural echoes) Hamlet's initial meeting with his father's Ghost on the ramparts (I.iv). By privileging this turning point, this image (re)constructs the narrative, influencing the reader's perspective before she even turns to the text's first page. Viewed as a document in the history of the book, Rowe's engraving partakes of a readers' theatre: if performance figures in the image, it is only as a latter-day Oedipal, post-Freudian ghost.

The persistence of performance memory

To move from the Rowe engraving to Daniel Maclise's painting, *The Play Scene in Hamlet*, first exhibited at the Royal Academy (1842) and reproduced in engraving, mezzotint and watercolour, is to enter an entirely different phenomenological world, one which draws together currents of historical and literary painting, critical reading, iconographic convention and theatrical memory to capture, in deep socio-historical detail, an idealised vision of a performance event as seen by a theatre spectator (Fig. 25). Writing as Michael Angelo Titmarsh, William Makepeace Thackeray called *The Play Scene* one of the 'most startling, wonderful pictures that the English school has ever produced'.[6]

What was so startling? An elaborately designed setting, showing massed figures ranged on either side of the performed scene, framed centre within a proscenium replicating the painting's frame; glowing colours; expressive figures, their moods intensified by chiaroscuro: even a cursory glance catches a viewer up within a revelatory moment of the action, aligning her with the painted spectators, positioning her as though she were watching the scene in the theatre. The composition's formal structure brings the scene into a single, sharp focus on Hamlet's figure – 'author' and spectator of the painting's spectacle: an open playbook, presumably including Hamlet's 'dozen or sixteen lines' (II.ii.535), lies before him; he gazes intently at Claudius, seated at right with Gertrude. Hamlet's posture echoes that of the sleeping king in the framed play scene – where the players' shadows, projected on the back wall, generate the eerie sense that the murder persists in memory; his half-shadowed face contrasts with Ophelia's brightly lit figure at left, her white dress and down-turned eyes proclaiming her innocence. Behind her a statue of Prayer stands before tapestries depicting the temptation and expulsion of Adam and Eve from Eden; at right, above Claudius and Gertrude, a statue of Justice bearing scales and sword and a tapestry showing Cain's murder of Abel from which Claudius turns away, hiding his face from the play and its painted spectators. Situated at the apex of a triangle between Ophelia and Horatio on the one hand and Claudius and Gertrude on the other, Hamlet's figure calls attention to the tense observation haunting Elsinore's court, a trope that some twenty-first-century stagings have visualised as pervaded by surveillance technologies.

In its use of allegorical and iconographic conventions, Maclise's image reveals a deep comprehension of textual resonances and characterological thinking that not only exceeds the Rowe engraving's sense of 'readers' theatre' but also over-reads the play's oppositions between good / evil, innocence / guilt. Yet Maclise's picture goes beyond mere illustration, for performance

25 Daniel Maclise, *The Play Scene in Hamlet*. Watercolour copy, possibly by Alice Bolton.

constitutes one of the causal factors behind the painterly image, which, based on the Hamlet-figure's resemblance to portraits of the actor William Charles Macready and confirmed by eyewitness accounts (the detail of Claudius hiding his face accords with his promptscript[7]), documents Macready's 1823 performance of Hamlet with remarkable accuracy. George Scharf's outline drawings, produced 'to assist the recollection of play-goers in recalling [Macready's] splendid and tasteful scenic arrangements', show allegorical figures flanking the stage as in Maclise's painting.[8] Moreover, not only did Maclise frequently visit Macready's rehearsals and attend his performances but he also discussed the painting-in-progress with Macready. For theatre historians, Maclise's painting is also famous for recording a defining gesture, one delineating a player in a particular moment. Known as Hamlet's crawl, this stage business originated not with Macready but with Edmund Kean's 1814 Hamlet. Although William Hazlitt praised its 'extreme boldness',[9] the *Morning Herald* deplored Kean's ungentlemanly behaviour: 'he not only exposed his *derrière* to his mistress, but ... crawled upon his belly towards the King like a wounded snake in a meadow'.[10]

Because Maclise's painting captures the moment before the crawl, it requires a viewer who knows the history to re-animate it. Even so, by preserving Macready's surrogation of Kean's behaviour, Maclise becomes what Roach calls a 'meticulous curator of cultural memory, a medium for speaking with the dead':[11] serving as a touchstone for subsequent performances, his image shifts the usual direction of borrowing from stage to painting. With the power of performance tradition behind it, Hamlet's crawl became stage business that audiences approved, even demanded, as though no performance of the play scene seemed complete without it: even if a player omitted it, images alluding to his performance sometimes included it. Haunting *Hamlets* for two centuries, the gesture passed (the list is incomplete) from Macready to Irving (where it reached melodramatic heights) to Johnston Forbes-Robertson (in his 1913 film, though not his 1897 staging) and, in a vestigial quirk, to Richard Burton's 1964 performance, directed by John Gielgud. And this 'startling, wonderful picture' had another, equally persistent afterlife, for, according to the *Quarterly Review* (1876), an Art Union print of Maclise's *Play Scene* – carrying marks of genre historical painting and commemorating Shakespeare, by now Britain's national poet – was 'as common in dining-rooms now as the mezzotint copy of Lawrence's portrait of John Kemble as the Prince was thirty years ago'.[12] By entering private living spaces, Macready's Hamlet, or a memory of his performance, points towards a mid-twentieth-century moment when television brought theatre, or its simulacrum, into the home.

The persistence of visual memory

Maclise's *Play Scene* may have graced dining rooms and front parlours, but portraits of actors and actresses – marked as second-rate paintings of disreputable people – were relegated to men's smoking rooms. By the mid-nineteenth century, however, as photography became increasingly affordable and obtainable, photographic images of performers not only gained respectability but also began appearing beside pictures of family members in photo albums.[13] Taken in a portrait photographer's studio, such photographs figure as re-enactments, simulacra of costumed-performers-in-role, designed to capture a particular attitude. Even though by the 1870s, the London Stereoscopic Company was making photographs for Henry Irving's Lyceum Theatre, existing technologies were not yet capable of taking images from performance: for the most part, 'freeze-framing' theatre remained the province of the painter or sketch artist, as in this 1874 wood engraving[14] (Fig. 26). Signed 'A.H.'[15] but undated, it re-imagines the moment in Irving's performance (which had opened on 31 October) when Hamlet breaks away from Horatio and Marcellus and follows the Ghost towards a stage-left exit.[16]

26 Wood engraving, Hamlet and Old Hamlet's Ghost, 1874. The missing caption reads, 'Unhand me, gentlemen! By Heaven, I'll make a Ghost of him that frets me! I say away! Go on, I'll follow thee.'

Not only does it offer a full-scene view rare in nineteenth-century visual records of theatrical activity, it also captures Irving's over six-foot-tall frame, extremely thin legs, awkward forward movement and angular hand gesture, his fingers held stiff and straight. Given the number of contemporary sources that agree with it, the *Graphic* image has considerable value as a document of re-membered performance. Yet why did A. H. choose to record this particular moment? Possibly he desired to capture some aura of what so impressed Tomaso Salvini: the 'perfect' moonlight achieved by blending dim green light from the footlights with dimmer blue light from rows of overhead gas jets behind the proscenium arch; as the Ghost appeared, the footlights dimmed, distant 'Ghost music' played and limelight illuminated the vision.[17] The engraving also marks an innovative moment of Irving's performance: rather than seeming terror-stricken by the Ghost, his outstretched hand and drawn sword, pointed at the ground, suggests his willing acceptance of this spirit as his father, to whom he spoke in 'tones of ... filial reverence, and awestruck submission', seemingly drawn onward as 'by a mesmeric spell'.[18] But whereas Victorian audiences might recognise Irving's familiar likeness, a latter-day historian viewing this drawing might just as easily read his figure as parody or caricature.

No history of *Hamlet*'s visual record would be complete without the image that definitively marks (and markets) his figure and has become his quintessential DNA: Hamlet holding a skull. That icon originates with the figure of Amblett, Hamlet's Danish predecessor: a 1597 illustration shows him holding a globe, an emblem representing worldly dominion that morphs into Hamlet's head as 'distracted globe' (I.v.97) and, finally, into Yorick's skull.[19] W. G. Baxter's drawing of Irving, 'sketched from life' in this *carte-de-visite* image, one of many readily available to collectors as souvenirs, represents the Hamlet-skull interface (Fig. 27). Although clearly a caricature – Baxter has endowed Irving with the big nose, enlarged head and spindly legs of his popular strip cartoon character Ally Sloper – it nonetheless suggests Irving's look, his exceptional powers of concentration. Highlighting his raven-black hair, heavy eyebrows and thin, wide mouth, the sketch accentuates his glittering eyes and penetrating glance, the gaze fixed outwards, revealing how the power and intensity of his acting, so frequently mentioned in eyewitness accounts, derived from the constant play of facial expressions.

But this particular caricature also has a fascinating historical doubleness, for Irving's attitude parodies that of John Philip Kemble's Hamlet in Sir Thomas Lawrence's romantic portrait (1801): bearing no resemblance to the stage, it shows Kemble posed before a sombre churchyard landscape in splendid isolation. Wrapped in a sable cloak and elaborate mourning bonnet

27 W. G. Baxter, 'Hamlet'. The Irving Portrait Gallery.

with feathers, he looks aloft, not at the skull, held decorously at his side, one thumb inserted in an eye-socket so that no reminder of grinning death detracts from the poetic Prince. Ten years before his Lyceum Hamlet, Irving participated in a series of readings by Charles Calvert marking the tercentenary of Shakespeare's birth by imitating Kemble's Hamlet in an accompanying *tableau vivant*.[20] A photograph commemorating that occasion shows Irving wearing a plumed hat and a cloak and gesturing with one hand towards Yorick's skull, held in the other, calling attention (as do other rare photographs) to his long, delicate fingers and striking facial architecture. In some respects, Baxter's drawing of Irving's figure, posed amid a tumble of grave monuments, is an even more direct descendant of its upmarket 'source' and of Irving's 1874 performance than the earlier photograph, for it not only references the portrait's solitary figure but also replicates Irving's copy of Kemble's elaborately plumed hat – to which critics objected, viewing Irving's more naturalistic stage conventions as at odds with Kemble's stagey style; here, the hat, held in one hand, balances the skull – the death's head visible, not turned away – held in the other. Looking at Irving's mask-like face and oddly disjointed figure, it even seems possible to see through the caricature to the actor contemporaries praised and revered.

The force of the photograph

Whereas the engraver, painter, sketch-artist and caricaturist clearly manipulate theatrical truth (a pertinent oxymoron), the photograph seems to stake out firmer evidentiary claims. Despite knowing that photographer and photographic processes alter or disturb documentary reality and that a photograph is subject to both the maker's and viewer's ways of seeing, 'reasonable accuracy' remains the flexible standard for photographic evidence in legal protocols. Theatre historians, however, mount a critique of theatrical photographs based on common assumptions that the photograph is an index of reality. Thomas Postlewait writes of how extraneous as well as extrinsic causes modify, limit or distort a photograph's documentary value: situating his comments within archaeological paradigms for deriving meanings based upon material, formal, efficient and final causes, he argues that when a photograph's final cause is a publicity shot or its formal cause the aesthetic principles of portraiture, such mediations subvert its use-value as a record of performance.[21] Taking a more inclusive stance, Dennis Kennedy advocates exercising care in choosing and using photographs, advises corroborating them with other available records and claims that the full-stage photograph showing relationships of actors to set represents the most accurate index of performance conditions.[22]

Given such caveats, consider Angus McBean's photograph of John Gielgud's 1937 Hamlet (Fig. 28). As with any McBean still, but especially his portraits, this one not only collapses distinctions between painting and photography but also seems prompted by the desire to reincarnate theatre as high art, theatre haunted by the ghost of painting. And as the boundary between the photograph and other performative media has become increasingly porous, the one absorbing the other, the still often seems to be doing the haunting. A descendant of the nineteenth-century cabinet or boudoir portrait photograph, this image is marked by similarly compromising conditions – a half- or full-day photo call, imported studio lighting, pre-arranged poses

28 John Gielgud as Hamlet, 1937. Photo by Angus McBean.

determined by McBean himself. Like the performance from which it derives its life, it is a staged event directed by McBean's I / eye: his gaze controls the shot; what emerges is the theatrical still as performance art. The patterns of contrast, exploiting highlight and shadow to carve out the actor's facial architecture, lend Gielgud an incandescent glamour: he becomes an icon of himself in role. Does it provide direct access to performance? No. And yes. For even though it may not precisely reference performance, it offers a metacriticism of Hamlet's characteristic solitude. Tangential to performance yet simultaneously perfecting it, the image strives to make visible the invisible: a flicker of thought, a glimmer of mental and emotional energy released into the image as markers of Gielgud's enigmatic, aloof, austere Hamlet – a logical, mannered, highly intellectualised performance. Both memory and mnemonic of performance (it was so when it was taken), McBean's image reveals what the still camera can do for performers – and for the theatre historian – that an archival video or streaming video cannot. Like any theatrical still, it is endowed with a seemingly timeless aura, for not only does it outlive the performance that it serves (or surrogates) but also, through the auspices of its presence in the archive, the event it commemorates continues to happen.

The photo call, usually though not consistently involving pre-arranged poses, was the primary means of documenting performance throughout the 1960s at the RSC. But it was not alone, for from the 1970s and well into the 1980s, Joe Cocks and Tom Holte, ex-journalists, were photographing entire dress rehearsals, resulting in an unusually full visual record for any one performance – images which, though obviously mediated, offered a direct, 'raw' look at performance. The practice of photographing dress rehearsals survives, but is usually confined to performances deemed significant, based on the celebrity value of players and/or directors; often, the full complement of images is available only by contacting the photographer. Thus, although one might imagine that the present-day visual record for any one production would increase exponentially, within the last ten to fifteen years the politics governing how stills are taken, manipulated and archived has been undergoing rapid and dramatic changes.

Characterising Victorian practices, David Mayer speaks of the 'symbiotic three-way relationship between performer, photographer and consumer' through which the portrait photo marketed play and performer and the play and performer marketed both performer and photograph.[23] Currently, however, not only do press departments control which images are taken and choose which will best market a performance, but the resulting media campaigns have a quickness and urgency that the nineteenth century's interlocking strategies lacked. The National Theatre (NT), the Royal Shakespeare Company (RSC) and Shakespeare's Globe share similar practices: following a photo call, the press officer, often consulting with the director, chooses around ten to fifteen images, mixing landscape (full-stage) and portrait images, looking for key actors in revealing poses, several crowd shots and images summarising key moments or telling the story; a selection is then made available to the press on password-protected websites and later archived.[24] And just as the still's publicity use-value takes precedence over documentary value, the politics of visibility at work here means that many performance features become literally invisible, available only (if at all) on archival videos. Although this may be partially dependent on curatorial logic, one way in which this tension between documentary and market value matters is that archival availability dictates, to some extent, the kinds of performance histories that can be told. Yet because theatrical stills function to sustain desire for Hamlet, *Hamlet* and Shakespeare, to see the present-day visual record as commercially tainted is to desire a utopian space where theatre – and theatre history – exist outside today's competitive media marketplace, one increasingly dependent on corporate funding rather than state or institutional subsidy. Consequently, current practices invite historians to reconsider past protocols about what constitutes documentary evidence of performance.

The following stills exemplify the current poetics and politics of photographic protocols at the RSC (and, by analogy, at the NT and the Globe). Both were taken by official production photographers, chosen by the director in consultation with the press office: one at a photo call where three to four scenes were staged; the other at a dress rehearsal. The first, Manuel Harlan's shot of Polonius's murder from Steven Pimlott's 2001 *Hamlet*, differs from usual images of the closet scene showing Gertrude, Hamlet and the Ghost (Fig. 29). Seemingly over-composed, its sharp angles and pyramidal design heighten the stark contrast between brightly lit foreground and dark background, throwing Gertrude's and Hamlet's black-suited figures into outline, replicating Polonius's silhouetted figure projected on the screen. A two-shot of lead actors, the still represents one kind of ideal image desired by both publicists and archivists: not only does it show the minimalist production design (thus functioning as a semi-landscape shot) but it also features major actors in key roles. As though evoking the Rowe engraving's gesture, Gertrude's raised hands echo those of the silhouetted figure on the screen; Hamlet's gun and the angle of his head point a viewer directly at the projected vision of Polonius, which resembles a portrait. More tellingly, since the shot is taken from Hamlet's point of view, it invites a double reading: although it portrays Polonius as the silhouetted monster, it also reads as Hamlet's projection of the figure he believes is behind the arras-screen: Claudius, the monstrous father.

The second, Ellie Kurtz's photograph of David Tennant's Hamlet in Gregory Doran's 2008 RSC staging, captures him about to exit on 'The play's the thing / Wherein I'll catch the conscience of the King' (II.ii.600–1) (Fig. 30). Occurring only in performance and on the archival video, the moment is absent from the later DVD, a second-generation, surrogate staging. Seeing Hamlet-in-motion is unusual for a figure often posed (in the archival record) at rest; Hamlet as cheeky barefoot boy keys into Tennant's manic energy, his mercurial ability to spin from one attitude to another on a dime, as though putting on and taking off hats in a comic routine. Image details – his bandage-wrapped hand, resulting from carving a *memento mori*

29 The 'Closet scene' in *Hamlet*. Photo by Manuel Harlan.

on his palm with a flick-knife, his crumpled red tee-shirt – stress this Hamlet's informality, lending him the aura of a rock-band performer. Although many eyewitnesses read the shirt's design as a skeleton, that it was a knock-off of a popular muscle shirt pulls a characteristically Shakespearean ambiguity into reading the still: Hamlet as both macho man-of-action and death's double. Clearly a landscape shot, the still reveals hints of the production's elegantly-chandeliered Elsinore where walls of dark mirrors loomed over a jet-black shiny stage floor, producing 'shimmer[ing] eerie doubles of everybody,

30 David Tennant as Hamlet. Photo by Ellie Kurtz.

including the encircling audience', a design 'perfectly suited to a drama where the hero is famously in two minds ... obsessed with theatrical counterfeits'.[25] Encapsulating Hamlet's most decisive moment, Kurtz's still enacts the tension between his larger foreground figure poised as though moving forward (out of the frame) towards action, leaving behind his former self, reflected upstage on the darkened mirrored floor – the double selves neatly encompassing the trajectory of Hamlet's role.

The play scene redux

Given what I sketched out earlier as the ideal image desired by a historian of Shakespearean performances, this photograph, of Giles Block's 2000 *Hamlet*, would seem to claim priority of place, to have 'pure' documentary status. (Fig. 31) Taken at Shakespeare's Globe, a theatre that reproduces the contours of early modern performance spaces, it shows costumed players in a familiar scene, seated spectators and the (famously infamous) groundlings. The image is as formally composed as a painting: marbled columns, players and musicians dressed to replicate an Elizabethan reality, hints of a garden setting

31 The play scene in *Hamlet*. Photo by John Tramper.

(the arboured backdrop, the flowered mound before the King and Queen) suggesting the space of Claudius's crime, the tightly controlled space fronting the stage where the audience stands. Does this still evoke a history of previous visions of performance? Vestiges, perhaps, though here Claudius turns away from the play and from Hamlet, not hiding his face (as in Maclise's painting) but kissing Gertrude's hand. The half-circle formed by the line of actors and the stage barrier frames Hamlet and Ophelia at the still centre of a turning world; Hamlet gazes, not on Claudius but on the parading players. Yet the very attempt to preserve this moment of playing – as in Maclise's painting, an instant preceding the scene's major event and the ensuing revelation – in a photograph seems anachronistic. Indeed, the image resembles what Peggy Phelan has called 'a pop-up anatomical drawing that stands in for the thing one most wants to save, the embodied [*original*] performance'.[26] Strikingly double, the image mingles times and spaces, evokes mythologised narratives and counter-narratives, has a conflated genealogy. It tantalises by offering spectators – and players – the sustaining illusion that they inhabit the space (and time) where Shakespeare himself was once a player.

But a tension between historical reconstruction and present-day market-place leaks into this image: staging a performance in the present, it also bespeaks, more explicitly than other photographs, the loss of performance past. For, as Catherine Silverstone writes, these contemporary actors 'function as supplements in relation to the material conditions of the early modern theatre'; they can never be 'the thing itself', only a simulacrum.[27] On the one hand, much of what those who work at the Globe have written about their attempts to bring back what is lost is shot through with anxieties about reproducing an early modern past, anxieties encompassing concerns about Shakespeare, authenticity, sex and gender in performance and spectatorship. On the other, more cynical spectators have compared the Globe experience to that of a theme park. Looking at a fantasy of early modern playing attended by (post)modern playgoers, does the viewer of this photograph become a cultural tourist, participate in the fictions and frictions of (replicating) presence on offer? If the narratives currently burring onto this image preoccupy present-day historians, what narratives will tomorrow's historians, whose gaze may differ, construct?

Looking on these pictures – again

In addition to the changes taking place in photographic protocols, what developments impact the future visual record of Shakespearean (and other) performances? First of all, the very status of performance is in flux: as performance itself circulates outside theatre buildings, in venues such as NT Live's HD-TV broadcasts, the boundary between live and digitally mastered performance has become blurred. Ancillary to that shift is the increased – and instantaneous – circulation of performance images. Both the NT and the Globe are currently retro-converting archival videos to DVD (itself a waning technology). The NT, the RSC and the Globe also maintain active websites where a photographic gallery and/or small segments of streaming video function as teasers, marketing performance stilled and in movement. Moreover, such images may circulate even more widely when clipped and/or collaged with other materials on YouTube videos, whether made under the aegis of the theatre company or in ready-made videos put up by individual users.

The move from analog to digital images has occasioned a massive shift in the quality of the image: even hi-res digital copies entail a loss of definition. As contrasts diminish, the image leeches out, a pale imitation of itself; the black-velvet depths of a McBean image are suddenly not quite so deep. Yet, although digital images can be easily and quickly transmitted from archives to individuals or publishers, permissions fees remain high (an average cost of £130 for four of the images reproduced here). Even in the recent past, this has meant that the visual image has existed in many performance histories as a looming absence, surviving only through verbal description. The upside, however, is that several archives recently have made some images available for print publication either free of cost or at a nominal fee.[28] Also, the Globe has recently granted permission for screen captures from archival recordings to academic journals (with each case carefully reviewed); provisions in Equity contracts, however, condition how such records can be made publicly available. At the time of this writing, it is difficult to assess the long-term effects of these practices on publishing visual images, for even if permissions fees are reduced, printing remains expensive and many publishers depend on authorial subventions and on CDs or websites accompanying print publication.

What, then, will constitute good looking? How will images be caught up in systems of public and private ownership? How, if at all, will images other than photographs be incorporated in these changes, made more available? In terms of present-day performances, will the photographic still become obsolete, replaced by captures from archival footage? If theatre historians have limited power to question or revise dominant politics of documentation and archiving, perhaps we can map out a materialist poetics of visual evidence that re-envisions how theatrical images, embedded as they now are within a series of authorised and un-authorised public practices, might perform in networks of viewing relations, in the dialogic of gazes. But then, what desires are or should be driving such future histories?

NOTES

1 Citations to *Hamlet* are from Harold Jenkins (ed.), *Hamlet*, Arden Shakespeare, 2nd edn (London: Methuen, 1982).

2 Joseph Roach, *Cities of the Dead: Circum-Atlantic Performance* (New York: Columbia University Press, 1996), pp. 22–7.

3 Stuart Sillars, *The Illustrated Shakespeare 1709–1875* (Cambridge University Press, 2008), p. 31; see also pp. 2, 31, 35, 38.

4 *The Laureat* (1740), p. 31; cited in William A. Buell, *The Hamlets of the Theatre* (New York: Astor-Honor, Inc., 1968), p. 10.

5 Charles Gildon's *Life of Mr. Thomas Betterton*, cited in Roach, *Cities*, p. 100; see also pp. 73–118.

6 Quoted in Finlan Cullen, 'Maclise and Shakespeare', in Peter Murray (ed.), *Daniel Maclise 1806–1870: Romancing the Past* (Cork, Ireland: Crawford Art Gallery, 2008), p. 174.

7 Shattuck's promptbook no. 24, cited in Alan R. Young, *'Hamlet' and the Visual Arts, 1709–1900* (Newark: University of Delaware Press, 2002), p. 192.

8 See *Recollections of the Scenic Effects of Covent Garden Theatre during the Season 1838–39* (London: James Pattie), n.d., n.p.

9 London *Morning Chronicle* (14 March 1814).

10 *Morning Herald* (14 March 1814), p. 245, cited in John A. Mills, *Hamlet on Stage: The Great Tradition* (Westport, CT: Greenwood Press, 1985), p. 83.

11 Roach, *Cities*, p. 78.

12 See Young, *Visual Arts*, pp. 248–50.
13 See David Mayer, ' "Quote the Words to Prompt the Attitudes": The Victorian Performer, the Photographer, and the Photograph', *Theatre Survey*, 43:2 (2002), 223–51.
14 Other performers include Tom Mead (Ghost), George Neville (Horatio) and Frank Clements (Marcellus); setting by Hawes Craven.
15 Possibly either Arthur Hopkins or Arthur Houghton; both worked for the *Graphic*.
16 Supported by J. H. Allen's souvenir promptbook, Harvard Theatre Collection. The original caption reads 'Unhand me, gentlemen! By Heaven, I'll make a Ghost of him that frets me! I say away! Go on, I'll follow thee'.
17 Salvini's *Autobiography* (1893), quoted in Alan Hughes, *Henry Irving, Shakespearean* (Cambridge: Cambridge University Press, 1981), p. 39.
18 Charles Lamb Kenney, 'Mr. Irving in *Hamlet*', quoted in Hughes, *Henry Irving*, p. 39.
19 The illustration (National Library of Sweden) appears in Marvin W. Hunt, *Looking for Hamlet* (New York: Palgrave, 2007), p. 6.
20 See Martin Meisel, *Realizations: Narrative, Pictorial and Dramatic Arts in Nineteenth-Century England* (Princeton, NJ: Princeton University Press, 1983), p. 405.
21 See Thomas Postlewait, *The Cambridge Introduction to Theatre Historiography*, Cambridge: Cambridge University Press, 2009), pp. 245–6.
22 See Dennis Kennedy, *Looking at Shakespeare* (Cambridge: Cambridge University Press, 1993), pp. 20–4.
23 Mayer, 'Quote the Words', 231–2.
24 My thanks to Nada Zakula (RSC), Margherita Orlando (NT) and Sian Estelle-Petty (Globe) for this information.
25 Kate Bassett, *Independent on Sunday* (10 August 2008); see *Theatre Record* 28: 16–17 (28 July–24 August 2008), 957.
26 Peggy Phelan, *Mourning Sex: Performing Public Memories* (London: Routledge, 1997), p. 3.
27 Catherine Silverstone, 'Shakespeare Live: Reproducing Shakespeare at the "new" Globe Theatre', *Textual Practice* 19:1 (2005), 31–50, p. 37.
28 For instance, Victoria and Albert Museum Theatre and Performance Archive, Folger Shakespeare Library, Harvard Theatre Collection; some archives refuse permissions for e-books.

FURTHER READING

Barthes, Roland. *Camera Lucida: Reflections on Photography*, trans. Richard Howard (New York: Hill and Wang, 1980).
 'The Photographic Message', in Stephen Heath, ed. and trans., *Image, Music, Text* (New York: Hill and Wang, 1977), pp. 15–31.
Hodgdon, Barbara. '"Here Apparent": Photography, History, and the Theatrical Unconscious', in Edward Pechter, ed., *Textual and Theatrical Shakespeare: Questions of Evidence* (Iowa City: University of Iowa Press, 1996), pp. 181–209.

'Photography, Theater, Mnemonics; or, Thirteen Ways of Looking at a Still', in W. B. Worthen with Peter Holland, eds., *Theorizing Practice: Redefining Theatre History* (London: Palgrave, 2003), pp. 88–119.

Merchant, W. M. *Shakespeare and the Artist* (London: Oxford University Press, 1959).

Sillars, Stuart. *Painting Shakespeare: The Artist as Critic, 1720–1820* (Cambridge: Cambridge University Press, 2006).

17

FIONA MACINTOSH

Museums, archives and collecting

Dionysius, the Syracusan tyrant, was an aspirant playwright and was also said to have been the proud owner of the writing tablets, desks and lyres that in the previous century had belonged to the tragedians, Aeschylus and Euripides. Some two and a half millennia later, devotees of Noel Coward are being invited to bid for a lock of Coward's hair, attached to an interview script dating from 1968.[1] While many such objects have been cherished by fans over centuries, others have only survived on account of their neglect in public institutions: a random list might include a pair of Lydia Lopokova's ballet shoes, David Garrick's gloves, and, more bizarrely, the amputated leg of Sarah Bernhardt, which was recently rediscovered in the anatomical collection at the University of Bordeaux.[2]

Collecting of all kinds has a long and fascinating history, and the desire to possess the relics of star performers, in particular, has resulted in a lucrative trade for dealers in recent years.[3] Many observers have pointed to the erotic impulses behind collecting – Benjamin speaks of 'the final thrill, the thrill of acquisition'[4] – and it is the 'thrill' of the chase, especially, that fuels the ardour of the collector. As Phillip Blom has noted, 'The most important object of a collection is the next one.'[5] And when the object itself is sexually titillating – as is the case with much ancient sculpture – there has often been a self-conscious awareness on the male collector's part of the interrelations between the sexual pursuit of a beautiful woman and the allure and 'penetration' of antiquity.[6]

Of equal longstanding has been the desire to put the objects in a collection on display, even if in the early years viewing was generally reserved for the privileged few. Whilst the nineteenth century witnessed the foundation of public museums, which housed collections formerly built up by and confined to the private realm, theatrical memorabilia – both relics and archival documents – took longer to become centrally held and preserved and considerably longer to be put on display. The ancient Athenians, by contrast, kept detailed records of their annual dramatic contest, the Festival of Dionysus, which

included the names of the winning plays and playwrights (who were originally the principal actors in their own plays), and from 449 BCE onwards the
names of the best actors as well. These lists are the earliest extant dramatic
records, and details of the dramatic contests were most probably kept from
the late sixth century BCE.[7]

Record keeping was often haphazard until the twentieth century –
sometimes carried out more or less efficiently by prompters but also recorded
by those who were dependent on unreliable sources[8] – and the documentary
evidence of performances survived, if at all, by chance rather than design. In
the early 1960s, most London theatres did not hold systematic records; the
hope of an editorial in *The Stage* in 1963 was that Kenneth Tynan, on his
appointment to the role of Literary Manager at the National Theatre, would
serve as the Theatre's archivist as well. But it was only some thirty years later,
in 1993, that the National Theatre established its own archives.[9]

This chapter examines the reasons for the relative belatedness of public
theatre collections and looks at the new ways in which theatre archives are
being developed in accordance with both current thinking about theatre
historiography and recent advances in archival theory. Long gone are the
days of privileging isolated documentary data in theatre history as theatre
historians now insist on the need to examine the multiple contexts of performance histories.[10] Since the 1970s there has been a parallel 'contextual turn'
in archive theory: whereas previously the collections housed within archives
were considered solely as physical entities, preserved within their original
order of acquisition, now archivists are encouraged to examine the institutional factors that shaped their collections and to think of their role as
'liberators' of their collections.[11] Indeed the archivist, whose previous focus
on the individual record often led to an inability to glimpse the significance of
the whole collection, provides the theatre historian with both a theoretical
and a practical partnership, which charts a path beyond the 'micro-theatre-
history' model.

From the cabinet of curiosities to the public museum

The traditional story of collectors and collecting begins with princes acquiring
rare and precious objects to reflect and reinforce their power. It moves on to an
account of the indefatigable humanists of the late sixteenth century who
believed they were descendants of Aristotle and Pliny, but who had, in the
wake of the discovery of the New World, another half of the world to document and assemble in their cabinets of curiosities. In the eighteenth century,
there begins to emerge a 'scientific' collector, who collects and classifies in
accordance with a rational system where all objects have a logical place.

Until relatively recently, the consensus was that the major difference between a pre-modern and the post-Enlightenment collection was that the first contained curiosities, the second 'representative' objects. The pre-eighteenth-century collector wanted to inspire awe and wonder in the onlooker while the modern collector aims, often within a museum context, to 'educate' the viewer. Whilst there is some truth in this overview, it adopts an outmoded reading of the history of collecting, according to which public museums were the only means of providing order and appropriate preservation for objects previously subjected to a chaotic and largely aristocratic and amateur care.[12] This account, moreover, downplays the spirit of scientific inquiry behind many early collections that served as both 'instruments of scholarship and realizations of encyclopaedic knowledge'.[13] Archives from the beginning were fuelled by serious research.

It is also mistaken to infer that early collections were simply shaped by the zeal and taste of aristocratic collectors: from the outset, collecting was in fact driven by precarious political and economic factors. Cottman's trawl through the records of ancient marble statues in the eighteenth century reveals a story of hard-dealing brokers, the imperial aspirations of patrons, political double-dealing on the high seas (notably between the French and the British during the war over the American colonies) and perilously long journeys across inhospitable terrain once the sculptures had arrived in Britain. It could often take as long as four years for the marbles to reach Britain from Livorno in Italy, occasionally making their way via the Irish ports of Dublin or Cork to avoid import duties.[14]

The emergence of the public museum was inextricably linked to political developments, both the overthrow of the monarchy in the French Revolution and the emergence of Romantic nationalism. Enlightened monarchs of Europe had begun to open their collections to public view during the course of the eighteenth century – both to signal their role as public 'educators' and to proclaim themselves as arbiters of taste – and just nine days following the storming of the royal residence and the effective fall of the French monarchy, work was begun on a museum to display the monarch's paintings. One year later, the museum at the former royal palace, the Louvre, and its collections were opened to the public. From 1803 the collections (now greatly enhanced by objects looted during Napoleon's recent victories across Europe) were organised chronologically, according to 'national' schools.[15] Gaps in collections were filled with plaster casts; and museums across Europe and the New World began to follow the French example in using museums to forge national identity and as a pedagogical device.[16] The educative goal was viewed by museums in Britain, in particular, as a way of 'civilising' the lower classes and was pursued 'with wholehearted ferocity: a Victorian missionary bringing to childlike natives the gospel of the rules of cricket'.[17] In a post-Enlightenment and increasingly secular Europe, culture was becoming sacralised.

Nationalism, national socialism and performing arts collections

Whilst the nineteenth century witnessed the birth of the modern, public museum, theatre collections languished in private hands well into the twentieth century. There are plenty of reasons for this delay, not least the still widely held assumption that theatrical memory is something that should be enshrined in the practitioner's art: inscribed in the bodily memory and then passed on over the generations through practice. The absence of central collections was also due to the fact that 'Theatre has no home': few companies or managements have owned the theatres they occupy, putting space at a premium.[18]

The Paris Opéra was the exception to the rule concerning collections: from the outset copies of musical scores were kept for revivals, even though none of these has survived from before the mid-eighteenth century, owing to the absence of public accountability. From 1749, when the administration of the Opéra was placed under the City of Paris, proper records had to be kept. In 1866, shortly after the publication of Castil-Blaze's two-volume history of the Opéra, the first archivist, the librettist Charles Nuitter, was appointed; in 1875 in the new theatre, Palais Garnier, a library was opened for study and in 1881 a museum.[19] The example of the Opéra serves to illustrate the paradox that benign neglect is often the best means of survival: if the collection had always remained with the company, rather than with the city records, it would certainly either have been consumed by fire or destroyed during the turbulent years following the Revolution.[20]

There are numerous reasons why the desire for the centralisation of performing arts collections should have come to the fore in Britain at the beginning of the twentieth century. Undoubtedly the most significant of these was the promotion of an increasingly nationalist cultural consciousness. Tours by the Comédie Française towards the end of the nineteenth century led to Matthew Arnold's call for a national theatre company in Britain, and from 1909 onwards the Ballets Russes acted as a strong spur for both a national theatre and a national ballet company.[21] Following the campaign for a national theatre, and with plans afoot to found the Shakespeare Memorial National Theatre, came the beginning of numerous attempts to establish a central collection of the performing arts. Gabrielle Enthoven began her campaign for a National Museum of

Theatre Arts in 1911; in 1924 she gave her own sizeable collection to the Victoria and Albert Museum, thereby inaugurating the V&A's Theatre Collection, and she worked on the collection as a volunteer until the late 1940s.[22]

The nationalist cultural impulse in Britain in the years leading up to the First World War found a rallying point in Shakespeare but was by no means confined to him. Fuelled by anxieties about and antipathy towards Germany both before and during the First World War, British cultural nationalism pervaded wide intellectual circles.[23] A series of lectures on theatre history given by Max Hermann at the University of Berlin in 1900 had led to the inauguration of the Max Hermann Theaterwissenschaft Institut (Institute of Theatre Science) in 1923. It was becoming more imperative than ever to promote a distinctly British theatre history.

Just as opera companies needed to keep musical scores for revivals from the outset, dance companies were similarly dependent on records as they too would regularly revive a complete production. For this reason, dance research was at the forefront of the establishment of archives for the performing arts in Britain owing to the riches residing within personal collections.[24] But dance was also at the forefront of the formation of central collections in Britain in the early twentieth century because events in Nazi Germany were even more keenly and immediately felt within the very international world of dance than they were within the more narrowly conceived national schools of Western theatre.

In July 1934 *The Dancing Times* announced the foundation of the Société Internationale de la Danse in Vienna, whose aim was to look for ways of establishing international co-operation within the dance community. Its members were urged to donate their collections of dance material to the Archives Internationales de la Danse, founded by Rolf de Maré two years earlier in Paris.[25] During the 1930s, anxieties concerning the dispersal of private collections increased as refugees were forced to flee their homes across Europe and seek shelter elsewhere.[26] The need to centralise collections for posterity became paramount: in 1944, in particular, there was considerable concern about the safety of the Paris Archives under the Occupation. The Ballet Guild began to build 'The London Archives of the Dance', under the chairmanship of Cyril Beaumont, which was finally founded in January 1945 with an archivist and a librarian. The central collection for the new Archives consisted of the Ballet Guild's 3,000 volumes, programmes and pictures, all of which are now in the collection of the Victoria and Albert Museum. The express intention was to set up a research centre for the post-war period, which would promote knowledge of the past in order to appreciate the performances of the present.[27]

Performing arts collections and the academy

Many collectors began collecting because they were involved in the profession in some way – the two founders of the Mander and Mitchenson Collection were both actors and acquired many important artefacts from friends such as Noel Coward, John Gielgud and Sybil Thorndike.[28] The other equally important catalyst for collecting is research: it is not simply the case that performance archives prompt research but that research proper (as was the case with the early humanists) leads to the creation of archives. Just as the publication of Castil-Blaze's two-volume *L'Académie impériale de musique de 1645 à 1855* (1855) had led soon after to the appointment of the first archivist at the Paris Opéra, so Harold Rosenthal's research for his *Two Centuries of Opera at Covent Garden* (1956) led to his taking up, albeit temporarily, the archivist post at the Royal Opera House at Covent Garden, and eventually to the appointment of a full-time archivist in 1969.[29] In 1945 The Society for Theatre Research was founded, and the preliminary discussions that year about the establishment of departments of drama within universities further strengthened the desire for the centralisation of performing arts collections.

Although the University of Oxford despatched a team of academics to the United States in March 1945 to examine the work in drama at Harvard and Yale, it was at Bristol in 1947 that the first British drama department was established. In 1952 at a conference on university drama departments at Bristol, the theatre designer, co-founder of The Society for Theatre Research and subsequently university lecturer in drama at Bristol, Richard Southern, advocated: 'we need a library where every known picture or plan relating to the development of the British stage up to the eve of modern times is available, whether in the original or in reproduction'.[30] According to Southern, it was not a museum that was needed for the performing arts, but 'the "Back Room" work of a museum – the models, the experiments, the uncased specimens, the notes, the photographic records, the list of references – the wood shavings and the carpentry of this research'.[31] And it was the universities, he argued, that needed to assume the responsibility for providing such a 'research station'. In 1957 Glynne Wickham, the first university lecturer in drama to be appointed in Britain and subsequently the first British Professor of Drama, purchased the founding object of the University of Bristol's Theatre Collection, a portrait of the eighteenth-century actor Charles Kean playing King Lear.[32]

Concurrent with the emergent new academic discipline of drama were the developments in the training of archivists in the post-war period.[33] In 1948, with the help of UNESCO, a meeting was convened in Paris to strengthen ties between archivists, which led to the foundation of the International Council on Archives (ICA). Behind these developments lay not only the post-war spirit of co-operation and collaboration, but also an anxiety dating back to the 1930s that European collections would head across the Atlantic where large sums of money were readily available. It was not, however, until 1965 that America's pre-eminent repository for theatre collections, The New York Public Library for the Performing Arts, was opened to the public.

Archival training was fuelled by a realisation that Europe needed both to appreciate the value of its historical records and, in the case of Britain in particular, to learn how to look after them.[34] With education and social policy high on the post-war agenda, 1947 witnessed not only the inauguration of Bristol's Department of Drama but also the institution of archival training within higher education.[35] At long last, there was a growing profession of archivists who were trained in and committed to the preservation of the nation's history for posterity.

'Re-opening' performance archives

The role of the archivist has changed considerably over time, both in theory and in practice.[36] The archive has ceased to function as a custodial setting where materials are locked away for safekeeping. Today the archivist focuses on how the records have been re-contextualised and often radically altered by the archival process itself. The context of the archive engenders a new understanding of the records, which means in turn that the history of the collection, and the various other societal and institutional contexts within which the records were produced, need careful scrutiny.

The way in which the archive itself is structured therefore becomes part of the object of study, and the fact that it functions as a creator of meaning rather than simply serving as a repository of knowledge is now widely acknowledged.[37] The digital performing arts archive, Sarma, was founded in Brussels in 2000 upon the belief that all archives are thoroughly subjective. Its core collection is made up of dance reviews from seventeen or so critics from eleven countries, alongside which are transcripts of discussions and workshops. Sarma's aim is to 'become a rhizomatic resource for dance discourse, a place where writers join their readers with respect for the polyphony of voices and opinions'.[38] Another archiving project, entitled 'My Hotel Medea: The Audience as Document', which was developed at the Victoria and Albert Museum in London in March 2011, involved two groups, one consisting of those who had watched an all-night show entitled *Hotel Medea* at the Arcola Theatre, London, in February 2009 and another of people who had missed the production. The archiving process in this instance involved not only recording first-hand experiences of a show but also capturing information from those whose knowledge had been acquired at second or even third hand.

The archivist who was formerly the custodian of individual records or objects is now understood to be engaged in the process of 're-opening' or 'liberating' collections to a wide range of people, from school students to scholars, from the local community to the international public who may 'visit' the archive remotely through the digitised objects within collections.[39] The 're-opening' of theatre archives, in particular, has come about through improved communications between different archives. TIG (Theatre Information Group) was founded in the 1980s to bring together those working with performing arts collections. Initially it involved only collections based in London, but it is now the UK centre of SIBMAS, the International Association for Libraries and Museums of the Performing Arts founded in Paris in 1954. Alongside this formal networking, indispensable guides to the various performing arts collections have appeared, in hardcopy and now online.[40] In Britain plans are currently underway to create a National Performance Database linking the collections held by the main performing arts archives, namely The Royal Opera House, the Victoria and Albert Museum, The University of Bristol Theatre Collection and the National Theatre Archive.

One important example of the 're-opening' of the archive is The National Theatre Archive, which moved in 2003 from the National Theatre's Prop and Costume Store in Brixton in South London to the National Theatre Studios, based round the corner from the theatre itself. Under the management of the National Theatre's Artistic Director Nicholas Hytner and its Executive Director Nick Starr, the National Theatre Archive was deemed to have a key role to play not only as storehouse of the Theatre's memory, but also in the creation of new work. In marked contrast to the other principal performing arts archives in Britain, such as The Shakespeare Institute in Stratford-upon-Avon, the National Theatre Archive is sited at the heart of the organisation and enjoys therefore a real interaction with practice. According to the National Theatre's Archivist, Gavin Clarke, the Archive functions very much like the engine room of the organisation, where its 'mechanical' parts and its fuel are stored and where there is a regular interchange of ideas as studio work is often punctuated by consultation of archival material.[41] It also demands of its Archivist the role of 'liberator' of the collection: while Tynan in the 1960s was expected to double as literary manager and archivist, Gavin Clarke is today both records manager and educator, with links to both nearby South Bank University and King's College London.

A relatively recent and much smaller scale archive, which also seeks to function as the 'engine room' for research and practice as well as seeking to 're-open' its collections, is the University of Oxford's Archive of Performances of Greek and Roman Drama (APGRD). Founded in 1996 by Edith Hall and

Oliver Taplin with a grant from the Leverhulme Trust, its aim was to document the history of performances of ancient drama from the Renaissance to the present. Since those early years, the APGRD has extended its remit: back in time to include the performance history of the ancient plays in antiquity; across genres by including performances of epic as well as dramatic texts, encompassing opera and dance within the orbit of modern performance; and across media to include performances on film, radio and television.[42]

Given the belated centralisation of theatre collections in Britain, the APGRD may not itself appear belated, but in many ways it was: literal amateurs of ancient drama, like Taplin himself, had amassed their own collections of memorabilia relating to performances of ancient drama in the modern world and yet there was no equivalent of the Shakespeare Institute at Stratford-upon-Avon (founded in 1951) within which to house such material. This absence was, perhaps, not surprising given the international impact of the classical world and, since the Second World War at least, the global presence of ancient drama in modern performance, which meant that there was no one obvious centre for such a collection. The nearest equivalents were scattered collections in Greece where performances of ancient plays had played a key part in the forging of national identity and nationalist politics.[43]

Like other collections, then, there were personal collections at the APGRD's foundation, and personal passion had been fuelled by involvement in research and in practice.[44] Whilst Shakespeare's rich tradition of reperformance was increasingly recognised as central to an understanding of his plays in the present, classical drama was studied well into the 1970s primarily as philological text, and performance histories of the plays were confined to the realm of the anecdotal or to the pedagogical margins. The founding of the APGRD was inextricably bound up with the desire of Taplin and Hall to promote further research: to demonstrate that an understanding of the performance history of the ancient plays was essential to an understanding of ancient theatre itself, and to broaden and shape the emergent discipline of 'classical reception studies'. Research Hall and I conducted at Reading University from 1991–4, documenting the performance history of Greek plays on the British stage from 1660–1914, had produced a sizeable collection of records and artefacts, which supplemented Taplin's twentieth-century-focused personal collection.[45] Through the research carried out at the APGRD and its burgeoning collections, theatre history has been recognised as an integral component in the study of Classics. The APGRD has, perhaps, more importantly allied theatre history to the history of classical scholarship and to the history of ideas. In the absence of any formal focus for theatre research within the University of Oxford as a whole, it is often said that the

APGRD has become by default the 'Theatre Department' that failed to materialise in 1945.

The physical location of a collection is significant. In 1996 the APGRD was based in the European Humanities Research Centre in Oxford but in 1999 it moved to a newly built Classics Centre. No longer the poor relation left to seek shelter with distant cousins in Modern Languages, the APGRD became part of the research culture within Oxford Classics alongside the Centre for the Study of Ancient Documents and The Classical Art Research Centre and the Beazley Archive. The APGRD's collection, built up over the years by researchers and by the donations from friends and colleagues around the world, boasts a sizeable collection of books, CDs and DVDs, production files containing programmes, photos and reviews, as well as original manuscripts, rehearsal scripts, set designs and oral histories.

Starting its life as a research centre, the collection was largely hidden from public view, visible only as sources for an online database, until the arrival of a professional archivist in 2010.[46] Indeed until then no one had particularly thought about the collecting process in any systematic way. There were discussions about whether tickets should be kept (the exorbitant price of a ticket for the epic-length *Tantalus* at the Barbican in 2001 had prompted that decision), and considerable thought was given to the widening of the remit of the collection to include loose adaptations, performances within antiquity, dance and opera, and more recently performances inspired by the ancient epics.

The APGRD collection is now 're-opening', in accordance with current archival theory, and continues to grow thanks to the increasing consensus that the written documents, oral accounts and the artefacts relating to the performances of ancient plays need to be preserved – as part of theatre history and of the story of how the classical world has shaped modern life. Whilst there has been no conscious sense of imposing control and exclusion in the way that Derrida identified as characteristic of archival practice in general, there are inevitably gaps and elisions, which have come about through unconscious prejudice as well the inevitable imbalances that derive from an attempt to collect material worldwide.[47] It is essential to reflect upon the institutional context of the APGRD, within what has been deemed an elitist discipline and an elitist university. Classics and class are inextricably linked, as has been well documented, but the APGRD's holdings and research have demonstrated how the ancient plays have been used as much to challenge as to reinforce the social and educational elite, for whom knowledge of antiquity was a mark of exclusion and privilege.[48] Histories of classical scholarship are now in a position to include the countercultural discourse of eighteenth- and nineteenth-century classical burlesques, as well as to examine the often radical purposes of productions of ancient plays across the globe since the Second World War.

A particular collection of material within the APGRD dating from the 1920s–1950s, which had belonged to a German Professor of Rhetoric at Humboldt University, points to other ways in which ancient plays have become embroiled in politics. Wilhelm Leyhausen spearheaded the post-Second World War Delphiad series of performances in ancient theatres across Europe, which were staged in order to bring young people together in the spirit of international cultural exchange and co-operation. A former participant in the series put us in touch with the current owner of the material, who was very keen to rid himself of numerous boxes languishing in a damp basement in Frankfurt. In addition to the Delphiad productions, the collection includes Leyhausen's own musical settings for Greek tragic odes and contains much material that documents the wider European avant-garde developments in 'total' theatre during the 1920s and 1930s, for which ancient drama was a major site for exploration and experimentation. Leyhausen's development of *Sprechchor* (speaking chorus) was contemporary with Rudolf Laban's *Bewegungschor* (movement choir) and must be seen in the wider political context of the Hitler youth and the Nazi mass rallies of the 1930s. Leyhausen's ability to remain in post throughout the war years and his reverence for ancient drama are symptomatic of fascism's investment in the ancient world. The theatre archive thus helps classicists and producers of classical drama to interrogate the practice of their own activities.[49]

Like most modern archives, the APGRD is a real space with objects and documents; it is also a virtual space through its online presence, its database and its increasingly digitised collections. More unusually, it has also acquired a further function thanks to the Onassis Foundation, which enables it to commission and produce new works inspired by ancient plays.[50] Finally, it is a 're-opened' space in which researchers, fledgling and seasoned, amateur and professional, scholars and practitioners, can access information, share ideas, create new work and write theatre history. In 1952 Richard Southern spoke of the need for universities to provide a 'Back Room' for the performing arts: the 're-opened' theatre archive promotes research, pedagogy and creativity and demonstrates that they not only can co-exist but that such co-existence needs to underpin theatre history.

NOTES

1 http://modernfirsteditions.co.uk/product/asignedcopyofan4183760.html.

2 A family friend has a number of Lopokova's personal items in her possession that she inherited from a balletomane grandmother; the RSC has one of two identical pairs of gloves that were worn by Garrick and allegedly once belonged to

Shakespeare. For the macabre story of Bernhardt's leg, see www.factsandarts.com/articles/the-curious-story-of-sarah-bernhardts-leg, accessed 28/4/2011.

3 P. Blom, *To Have and To Hold: An Intimate History of Collecting* (London: Allen Lane, 2002), esp. pp. 158–68.

4 W. Benjamin, *Illuminations*, trans. H. Zohn (New York: Harcourt, Brace & World, 1968. See, esp., 'Unpacking my Library: A Talk about Book Collecting', pp. 59–69.

5 Blom, *To Have*, p. 157.

6 V. Cottman, *Classical Sculpture and the Culture of Collecting in Britain since 1760* (Oxford: Oxford University Press, 2009).

7 P. Wilson, *The Athenian Institution of the Khoregia* (Cambridge: Cambridge University Press, 2000), pp. 214–18.

8 J. Bratton, *New Readings in Theatre History* (Cambridge: Cambridge University Press, 2003).

9 *The Stage*, 15 August 1963, cited at www.nationaltheatre.org.uk/7134/archive-collection/collection-holdings.html, accessed 28/4/2011 and subsequently inaccessible.

10 Bratton, *New Readings*; T. Postlewait, *The Cambridge Introduction to Theatre History* (Cambridge: Cambridge University Press, 2009); and H. Bial and S. Magelssen (eds.), *Theatre Historiography: Critical Interventions* (Ann Arbor: University of Michigan Press, 2010).

11 T. Cook, 'The Concept of the Archival Fonds in the Post-Custodial Era: Theory, Problems and Solutions', *Archivaria*, 35 (1993), 4–37.

12 T. Bennett, *The Birth of the Museum: History, Ideas, Politics* (London and New York: Routledge, 1995); and Cottman, *Classical Sculpture*, for a critique of A. Michaelis, *Ancient Marbles in Great Britain* (Cambridge: Cambridge University Press, 1882).

13 Blom, *To Have*, p. 15.

14 Cottman, *Classical Sculpture*, pp. 150–1.

15 Blom, *To Have*, p. 113.

16 E. Crooke, *Politics, Archaeology and the Creation of a National Museum of Ireland* (Dublin: Irish Academic Press, 2000); J. J. Sheehan, *Museums in the German Art World* (Oxford: Oxford University Press, 2000).

17 Blom, *To Have*, p. 120.

18 Muriel St Clare Byrne's address, 'Theatrical Records' (1957), cited in C. Hudson, 'Sixty Years of Collecting', unpublished lecture for The Society for Theatre Research, March 2008. I am most grateful to Claire Hudson for sending me a copy of her notes for this lecture.

19 Castil-Blaze, *L'Académie impériale de musique de 1645 à 1855* (Paris: Castil-Blaze, 1855). See I. Guest, 'Archives of the Dance [8]: Dance Material in the Archives of The Royal Opera House, Covent Garden', *Dance Research*, 6 (1984), 78–82.

20 *Ibid.*, 76.

21 M. Arnold , 'The French Play in London', *The Nineteenth Century*, 5 (1879), 242–3; J. Lawson, 'An English School of Dance', *The Dancing Times*, August (1942), 60–6; and E. Evans, 'Nationalism and the Ballet', *The Dancing Times*, April (1943), 309–10.

22 Hudson, 'Sixty Years'; A. Schouvaloff, 'The Theatre Museum: Where is That?' (2007), at www.theatremuseumguardians.org.uk/TheatreMuseum/curatorspeaks.

html (accessed 5/5/2011 and subsequently inaccessible). The Theatre Museum was based in Covent Garden from 1987–2007. The collections are now held in the dedicated Theatre and Performance galleries in the Victoria and Albert Museum, Kensington, and at the Museum's premises in Blythe House, Kensington Olympia.

23 C. Baldick, *The Social Mission of English Criticism 1848–1932* (Oxford: Oxford University Press, 1987), pp. 70–108.

24 J. Pritchard, 'Archives of the Dance (7): The Rambert Dance Company Archive', *Dance Research*, 6.1 (1988), 59–69.

25 *The Dancing Times* (July 1934), 391–2.

26 *The Dancing Times*, (March 1942), 296.

27 K. Sorley-Walker, 'Archives – Positions and Problems', *The Dancing Times* (February 1944), 113–14; *The Dancing Times* (February 1945), 208; *The Dancing Times* (May 1945), 353. Cf. earlier concerns in *The Dancing Times* (July 1934), 391–2; (March 1942), 296; (December 1939), 125, (March 1942), 296.

28 The Collection is now part of The University of Bristol Theatre Collection.

29 F. Franchi, 'Archives of the Dance [3]: Dance Material in the Archives of The Royal Opera House, Covent Garden', *Dance Research*, 6 (1988), 78–82.

30 R. Southern, 'Theatre Research and the Universities', in D. G. James (ed.), *The Universities and the Theatre* (London: G. Allen & Unwin, 1952), p. 97.

31 *Ibid.*, p. 100. The University of Bristol Theatre Collection dates from 1951.

32 M. White, 'Professor Glynne Wickham', Obituary, *The Independent* (11 February, 2004). The painting was purchased after he persuaded the University to put up the requisite £110.

33 E. Shepherd, *Archives and Archivists in Twentieth-Century England* (Aldershot: Ashgate, 2009).

34 Cf. France and Spain where training was offered from the nineteenth century onwards. *Ibid.*, p. 218.

35 At UCL, Liverpool, and Oxford. *Ibid.*, pp. 175ff.

36 For archival theory, see T. Cook, 'The Concept of the Archival Fonds in the Post-Custodial Era: Theory, Problems and Solutions', *Archivaria*, 35 (1993), 4–37; T. Nesmith, 'Reopening the Archives: Bringing New Contextualities into Archival Theory and Practice', *Archivaria*, 60 (2005), 259–74.

37 P. Michelakis, 'Archiving Events, Performing Documents: On the Seductions and Challenges of Performance Archives', in E. Hall and S. Harrop (eds.), *Theorising Performance: Greek Drama, Cultural History and Critical Practice* (London: Duckworth, 2010), pp. 95–107.

38 www.sarma.be/nieuw/about/about.htm (accessed 5/5/2011 and subsequently inaccessible).

39 Nesmith, 'Reopening', 274.

40 E.g., Diana Howard's pioneering *Directory of Theatre Research and Information Resources* (London: Arts Council of Great Britain, 1980). The third much expanded edition by Francesca Franchi appeared as *Directory of Performing Arts Resources* (London: Society for Theatre Research and the Theatre Museum, 1998). In 2002 Backstage database appeared, the records for which have now migrated to the Culture Grid (www.culturegrid.org.uk).

41 In conversation with the NT Archivist, Gavin Clarke.

42 Two five-year AHRC grants, support from the Mellon Foundation and the Classics Faculty at Oxford, and a further grant from the Leverhulme Trust have made this possible.

43 G. Sideris, *To Archeo Theatro sti Nea Elliniki Skini 1817–1932* (Athens: Icarus, 1976).

44 Taplin had acted as academic consultant on the 1981 *Oresteia* at the National Theatre and had more recently written a book (1990) based on his Channel 4 series *Greek Fire*.

45 This research was eventually published as E. Hall and F. Macintosh, *Greek Tragedy and the British Theatre 1660–1914* (Oxford: Oxford University Press, 2005).

46 The online database contains details of over 9,000 productions (www.apgrd.ox. ac.uk/database). The APGRD has published nine volumes to date (one due in 2013) and numerous monographs by its researchers, who are both senior and emergent academics.

47 J. Derrida, *Archive Fever* (Chicago: University of Chicago Press, 1996), trans. E. Prenowitz.

48 Hall and Macintosh, *Greek Tragedy and the British Theatre*.

49 Dr Eleftheria Ioannidou (Humboldt Postdoctoral Fellow, Freie Universität, Berlin) is working on this collection for a monograph on Greek drama under totalitarian regimes.

50 www.onassis.ox.ac.uk.

FURTHER READING

Bennett, T. *The Birth of the Museum: History, Ideas, Politics* (London and New York: Routledge, 1995).

Blom, P. *To Have and To Hold: An Intimate History of Collecting* (London: Allen Lane, 2002).

Bratton, J. *New Readings in Theatre History* (Cambridge: Cambridge University Press, 2003).

Cook, T. 'The Concept of the Archival Fonds in the Post-Custodial Era: Theory, Problems and Solutions', *Archivaria*, 35 (1993), 4–37.

Nesmith, T. 'Reopening the Archives: Bringing new Contextualities into Archival Theory and Practice', *Archivaria*, 60 (2005), 259–74.

Shepherd, E. *Archives and Archivists in Twentieth-Century England* (Aldershot: Ashgate, 2009).

Sincere thanks are owing to the APGRD Archivist, Naomi Setchell; to Gavin Clarke, National Theatre Archive's Archivist; to Claire Hudson, Head of Collections, V&A; and to Eileen Cottis, Secretary for The Society for Theatre Research.

18

GILLI BUSH-BAILEY

Re: Enactment

> What are we to do about reenactment? ... One easy answer is to say of
> reenactment as of sexually transmitted disease, that there is a lot more of
> it about nowadays.[1]

Following the lead in the next chapter, a cursory glance at Wikipedia delivers
a list of over 178 historical re-enactment groups of which at least 48 organisations are identified as UK-based, over 40 are in the USA, with others
offering cross-national membership in groups as far afield as Romania and
Taiwan. Their activities chiefly offer involvement in battles and military
events, dating from as early as 284 CE to the South African border wars in
1989.[2] The long-established practice of reconstructing and re-enacting military engagements is far from the only area upon which scholarly interest
around re-enactment has begun to focus. The desire to 'know' about one's
own past, the individualised genealogical quest for a personal family history,
has elided with a public desire for a shared cultural memory, both coming
together to satisfy what cultural historians recognise as a 'yearning to experience history somatically and emotionally – to know what it felt like'.[3] British
television companies have embraced this appetite for popular histories with
re-enactment programmes on life in Edwardian country houses, Victorian
pharmacies, Georgian town houses and village high streets down the ages.
These places are all brought to life by teams of historians, behind and in front
of the camera, aided by willing (re-en)actors, offering a stream of entertainment that is educational in remit and, crucially, economically successful.
Worldwide spin-offs promise participants and their audiences a 'just-as-it-
would-have-been' experience, which often, as Anja Schwartz observes of the
Australian *Outback House* (Australian Broadcast Corporation, 2005),
'mixes traditions of re-enacting historical events in period dress with documentary television and *Big Brother*'s "fly-on-the-wall" format that portrays
participants subjected to a group endurance test'.[4] For those wanting more
than a couch-bound experience, Google offers a calendar of re-enactment
events and a portal to a tempting array of retail outlets for chainmail,
medieval shoes, and battle-ready helmets, with specialists like Seraphima
Needlework offering to provide tailor-made 'bespoke garments' for male
and female re-enactors who '"play" in the Napoleonic period'.[5] It is this

crossover between play and performance, this slippage between the real and the imagined, that provokes the academic unease expressed in my epigraph. That half-joking analogy between these activities and the diseases of sexual promiscuity goes to the heart of the matter: we are deeply alarmed by the fetishistic attention to, and visceral excitement of, the embodied engagement with the past.

This chapter looks at the ways in which the concerns of historiography, particularly the performative approaches of re-enactment methods that seek to provoke an emotional experience, intersect with moves in performance theory and theatre historiography. The gap between the re-enactor and the actor/performer is increasingly blurred. Re-enactment is no longer a private experience but more often a public event, involving spectators and, in the case of the televised examples above, a growing worldwide audience. Professional historians are also entering into re-enactment, becoming re-enactors in their own archival projects.[6] Similarly, professional performers are undertaking scholarly reflections on past performance practices, bringing into play their own archive of embodied knowledge through practice as research. The connections and dissonances between reconstruction and revival, the archive and the body, are being employed to explore and contest the assumptions of distance and difference between the past and the present. As Joseph Roach puts it, '[t]ime doesn't flow, it percolates'.[7] What now follows is concerned with the place of theatre history in narrating stories that seep through the porous filters of the archive: stories told and retold, written and performed, textual and embodied both in performance and in my own kinaesthetic imagination as a sometime-practitioner theatre historian.

Benchmarks on the body of theatre history – and cultural heritage

As the introduction to this volume makes plain, at a time when history has a growing popular appeal, with television channels devoted entirely to the subject and employing marketing devices more usually aligned with fresh food in the supermarket industry – 'History: made every day,'[8] theatre historians feel somehow besieged. We fear being caught out, squeezed between the tectonic plates of history and heritage. The energetic focus on the importance of local histories, the histories from beneath that continue to add new dimensions to our understanding of community identity, finds itself at odds with the current political desire for the 'big stories', the 'facts' to be reinstated in our schools and university programmes.[9] This volume seeks to offer challenges to that limiting set of binaries. Another important move, to which this volume contributes, is the gradual cessation of sometimes hostile suspicion between theatre history and performance studies, a contestation that Henry Bial and Scott Magelssen work to erase in their collection of essays *Theatre Historiography: Critical Interventions* (2010), a volume welcomed as 'a veritable hotbed in which theatre history and performance studies productively, even seamlessly intertwine'.[10] And yet, a defensive turn can be felt in a number of other recent publications in theatre history and historiography that appear to offer a narrowing focus on the processes and protocols of the discipline, recapitulating the demand for 'facts' and retreating from the affective turn of cultural theory to reconstitute a cloak of objectivity, a barrier that safely shields the historian from her or his subject of enquiry.[11] So where in this shifting ground of academic discourse and exchange does the work of historical re-enactment sit, and how does the theatre historian apply historiographical methods and protocols to such a complex set of engagements? Can the cross-currents of performance studies and the heritage industry create a matrix from which new historiographies can emerge?

In *Representing the Past* (2010), a companion piece to the ground-breaking *Interpreting the Theatrical Past*, published twenty years earlier in the whiteheat of cultural theory, Tracy C. Davis and Bruce McConachie (also both contributors to that earlier volume of essays) include in their discussions the impact of re-enactment on contemporary performance and for theatre history.[12] Tracy Davis draws attention to the economic importance of the heritage industry and its performative pleasures, arguing that '[t]he way that many heritage sites infuse artificiality amid authenticity – a presentational exigency borrowed from theatre, making veracity relative – gives professional historians pause yet is precisely what enhances many visitors' enjoyment'.[13] The embodied, visceral response – the affective turn – is central to historian James Walvin and his concerns about the work of Liverpool museums in the 1990s, presenting a disturbing account of the debates on how, and indeed whether, Liverpool's role in the slave trade should be represented by a reconstruction of the interior of a slave ship:

> Efforts to present accounts of the stink of a slave ship, the shrieks of the mad and the distressed, and the agonies of the dying raised the fundamental question of our obligation to the visiting public. Do we want to rub the visitors' noses in the slave mire in order to make a (perfectly valid) point? What role should affect play in historical sites?[14]

Walvin raises questions about the usefulness of 'immersion' experiences, asking 'how do we know what the past smelt like, and how do we know what historical actors considered to be a bad smell?'. Describing the 'less sensational' but surely highly theatrical device of using 'flickering images in a darkened room to the sound of a creaking ship and hushed voices', Walvin notes that, '[e]ven in so muted a form, this proved to be one section of the exhibit which often caused the greatest distress to black visitors'. Walvin's larger concern is with the occlusion or, worse still, the romanticisation of the black presence in the political and cultural life of British (and American) culture and the concomitant limitations of the connections between the past and the present. 'The question remains', he asks of the museum's slave ship experience, 'does it increase historical understanding?'.[15]

An important intervention in the field has been made by the Performance, Learning and Heritage research project (2005–8), funded by the British Arts and Humanities Research Council, and led by Professor Anthony Jackson from Manchester University. The major findings and reflections on the project are gathered together in *Performing Heritage* and, as Jackson and Kidd explain in their introduction, the contributors work to engage with the '[w]ider debates in the heritage sector around ownership, authorship, participation, materiality and, not least, pedagogy [which serve] to highlight the role of the performer'.[16] Jackson goes on to discuss the research group's preference for using the term 'performance' rather than 'museum theatre', arguing '"performance" is a more all-embracing term that includes not only theatre performances that are clearly recognisable as such, but also "first person interpretation"'.[17] First-person interpretation is particularly important to the negotiations made in *This Accursed Thing*, a partnership project between PLH researchers and Manchester Museum in 2007, marking the bicentenary of the abolition of the British slave trade. Moving beyond Walvin's concerns, this project embraced the potential of the visitor's emotional experience in a promenade performance that began and ended with an actor performing the role of a museum curator: 'the subject of the performance was thus both the museum (and its past failure to acknowledge its links with the history of slavery) as well as the transatlantic slave trade itself'.[18] Helen Rees Leahy describes the decisions and choices that visitors made as they followed the promenade performance from space to space, standing close, or drawing back from the actors, showing how such positions brought them into 'direct dialogue' with the performers, particularly in

> a scene in which a black African sells people whom he has captured to a white European trader. At the end of the scene, the white trader challenges the viewers to criticise his actions; the well-prepared actor has a deft answer to all the objections that they raise. It is a piece of skilled improvisation which fuels precisely the kind of debate (and position-taking) that the performers intended.[19]

Unsurprisingly, Leahy records that 'for many people *This Accursed Thing* was a moving and sometimes painful experience'.[20] The 'skilled' improvisation, the move from first-person to third-person interpretation, also demands that the performer immerse her/himself in the character being performed (first person) and in the practice of historiography as the third-person interpreter, that is, to embody in their performance not only what happened, but as third-person interpreter to convey how and why the events have been constructed.[21]

A less emotionally loaded experience of first- and third-person interpreters raised further questions for me about the relationship between history, heritage, performance and historiography on my visit to Blists Hill Victorian Town in Ironbridge, Shropshire, on a hot day in spring 2011. The site for the BBC series, *Victorian Pharmacy* (2010), the Victorian town is one of ten museum sites in and around Ironbridge. Visitors roam around the reconstructed streets, taking horse and trap rides, avoiding the newspaper boys running past in heavy boots, entering the many shops to buy 'Victorian' produce with Victorian coins (a visit to the bank where 'local' currency can be obtained is one of the highlights). Cards and letters can be posted at the Post Office where the postmaster, in full official regalia, explains (in first-person role) the workings of the post and, with some prompting from this visitor, moved to third-person role to expand upon his duties across several of the area's museum sites. As a trained curator, he was pleased to share his professional expertise with a self-confessed theatre historian and express his commitment to the move from the display of objects to an emphasis on visitor experience in the heritage industry as a whole, shifting swiftly into his 'role' as postmaster on the entrance of another set of visitors. Moving on to a 'squatter's cottage' on the outskirts of the town, I encountered a female squatter carrying a basket (see Fig. 32).[22] Again, the first-person role was embodied as she moved into the cottage to take up her place by the cooking fire and, again, she was pleased to slip out of that role to tell me about her own research processes, and how the cottage had been moved from its original site some miles away to be reconstructed at Blists Hill. Her job demanded local knowledge and a surprisingly deep historical understanding of squatting, the rights of the squatter, the number living in this and similar squats in the nineteenth century, survival rates of children and the demands for families attempting to live in such circumstances. Watching her move around the cottage, demonstrating domestic skills and responding to visitor questions, I was aware of the very porous space between the visitor and the audience, a theatrical experience that is established in the process of entering the Victorian town via the shiny twenty-first-century museum shop at which the entrance fee is taken. The visitor is then directed toward an unmarked domestic door, opening unexpectedly into a high darkened space filled with projections of the industrial past, its processes and its workers larger than life-size on every surface. Surrounded by the startling sights and sounds of iron foundries, blazing red

32 Re-enactor at Blists Hill.

and white furnaces with men lifting huge shovels of molten ore, this immersive experience leads toward another door, marked simply 'to the town', from which you enter the streets of a Victorian town.

Performing Heritage is interested in 'how visitors *become* audiences and often participants in performance'.[23] Theatre historians grapple with this question too but from the other side: how do audiences *become* visitors? Questions around the quite different, but equally contentious, 'heritage' experiments in spatial reconstructions of theatre and performance have circulated in discussions between theatre-makers and theatre historians for some time. Robert K. Sarlos's minutely detailed reconstruction of the medieval

286

passion play of Lucerne is prefaced by an impassioned argument for theatre historians to engage with performance reconstruction:

> No matter that it cannot be an exact replica of the original work – it will bring all the participants, including spectators, closer to a sensory realization of the style and atmosphere, the physical and emotional dynamics of a bygone era … intensif[ying] the imaginative stimuli, extending them into auditory, tactile, and olifactory realms, with a force and urgency beyond the reach of written language.[24]

Sarlos was writing in 1989. A similar passion for reconstruction, '[r]ecapturing the *spirit* of the Shakespearean staging tradition',[25] with all its attendant dangers of romanticising past theatre as a 'golden age', has been realised to some extent with the opening of 'Shakespeare's Globe' theatre on London's South Bank in 1997. Visitors are invited to see an exhibition and take the Globe tour 'to explore the life of Shakespeare, the London where he lived and the theatre for which he wrote'. Demonstrations of costumes, props and special effects are on offer, and, while there are no first-person interpretations (as yet), the Globe's website does promise an experience of the past in the present:

> Our expert guides will take you on a fascinating tour of the iconic Globe Theatre and auditorium, bringing the space to life with colourful stories of the 1599 Globe, of the reconstruction process in the 1990s, and of how the 'wooden O' works today as an imaginative and experimental theatrical space.[26]

As the theatre is also used for performances, the shift from visitor to audience is perhaps clearer here than in the museum sites discussed above. Even without Sarlos's '[n]oises, scents and other stimuli external to the work itself',[27] the Globe experience, whether for visitors or audience (or both), begs the question of how deeply the modern-day 'groundlings' are engaged on a sensory level, especially when plied with very modern bottles of water on the few hot summer days or provided with waterproof ponchos to deal with the London summer rain that is the more usual experience of outdoor theatre. The aesthetic pleasures of the oak timbers and the intimacy of the space are undeniable, but does the Globe experience materially affect Shakespeare's place in the cultural memory of its audiences and, crucially, in the long history of the theatrical repertoire?

The Theatre Royal at Bury St Edmunds has also combined a heritage restoration programme on its Regency building (1819) with a programme of revivals of plays familiar to a nineteenth-century audience. With guided tours, play-readings and full productions, it aims 'to do for the Georgian theatre what the Globe has done for Shakespeare!'[28] As a receiving house, the programming is dominated by modern productions, but its 'ReVisit' programme includes workshops and backstage tours that promise the experience of a nineteenth-century working theatre. Other recent reconstructions in theatre history have been employing practice-as-research as part of scholarly research, and these findings are increasingly disseminated via online and digital resources, such as Martin White's *Chamber of Demonstrations* which reconstructs a Jacobean theatre, providing examples of performance and, crucially, different sightlines for the spectator seated in the pit, stage boxes and gallery.[29] Virtual visitors, or audiences, have a growing number of opportunities to experience the past in the present. Richard Cave's project, *Richard Brome online*, augments a complete collected edition of this seventeenth-century dramatist's plays with video-stream of workshops in which 'real' performers explore Brome's 'theatricality visually, serving as inspiration to encourage more frequent staging of Brome's works'.[30]

The projects discussed above all seem to respond to Sarlos's argument that 'performance reconstruction should be undertaken in order to enhance vital links between past and future theatre practice, and at the same time to restore a balanced relationship between scholars and artists',[31] an argument that is at the heart of the editors' intention for this volume as practising historians work with and teach theatre-makers of the future. But should theatre historians not heed Baudrillard's warning that 'the simulation – the simulacrum – is more real than the thing itself'?[32] To put this caveat simply, if we were able to step back in time and enter an Elizabethan, Jacobean or Regency theatre, would the experience of the reconstruction enable us to recognise the 'real thing', or would we find that experience so alien that the reconstructed, simulated, re-enacted representation appears more 'real' to us? The temptation, as John Brewer sees it, lies in 'the tendency to collapse the distance between past and present, reducing it to zero so that the re-enactor inhabits a sort of overwhelming timelessness in which the present self and past other merge into a single identity'.[33] As visitors or audiences in the theatre yard or gallery, we are, in effect, re-enactors, being encouraged to connect ourselves with the theatre-going experience of earlier generations. Brewer goes on to argue for the importance of working *with* distance, rather than seeking to erase it. It is here that projects like Performance, Learning and Heritage have much to offer by recognising that the visibility of the historian at work, *in* the work, is vital.

That very visible presence has been embraced by popular public historians. Simon Schama and David Starkey are among the familiar faces of authoritative history on British and American television screens, continually augmented by new historians and rising stars, including one of the few female voices, Professor Amanda Vickery, whose successful television series

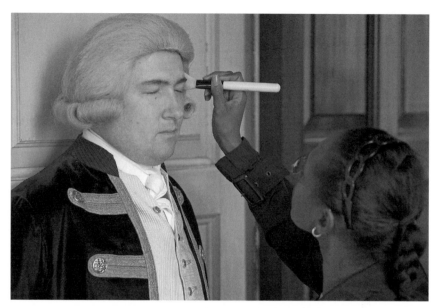

33 *At Home with the Georgians*. BBC, 2010.

At Home with the Georgians was screened by the BBC in 2010. This three-part series took the viewer on a journey through the development of the 'home', focusing on the relationships between men and woman in Georgian society as houses were secured, furnished and decorated according to the advancements and consumerist tastes of the day. Vickery was always 'herself' on screen, the historian walking through the streets, houses and rooms that were then peopled by (re-en)actors who demonstrated the action described (Fig. 33). These scenes were augmented by Vickery's re-enactment of her own historical process, notably when she was seen walking freely (and surely only because she had a television crew with her) through archive stacks, reaching for boxes of letters and personal documents that had provided the intimate accounts of the past that she had garnered over many years of research, and demonstrating technological advances in research by referring to documents stored on her iPad.

While high-profile popular historians have a wide and enthusiastic following for their performances, historians of theatre and performance are, paradoxically, far from visible. Until now they have normally appeared as 'the expert', a talking head in a documentary, while the figure offered to the viewer as the real expert is a well-known performer hosting and sometimes re-enacting the performer and performance of yester-year. But new scholars and new forms of scholarship are beginning to emerge, as practitioners engaging with the histories of their craft in self-reflexive and critical research seek to situate their own practice within a historical context. Much of this work has emanated from the field of dance. Susan Leigh Foster is a leading practitioner-historian who demonstrates the power of gesture, expressive movement held and remembered in the body, in an argument that works to establish that we might 'allow movement as well as words the power to interpret', that we might 'find in choreography a form of theorizing'[34] that embraces memory and embodied histories of theatre practice. Placing living memory, gestures and movement in juxtaposition with historical records in a move that acknowledges an embodied archive is described by theatre historian Joseph Roach as kinaesthetic imagination,[35] which leads me to insert my personal experience into this history – and into the emerging practices of historiography.

Scars and traces

As a professional performer, I have been familiar with the experience of having my hair put in rags overnight, to maintain the curls favoured for young Edwardian girls as depicted in *The Railway Children* (BBC, 1967). Aged fourteen, I felt none of the visceral excitement expressed by women donning corsets for re-enactments and was delighted when my mother suggested secretly removing every other bone in the corset to give me some comfort while performing as Jane Seymour's sister in *Six Wives of Henry VIII* (BBC, 1969). As an actress, I learnt to move and sit within the costumed constraints of the past, but however many dialect coaches or dance instructors were imported to bring authenticity to our actions, I was always aware that I was acting in fictional narratives. In 1978, I played Charlotte Brontë in a drama-documentary (BBC, *Blue Peter Special Assignment: The Brontës of Haworth*). Filmed in the lovingly restored Brontë parsonage in the Yorkshire village of Haworth, the film crew had access to the usually cordoned-off spaces, and we silently enacted many of the famous moments and scenes in the Brontës' lives, to which the voice-over commentary would be later added. While filming, I read Charlotte's novels and found myself immersed in the 'Brontë experience', especially when it came to (re)enacting her last walk on the moors when, a few months pregnant, Charlotte and her curate husband were caught in a rain storm (provided for the moment of our reconstruction by the local fire brigade who doused us with water from their hoses). Charlotte's death scene was played out in the actual room in which she died of pneumonia and dehydration exacerbated by sickness in the early months of her pregnancy. I too was four months pregnant in the spring of 1978, a condition that gave great concern to the costume department as they tightened my corset and fed me into the constricting skirts of 1854. The eerie experience of performing Charlotte's dying moments in that small, candlelit upper room in the parsonage has always stayed with me. In retrospect I might say that it marks a transition moment between acting and re-enacting, which now has significance for me as a historian–practitioner. The presence of the film crew did of course emphasise my role as an actress, but the shared embodied knowledge of my, and Charlotte's, pregnancy enabled me also to recognise the powerful sense of having 'really lived' an experience of the past, a sense expressed by so many re-enactors and heritage performers.

I initially moved into the scholarly pursuit of theatre history with the idea of creating some distance from my performing past. Coming from three-deep generations of actresses, I did not recognise myself or the experiences of my mother and grandmother in stories I read about the history of women in theatre. I felt a need to interrogate their history and, ultimately, my own experiences as a performer, so I set about learning a new scholarly trade, embracing the rigours of engaging with the archive as I explored the working lives of the first actresses and female playwrights of the Restoration stage. I could not wholly resist the belief that to see costumed bodies in performance would reveal some historical secret, hidden from view in textual accounts of the period; however, while my faltering attempt to reconstruct the staging conventions of the Restoration playhouse in the found space of a Victorian boilerhouse told me much about the assumptions around acting style of the period, I was aware that the problems of engaging with historically distant comedy encountered by my inexperienced student performers told me more about my own ineptitude in directing an informed, but nonetheless imagined, reconstruction of actresses working in 1695. I recorded the event, but when I submitted my Ph.D. in 2000, the first year that London University admitted practice-as-research Ph.D.s, I did not submit my practice to be examined, including it merely as an appendix to my conventionally written thesis. This was a wise move: my examiners chose politely to ignore the video of the work.

A more successful experiment was undertaken with Jacky Bratton and a class of students working on the fragmented performance text of Jane Scott's Romantic melodrama, *Camilla the Amazon* (1817). Building on the students' familiarity with the complex and intimate narratives of contemporary soap opera, combined with the spectacular and comic genre of the adventure film, we were able to lift a sometimes confusing nineteenth-century performance text from its place of hiding in the archive and realise some of its impact as a live piece of popular entertainment. This led to a research grant to take Scott's work further in a series of workshops with a company of professional practitioners. 'Working it Out' (2002) revealed the presence and strength of the embodied knowledge of performers, guided and directed by a phalanx of historians specialising in music, dance, theatre, stage fights and, crucially, costume. The opportunity to experiment with authentic early nineteenth-century clothes revealed the vast difference in body shapes between past and present. The small-armed, fitted jackets of the period were impossibly small for the more developed upper body of our twenty-first-century actors, while the capacious buckskin trousers, we discovered, were fitted for thighs and calves that were more used to walking or riding than travelling in cars, trains and buses. A move to experiment with a period absence of under-garments beneath the flowing dresses for the women was roundly rejected by twenty-first-century actresses. On the other hand, the use of gesture with text and music creating a meta-language of performance was exciting to the modern performers, both effective and, for our modern-day audience, affecting. Yet, as historians, in our decidedly off-stage position, we perhaps did little more than give the findings of our performers the air of scholarly authority. A CD-ROM documenting the project was this time included along-side conventional academic writing in a special edition of *Nineteenth Century Theatre and Film* (29:2, Winter 2002). Although this research project resulted in invitations to lead workshops in Canada and America and informed the performance approaches employed by companies producing plays at the Theatre Royal, Bury St Edmunds, there remains something unsatisfying in a procedure that is so close to practice, yet situates the theatre historian outside the event. For the Scott project, we were the narrators, commenting on the work of the re-enactor/performers; having situated ourselves on the margins as a sanctioning authority, we were, at most, seen as doing the preparatory scholarly work that informed the embodied research of others.

There is, I suggest, another step to be taken, one that emerges from the matrix of historian-re-enactors, historian-presenters and heritage performers, a step that can be made through extending the historiographical practice of the usually more distant theatre historian. I have only recently begun to explore the possibilities of such a move in my own research on the perfor-mance history of Frances Maria Kelly, a nineteenth-century actress who performed what is probably the first English one-woman show, in 1832. A popular actress on the stages of London's Drury Lane and Lyceum theatres, Kelly used her own life stories, and her own memories of the theatre profes-sion and its audiences in London and the country theatres where she appeared, as material for *Dramatic Recollections*, a fund-raiser to build a theatre behind her home in Dean Street, Soho, from which she would run a Dramatic Academy. Having transcribed her text to become the first-ever published edition of Kelly's performance text and prepared a performance biography for publication, I faced the pressing question of how to realise some of this material beyond its textual form.

Even though the Theatre Royal at Bury St Edmunds could provide a perfect setting in the newly restored Georgian theatre in which Kelly appeared, and to which she returned for a performance of *Dramatic Recollections*, the notion of donning a costume and simply performing the material seemed unsatisfactory. A televised documentary on her life and work, with actors performing the material, seemed an exciting but unlikely project in today's hard commercial world of television commissioning where the emphasis on the fame of the subject (or historian-presenter) is paramount. The route that has therefore suggested itself is performative – and also personal. It is tied in with Kelly's frequent references to her own years as a child performer and empathetically touched by my own understanding of that sometimes strange childhood experience. The performance paper based on this confluence is still a work 'in progress'. It pulls on the tensions between autobiographical performance and a conventional academic paper in theatre history. It situates the theatre historian, me, in the real space of negotiation between Kelly's anecdotes of her early professional life and my own life, between her own material for performance and my performance of that material. The dangers of presentism are not buried but embraced, just as historical distance is not ignored but worked with. By drawing attention to the role and place of the 'real' theatre historian, the work sits between re-enactment and practice as research. It seeks to open up the hidden history of women in theatre, interweaving my own performance history with Kelly's story. The juxtaposition of these stories produces a new history and, I hope, explores a new historical methodology.

34 Gilli Bush-Bailey in *Performing Herself* (2012).

Jonathan Walker's 'textual realism' provides a useful reference point for the performative strategy I am seeking to mark out. 'It is a self-conscious and critically engaged form of intertextuality', not to be confused with what Walker identifies as the 'blank stare of pastiche'. In this practice, textual realism 'replaces imitation with selective, critical quotation and commentary – that is, with interpretation – but this interpretation proceeds through drama-tisation rather than exposition through re-enactment'.[36] Walker's essay uses illustration, in the form of a comic strip that depicts the historical moment he is exploring but includes himself, the historian, as one of the cartooned characters in the dramatic action (Fig. 35). In the same way, my own presence in the performance as a theatre historian is always visible to the audience. For Walker, '[a]nachronism is deployed as a critical technique',[37] and, in a similar move, I step to and fro between historically different pasts, unsettling the distance by my presence as both subject and object of my historical research.

Such unsettling of past and present is of course central to the work of heritage performance. The performers in *This Accursed Thing*, discussed above, stepped in and out of role, entering into dialogue with their visitor audience in what Anthony Jackson sees as a manifestation of Bakhtinian heteroglossia.[38] As part of a related project, Anna Farthing reflects upon her creation of *Destination Freedom*, a half-hour piece for two performers based on the biographical narrative of William and Ellen Craft, who fled enslavement in America to freedom in Britain in the mid-nineteenth century. Farthing discusses the setting of the piece in an abolitionist meeting in Liverpool with a member of the museum staff inviting the visitor/audience to 'imagine themselves at an anti-slavery meeting in 1850'; the power of touch, as the actors shook hands with as many people as they could, 'con-firm[ed] the enrolment of the audience into a shared double consciousness of imagined time as well as space, 1850 and 2007'.[39] Farthing describes the powerful encounters as, following the performance, 'the actors came out of role', answering questions about the Crafts but also asking questions about present race relations in Liverpool, with particular reference to race hate crimes, including the murder of a local black teenager to whose memory the performance was dedicated. Powerful as Farthing's description is of the theatrical experience she had created for actors and audience, Farthing, as dramatist (and historian), was absent from the performance.

This absence brings me back to the deliberate fracturing of the word 're-enactment' in the title of this chapter. As historians, of whatever kind, history matters to us, and we are interested in enacting our roles as historians, playing a part in bringing what matters from the past onto the stage of this present moment in life. The practices of historical re-enactment and performance studies in heritage contexts have much to offer us and, I suggest, we have

35 Jonathan Walker in a medieval 'dance of death'.

much to offer in return. With Walker, I would argue that, as *theatre* historians, we commonly work in a disembodied digital world on the one hand, yet have an increasing appetite for somatic engagements with the past on the other. As Farthing puts it, 'in order to reuse and recycle our material, to say something new with it (and if we are not saying something new, then why say anything at all?), we must first take it to bits, gut it and expose the bare brick underneath. We must, in other words, violate its integrity by exposing its relativity, along with our own.'[40] It is an irony that perhaps it is time to confront and expose the truth – that as theatre historians we are often particularly afraid of performance. It is as if in our desire to remedy the lamented ephemerality of theatre and performance we feel safe only with the reality and durability of the text. Theatre historians should acknowledge what we know but often leave to be realised by others: that text may be embodied and that, without the body, theatre is only a place of the imagination.

NOTES

1 John Brewer, 'Reenactment and Neo-Realism', in Iain McCalman and Paul A. Pickering (eds.), *Historical Reenactment: From Realism to the Affective Turn* [hereafter referred to as *Historical Reenactment*] (Basingstoke: Palgrave Macmillan, 2010), pp. 79–89, p. 79.

2 Wikipedia, www.wikipedia.org/wiki/List_of_historical_reenactment_groups (visited 08/01/2012).

3 Iain McCalman and Paul A. Pickering, 'From Realism to the Affective Turn: An Agenda', in *Historical Reenactment*, pp. 1–17, p. 2.

4 Anja Schwarz, '"...Just as it would have been in 1861": Stuttering Colonial Beginnings in ABC's *Outback House*', in *Historical Reenactment*, pp. 18–38, p. 20.

5 www.seraphima.co.uk/, visited 08/01/2012.

6 See, for example, Stephen Gapps, 'On Being a Mobile Monument: Historical Reenactments and Commemorations', in *Historical Reenactment*, pp. 50–62, and Jonathan Lamb, 'Historical Re-enactment, Extremity and Passion', *The Eighteenth Century*, 49:3 (2008), 239–50.

7 Joseph Roach, *It* (Ann Arbor: University of Michigan Press, 2007), p. 13.

8 www.history.com/shows regularly advertises its programmes with this tag.

9 See Introduction, pp. 3–4.

10 Henry Bial and Scott Magelssen (eds.), *Theater Historiography: Critical Interventions* (Ann Arbor: University of Michigan Press, 2010), back jacket quotation by Kim Marra, University of Iowa.

11 Robert Hume's *Reconstructing Contexts: The Aims and Principles of Archeo-Historicism* (Oxford: Clarendon Press, 1999) is an obvious example, but even Thomas Postlewait's *The Cambridge Introduction to Theatre Historiography* (Cambridge: Cambridge University Press, 2009) is described in the front matter as 'an indispensible "how to" guide for students and teachers alike', suggesting a leaning toward goals of objectivism.

12 Tracy C. Davis, 'Performative Time', pp. 142–63, and Bruce McConachie, 'Reenacting Events to Narrate Theatre History', pp. 378–403, in Charlotte M. Canning and Thomas Postlewait (eds.), *Representing the Past: Essays in Performance Historiography* (Iowa City: University of Iowa Press, 2010).

13 Davis, 'Performative Time', p. 151.

14 James Walvin, 'What Should We Do about Slavery?', in *Historical Reenactment*, pp. 63–78, p. 68.

15 *Ibid.*, p. 69. This gallery made way for a new museum of slavery as part of the 2007 anniversary of the abolition of slavery and Liverpool's status as a European City of Culture in 2008.

16 Anthony Jackson and Jenny Kidd (eds.), *Performing Heritage: Research, Practice and Innovation in Museum Theatre and Live Interpretation* (Manchester: Manchester University Press, 2011), p. 1.

17 *Ibid.*, p. 1.

18 Helen Rees Leahy, 'Watching Me, Watching You' in *ibid.*, pp. 26–38, p. 36.

19 *Ibid.*, p. 37. *This Accursed Thing* and the challenges of 'unsettlement' for all participants is also described in Anthony Jackson's chapter, 'Engaging the Audience', in Jackson and Kidd (eds.), *Performing Heritage*, pp. 11–25.

20 Leahy, 'Watching', p. 37.

21 Here, I am citing and paraphrasing Bial and Magelssen's useful definition of historiography in *Theater Historiography*, p. 1.

22 My thanks to Lorraine Ratcliff for kind permission to include this photograph taken on my visit on 9 May 2011.

23 Jackson and Kidd, *Performing Heritage*, p. 5.

24 Robert K. Sarlos, 'Performance Reconstruction: The Vital Link Between Past and Future', in Thomas A. Postlewait and Bruce A. McConachie (eds.), *Interpreting the Theatrical Past: Essays in the Historiography of Performance* (Iowa: University of Iowa Press, 1989) pp. 198–229, pp. 201–2.

25 *Ibid.*, p. 202.

26 www.shakespearesglobe.com.

27 Sarlos, 'Performance Reconstruction', p. 28.

28 www.theatreroyal.org/PEO/site/home/.

29 www.bristol.ac.uk/drama/jacobean/iportal1.html. Users have to buy the DVD to see the full range of this work.

30 www.hrionline.ac.uk/brome/about.jsp.

31 Sarlos, 'Performance Reconstruction', p. 228.

32 McCalman and Pickering, 'From Realism to the Affective Turn: An Agenda', in *Historical Reenactment*, p. 6.

33 Brewer, 'Reenactment', in *Historical Reenactment*, p. 81.

34 Susan Leigh Foster, 'Organizing and Narrating Dance's History', in Canning and Postlewait (eds.), *Representing the Past*, pp. 333–50, p. 337.

35 See Joseph Roach, *Cities of the Dead: Circum-Atlantic Performance* (New York: Columbia University Press, 1996).

36 Jonathan Walker, 'Textual Realism and Reenactment', in *Historical Reenactment*, pp. 90–108, p. 90.

37 *Ibid.*, p. 91.

38 Jackson, 'Engaging the Audience', p. 21.

39 Anna Farthing, 'Authenticity and Metaphor: Displaying Intangible Human Remains in Museum Theatre', in Jackson and Kidd (eds.), *Performing Heritage*, pp. 94–106, p. 97.
40 *Ibid.*, p. 105.

FURTHER READING

Davis, Jim, Katie Normington, Gilli Bush-Bailey with Jacky Bratton. 'Researching Theatre History and Historiography', in Baz Kershaw and Helen Nicholson, eds., *Research Methods in Theatre and Performance* (Edinburgh: Edinburgh University Press, 2010), pp. 86–110.
Gale, Maggie B., and Viv Gardner, eds. *Auto/biography and Identity* (Manchester: Manchester University Press, 2004).
Groot, Jerome de. *Consuming History: Historians and Heritage in Contemporary Popular Culture* (London and New York: Routledge, 2009).
Heddon, Deirdre. *Autobiography and Performance: Theatre and Performance Practices.* (Basingstoke: Palgrave Macmillan, 2007).
McGillivray, Glen, ed. *Scrapbooks, Snapshots and Memorabilia: Hidden Archives of Performance* (Bern: Peter Lang, 2011).
Roach, Joseph. *Cities of the Dead: Circum-Atlantic Performance* (New York: Columbia University Press, 1996).

19

JACKY BRATTON AND GRANT TYLER PETERSON

The internet: history 2.0?

Valorising liveness, in the face of a threat from the endlessly remediated art of the day, performance studies has tended to reject the historical; on the other hand, documentation of the live event has become not only a funding imperative but a personal obsession with many practitioners. It is not enough to do what we do; we must record it, and put it on YouTube. In the spirit of this take – or assault – upon historiography, this essay begins with a live moment that has led to a revision of the plan of this book, and continues with some perhaps uncomfortable historiographical questions.

On 18 June 2010 the editors called together a conference of the contributors to this volume, and an audience of interested scholars and postgraduate students, to discuss and co-ordinate approaches to its content. I (Jacky Bratton) spoke late in the day, with a brief to address the history of 'the comic' – solo performers of humorous material – and to suggest how the dominant aesthetic has variously appropriated, discarded, hidden or demonised the 'popular' art of the entertainer, and then suggest what the historian might do about this. I decided to demonstrate the complexities by showing a picture (Fig. 36) found on a calendar and asking delegates to name the performer. Of course they could not; as I had hoped, they did not even guess right as to the gender of the figure posing perfunctorily as a monster chicken, clamp-jawed, toothless and befeathered, in skull cap and big three-toed comedy boots.

That anonymity, that absence from history, was the point I wanted to make, but I had realised somewhat belatedly that in order to fill the second five minutes of the presentation I myself needed to know more about this woman. The image is captioned 'Elizabeth "Betty" Green, known as "Koo Koo", c. 1930'. So I had reached for the obvious resource for popular entertainment history: Google. And sure enough, Wikipedia proffered a biography, but another site, devoted to the now-cultish movie *Freaks*, offered a quite different story, claiming to be about the same woman, but probably

36 Betty Green, known as Koo Koo, circa 1930: an image included in the Circus Calendar published by Taschen in 2009, and to be found on many websites about 'freaks' and variety performers.

concerning someone else. This uncertainty was another useful approach to the topic of the loss of the history of the popular, and I conveyed it to the meeting.

But from this point a quite different history takes off. At the end of the meeting I was approached by a 3rd-year Ph.D. student in the department, Grant Tyler Peterson, eager to discuss not Koo Koo, but Wikipedia. This, he said, was something he had been waiting in vain for all day, as speaker after speaker had voiced and apparently explored our anxieties about our discipline and its strategies, without, at any point, mentioning the internet. He spoke of his own anxiety, induced by the new technologies, about supercedure and the redundancy of our whole endeavour: these concerns are the elephant in the room of historiography.

And we embarked upon a very twenty-first-century scholarly relationship: at a distance, virtual, and intergenerational, between a senior Englishwoman and a young man from the United States. Here (to call it by one of the less felicitous new words of the digital age) is the mash-up of our exchange:

JACKY: Grant, what makes you say the field of theatre history has generally ignored digital media resources, and why should this book address this topic?

GRANT: Well, I find it troubling how theatre and performance historians regularly traverse the internet's rapidly developing landscapes, yet are slow to critically inquire how our field should engage with or resist the internet's political, economic, social and pedagogical structures.

Recent publications share a troubling lacuna. As Marvin Carlson has mentioned in his chapter in this book, the 2010 second edition of *Theatre Histories: An Introduction* impressively offers a complementary website hosting references and links to literary, audio and visual material supporting each chapter. But despite this employment of the internet's hyperlinking structures, the book and its website provide only a paragraph about the possible pitfalls and challenges of using the internet as a record of history, thus missing the opportunity to engage critically with the implications of such structures for the practice of history.[1] The anthology *Representing the Past: Essays in Performance Historiography* (2010) all but leaps over the internet. Editors Charlotte Canning and Tom Postlewait regret that 'far too much of the historical scholarship in our discipline fails to do justice' to academic standards, but seem to suggest that principles and methods of performance historiography should be gleaned from reading primers from the canon of general history and historiography.[2] They give six examples published before 2003, none of which directly engage with the challenges or opportunities presented by the internet. Hidden in a footnote, however, is a mention of the 2007 *Information-Literate Historian*, which does devote a chapter to the internet.[3] Similarly, Postlewait's 2009 *The Cambridge Introduction to Theatre Historiography* uses a footnote to recognise that 'guides to and training in Internet research are also essential today' but regards this topic as outside the scope of his project.[4] At the same time as flagging attention to this gap, I think it's worth noting how the production of a printed textbook as an educational tool in the twenty-first century increasingly becomes a pursuit plagued with contradictions. Sometimes referred to as 'digital natives', students born after 1980 are part of a generation immersed in digital media and are thus considered – wrongly or rightly – more adept with forms of digital literacy than older generations who have received the equally problematic label 'digital immigrants'. This polemic implies that the use of printed textbooks, as a format for knowledge exchange, is becoming in the twenty-first century what Greek and Latin were in the English Reformation: linguistic relics of previous cultural and political orders.

Although such generational divisions and historical comparisons are over-simplified, the tensions they raise warrant attention. Born in 1979, I am placed ambiguously on the cusp of this strange imaginary divide, with a keen interest in new informational techniques, in large part because I feel they undermine academia's traditional modes of reading and thinking – a healthy challenge to the old guard, if you will.

How the 2012 *Cambridge Companion to Theatre History* will operate as a tool of information (and of education) will, in part, be determined by its engagement with and accessibility to digital culture. After all, more people may read this book through the 'limited view' option on Google Books or Amazon than buy or borrow a print copy. This book will also be available as an institutionally purchased e-book, but here we see how digital access to books, including free portions of books, raises a host of difficult questions. It brings into sharp focus the economic and cultural practices of print culture (prices of books and journals, selective distribution, product rigidity) by foregrounding the innovative promises of digital media (lower costs, wide access, product mutability, advanced search abilities, interlinked contexts, participatory formats).

This is not just a printed book, but also a digital representation of a book on the internet with distinctly separate effects and viewers. Isn't this a key principle of theatre historiography, to interrogate the terms and conditions of authorship and audience?

JACKY: OK, yes, but what about the level before this – not our commentaries, but the raw materials? There are two huge divisions of material to consider before we get to the distribution of what we write ourselves. First, there are the products of digitising programmes: for example, the catalogues in print and picture form that most libraries and collections now have online and the journalistic materials turned into massive pay-per-view databases – these constitute a core area in which we need constantly developing investigative skills. Second, there are the different challenges to our analysis posed by the new, rather than made-over, materials that are posted to the web as publicity for live performances or directly as performance themselves. The already huge collection of data, much of it short-lived, created by theatre companies and individuals bent upon performing themselves are the materials of future histories.

GRANT: Well, yes, I think digital technologies open up profound opportunities, particularly for sourcing materials for theatre history. Videos of past performances once hard to find, or costing high prices, are now available on

YouTube for free. I once spent 50 dollars on a DVD of *Dionysus in 69* for teaching purposes only to find later that my students could view the film on YouTube. The growing amount of performance material in digital form forces us to rethink how we operate as researchers and teachers.

Not only is the 'canon' of theatre and performance history finding its way onto YouTube, but as you say, the internet's floodgates are open to performance histories that would have otherwise remained in the margins. Google has – in less than a decade – digitally scanned 15 million books and plans to have nearly 130 million scanned by 2020. It intends to make these books available (under various free and cost-based models) as it did with 3 million books in 2010. Google's resources, and its dominance as a free information gateway, have created an alarming consequence: many students behave as though something that cannot be found there cannot exist. What most people are even more familiar with, of course, are popular commercial websites like YouTube, blogs and social networking platforms. These websites exploit the user-contributed-content model and are amassing large banks of cultural material that includes many treasures.

JACKY: This last is of course how I came to this issue. In the Koo Koo example, Google gave me two, entirely incompatible, stories, as well as video and stills by which I could attempt to determine which one applied to my calendar image. So I might say that the conflict was productive, since I thought about the materials I found instead of just grabbing them. In this case. But I needed to supply the skills, my old skills as an historical researcher, which one may do, so long as it remains obvious and universally accepted that such a judgement is required.

There is also the matter of the transience of these websites, of endeavours that crash all the time, from the commercial to the institutional – issues of durability that do not afflict the book. There is almost always another copy of a book, though of course the ticket or the rehearsal photo is another matter – maybe one is back to the issue of the evanescence of the performed moment, which is the constant refrain of the theatre historian, moved into another key. It's on YouTube now, but will it be there in ten years' time? Probably not. I met a scholar – admittedly from Oxford University – who had embarked upon a massive comprehensive calendaring endeavour, to continue *The London Stage* into the nineteenth century, and was determined upon print publication in the first instance.[5] I was incredulous, but, in retrospect, I can see his point. However, he is now working on a database.

GRANT: Wow. So, if the internet is an elephant, does that mean he has mounted the beast, or is just being sat on? As much as I promote digital cultures, I can relate to his ambivalence. But I do think theatre and performance historians should be leading the academic charge to tame (and claim) new territory in the internet's wild west. Not only were practitioners of theatre and performance early pioneers in the digitisation of performance and the virtual and cyber extensions of its practice, but the foundation of performance studies tackled early on what many academic fields find so troubling about the internet: the destabilisation of binaries like spectator/participant, amateur/professional, singular/collaborative authorship, fixed/improvisatory. Leaders in the field of performance studies continue to point the way: Baz Kershaw, for example, in a chapter in *The Cambridge Companion to Performance Studies* (2008) discusses digital or 'distributed archives' and intermediality.[6] The internet's abundance of material troubles traditional notions of value and 'liveness', a challenge to which the field of theatre and performance history is well accustomed.

Our field of study, perhaps more than others, is heuristically equipped to engage with the anxieties, questions and problems arising from the birth pains of internet culture. As search engine technologies increasingly add data from theatre playbills, scripts, art, maps and recordings, historians in theatre and performance can trace new relational patterns and genealogies of our subject material. I feel the internet should demand greater attention and involvement from our field – not only as consumers of its data, but as active agitators, responsible interpreters, and possible organisers.

In this role, the theatre and performance historian is crucial. The mathematical logic governing much of the mining and the analysis of digital data will always be vulnerable to misinterpretation and misuse. Computer science algorithms that determine significance will always (or at least *should* always) come into conflict with shifting interpretive and cultural perspectives that will challenge what is significant and meaningful. Historians can use the quantitative abilities of the internet not only to extend interpretations about relationships between the past and the present, but to discover and explicate qualitative intertheatrical connections between texts and their users.

JACKY: Yes, indeed; there are many ways in which our discipline in particular is served by the developments in what is currently called digital humanities. I am excited about this change, despite being cast in this particular dialogue as the old guard. I lived through the explosion of literary and cultural theory, in which I was on the new-scholar side and which shaped my academic life entirely, so I can easily see these things are cyclical and organic. Digitisation is the next big turn of the wheel. But I get a sense of rising urgency – panic, even – from the many new initiatives that are beginning to attempt academic, institutional control of the digital world. At an accelerating rate since the turn of the century, dozens of conferences have been called, projects begun, institutional initiatives set up, under the wings of universities in America and Europe and various national institutions. One feels the likes of the Association for Computers and Humanities in the US and the Centre for Computing in the Humanities at King's College London[7] are trying to set out pipes – or even just put up umbrellas – to deal with a flood that is already pouring over them. The tone of the various calls for papers and participants has moved from excited dreams and descriptions of what might be done by bringing computing power to bear upon arts disciplines to a dismayed recognition of its problems and huge expenses, from proclaiming a rescue bid to preserve ephemeral heritage to realising the greater ephemerality of all websites, from starting brave new forays into the past to discovering the need for protocols and standards in what is created. The London Charter for the computer-based visualisation of cultural heritage[8] is an instructive document. It was created in 2009 to deal with some of the basic academic concerns that should underpin undertakings such as computer-generated views of theatres that are no longer, or have never been, physically there. One of these, the debate about whether, or how far, any picture on a screen can represent or substitute for the textured, embodied, live experience of the thing itself, is far too large and general for this discussion , but two of its concerns, 'transparency' and 'authority claims', are, I think, central to historiographical thinking.

Transparency is the basic scholarly requirement that everything you say – or, in the case of these models of lost theatres, generate visually on a screen – has to be referenced, so that the audience can know why it is as it is, in your picture, and where they might go for the information that would enable them to make a different picture of their own. This requirement presents one huge but relatively obvious problem in web-based materials: how should such annotation be done? 'Authority claims' are more difficult but are linked to the same issue: who has the right to say what happened, what Lincoln's Inn Fields theatre looked like, whether Ellen Terry slept with Henry Irving? Is it a fully certified historian with a Ph.D. and two years of official funding for their project, or a hobbyist who has done a lifetime's research on the subject and set up a DIY website? The person with institutional access to the most expensive archival database, or the actor's great-grandchild? Unchallenged and uncheckable authority goes to those organisations with the money and expertise to create and sell archives, such as Googleartproject.com – promulgating their version of the information, making decisions about what is and is not known and to whom, they give an appearance of universal accessibility of all facts that is entirely spurious, their creation and maintenance a political move. This is the question of the control exercised by the preservers and transmitters of documents and other remains in archives writ large. It digs below the level of which people and institutions can afford to pay for access to digitised resources, to decisions made about what should be preserved at all. The story now is that everyone has the opportunity to make their own records and make them available, so there is no authority making such decisions. There is, but how and who shifts all the time, and the impression for students is, as you say, that anything not in the realm of free content does not exist, or, when they find there are databases that have to be paid for, that these have some extra special authority for that very reason, and certainly exhaust all possibilities.

GRANT: Some have compared the introduction of the internet to such historical shifts as those presented by the printing press in the fifteenth century and the institutionalisation of public libraries in the seventeenth century.

JACKY: *(disgruntled political interjection)* And the destruction of such libraries in the twenty-first?

GRANT: *(not put off)* Of course, if we are at the beginning of a digital (or cyber) shift, we must ask whether its importance has become overplayed. In the midst of a shift, it's difficult to assess how big the turning of the wheel will be. The inherent 'democratising' power often championed by internet idealists has been challenged by digital sceptics who point to political and economic forces that censor, exclude and can, with a click of a button, prevent democratic activism. Evgeny Morozov, from the former Soviet Republic of Belarus, is possibly the most outspoken critic pointing to ways authoritarian governments actually leverage the internet to enhance methods of surveillance, censorship and suppression of democratic social action.[9] Of course, there are various outcomes when governments meddle with the internet; in early 2011, Egypt shut down the country's internet access but failed to thwart revolution, but other governments, such as China, Iran, North Korea and Saudi Arabia, have been more successful at controlling what voices are heard and which histories get told. Thus, the internet is not a deterministically democratic medium.

The 'worldwide' aspect of the internet fails to withstand even the simplest scrutiny, as do claims of its post-modern embodiment of non-hierarchical structures. The 'cloud' of the internet does not reach the entire world, and it does indeed have a centre (or centres) as well as edges, margins and even shadows. Victorian scholar Patrick Leary cleverly coined the term 'offline penumbra' to describe the cognitive lapse among internet users who assume that, if something cannot be found online, it does not then exist.[10]

JACKY: I suspect that this last point, to which we have both returned more than once – the 'cognitive lapse' that might be called credulity and laziness – is something the digital natives will sort out in their own heads; it really is no good going on about it in dense and learned books. But there are concerns that have to be addressed by us digital migrants and riders of the cusp like yourself, which were expressed by some attendees at the conference: our digital stage-fright, if you like. We have the sense that, in the internet landscape, a tide of popular information that has no discernible structure or intellectual content at all is sweeping away not only top-down received accounts but also the counter-histories many of us have sought to erect, deploying Leftist, feminist, queer and other theoretically charged agendas to challenge the hegemonic story by outgunning their own intellectual and scholarly weapons. Moreover, there are stories about institutional capitulation to pressure from what is perceived as this new form of history, so that universities and publishers sideline or withdraw funding from the writing of analytic and 'authoritative' historical narratives in order to deploy all available expertise upon the generation of encyclopaedic information to be posted online and left somehow to speak for itself. However expertly created, such material simply stands beside masses of other data – as if, suddenly, a new book by Tracy Davis or Susan Bennett had the same status as the little lovingly preserved piles of programmes for Sadler's Wells in the 1950s or the million surviving postcards of Zena and Phyllis Dare.

GRANT: But, is there such a thing as too much data? Is there a point when this seemingly endless abundance of material becomes a hindrance?

JACKY: No, really – no. I have spent all my life seeking out the other, othered, materials that challenge the slipshod, reach-me-down received wisdom. I chose to work in the nineteenth century at least partly because there is so much data about it still available and underused. But I have therefore had to develop certain specific methodologies for dealing with that plenitude: signs within the materials that tell me when to stop looking for more; ways of describing and discussing what I have found when I have simultaneously to make it available to readers who have not seen it. Purposeful historical arguments are my responsibility, and I do not want to weave new cloth out of old yarns, so I welcome all this material and make use of it.

GRANT: So – you have established yourself as an expert. But the internet's abundance of 'authors' troubles culturally dominant notions of 'authority' and 'expert' – notions on which the academy fundamentally relies. The distinction carried by scholars, in other words, our (scarcity) value within economies of information, is brought into question by the increased availability (and cheaper costs) of alternative sources. The internet's accessibility undermines academic hegemony: hence, our stage-fright.

For historians, the idea that rare books, once only accessible in special collections or at large research universities, are now available online probably induces both joy and panic: joy for those not previously privileged with easy access, but also panic in imagining how open access to everyone might invite the common 'misuse' of information or result in bad scholarship – or possibly, even more worrying to some, allow entry into intellectual territory that must be defended or shared. Although there have always been grey areas, perhaps especially in our kind of history, between 'experts' and knowledgeable 'amateurs', the internet offers a platform where conflicts between the two are played out in surprising ways.

JACKY: We set ourselves up as experts and regard the new resources as our raw materials. This has always been how I've dealt with memoirs, local histories and the like. But are you suggesting that the internet has shifted this relationship, and that Wikipedia and its cultural commons methodology offer the possibility of a radically different understanding of expertise?

GRANT: Yes, cultural commons information aggregation presents a significant shift in the way relationships operate between the 'crowd' and the 'expert'. Going against the grain, digital humanities pioneer Roy Rosenzweig suggested in 2006 that Wikipedia could act as a training ground for novice historians. Despite its maligned reputation, Wikipedia's guidelines, he claimed, 'sound very much like the standard manuals offered in undergraduate history methods classes'.[11] Volunteer contributors are provided with specific instructions regarding citations and the 'verifiability' of primary and secondary sources and are overseen by a collective of 'quality' enforcers. Although vulnerable to misuse and presenting a homogenised 'objective' style, Wikipedia nonetheless offers a valuable – if imperfect – methodology of history writing. Moreover, under the layer of each subject page (clicking on the 'history' tab), Wikipedia presents the changes, dialogues and debates that determined the front-page content – a strong gesture towards leaving a historical trail.

Wikipedia, of course, privileges the popular over the particular, sometimes siding against established historians and 'authorities' (especially excluding corrections offered by the subjects themselves), and this can result in significantly skewed versions of the 'truth' and of history. Authority on Wikipedia is determined on the 'authority' of other citable and linkable references – with questionable standards of quality. As long as a 'fact' has been cited in previous sources, it doesn't always matter if it has been debunked. Further, no 'original' content or 'opinion' is accepted. The sum result is a history of and from the popular, narratives approved by the collective.

JACKY: And this seems to be a real problem for the academy, which is challenged at a basic level by the notion of collective approval, mere aggregation – since the class will always outnumber their instructor.

GRANT: Yes. Computer scientist Jaron Lanier calls this a form of 'digital Maoism' and warns that if future methods of communication and education 'take place through anonymous Internet aggregation ... we could become vulnerable to a sudden dangerous empowering of the hive mind'.[12] Lanier's point raises legitimate concerns about the popular use (and misuse) of

Wikipedia, but this argument would be better balanced if he offered a parallel critique of the encyclopaedic format in general.

JACKY: This very book has been materially changed, however, by the tendency of at least one academic institution to be seduced by the promise of comprehensive information and democratic inclusiveness that the digital encyclopedia holds out. Temple Hauptfleisch, of the University of Stellenbosch, was to contribute a chapter, but his University decided to transform a book-based history into a comprehensive Encyclopaedia of South African Theatre and Performance 'as a web-based, online and open-access "wiki"-driven reference resource'. He found himself obliged 'to load the over 15,000 entries ... produced so far, get it set up and edited in the wiki programme, and then open it for public access by late March 2011'[13] and therefore could not pursue his own historiographical work.

GRANT: This highlights (again) how the economies of information are quickly reshaping the ways we operate as historians and educators. Perhaps the training gap in our field identified by Canning and Postlewait can begin with an 'outing' of Wikipedia – rather than remaining a dirty secret or shunned pariah, Wikipedia can be critically employed as a pedagogic tool for historiography. It not only offers a relatively safe (and free) laboratory to experiment with ways of articulating history and a platform that reveals the limitations of anonymous collective authorship, but Wikipedia operates on a set of digital literary skills (for example, html basics, hyperlinking, etc.) that benefit scholars who wish to strengthen their internet capabilities.

JACKY: This is pedagogy, training for the theatre historian or any modern historical writer, but is there actually a new *research* methodology, new historical practice, to be learnt from our experience of using the internet?

GRANT: Well, perhaps more important than learning the scale of the internet's digital resources is the manner (and language) in which information is re-organised across its digital structures. Wikipedia's interlinked document format is, in many ways, a foreshadowing of the likely shape that future digital books may take. In this sense, the true revolution of the digital age lies not in the millions of items being scanned, but in the ways in which the transposition of these items involves information overlay. Google Books provides an early glimpse of this process in the way books' tables of contents, indexes and footnotes are sometimes hyperlinked to their respective pages. It is not a far step forward to then hyperlink bibliographies, in-text citations, and illustrations to external sources that are in turn hyperlinked to more external sources. In this way, a single book will not exist independently in the way it used to; rather, it will become a thread within a larger, interconnected tapestry of other data points. Marvin Carlson's argument in this volume helpfully extends this idea to how the internet, as he believes, 'is the only way to deal with the concept of global theatre history' because it enables 'a paradigm shift that replaces the narrative model of the European nation-state with . . . the model of the rhizome'.[14]

Crucially, the rhizomatic structures of the internet not only connect history in new ways, but mobilise the user of that history differently. The reading practice (and offence) of note-making in books is transformed (and liberated) in digital media. The online Shakespeare Quartos Archive, for instance, offers the ability to read pre-1642 editions of *Hamlet* and add page comments that can be set to private or public views. Analysis by experts and novices alike can be viewed through these data overlays. Google plans to develop similar technology. In this sense, the flat static print book becomes a digitally inscribable, multi-layered, interconnected, and participatory collection of data. How these layering practices can be applied to digitised theatre and performance records is an endeavour in its infancy.

But, as traditional formats and structures of information (the book, article, footnote, index, appendix) are translated to suit internet structures and digital literacy, how might our processes of knowledge acquisition – and therefore, our sense of history and history research – be changing? Are readers being suffocated with information, or are they becoming more participatory? How might traditional methods of historical narrative be challenged, rearranged and maintained in internet landscapes? How might the portals and hyper-linked avenues of these spaces re-map our cognitive sensibilities? Is the ability to keyword-search millions of books and billions of webpages transformative of the way we can learn, think and document the intertextuality and inter-theatricality of our subjects?

JACKY: I'm afraid I have no answer to the string of questions here, only another one raised for me by your enthusiasm for individual readers as contributors to a text – the suggestion that every word of response joins with and effectively becomes a layer of meaning, a 'data point': are we not back with the literary battles about close reading, the debatable value of each personal response?

The substantive issue to which we here return, I think, is the matter of 'authority claims'. If everyone can tell their story, and all stories are equal so I can choose whichever I like to believe, then possibly there is no history at all, only a lot of competing accounts, which I am free to multiply and make up. It seems to me that you could look upon this as a development you and your generation have to tackle, as the would-be authorities of your cohort; you have to buy in to the new modes of knowledge transfer and at the same time challenge them, discovering and voicing the oppositional positions that are part of the role of the academy. I guess my role at this point is to make – well, point out – difficulties. So I would offer the proposition that you are in trouble here because the digital realm offers you nowhere to stand, as an authority. Suppose that what you publish has no greater status than a family-history website put together by an enthusiastic amateur. How are you to assert that your view of the larger topic in hand, say the company in which that amateur's father played a minor role, is worth more than his view, that the sun does not revolve around the earth?

GRANT: Well, I remain optimistic. It may not be worldwide, but the global stage of the internet is a malleable place where history can be played out to new audiences in new ways.

This brings me to my answer to your challenge: if the abundance of information in digital media lacks a sense of authority and verifiability and I need a place to stand, then perhaps that is the problem to solve. The internet's fount of information has resulted in abundant material that raises content judgement issues. One of my roles as an academic is to be an 'expert' on a certain area; in that role I must be able to organise that information. So, in many ways, academics can be the ones who help solve the abundance issue. We can develop the critical acumen to discern, navigate and critique these new forms of information. We can expand our cognitive maps of our subject to include, accommodate and filter a multitude of sources that engage with our subject and also to possibly address new and larger audiences. This is, perhaps, a weighty – if not impractical – responsibility.

JACKY: Yes, all very well: it is the role of the academic to winnow the cascade of information into some sort of balanced and verifiable account, to act as historian rather than annalist. But my worry is that there is no longer an acknowledged place for this activity: the strength of the academy, the prestige of the academic press, the imprimatur of the peer review process are no longer felt to be of the essence by the digital natives in the knowledge economy. This leaves even Left-leaning opponents of authority, like me, without a platform on which we may climb in order to challenge the incumbents and hope to be heard above the noise. No one need attend to any individual voice.

GRANT: Is that why this chapter is in dialogue form? Are we two bee-keepers – or just two bees? Despite the anxiety, I think the shake-up of power is healthy. My stand is unashamedly populist. If theatre and performance history matter, and if the internet represents a repository of significant influence and power, then how the internet's architecture and language operate is important to understand if we want to participate and possibly effect change as historians. In the first ten years of the twenty-first century, the internet underwent a key transformation known as Web 2.0, which changed the format from an architecture that displayed information to a platform that enabled participatory experiences. As the digital age continues to mature and our digital literacies expand, I think we should not only adapt our print culture formats, such as books and journals, to suit digital hyperlinking and participatory structures, but we should increasingly think, operate and perform within these spaces as digital historians.

Issues of authority and expertise are contested in new digital landscapes, often viewed as a danger. Mostly, I find inspiration in the uncertainty and am excited by the spontaneity that this landscape demands of me, my fellow academics, and my students.

As someone on the cusp of being a 'digital native', I do not fully understand the language and the scripts I seem to be following. I improvise as much as I follow the lead of those around me. But I know the future is in the making, and how history will be treated in this future is a project in which we can all be players. I feel like the curtain has just risen, or perhaps, the screen has just turned on. What are my lines? Where do I click?

JACKY: Go for it, young man. Oh – and can you tell me anything about a woman dressed up as a chicken?

NOTES

1 Phillip B. Zarrilli, Bruce MacConachie, Gary Jay Williams and Carol Fisher Sorgenfrei, *Theatre Histories: An Introduction*, 2nd edn (New York and London: Routledge, 2010), p. xxv.

2 Charlotte Canning and Thomas Postlewait (eds.), *Representing the Past: Essays in Performance Historiography* (Iowa City: Iowa University Press, 2010), p. 5.

3 *Ibid.*, p. 27. They cite Jenny Presnell, *The Information-Literate Historian: A Guide to Research for History* (Oxford: Oxford University Press, 2007), pp. 136–56.

4 Thomas Postlewait, *The Cambridge Introduction to Theatre Historiography* (Cambridge: Cambridge University Press, 2009), p. 272.

5 *The London Stage, 1660–1800. A calendar of plays, entertainments & afterpieces together with casts, box-receipts and contemporary comment, compiled from the playbills, newspapers and theatrical diaries of the period.* 5 parts, 11 vols. (Carbondale: Southern Illinois University Press, 1960–8) provides a shelf-full of impressive volumes that offer an exhaustive calendaring of performances at the major playhouses; it has been a staple of eighteenth-century theatre research greatly envied by scholars working on the nineteenth-century, when the huge expansion of London and its entertainments has hitherto made it unthinkable to continue such an undertaking.

6 Baz Kershaw, 'Performance as Research: Live Events and Documents', in Tracy C. Davis (ed.), *The Cambridge Companion to Performance Studies* (Cambridge: Cambridge University Press, 2008), pp. 23–45, p. 37.

7 www.ach.org/, since 1997; www.kcl.ac.uk/schools/humanities/depts/cch/, since 1996.

8 www.londoncharter.org.

9 Evgeny Morozov, *The Net Delusion: The Dark Side of Internet Freedom* (New York: Public Affairs, 2011).

10 Patrick Leary, 'Googling the Victorians', *Journal of Victorian Culture*, 10:1 (2005), 72–86, p. 82.
11 Roy Rosenzweig, *Clio Wired: The Future of the Past in the Digital Age*, ed. Anthony Grafton (New York: Columbia University Press, 2010), p. 73.
12 Janor Lanier, 'Digital Maoism: The Hazards of the New Online Collectivism', *Edge: The Third Culture*, 183 (30 May 2006), n.p., http:/edge.org/documents/archive/edge183.html.
13 E-mail communication to David Wiles, 2 December 2010.
14 Pp. 157–9.

FURTHER READING

Center for History and New Media. George Mason University. http://chnm.gmu.edu/.
Cohen, D. J., and R. Rosenzweig, *Digital History: A Guide to Gathering, Preserving, and Presenting the Past on the Web* (Philadelphia: University of Pennsylvania Press, 2005) (Also available to read at http://chnm.gmu.edu/digitalhistory/).
Digital Humanities Now. Center for History and New Media. George Mason University. http://digitalhumanitiesnow.org/.
Knapp, M. M. 'EBay, Wikipedia, and the Future of the Footnote', *Theatre History Studies*, 28 (2008), 36–41 (Also available to read on Google Books at http://goo.gl/ToLih).
Rosenzweig, R. *Clio Wired: The Future of the Past in the Digital Age*, ed. Anthony Grafton (New York: Columbia University Press, 2011).
TDR Comment: 'Concerning Theory for Performance Studies', *TDR: The Drama Review*, 53.1 (2009), 7–46.

INDEX

Cambridge Companions To...

AUTHORS

TOPICS